SUNBURST

SUNBURST

The Rise of Japanese Naval Air Power
1909–1941

Mark R. Peattie

Naval Institute Press • Annapolis, Maryland

The latest edition of this work has been brought to publication with the generous assistance of Marguerite and Gerry Lenfest.

This book was originally brought to publication with the generous assistance
of Edward S. and Joyce I. Miller.

Naval Institute Press
291 Wood Road
Annapolis, MD 21402

First printing in paperback, 2007
ISBN 978-1-59114-664-3 (paperback)
ISBN 978-1-61251-436-9 (eBook)

The Library of Congress has cataloged the hardcover edition as follows:
Peattie, Mark R., 1930–
   Sunburst : the rise of Japanese naval air power, 1909–1941 / Mark R. Peattie.
     p. cm.
   Includes bibliographical references and index.
   ISBN 1-55750-432-6 (alk. paper)
   1. Japan. Kaigun—AviationHistory—20th century. I. Title.
   VG95.J3 P43 2001
   359.9'4'095209041–dc21

                         2001030220

♾ Print editions meet the requirements of ANSI/NISO z39.48-1992 (Permanence of Paper).
Printed in the United States of America.

22 21 20 19 18   10 9 8 7 6 5

Dedicated to the memory of
David Christian Evans,
1940–1999,

who is remembered by his family,
by his colleagues, and by this author as a shining emblem
of kindness, courtesy, integrity, and professionalism

Contents

Illustrations

FIGURES

Maps

Preface

Many years ago, while on a summer tour of the Caroline Islands for research on a book on the rise and passing of the Japanese in Micronesia, I thought I heard the roar of fighter engines. On the high island of Ponape, I was driving along a paved road southwest of Kolonia, the main town, looking for what I had been told had been one of the Japanese navy's two air bases on the island. It was high noon, still, and incredibly hot as I slowed the car about five kilometers out of town—about the distance I had been told that I should find the airfield, or what was left of it. Across the taro patches and through clusters of trees I saw the ribs of what I took to be a ruined aircraft hangar. After a rough and prickly trek through the weeds, I came upon the foundations of what must have been a barracks, some small construction locomotives, trenches, concrete bunkers, and other detritus of war.

I knew that fighter planes had been based on the island during the Pacific War. Indeed, during the course of the hour or more I spent at the site, I stumbled across the twisted remains of a Mitsubishi Zero more than a hundred meters from one the airfield's runways. Vines and grasses had pulled a shroud over the wrecked fuselage, and only the tail section, broken off from the fuselage, remained uncovered. I walked back to the airfield. All was heat and sun and somnolence. I looked out across the broad expanse of weeds and grass that had once been the runway, trying to make out the faded markings on fuselage and tail assemblies, wondering what the Zero must have looked like when, with its fellows, in full fighting trim and still bravely bearing its air group and pilot markings, it had touched down on this remote tropical airfield with the same airy lightness it would have brought to the flight deck of a carrier.

As I strained to imagine what must have been here, I began to catch the cough, the choke, and then the roar of engines as the fighters sped down the runway and lifted off to hurl themselves against the waves of the approaching aerial enemy. What had it been like here at this air base during those desperate months when the Japanese navy sent its men and planes to defend outlying defenses such as this, only to have them consumed in the furnace of American air power like moths drawn to a candle? What had been the nature of the combat unit of which they had formed a part, and what of the skills and fighting qualities of the pilots who had flown with it? What of the assumptions that had gone into the conception and design of this abandoned relic? How, indeed, had it figured in the plans of a navy fixated on the idea of great battleships and titanic surface battles at sea? I climbed back into my car that hot afternoon in the Carolines, believing that someday I would follow the prop wash of the Zero but recognizing that, for the time being, I had a different book to research and write.

A year later, chance offered a liftoff to my interest in Japanese naval aviation, though it was to take it across the oceanic expanse of a greater subject. I had returned to my teaching duties at a public university in New England when the Naval Institute Press proposed that I undertake a history of Japanese naval strategy in the Pacific War. With the late David Evans as my invaluable collaborator, I spent the next decade and more in this effort, during which time the focus of my research shifted once again. Concern with the wartime strategy of the navy gave way to a study of the prewar navy in its strategic, tactical, and technological aspects. The result was *Kaigun: Strategy, Tactics, and Technology in the Imperial Japanese Navy, 1887–1941* (Naval Institute Press, 1997).

Because of my continuing enthusiasm for the subject and because of its major importance in the rise and fall of the Japanese navy, our original manuscript had included four long chapters on the Japanese naval air service. But upon completing our work, we had concluded, along with the press, that such extensive attention to the rise of Japanese naval aviation made for too bulky a manuscript, and that in any event the story deserved to stand on its own. In the published work, therefore, the four chapters were excised and the subject summarized in one.

The core of this present book thus comprises the original treatment of Japanese naval aviation in the earlier work, plus additional chapters added to describe its prewar origins and wartime destruction. It is important to emphasize the genesis of this present study, since *Kaigun* provides the broader institutional and historical context of the Japanese navy. I thus refer the reader to *Kaigun* for much that has been left out of this present work concerning the evolution of the Imperial Japanese Navy as a whole, particularly matters of strategic planning and decision prior to and during the great conflict in the Pacific. The present work is an attempt to provide an outline history of the evolution of the organization, doctrine, tactics, training, and technology of Japanese naval aviation—its aircraft, its ships, and its personnel—from its inception up to the beginning of the Pacific War. I conclude the story with a chapter that sketches the victories of Japanese naval air power early in that conflict and analyzes the progress of its utter destruction by 1944. While this work makes no attempt to be encyclopedic in the coverage of its subject, I have added a number of appendices that deal with the personalities, organization, technology, and tactics of Japanese naval aviation. The individuals and aircraft listed in appendices 1 and 6 are identified, respectively, with the symbols † and • where first discussed in the text.

In the introduction to *Kaigun* David Evans and I attempted to outline the difficulties of writing and researching Japanese naval history. I shall not readdress these issues here in detail, but since they are relevant to the present study and serve to explain why it is not always possible, when writing about the Japanese navy, to answer with certainty all the questions of "how" and "why" and "by whom," they deserve summary repetition, at least.

There is, to begin with, the problem of the ambiguity of the Japanese language, which often obscures sharply delineated meaning. Further, the absence of adequate documentation because of the wholesale destruction of files and documents at the end of the war means that numerous issues of major importance about the Japanese navy may never be resolved. Nor can one turn to a large body of biographies, autobiographies, memoirs, and reminiscences by knowledgeable Japanese naval personalities for "the final inside story" of prewar and wartime naval affairs, since the norms of Japanese culture and society in general, and the reluctance of the survivors of a defeated navy in particular, often blanch such documents of controversy and incisive judgments. Finally, there is the reality that the authors and editors of some of the major multivolume studies I have used for this work—the *Senshi sōsho* (War history) series published by the Japanese Self-Defense Agency, the *Nihon kaigun kōkūshi* (History of Japanese naval aviation), and the *Shōwa zōsenshi* (History of shipbuilding in the Shōwa era), for example—are voluminous in detail but often omit questions of primary importance to the Western historian. All these difficulties challenged the completion of this work as well as of the earlier study.

A few technical points mentioned in the introduction to *Kaigun* need to be repeated here for the sake of clarity, particularly those dealing with my use of systems of spelling and measurement. In writing Japanese I have used the Hepburn system of transliteration, and in writing Japanese personal names I have followed the Japanese word order—that is, family name first, given name second (the exceptions being adherence to Western word order in the case of American citizens and in cases where English-language publications provide authors' names in Western word order). For place names in China, I have generally followed the Wade-Giles system except for those prominent cities—such as Hankow, Canton, and Tientsin—whose names in the period between the world wars were usually transliterated according to the old Chinese postal system. For major places in Korea and those major places in China (mainland China and Taiwan) that were under formal Japanese administration between 1909 and 1941, I have given the Japanese name and have sometimes added the indigenous name in parenthesis. I have also used a few common Western names that had general acceptance before World War II, such as Port Arthur and the Pescadores Islands.

The problem of measurement is a complicated one in writing about the Japanese navy, since the navy itself was not always consistent, sometimes using the English system of measurement for length, distance, and weight, and sometimes the metric system. My recourse, in most cases in the text, has been to use the system of measurement used by the navy at the time and to put in parentheses the equivalent conversion in the other system, with the figure given in round numbers.

Unless otherwise indicated, displacements are given in long tons (English tons of 2,240 pounds) and denoted simply as tons. The Washington Naval Treaty of 1922 introduced "standard" displacement, which indicated the displacement of a ship fully loaded and ready for sea, but without fuel. I have used standard displacement as a general rule. I have attempted to be accurate, but displacements sometimes changed as ships were modified, and sources are often ambiguous and occasionally disagree. I have resolved such issues by using my best judgment.

For distances, in most cases I have followed the Japanese practice of measuring longer distances in nautical miles. I have defined range of aircraft as the total distance an aircraft could fly on a given supply of fuel, for a given speed. By "radius" I mean the distance an aircraft could fly, perform its mission, and return to base with sufficient fuel to land safely.

Acknowledgments

When, more than fifteen years ago, I received the invitation from the Naval Institute Press to write a book on Japanese naval strategy in World War II, I was eager to try my hand, since it was a subject that had interested me for more than a decade. Yet I had a feeling, of only the shadowiest sort, that such a scholarly task would prove more taxing and time-consuming than any I had attempted. I also knew that in addition to my full-time duties in the university where I was teaching, I had made commitments to several other projects, all of them with onrushing deadlines.

It was clear, therefore, that I would need a collaborator, someone steady, someone with a firm grip on the written Japanese language, someone with some knowledge of the subject put before me, and someone with whom I could work collegially, day in and day out. There was only one person who could meet all these requirements: David Evans, a friend of some years, then teaching on the history faculty at the University of Richmond. I was delighted when Dave was willing to come on board for our long and arduous voyage toward what eventually became the comprehensive work that I have introduced in the preface. How lucky I was to have made this choice, the unrolling years were to reveal.

Dave had an M.A. in Japanese language and literature and a doctoral degree in modern Japanese history from Stanford University, the same institution where he had done his undergraduate work. His Ph.D. thesis on the Japanese naval officer corps of the Meiji era was a solid work that displayed not only his skills as a historian but also a deep reading in the esoteric Japanese literature of the field. As I was to learn, it was also the product of his wide-ranging familiarity with all in Japan who were knowledgeable about Japanese naval history. Dave knew everyone in that community, from aging former officers of the prewar navy, like the piratical-looking old gunnery expert Capt. Mayuzumi Haruo, who strode around veterans reunions with a patch over one eye, to that quiet young librarian back in the third office of the Navy Archives who knew just where you could get your hands on the single extant copy of the navy's secret "Battle Instructions" of 1934. Dave knew them all, and they trusted him. That trust was to be precious currency in the gathering of information and materials for our work.

In the fifteen years that Dave and I collaborated, we were often separated by great distance but were blessed that our collaboration matured with the evolution of the computer and e-mail, which let us be in touch almost daily. During those years, as we struggled with the complexities of Japanese naval institutions and technology, the centrality of his contributions became manifest. Was there a passage in some Meiji-era text in stiff, formal Japanese that seemed unfathomable? Dave would quickly render a logical and elegant translation. Was there a fact, a source, or a judgment that could only be obtained from Japan? Dave located it and brought it to the mill of our work. Was there a naval term that I had carelessly misused? Dave corrected the error with courtesy and expertise. Each summer Dave would generously come for several weeks to whatever home my peripatetic academic life had brought me, to go over with me the latest chapters of our work. During these sessions, with tact, humor, and dedication he applied to the manuscript his rigorous demands of logic and style. No paragraph that I had hastily or illogically constructed escaped his attention, and with a jeweller's eye he dissected and then reassembled my overreaching sentences. No page left his hand without being the better for it. It was Dave, moreover, who accomplished the arduous task of pulling together all the illustrative material—maps, charts, and schematics—and integrating them effectively into the text. Gentle as a feather and as enduring as carved granite, David Evans left his mark on *Kaigun*.

All this he did while serving as a dedicated, stimulating, and enthusiastic teacher at the University of Richmond, to which he later added his role as a resourceful, caring, and effective administrator. Along the way, he wrote a number of articles on Japanese naval history and edited a new and expanded edition of a widely acclaimed collection of reminiscences and eyewitness accounts of Japanese naval actions in World War II. And all the while, we kept up a running exchange on literature (about which he taught me much), Stanford sports (we were both loyal fans), exotic beers, and movies (he was an avid exponent of film noir).

When we had finished *Kaigun* we turned to the manuscript of this present work, which, as I mention in the preface, has been a sort of spin-off from that earlier study. Dave and I had worked through a first draft when, at the outset of 1999, he felt the first pains of the malignancy that was to wrack his body but leave his soul untarnished. As the disease worsened, direct communications between us became less frequent and more abbreviated. He fought on throughout the spring, displaying courage as great as that on any battlefield, and then, in June, he was gone. To say that I have lost a great friend hardly plumbs my sorrow. To say that I profoundly miss a priceless collaborator better encompasses the situation in which I have had to complete the substantial revisions of this work without his skilled and dedicated participation.

Fortunately, the counsel, insights, and encouragement of a corps of knowledgeable friends, colleagues, and acquaintances have fortified me in my efforts to complete this sequel to *Kaigun*. First among these has been Jonathan Parshall, a senior business analyst for a Web development firm in Minneapolis, a longtime naval history enthusiast, and a superb graphic artist. I first learned of Jon through his handsomely crafted and instructive website on the Japanese navy. Dave Evans suggested him as the ideal person to undertake most of the graphics for *Kaigun,* and the quality of his work for that volume has been central to its success. Subsequent and frequent correspondence with Jon made clear that his knowledge of naval technology went far beyond that of the ordinary buff. It also revealed an interesting as well as interested mind. For all these reasons, Jon's role in the production of this volume was far greater than his valuable contributions to *Kaigun*. He read and critiqued every page, and contributed both insights and actual wording throughout the manuscript, particularly with regard to Japanese carrier design and operations. He drafted a significant portion of the appendices and was responsible for all the graphics. Moreover, he undertook, without complaint, the onerous task of preparing the final physical copy of the draft manuscript, with its innumerable details of computer formatting and graphics output, for the Naval Institute Press. It is clear that *Sunburst* could not have been published or even finished without him.

The contributions of Frederick Milford as technical advisor and general counselor to the research and writing of *Kaigun* were of such magnitude that David Evans and I dedicated that work in part to him, and we provided significant space in our acknowledgments to explaining why we had done so. Since much of what appears in these pages was part of the earlier work, his insights continue to illuminate my general understanding of naval technology. Further, he reviewed this sequel manuscript in its entirety, and once again his expertise, incisive comment, and judiciously wielded blue pencil were fundamental to its improvement.

Few know more about the Japanese naval air service than Osamu Tagaya, investment banker and aviation historian par excellence. "Sam" Tagaya read the manuscript twice, offered insights from a wealth of reading, and saved me from many gaffes, both large and small. He has, moreover, generously guided me to many of the Japanese-language sources cited in these pages. David Dickson, state counsel for a national title insurance company and collector extraordinaire of the details of Japanese naval tactics and technology, read the entire manuscript and offered useful comments in addition to generously sharing with me his large collection of translated documents on these subjects. John Lundstrom, the doyen of the historiography of naval air combat in the Pacific War and author of two classic studies on that subject, read various parts of the manuscript and never failed to answer questions from Jon Parshall and me with authority, patience, and courtesy. James C. Sawruk shared with me his minute knowledge of the formations, tactics, and aircraft and personnel losses involved in the great carrier battles of 1942. In numerous conversations and communications, Eric Bergerud, whose magnificent study of the air combat in the southwestern Pacific is cited frequently in these pages, illuminated for me a whole world of aviation lore.

Halfway through the research for this book Quinn Okamoto, a widely traveled corporate attorney and longtime student of Japanese naval aviation, generously volunteered his research and translation services toward its progress. Without reward, other than this acknowledgment, Quinn selflessly gave of his time to help me work quickly and thoroughly through a number of Japanese materials that would have otherwise consumed a great deal of my time in plodding translation.

Thomas Wildenberg, a specialist on U.S. naval aviation, read through the entire manuscript and provided valuable corrections to my understanding of American naval aircraft and tactics. H. P. Willmott also read through the manuscript and, as usual, offered comments that were provocative and sharply worded but always illuminating.

In Honolulu, John De Virgilio, who has made himself the premier expert on the ordnance and methods used in the attack against the fleet units at Pearl Harbor, was of assistance in helping Jon Parshall and me understand the configurations of the special bombs and torpedoes used in the operation. Nathan Okun, an expert in World War II ordnance, fire control, and ballistics, contributed his expertise in these matters. Tadashi Kuramatsu, doing doctoral work in diplomatic history at the University of London, helped clarify certain issues regarding the navy's position on carriers during the interwar international arms limitations negotiations. Kirk House, curator of the Glenn H. Curtiss Museum at Hammondsport, New York, generously provided photographs of early Japanese aviators in training at the Curtiss flying school that appear in this volume. In New York, J. D. Louie, collector of materials on air combat during Japan's war in China, shed light on Chinese air operations during that conflict. Martin Favorite's website on the Japanese air services on the eve of the Pacific War has been a useful source of information on the disposition of Japanese naval air units at the time. Todaka Kazushige, on the staff of the Shōwa Museum in Tokyo, was of great assistance in providing me with certain data necessary to the biographical entries in the first appendix to the volume. Also in Tokyo, I am grateful to Best Sellers, Inc. for permission to reproduce photographs 3-1, 3-2, 4-1, 7-1, and 7-3 and also for permission to adapt figure 3-2 for use in this work. Jon Sumida, Yoshida Akihiko, Geoffrey Till, Alan Zimm, Mark Campbell, Hans Lengerer, and Wayne Hughes are among those who read portions of the manuscript when it was part of the larger, earlier work and offered helpful comments and criticisms. My brother Noel, whose grip on the English language is unrivaled, saved the text from various small infelicities of style, and in Mary Yates, who read the manuscript with a jeweler's eye, I could not have had a more skilled, painstaking, and resourceful copy editor.

I also feel deep gratitude to Edward Miller, a former industrial executive and a fine naval historian himself. Ed has been the benefactor of a number of publications of the Naval Institute Press, including *Kaigun*. I am happy to acknowledge that the publication of this present work has also been greatly facilitated by his generosity.

Finally, I wish to thank the Hoover Institution on War, Revolution, and Peace for the office space it has provided to me over the years and for its continued logistical support. Without either of these, the research and writing of this study would have been difficult indeed.

Whatever errors of fact and interpretation remain are, of course, solely my responsibility.

SUNBURST

1

THE NAVY TESTS
—*Its*—
WINGS

Japanese Naval Aviation, 1909–1921

When the Imperial Japanese Navy was established in the 1870s, there existed a formidable gap between Japan and the Western maritime powers. These powers, led by Britain, had made epochal advances in naval technology, the tactical coordination of fleets, and the applications of sea power to achieve strategic objectives. Decades and in some cases centuries of naval evolution in the West confronted Japan with a daunting challenge. The Japanese navy was able to narrow this gap dramatically, but only through extraordinary effort intensified by a consciousness of Japanese inferiority and backwardness.

In the development of aviation, specifically naval aviation, the comparative situation was different. While manned flight in balloons had been undertaken in the West in the eighteenth century and powered lighter-than-air craft had been successfully tested in the middle of the nineteenth, heavier-than-air flight was not demonstrated as practical until the opening of the twentieth. When, in 1909, the Japanese navy first made a decision to develop a capability in this new medium, the Wright brothers' flight at Kitty Hawk and Samuel Langley's abortive experiments on the Potomac River had occurred only six years before, and none of the pioneer endeavors of powered flight had yet demonstrated that aviation could contribute to the conduct of war on land or at sea. Yet soon thereafter, progress in aviation came with remarkable rapidity, and its principles were widely disseminated. The pace of this dissemination thus allowed Japan to participate in the general liftoff of aviation within a far shorter time than it had taken the nation to join the ranks of the great naval powers. Of course, Japan's smaller resource base in science, technology, and materiel meant that the navy's first decades of powered flight were greatly dependent on Western developments in aviation. In the long run, moreover, the rise of Japanese naval air power, as stunning as it proved to be by 1941, must necessarily be viewed against the material dominance of the West.

By 1911, naval aviation already offered two paths for development: the seaplane and the wheeled land-based aircraft. Because it was waterborne, the seaplane[1] seemed the logical type of aircraft for naval operations. At San Diego that year, the American engineer Glenn Curtiss, who was pioneering the development of seaplanes, undertook the first waterborne flight, landing alongside a warship that then hoisted the aircraft aboard. Other seaplane records were set over the next ten years, and a mother ship, the seaplane tender or carrier, was developed by the leading naval powers as a new warship category. Yet the use of seaplanes with the fleet presented problems. They took too long to launch and recover, the mother ship having to stop and lower or retrieve her aircraft over the side.

The second approach to naval aviation was the employment of shore-based aircraft, but their range at that time was so short that they could not operate with the fleet. As early as 1910, the United States Navy made a historic effort to solve this problem by launching ship-borne aircraft. At Hampton Roads, Virginia, that year, an aircraft was flown off the temporary platform deck of an American cruiser, an event followed a few months later by the successful landing of an airplane on the temporary deck of a cruiser in San Francisco Bay. Yet these were flights by single aircraft from and to ships riding at anchor. No navy had yet attempted to launch or recover aircraft from a ship under way. Nor had any maritime power yet determined the role of such aircraft in the operations of its navy, though many naval professionals saw the function of both sea- and ship-borne aircraft as most likely one of reconnaissance, not combat. It would take World War I to change this limited perception of naval aviation.[2]

In that conflict, the impact of aviation on the war at sea was far less dramatic and wide-ranging than its effect on land war, but the airplane had, in isolated instances, demonstrated its potentially versatile role in naval operations. In 1913, even before the world war, a Greek seaplane carried out a reconnaissance sortie over a Turkish fleet in the Dardanelles. A British seaplane made a practice drop of a standard naval torpedo in 1914, and the next year British seaplanes heavily damaged a Turkish military transport in an aerial torpedo attack. In 1916, Austro-Hungarian seaplanes sank a French submarine at sea by bombing. Jutland itself was the first naval battle that involved naval aviation, though in a small role, when an aircraft from a British seaplane tender attached to the Grand Fleet spotted the advancing German battle cruiser squadron and reported the enemy's movements accurately, though the British flagship did not receive the information because of a communications breakdown.[3]

Despite these "firsts," however, the limitations mentioned earlier—the time-consuming process of launching and retrieving seaplanes at sea and the difficulty of launching more than a single aircraft from the temporary platforms installed on regular warships—kept naval aviation from playing a significant scouting or striking role at sea. To operate wheeled planes from ships under way called for a new kind of warship with wide and permanent decks for the launch and retrieval of numerous aircraft. In converting the battle cruiser *Furious* in 1917, so as to provide a permanent flight deck forward, the British navy produced the prototype of the modern aircraft carrier. In August of that year the first landing on a ship under way took place on its flight deck. The next year a landing flight deck was extended aft, though the warship's funnel and superstructure still separated it from the takeoff deck forward.

FIRST FLIGHTS
The Japanese Navy Finds Its Wings, 1909–1914

In all such developments the Japanese navy had as yet little direct experience. At the end of the first decade of the new century, the issue of aviation in Japan was largely theoretical, tested in the press rather than in the air, since there were no aircraft of any sort in the country. But there were those who had at least begun to think boldly about the new subject of "aeronautics." In the navy, a few officers, stationed abroad, including Comdr. Iida Hisatsune, resident at the Royal Navy's Gunnery School in Portsmouth, and Lt. Comdr. Matsumura Kikuo, resident officer in France, had become interested in Western developments in powered flight and had begun to send reports back to Tokyo.[4] But it was Lt. Comdr. Yamamoto Eisuke[†]—nephew of the powerful Meiji-era naval figure Adm. Yamamoto Gombei, but no relation to Adm. Yamamoto Isoroku of Pacific War fame—who can properly be called the conceptual father of Japanese naval aviation. While serving on the Navy General Staff, Commander Yamamoto became intensely interested in aviation through stories in the press about Western advances in the field. He subsequently drafted a number of pronouncements in which he urged the navy to address seriously the question of "flying machines" (*tako-shiki kūchū hikōki,* literally, "kite-type flying machine"). In his "Statement Concerning the Study of Aeronautics" *(Kōkūjutsu kenkyū ni kan suru ikensho)* of March 1909, Yamamoto predicted the advent of "aerial warships of awesome potential" and went on to argue that while naval warfare up to then had been two-dimensional, in the near future, with the addition of flying machines and submarines, it would be conducted within three dimensions.[5] This view prefigured the arguments of air power advocates in the Japanese navy in the years to come. It obviously implied a challenge to the orthodox belief in the dominance of surface fleets, but it ascribed to aviation capabilities that it was decades from achieving—this at a time when "flying machines," with their delicate assemblies of wood and wire and cloth, had the structure and the performance of a crane fly, and in a year when there was not as yet even one of these odd contraptions in Japanese military service.

In any event, Yamamoto's various memoranda came to the attention of Navy Minister Saitō Makoto, who was sufficiently impressed with their dramatic claims to enter into negotiations with the army minister for a joint program to study the military application of flight to the conduct of war. The timing was fortuitous, for just about that time the army was beginning to move in that same direction. In 1909 the two services established a "Provisional Committee for the Study of the Military Application of Balloons" (Rinji Gun'yō Kikyū Kenkyūkai). Despite this oddly narrow focus for the study of military aviation, both the army and the navy continued to pursue heavier-than-air flight. The army sent several officers to Europe for flight instruction in the latest flying machines. Upon their return in 1910, they brought with them two aircraft for a public demonstration of the first heavier-than-air flights in Japan. The interest engendered in the army high command by the experiment led to the establishment of the first military airfield at Tokorozawa the next year.[6]

But the Japanese navy was determined to acquire its own wings. Given the friction that had existed between the two services since their creation, it was inevitable that the nature of the Provisional Committee—chaired by an army general, dependent entirely upon the army's budget, and heedless of the navy's interest in waterborne aircraft—would cause restlessness among its navy members. Most of those officers urged the navy to withdraw from the committee and to form its own aviation research organization. Thus, in 1910 the navy set out on its own course by establishing a "Committee for the Study of Naval Aeronautics" (Kaigun Kōkūjutsu Kenkyūkai), headed by Capt. Yamaji Kazuyoshi[†] and twenty-one other naval officers, most of whom went on to become the pioneers of Japanese naval aviation. This navy initiative caused a good deal of resentment in the army and marked the beginning of a bitter rivalry in aviation between the two services that lasted to the end of the Pacific War.[7]

The obvious first step in aviation for the Japanese navy was the development of a core of young naval officers who could fly and who then could teach others to fly. This, in turn, required that a few selected officers be sent abroad for flight training. While there, they could purchase and ship home the latest flying machines. Because France and the United States seemed to be making the greatest progress in aeronautics, it was to those two countries that the first Japanese officers, most of them members of the navy's Aeronautics Committee, were dispatched.

In 1911 to 1912, lieutenants Kaneko Yōzō,[†] Umekita Kanehiko, and Kohama Fumihiko were dispatched to an aviation school in Paris, and lieutenants Kōno Sankichi, Yamada Chūji,[†] and Nakajima Chikuhei[†] were sent to the Glenn Curtiss aviation schools in Hammondsport, New York, and in San Diego.[8] At Hammondsport the Japanese trainees learned to fly the newly designed Curtiss seaplanes on nearby Keuka Lake and later took training on the Curtiss wheeled aircraft, popularly known at Hammondsport as "grass cutters." Actually, only Kōno and Yamada were under orders for flight instruction on Curtiss aircraft. Nakajima was charged merely with studying the production and maintenance of such machines,

Photo. 1-1. Pioneer Japanese aviators at Hammondsport, N.Y. *Left to right:*
Comdr. Takeuchi Shigetoshi (naval attaché, Japanese Embassy, Washington);
Lt. Yamada Chūji; Lt. Kōno Sankichi; and Engineering Lt. Nakajima Chikuhei
Courtesy of Glenn Curtiss Museum, Hammondsport, N.Y.

but he took it upon himself to obtain flight training from Curtiss instructors.[9]
Judging from American accounts, the Japanese students exhibited more zeal and
daring than natural skill, and as a result demolished several machines, much to the
frustration of their American instructors.[10]

Meanwhile, Commander Yamamoto had been dispatched to Germany to learn
all he could about European developments in military aviation. While there he cor-
responded frequently with Lieutenant Kaneko on the importance of aviation
research for the Japanese navy. Seeking ways to demonstrate to the navy brass the
possibilities for aviation, Yamamoto hit upon the idea of using the navy's newly
purchased foreign aircraft in the annual naval review held before the emperor. To
that end, he fired off a recommendation to the navy minister for such a demonstration. Many in the top echelon were opposed, being skeptical of the whole idea
of aircraft in naval warfare and fearful that an accident or a mechanical failure in
either one of the aircraft would ruin the demonstration and embarrass the navy. But
Navy Minister Saitō approved, and lieutenants Kōno and Kaneko were ordered to
hurry back from the United States with their aircraft—a Curtiss seaplane and a
Maurice Farman seaplane, respectively—to take part in the review. In the fall of
1912 these aviators made the first flights in Japanese naval air history at Oppama,
just north of Yokosuka, which was to become Japan's first naval air base. The
Farman seaplane was assembled at Oppama, and on 6 October 1912 Kaneko made

a test flight of the aircraft for fifteen minutes, reaching an altitude of 100 feet (30 meters). On 2 November, Kōno flew the Curtiss seaplane for about ten minutes, also reaching an altitude of 100 feet. Then, on 12 November, the two lieutenants put on a demonstration of their aircraft at the imperial naval review at Yokohama. Kaneko flew the Farman from Oppama, alighting on and taking off from the water near the ship carrying the emperor Taishō, and Kōno piloted the Curtiss in a circuit over the naval ships in the review.[11]

In such fragile and clumsy contraptions the navy had now tested its wings, but whether they would become anything more than an entertaining curiosity remained an open question for much of the navy brass. Still, there was now a sufficient, if small, core of aviation enthusiasts among the junior officers and a few interested flag officers to push along the development of aviation in the navy.[12] Keeping abreast of foreign aviation progress was obviously essential to that purpose, and in December 1912 Captain Yamaji and Lieutenant Kōno were sent to France, Germany, and Britain on a fact-finding mission. While in Europe they studied various kinds of airships, picked up rumors about airborne radio communications, watched a demonstration of aerial bombardment in France, and observed that in all three navies the preponderance of aircraft consisted of seaplanes.[13]

Among their observations was their assessment that ships able to launch and retrieve wheeled aircraft would be an inevitable development in future naval warfare, though they conceded that it was unclear how such a warship type and its aircraft would influence conventional surface warfare. In any event, they concluded, navy pilots should practice short takeoffs and landings on fields ashore until suitable ship platforms could be developed. In the meantime, however, they recommended a continued emphasis on seaplanes and the development of more coastal sites from which they could be launched.[14]

In late 1913 the navy's decision to push ahead with seaplanes led to the development of its first specialized vessel for handling waterborne aircraft. This was the *Wakamiya Maru,* a converted freighter, which had simple derricks and canvas hangars fore and aft and was capable of carrying two assembled and two disassembled seaplanes.[15] In the annual naval maneuvers off Sasebo that year, it was as a seaplane carrier that she loaded several Farmans at Yokosuka to test the usefulness of aircraft in fleet reconnaissance. The seaplanes aboard the *Wakamiya Maru,* organized into a "seaplane unit" *(suijōki butai),* served the "Blue Fleet" (the "attacking force") while three seaplanes were kept at Oppama to serve the "Red Fleet" in defense.[16]

As it was in the U.S. and British navies, lack of a rapid means of communication—between aircraft, and between aircraft and ships—was an early impediment to integrating aircraft with the Japanese fleet. Some tests using radio telegraph were carried out, but this means proved unsatisfactory because of the primitive nature of the equipment. In these early years, hand flags were used for communication from aircraft. One of the early naval aviation pioneers, Wada Hideho,† later recalled that when communicating with other aircraft, crewmen actually stood up in their seats

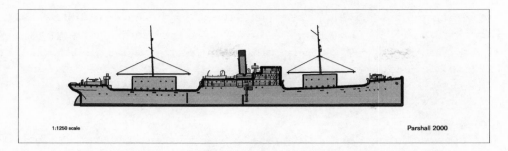

Fig. 1-1. Seaplane carrier *Wakamiya*

and gave arm signals with flags tied from elbow to wrist. For communication from aircraft to ships, Japanese naval aviators dropped weighted rubber balls with messages inserted into them and with colored streamers attached to make them easier to see when dropped.[17]

THE FIRST TEST OF COMBAT
Japanese Naval Aircraft in the Tsingtao Campaign, September–October 1914

While histories of Japanese naval aviation mention no particular feats by these flimsy aircraft during the maneuvers of 1913, the test of the navy's fledgling air unit in actual combat was not long in coming. In September of the next year, within two weeks of Japan's declaration of war on Germany and the preparations for the reduction of German territories in Asia and the Pacific, the *Wakamiya Maru* and her aircraft were assigned to the navy's Second Fleet. That force departed Yokosuka on 23 August to take part in the blockade and reduction of the German naval base at Tsingtao, China. Aboard were Lt. Comdr. Kaneko Yôzô (the senior air officer afloat), lieutenants Kôno Sankichi (the group's executive officer), Yamada Chûji, Wada Hideho, Magoshi Kishichi, and Fujise Masaru, and several other junior officers—nearly all the navy's "experienced" aircrew.[18]

Embarked on the *Wakamiya Maru* were four Maurice Farman seaplanes, aircraft that could attain a speed of 50 knots and had a ceiling of 500 meters (1,500 feet) when fully loaded. While their mission was expected to be principally reconnaissance, the navy also expected them to bomb targets of opportunity. But the means by which they were to do so were ridiculously slight by the standards of tactical bombardment that would evolve only a few years later. The planes had crude bombsights and carried six to ten bombs that had been converted from ordinary shells and were released through metal tubes on each side of the cockpit. The pilots were able to communicate with each other only by flag signals.[19]

On 1 September the *Wakamiya Maru* arrived off Kiao-chou Bay where the Second Fleet had already supported a Japanese army landing. Bad weather and a number of mishaps kept the ship's aircraft from taking off for some days. Then, on

Photo. 1-2. Farman seaplane being hoisted aboard the seaplane carrier *Wakamiya Maru,* 1915

5 September, in the first successful Japanese air operation, Lieutenant Wada, flying a three-seat Farman seaplane and accompanied by Lieutenant Fujise, piloting a two-seater Farman, rose clumsily into the air and headed toward the Bismarck battery, the main German fortifications at Tsingtao. When directly over the battery, Wada dropped several bombs that landed harmlessly in the mud—a disappointing beginning to the history of air bombardment. But the main value of the navy's early aviation was demonstrated almost immediately. Soaring over Kiao-chou Bay, the Japanese pilots were able to see which German ships were still at anchor and which had successfully reached the open sea. Their confirmation that the cruiser *Emden,* the most powerful remaining unit of Germany's Asiatic Squadron, was no longer in harbor was intelligence of major importance to the Allied naval command.[20]

On 30 September the *Wakamiya Maru* had the misfortune to be holed by a German mine, and after being patched up she was eventually sent back to Japan. Her aircraft were transferred to a strip of Japanese-held beach from which they continued to conduct reconnaissance and bombing missions during the remaining month of the one-sided campaign against Tsingtao. The best opportunity for aircraft-to-aircraft combat came about on 13 October, when Lieutenant Wada, in cooperation with three army aircraft, set out to attack the lone German navy airplane that had been used by the defenders for reconnaissance. The encounter was inconclusive; after much dancing about in the sky over the bay, the German aircraft, too nimble for its pursuers, escaped into a cloud.[21] By the end of the siege, the navy had conducted nearly fifty sorties against Tsingtao, had undertaken various search missions at sea, and had dropped nearly two hundred bombs, though damage to German defenses may have been slight. With the surrender of the fortress, the navy's air unit was withdrawn.[22]

In the greater scheme of World War I, the navy's air operations over Tsingtao were a footnote in a campaign that was itself a footnote in the history of the war. Certainly the meager operational results had given the navy brass no reason to suppose that these fragile bundles of struts and wires would supplant the surface battle line as the locus of naval power. Yet if nothing else, the Tsingtao operations confirmed for the navy's tacticians the fact that aircraft, far better than any surface vessel, could act as the eyes of the fleet. That in itself was a significant step forward for Japanese naval aviation. Viewing the air operations at Tsingtao as a whole, Charles Burdick, the acknowledged authority on the siege, has asserted that "the sophistication of Japanese aircraft employment—i.e., coordination with land forces, bombing equipment, and general mobility—was well ahead of any other country."[23]

WATCHING FROM THE SIDELINES
Development of Japanese Naval Aviation, 1916–1920

Japan's swift operations to seize the German territories in Asia and the Pacific were completed by November 1914, following which the nation became largely a passive belligerent. Except for the dispatch of light naval forces to the Mediterranean in 1917, Japan was content to watch from the sidelines as the endless and futile offensives dragged on in Europe. But such a posture cost the Japanese a firsthand understanding of the conduct of modern naval war. This was particularly true in the field of naval aviation, where, at the outset of World War I, Japan had gained experience ahead of the Western naval powers. By 1918, however, aviation had become a standard element in Western naval power, taking on new and important roles in reconnaissance and antisubmarine patrol work; naval aircraft had grown significantly in capabilities and performance, and naval aviation had been given its longest reach yet with the development of the first aircraft carriers.[24]

All this had yet to be mastered by the Japanese navy, which did its best to monitor the tactical and technological developments in the naval war through observers dispatched to the European theater. The evolution of naval aviation was a significant, though not major, element in the navy's interest in the conduct of the war in Europe. The navy not only made use of the reports of Japanese naval attachés stationed in Allied capitals but also dispatched observers with specific missions to collect information on Western progress in military and naval aviation. In this way, Lieutenant Kaneko was sent to tour Europe and the United States in 1916–17 to gather information on the construction of the first proto–aircraft carriers. Lt. Kaiya Masaru went to France in September 1916 to observe French army air groups and pilot training. Lt. Kuwabara Torao[†] spent the latter half of 1917 getting a detailed picture of British naval aviation. Kuwabara was able to observe naval balloon units and flying-boat operations at Felixstowe and to visit the construction site of the *Argus* (the Royal Navy's first flush-deck carrier). He then went aboard the proto-carrier *Campania* to experience two weeks of aerial patrols during British fleet operations.[25]

Of particular importance among the reports of these naval observers was the memorandum drafted by Capt. Torisu Tamaki,[†] who was an observer with the British navy, 1916–17. Included in his "Summary of Operations of the British Grand Fleet" was a section on aviation that detailed the British use of airships to patrol ahead of the fleet, warn of enemy attacks, reconnoiter enemy coastlines, and undertake photoreconnaissance. The report provided detailed information on the conversion of the *Furious* with a foredeck flight platform and alerted the Japanese navy to the construction of the *Hermes,* Britain's first built-for-the-purpose through-deck carrier (i.e., a carrier without any obstruction—funnels or bridge—across the flight deck).[26]

But the most detailed and influential policy statement on the development of aviation in the Japanese navy was a report—"On the Stagnation of Naval Aviation and Other Matters" *(Kaigun kōkū no fushin sono ta ni tsuite)*—issued by the Navy Ministry in December 1919. Drafted by Capt. Ōzeki Takamaro, the report pointed out that Japan's isolation from the recent war's main combat theater meant that Japan had fallen considerably behind the other Allied powers in naval aviation and that in order to catch up with these powers the navy needed to take a number of steps. First, the navy must decide on what sort of aircraft it required, and then it should begin to produce these in Japan, under licensing arrangements if necessary. Second, it needed to invite foreign instructors, most probably British, to provide instruction in flight operations from warships configured to carry wheeled aircraft and to provide counsel on the manufacture of aircraft in Japan. Third, naval air strength had to be augmented by increasing the number of land-based air units, by converting a conventional warship to an aircraft carrier, and by building two fleet carriers. All this should be accomplished within eight years. Finally, Ōzeki urged, the navy ought to investigate the naval air organizations of other countries and adopt the best features of each.[27]

THE VISIONARIES
The Navy's Early Air Power Extremists

These official reports and recommendations by aviation advocates were effective in promoting practical measures to develop aviation as part of the regular naval establishment, though Navy Minister Katō Tomosaburō, in Diet interpolations at the end of 1919, made it clear that the navy was still focused on a "battleship-first" policy.[28] Outside the range of the moderate approaches to aviation, however, there existed an array of radical visions and prophecies by a few naval officers who envi-

sioned aviation not merely as a supporting component of conventional surface wa
fare but as the dominant element of naval war. As we have seen, Command
Yamamoto had been one of the first to give voice to such an argument. Others
among the small and youthful band of aviation pioneers in the navy spelled out
more precisely how aircraft would be potent weapons in the naval tactics of the
future. In 1912, while training in France, Kaneko Yōzō had written to Yamamoto:

> Operating in good weather on either a moonlit or a moonless night, aircraft
> could, in cooperation with torpedo boats, attack enemy warships in harbor.
> Moreover, there would be nothing to prevent aircraft from entering a harbor
> fortified against surface attack and strike enemy warships from above. And,
> in the case of blockading operations, when enemy warships must inevitably
> try to escape, it is hard to imagine a more useful weapon.[29]

Others, with the passion of the newly converted, drew more sweeping pictures
of the future dominance of air power. Before World War I, one of the more daredevil figures to do so was Engineer Lt. Isobe Tetsukichi, who first demonstrated his
enthusiasm for aviation by building his own seaplane out of bamboo and flying it
for 60 meters (200 feet) at a height of 3 meters (10 feet) before the machine overturned—this a year before the navy imported its first seaplane. Isobe went off to
Germany in 1913 for flight training and returned in time to join the Tsingtao campaign. Flying an army aircraft in a test flight, he crashed. He was repatriated to
Japan because of his injuries but soon became restless and eager for more aerial
combat. He somehow managed to join the French army air service and participated
in the Verdun campaign but again crashed, this time suffering serious wounds, and
was once more sent back to Japan. His flying career at an end, Isobe put his convictions to paper. In 1918 he published a short work, "War in the Air" (Kūchū no
tatakai), in which he predicted that those nations able to dominate the air would
soon dominate the land and sea as well. Taking note of the ability of Germany to
bomb the British Isles during the recent war, Isobe argued that enemy aircraft based
at Vladivostok or Shanghai could just as easily strike at Japan. Foreshadowing the
destruction wrought by American B-29s at the end of the Pacific War, Isobe predicted that Japanese cities would burn like matchwood under such an aerial
assault.[30]

But the air power statement that most directly confronted naval orthodoxy had
been drafted three years earlier. In January 1915 the future aircraft industry mag-
nate Nakajima Chikuhei, then a young engineer lieutenant, had sent to the chair-
man of the navy's Aeronautics Committee a memorandum outlining his views on
weapons procurement for the navy. The thrust of the memorandum was that even
though the airplane was in its infancy, it was destined to be the decisive weapon of
the future, and the dreadnought battleship was now fatally threatened by the aeri-
ally launched torpedo and mine. For that reason and because aircraft technology
was advancing so rapidly, the considerable sums spent on the construction of

Photo. 1-3. Nakajima Chikuhei (1884–1949) as
a young naval officer

capital ships could be better spent on aircraft design and production. For example,
Nakajima argued, the immense costs of the construction of the battle cruiser *Kongō*
could have paid for some three thousand aircraft, each one of which could carry a
torpedo load more powerful than one of the *Kongō*'s broadsides (which, of course,
was a wildly inaccurate statement). On the eve of his resignation from the navy to
begin his career as a manufacturer, Nakajima had incorporated the main arguments of his memorandum into a circular letter that he had sent around to all his
friends and acquaintances.[31]

This was a very bold, if exaggerated, air power manifesto, the first made in any
nation, coming as it did substantially before that of Giulio Douhet in Italy or
"Billy" Mitchell in the United States. But it was the argument of a visionary, not a
realist. The realities of aircraft technology for the next several decades made it

hardly likely that such frail machines could accomplish all that Nakajima and the more extreme air power advocates expected of them. Moreover, given the naval wisdom of the day, it is not surprising that Nakajima's statement had little imme- diate impact on naval circles. Asked in the Diet, in 1916, about the impact of air power in relation to naval warfare as it was then understood, Navy Minister Katō Tomosaburō declared with confidence that there was as yet no aerial bomb that could put a warship out of commission. That didn't mean that the navy shouldn't make sure that in the future its warships were safe from aerial attack (by either bombs or torpedoes), but for the present, most of these dangers were largely theo- retical. For that reason, Katō assured his listeners, the Japanese navy did not regard the advent of aircraft as upsetting the traditional dominance of the battle fleet.[32] Considering the limited bomb loads, the ranges, the speeds, and the bomb-sighting systems of aircraft of the time, this was not an unreasonable assumption. But as air- craft technology evolved and the reach and destructive potential of naval aviation emerged, the arguments of the air power advocates increasingly came to challenge the battleship orthodoxy of the navy.

PRACTICAL ADVANCES
Air Training, Air Groups, and the Search for Administrative Unity

In the decade prior to 1920, the course of naval aviation was in the hands of those more interested in making solid organizational advances within the navy than in making sweeping theoretical claims for the future of air power. Over a five-year period, 1916–21, the reports and recommendations of the naval commentators already mentioned—particularly those of Captain Ōzeki—stimulated the navy to undertake a number of parallel efforts to further the progress of naval aviation: the beginning of a regular and systematic program of naval air training; the creation of the navy's first permanent shore-based air groups; an attempt to establish a single administrative organization for naval aviation; a brief exploration of the possibili- ties of lighter-than-air aviation; the construction of Japan's first aircraft carrier, and the creation of a training program for flight operations to be conducted from it; and the invitation of a British aviation mission to facilitate the development of naval air training and to promote the manufacture of naval aircraft in Japan.

The first and most critical steps in the enhancement of aviation's role in the navy was the expansion of the cadre of aircrews and the creation of a systematic program of flight training. In 1912, after the return from abroad of the pioneer aviators men- tioned earlier, flight training had begun at Oppama for selected personnel. Fol- lowing the practice in Western navies, this training was at first limited to officers, though noncommissioned officers were permitted to occupy the cockpit beginning in 1916. The training itself was largely confined to simple operational procedures, but in these early years of Japanese naval aviation, such training was incredibly haphazard and limited. Because of a shortage of aircraft, the average in-air training session lasted only ten to twenty minutes per pilot, and in an entire year of training few students received more than forty-five minutes in the air. Once a trainee went up solo, he was judged sufficiently qualified. Naturally, with such limited time in the cockpit, there were fairly frequent crashes and forced landings by the navy's pioneer aviators. Considering the rough handling the navy's few aircraft received, it is a wonder that there were not more such accidents; remarkably, there were none at all in the Tsingtao campaign.[33] Over time, flight training in the navy improved, but this came only with the establishment of permanent and specialized facilities, which in turn depended upon the creation of permanent air units.

The navy's seaplane unit, which had been assembled for participation in the Tsingtao campaign, had never been thought of as a permanent unit and was organized only on a temporary, annual basis for participation in fleet exercises. But with the dissolution of the original committee that had initiated naval aviation, funds were released in 1916 for the establishment of three permanent air groups *(kōkūtai)*, which were to be established in peacetime as needed at designated naval ports or naval bases. These groups took their designation from the names of those ports and bases, and fell under the authority of each local port or base commander. (A more detailed explanation of the *kōkūtai* system and an enumeration of the navy's land-based air groups, 1916–21, is provided in app. 5.) The first air group was established at Yokosuka in April 1916, and because the air base on which it was stationed was charged with responsibilities for naval air training and naval air development, for most of its early years the group had the character of a training unit. The first really operational naval air group was not organized until 1920 at Sasebo.[34]

Yokosuka and Sasebo were initially bases for seaplanes only, but a number of leading aviation pioneers, Lieutenant Commander Kaneko among them, had long believed that the navy needed land bases for wheeled aircraft as well. At the time, the army was dickering for the use of Kasumigaura, a lakeside base in Ibaraki Prefecture, north of Tokyo, ideal for both wheeled and pontoon aircraft. The navy bought the land, forestalling the army, and in 1922 a third air group was established at Kasumigaura. The Kasumigaura Air Base became the center for pilot training. At the same time, a fourth air group was established at Ōmura, Nagasaki Prefecture, which later in the decade became a fighter base.[35]

The creation of permanent land-based air groups and the increasing importance of aircraft in the navy's exercises and maneuvers provoked calls by aviation advocates for a single administrative organization for aviation. Until 1916, control of aviation had been held by the Navy Technical Department, but that year it was transferred to the Navy Ministry's Naval Affairs Bureau. Proposals for enhancing the importance and coordination of aviation ranged from the establishment of an aviation section within the Naval Affairs Bureau to the creation of a separate Naval Aviation Department. But the idea of a semiautonomous air agency was quickly set aside. The mainstream view was that because aviation was no different from gunnery or torpedo warfare, a separate administrative organization was not necessary. More important, perhaps, the top brass did not believe that aviation would be a critical element in naval warfare. On the other hand, uncertain as to what role aviation *would* play in the future, the navy brass did not wish to relinquish control over its direction. Thus, the greatest organizational identity that the navy would concede to aviation was a small Aviation Department created in 1919 within the Naval Affairs Bureau, later redesignated the Third Section of the bureau. When this office was abolished in 1923, there was no remaining naval air advocate with sufficient stature to resist the demands for the breakup of naval aviation. Hence, its various activities were divided among several bureaus and departments within the Navy Ministry.[36] It would be four more years before an officer of energy, foresight, and influence could give it a powerful and unified presence within the navy.

LIGHTER-THAN-AIR AVIATION IN THE NAVY

In the meantime, the Japanese navy continued its effort to keep abreast of developments in all aspects of aviation. Toward the end of World War I, both the British and American navies devoted considerable effort to the development of semirigid airships, in large part because of the effectiveness of German Zeppelins during the conflict. The Royal Navy had begun using airships in reconnaissance as early as 1917 and subsequently undertook research and training relating to such craft. The United States Navy, thanks to America's great supply of helium, which reduced the danger of explosion and made its airships somewhat safer, made even greater strides in this technology. In view of these advances, the Japanese navy began to investigate the utility of airships in its own tactical and strategic schemes. In 1918 it established a lighter-than-air unit at its Yokosuka base (later moved to Kasumigaura) and began acquiring airship technology from abroad. The first lighter-than-air craft acquired by the navy were simply large balloons *(kikyū)* that were tethered to warships and used for shell spotting and torpedo tracking. In 1921 the navy acquired several semirigid and self-propelled airships *(hikōsen)* from Britain, France, and Italy. After successful tests integrating these craft with fleet operations, the navy began to construct its own airships of this type. After 1921, rigid airships were attached to the Combined Fleet and regularly took part in the navy's annual maneuvers.[37]

During the 1920s a number of officers on the Navy General Staff saw the rigid self-propelled airship as a significant component of the navy's defensive strategy in the western Pacific. Because of its greater endurance, such a craft offered the possibility of locating enemy fleet units far beyond the range of winged aircraft of the time. Armed with bombs to attack enemy ships and machine guns to defend itself, the airship could, its advocates argued, provide the navy with a long-range strike capability. Yet major doubts persisted. To begin with, all three major navies suffered a number of accidents involving airships, the most spectacular being the crash of the American *Shenandoah* in 1925, which raised questions as to the reliability of airship technology. The Navy General Staff, moreover, pointed to the liabilities of the airship. It was vulnerable to damage or worse in rough weather, as the number of

shes in the British and American navies demonstrated. It presented a large, soft
;et for enemy fighter aircraft. It was expensive to build, and its supposed military utility was a matter of speculation, not proof.

Ultimately, the emerging potential of winged aircraft turned the Japanese navy
away from further development of the airship. Given the expense of rigid airship
construction and the continuing doubts as to its utility and viability in combat, the
winged airplane appeared to be a more promising agent for the navy's bid to enter
the new dimension of the sky. Undoubtedly too the airship—large, slow, and
ungainly—could hardly compete with the glamour of winged aircraft as an object
of enthusiasm for aviation advocates in the navy. For all these reasons, the navy
decided in 1931 to abolish its airship units and, over the next few years, to phase
out the airships attached to the fleet.[38]

FURTHER ADVANCES
Naval Aviation Extends Its Reach

In any event, the future of Japanese naval aviation rested on wings and engines, not
on airships. In such aircraft, navy pilots, with enhanced skills, flying better and bigger aircraft, began to make flights of increased time, distance, and height. In February 1914, Lt. Magoshi Kishichi, piloting a Farman seaplane, reached a height of
3,500 meters (11,500 feet), and a month later, flying the same sort of aircraft, he
flew nonstop for six hours. In the spring of 1918, three Farman seaplanes flew
from Yokosuka to Sakai nonstop. In April 1920, three Yoko-type seaplanes flew
from Yokosuka to Kure to Chinkai (Chinhae), Korea, to Sasebo and back to Yokosuka. The last leg took eleven hours and thirty minutes—a historic flight, since up
to that time no aircraft of any country had flown for more than ten hours without
landing.[39]

Aircraft also began to take an important role in the annual naval exercises. In
the grand maneuvers of 1919 a seaplane from the *Wakamiya,* attached to the "Blue
Fleet," was able to discover the main body of the "Red Fleet" far over the horizon
and to report this intelligence by dropping a marker on the deck of the "Blue Fleet"
flagship, an event regarded as a great success at the time. This achievement was
repeated by both fleets in the grand maneuvers south of Honshū two years later.
About the same time, navy aircraft also proved useful in the protection of Japanese
civilians in Karafuto and the Russian Maritime Provinces during Japan's Siberian
intervention by providing reconnaissance and aerial demonstrations. The campaign
was also an opportunity for testing cold-weather flight operations.[40]

During World War I, Japanese naval observers quickly noticed the different
emphases in aviation between the U.S. and British navies. The United States Navy
relied mostly on seaplanes and shore-based wheeled aircraft for its air capabilities,
while the British had come, by the end of the war, to emphasize carriers as the basic
naval aviation force. As it had in other, earlier naval matters, the Japanese navy
decided to follow the British rather than the Americans, for the time being. Recom-

mendations from Japanese observers aboard the Royal Navy's first carrier, the *Furious,* were undoubtedly instrumental in moving the Japanese navy toward plans for the construction of its first carrier, the *Hōshō.* This vessel was laid down in December 1919 in the Asano yard at Yokohama. After the British *Hermes,* she was the first warship to be designed from the keel up as a carrier and the first to be completed as such. Yet the construction of this 7,470-ton warship was an act of faith. There was as yet no doctrine for her employment, nor were there any aircraft suitable for flight operations from her deck. Indeed, the construction of the *Hōshō,* while undertaken with extensive British counsel, was largely a matter of experiment, reflecting the uncertainties of carrier design at the dawn of the air age.[41] Yet the decision to build a carrier was a significant step in extending the reach of the Japanese navy.

THE SEMPILL AIR MISSION TO JAPAN

While the Japanese navy had endeavored to monitor the progress of aviation in all of the three major Allied naval powers during World War I, by the end of the war aviation specialists in the navy had concluded that it was Britain that had made the greatest advances in naval aviation. For that reason, the Japanese government decided to seek British aid in acquiring a professional edge to this newest arm of the Japanese navy.

During the 1920s, Japan was of two minds about the strategic implications of aviation. On the one hand, like a number of European powers, Japan came to exaggerate the capabilities of air weapons as they existed at the time. Along with their opposite numbers in Britain, the Japanese military and political leadership, drawing upon the "lessons" of the early advances in aerial bombardment during the recent world war, came to fear the enormously destructive consequences of such a campaign launched against the home islands. The advent of the aircraft carrier and its seeming ability to bring aerial bombardment to Japanese shores appeared to confirm these pessimistic speculations. It is not surprising, therefore, that at international conferences on disarmament and on the conduct of war, Japan strongly condemned aerial bombing and supported limitations on carrier construction. Japanese representatives at the Washington Naval Conference and at the Hague Conference of Jurists urged the outright condemnation of, or at least restrictions on, aerial bombardment in general, and on the bombing of cities in particular. Before and after the Washington Treaty, therefore, the Japanese sought restrictions on carrier tonnage, though the navy wished to keep its options open concerning the construction of this type of warship.[42]

Yet as we have seen, the Japanese navy had not been slow to adopt the new aviation technology and training; its first pilots had taken to the air only a few years after pioneer military aviators in the West. Before the end of World War I, Japan had begun to develop its own aircraft industry; at the outset of the war, it had even undertaken minor aerial operations against enemy surface units; and it had launched one of the world's first carriers following the war. But in training and technology (one cannot really speak of a naval air doctrine in the immediate post-war years), Japanese naval aviation was still largely dependent upon the West. Many of Japan's pilots had trained abroad. Most of its aircraft were of foreign manufacture, and those few that were domestically produced were largely of foreign design. It is unlikely, moreover, that Japan's first carrier, the *Hōshō*, could have been completed so quickly without British technical assistance.

In these early years of Japanese naval aviation, the nucleus of specialists—pilots, gunners, navigators, and ground crews in the navy, and aircraft designers and manufacturers outside it—was neither sufficiently large nor sufficiently advanced technologically to keep up with the rapid pace of aviation developments elsewhere in the world, let alone capable of enabling the Japanese navy to pursue its own innovations. During the world war, the gap in aviation technology and aircrew proficiency between Japan and the West had widened considerably. Not only had the European belligerents gained valuable experience in aerial combat, but they had been able to mass-produce planes with dramatically better performance than prewar aircraft. The postwar decade in Japanese aviation was therefore marked by two related and intensive efforts: the infusion of considerable amounts of Western technological and training assistance and, at the same time, an effort by Japan to establish its own fledgling aircraft industry.

The Japanese navy's initiatives in aviation arose from both international and domestic competition. On the one hand, the navy had to be concerned with recent advances in naval air technology in the American and British navies that threatened to leave Japan in a distant third place as a modern naval power. On the other, it had reason to be chagrined at the rapid advances in Japanese army aviation made possible by the arrival of a French air mission under Col. Jean Faure, invited to Japan in 1919 at the behest of the army.[43]

It was for these reasons that the Japanese naval leadership, following the recommendations of the Ōzeki report, decided in 1920 to seek the assistance of the British navy in improving the proficiency of its naval air arm. That summer, through the good offices of the Japanese Foreign Ministry, the navy requested that a British naval aviation mission be sent to Japan.[44] As the Japanese navy's old mentor and as the world leader in naval aviation at the time, the Royal Navy was, of course, a logical choice. Yet more prescient, perhaps, than either the British Foreign Office or the British Air Ministry, the British Admiralty had serious reservations about granting Japan unrestricted access to British technology in what might become a formidable new weapons system. The hopes of the British aircraft industry for aircraft sales to Japan, however, combined with the British navy's dismissive attitude toward Japanese flying skills, led to a compromise. After a certain amount of backing and filling, the British government proposed to send an unofficial civil aviation mission to Japan, an offer accepted in November 1920 by the Japanese government. The mission of thirty men arrived at Kasumigaura in 1921. Its leader was Sir William Francis-Forbes (later Baron) Sempill, a former officer in the Royal

Photo. 1-4. The Baron Sempill and the Baroness Sempill in Japanese dress

Air Force, experienced in the design and testing of Royal Navy aircraft during
World War I. His hand-picked team members were largely men with experience in
naval aviation and included pilots and engineers from several British aircraft firms.

The Sempill Mission, which lasted a year, provided the Japanese navy with a
quantum jump in aviation training and technology.[45] Initially it emphasized flight
training. The mission staff provided some five thousand hours of in-flight training
to Japanese student fliers. But instruction was soon expanded to include air combat, particularly dogfighting as developed by the British during World War I, high-
level bombing, aerial torpedo attacks, reconnaissance, aerial photography, and the
handling and maintenance of various types of aircraft.[46]

As important as the training it brought to the development of Japanese naval
aviation was the considerable access to the latest aviation technology that the 33

mission provided. Not only did the trainees become familiar with the latest aerial weapons and equipment—torpedoes, bombs, machine guns, cameras, and communications equipment—but the mission also brought to Kasumigaura well over a hundred aircraft, comprising twenty different models, five of which were then in use in the Royal Navy's Fleet Air Arm. Several of these planes eventually provided the inspiration for the design of a number of Japanese naval aircraft during the 1920s.

Contemporaneous with the mission, technical and training assistance from British private firms was also made available to the Japanese navy. In February 1923, for example, a British pilot/technician, William Jordan, a former captain in the Royal Navy Air Service and now in the employ of the Mitsubishi Aircraft Company as an engineer and test pilot, was chosen to make the first takeoff and landing on Japan's new carrier, the *Hōshō*. Once he had demonstrated the techniques for proper flight operations off a carrier, he was followed by the navy's first carrier pilots, including lieutenants Kira Shun'ichi,[†] Kamei Yoshio,[†] and Baba Atsumaro.[47]

Thus, by the time the last members of the Sempill Mission had returned to Britain, the Japanese navy had substantially improved its naval air training program, had begun to understand the rudiments of carrier flight-deck operations, had become familiar with such naval air tactics as existed at the time, and had acquired a reasonable grasp of the latest aviation technology. The navy's task was now to use these advances to launch itself skyward on its own wings.

2

AIRBORNE

Japanese Naval Aircraft and Naval Air Tactics,
1920–1936

During World War I, each of the four future roles of naval aviation had been demonstrated on one or more occasions. These roles were fleet reconnaissance, spotting for naval gunnery, attack (against both maritime and land-based targets), and protection of friendly forces at sea or ashore. Such was the promise of aircraft to project naval power beyond the range of shipborne weapons that each of the world's major navies felt impelled to develop a naval air arm in one form or another. By the opening of the 1920s, each had included in its roster of warships at least one prototype of aircraft carrier: the *Langley* for the United States, the *Argus* and *Furious* for Britain, and the *Hōshō* for Japan.

Yet since none of the trials of naval aviation in the recent war had proved decisive, most of the thinking about the future of the new arm lay in the realm of speculation rather than experience. On the basis of recent history there was little evidence to shake the faith of naval establishments in the continued primacy of the big-gun battleship. During the 1920s the battleship-oriented brass in all navies had scant regard for the average aircraft of the day as offensive weapons, though they had already come to appreciate the role that aircraft could play in spotting for naval gunnery.[1] Small, fragile, capable of flying only short ranges, without adequate means of communication with ships or shore bases, equipped with only the crudest navigation systems, incapable of delivering their bombs with any accuracy, and subject to grounding in any sort of bad weather, early naval aircraft had few capabilities to suggest that they were a serious threat to surface ships. True, heavy bombers of the United States Army Air Corps had sunk an old German battleship anchored off the Virginia Capes, but the dubious conditions that surrounded this test made its outcome inconclusive. If anything, the circumstances of the experiment seemed to indicate that level bombing by aircraft could not destroy a well-defended battleship.

But the limited offensive power of horizontal bombing reflected the circumscribed capabilities of naval aviation as a whole.[2] During much of the period 1920–37, the modest performance of naval aircraft (in speed, range, ceiling, and payload), and thus their modest potential, meant that in all three major navies "command of the air" was seen largely in relation to the decisive surface engagement that would be fought by the big guns of the capital ships of the line far out at sea.[3] At the outset of the 1920s, the reconnaissance function of naval aviation had matured with the use of battleship and cruiser floatplanes as scouts for the fleet. In the United States Navy these same aircraft were being used to spot the fall of shot from the battle line, a task that in the Japanese navy began to be shared by carrier aircraft as they appeared in greater numbers. Because of the potential advantage provided by such spotter aircraft to the accuracy of surface firepower, the dominant battleship orthodoxy in both the U.S. and Japanese navies came to emphasize the problem of control of the air space above the battle fleet, or, more exactly, over the decisive battle area. Naval tacticians in Japan and the United States concluded that such control could best be secured by the use of carrier fighter planes to destroy or drive off the enemy's scouting and observation aircraft. By the beginning of the 1930s this had raised the question of how to prevent the enemy from doing the same. The eventual conclusion in both navies was that control of the air space over the battle area could best be achieved by sinking or crippling the enemy's carriers at the outset, an imperative identified by the U.S. Naval War College as early as 1921.

That tacticians in the Japanese and American navies viewed carriers, not big-gun capital ships, as the proper targets for naval air power is explained by the fact that at the beginning of the 1930s few naval professionals had much confidence that carrier-borne attack aircraft could actually destroy a capital ship, though there was increasing speculation that such aircraft could at least damage and thus slow down an enemy battle line. There was, however, increasing conviction that such aircraft could destroy or effectively disable aircraft carriers, given the vulnerability of the latter. During the 1930s the development of higher-performance aircraft—marked in particular by significant improvements in radial engine design and manufacture—made it possible for carrier aviation to attack enemy fleet units at several hundred miles' distance. Moreover, the development of two carrier-borne offensive systems—torpedo bombing and dive bombing—increased the vulnerability of both battleships and carriers (in proportional degree). These developments opened up a debate on the question of which should be the primary objective of carrier strikes: the enemy's battle line or his carriers. Different answers to this question were posed by the two most interested elements in the Japanese and American navies—big-gun proponents and aviation advocates—though the evolution of such carrier doctrine was somewhat different in each navy. But by the second half of the decade, it was the preemptive strike against the opposing carriers that seemed to promise the key to victory.

Moreover, it was not fully recognized at the time how rapidly a preemptive carrier strike could inflict damage, thus dramatically changing an inferior naval force's odds of defeating a numerically superior enemy. In this regard, the carrier age largely overturned the N^2 Law and the calculations of F. W. Lanchester. In 1914 this distinguished British engineer had demonstrated in algebraic form that in modern naval combat, gunnery conferred an expanding cumulative advantage on the side with the numerical preponderance of firepower. But now, not being the target of continuous fire by an enemy battle line, a numerically inferior fleet of carriers could, if it launched a preemptive aerial strike against a numerically superior foe, summon up the equivalent of a single enormous salvo, one that could destroy the enemy in one great "pulse" of firepower.[4] But the great carrier battles of the Pacific War that would demonstrate this new equation of firepower lay in the future. In the intervening decades, those responsible for aircraft design and manufacture struggled with problems of drag, weight, performance, firepower, and the rest of the challenges to aviation engineering that lay between them and the development of aircraft that could dominate combat in oceanic skies.

JAPANESE NAVAL AIR TECHNOLOGY
Aircraft Design and Manufacture

The Sempill Mission had not been the only source of foreign air technology in the postwar decade, nor was the navy the sole beneficiary. Until this time, Japanese naval aviation had been mostly dependent on the purchase of foreign-manufactured engines and airframes, or on their manufacture in Japan under foreign licensing arrangements. But at the beginning of the 1920s, Western technological assistance began to provide the basis for the development of an independent Japanese aircraft industry.[5] The first naval aircraft manufacturer in Japan was the Naval Arsenal at Yokosuka (Yokosuka Kaigun Kōshō, or Yokoshō for short). As early as 1914 the Yokoshō had turned out small numbers of seaplanes, the design for which had been based on foreign airframes.[6] In 1920, to escape the cramped facilities at Yokosuka, the navy had established another production center at Hirō, just east of Kure, as a branch of the Kure Naval Arsenal. It was to the Hirō Branch Arsenal (known by the acronym Hirōshō) that the navy invited a small group of engineers from the Short Brothers, the British firm noted for its manufacture of large flying boats. With this assistance the navy began what was to be a quarter century of production of outstanding aircraft of this type.[7] In 1923 the Hirō Branch Arsenal was upgraded to the Hirō Naval Arsenal, but it retained an aircraft department. In 1932 it was phased out as a center for aircraft development, and its technology was transferred to the Mitsubishi Aircraft Corporation. Thereafter the function of the Hirō Arsenal and its two branches at Ōita and Maizuru was to augment the production of aircraft and aircraft engines already developed by commercial manufacturers.

In their scramble for participation in an increasingly lucrative business, private firms in Japan were not far behind in the design and manufacture of aircraft. Established commercial and industrial firms began to build research and testing facilities, including wind tunnels and water tanks to study lift and drag. To master the new developments in aeronautical science in the West, they hired foreign technicians, sent their engineers abroad, and purchased foreign aircraft for intensive study and analysis. Mitsubishi had entered the new industry in May 1916 with the establishment of an aircraft fuselage facility in Nagoya, and two years later the company strengthened its participation with the production of fuselage and engine components at its facilities in Kobe. In 1923 the Mitsubishi Internal Combustion Engine Manufacturing Company was established at Ōemachi in Nagoya, the name being changed in 1928 to the Mitsubishi Aircraft Company. Mitsubishi was fortunate at the very outset of its aircraft venture, since it quickly secured a navy contract for the design, development, and production of three different types of aircraft for use with the carrier *Hōshō*, then nearing completion. It also obtained the services of a British design team headed by Herbert Smith, a talented former employee of Sopwith. Along with the ill-fated test pilot Frederick J. Rutland, Mitsubishi retained another former Sopwith employee, William Jordan, as a test pilot and designer. It was Jordan who made the first landing on a Japanese carrier deck when he touched down on the *Hōshō* in February 1923 in a Mitsubishi aircraft.

There were three variants of aircraft developed by the British employees of Mitsubishi. Two, the Mitsubishi 1MF (Type 10) carrier fighter,* the first fighter aircraft designed specifically for carrier operations, and the Mitsubishi 2MR (Type 10) reconnaissance aircraft,* based on the general design of the 1MF fighter, proved quite successful. Both remained standard aircraft in the navy until the end of the decade.[8] The third, the Mitsubishi 1MT1N (Type 10) carrier attack aircraft, the only triplane ever accepted by the navy, was not a successful design and lasted little more than a year before being replaced.

Another aircraft manufacturer, the Aichi Watch and Electric Machinery Company, established in 1920, began the production of water-based aircraft for the navy at its Nagoya plant that same year. Most of its aircraft were, like those of other manufacturers, of foreign design and produced under licensing arrangements with a foreign firm. Aichi made arrangements with the Heinkel Company in Germany, which eventually dispatched two members of the company to Japan, including the president, Dr. Ernst Heinkel. As a result, Heinkel provided technical assistance in the design of a new generation of naval aircraft.[9]

Nakajima was the oldest and in some ways the most unusual private aircraft-manufacturing firm in Japan. It was founded in 1917 as the Hikōki Kenkyūshō by Nakajima Chikuhei, the former naval officer and pioneer pilot who eventually became a formidably influential industrialist and politician. Because of his expanding need for capital, in 1918 Nakajima joined with Kawanishi Seibei, a manufacturer of woolen goods, to found the Japan Aircraft Works. The arrangement was soon dissolved after a business dispute, and Nakajima readopted the name Nakajima Aircraft Manufacturing Works (Nakajima Hikōki Seisakusho). While it initially built aircraft and engines from existing designs or through purchase of licensing arrangements for foreign designs, Nakajima was unlike other aircraft- manufacturing firms in that from the beginning it used mainly its own engineers and designers rather than hiring foreign experts. The firm became enormously successful during the 1920s, when it produced a range of first-rate aircraft types for both the Japanese army and navy. One outstanding aircraft that the company sold to the navy was the Navy Type 3 carrier fighter (Nakajima A1N1,* a modified version of the British Gloster Gambet), which replaced the aging Navy Type 10 (Mitsubishi 1MF). Its successor was the Navy Type 90 carrier fighter (Nakajima A2N1).* Based on several American and British designs, it was the first Japanese-designed carrier fighter that "could meet on equal terms the rest of the world's best fighters."[10] The firm also excelled in the design and manufacture of aircraft engines after the establishment, in 1925, of a plant at Ogikubo, a western suburb of Tokyo, for that purpose.[11]

Whereas Nakajima manufactured aircraft for both of Japan's armed services, Kawanishi became essentially identified with the navy, in large part because so many of its staff were former naval officers. After the dissolution of his partnership with Nakajima, Kawanishi Seibei tried his hand at machine-tool manufacturing and then at the production of airplanes for civil aviation for a number of years before turning to the design and construction of naval aircraft. The Kawanishi Aircraft Company was established in 1928, and that same year the firm, in cooperation with the Short Brothers, began work on the first of a number of highly successful flying-boat designs that it undertook on contract with the navy. Thereafter, the Kawanishi name was linked to some of the largest flying boats in the Pacific.[12]

While Yokosuka remained the center for the direction of aviation technology through the end of the Pacific War, in the early 1920s the navy moved toward a division of labor in the matter of aircraft production. In 1921 the Navy Technical Department was given the authority to issue competitions for the design of aircraft according to certain specifications provided by the Navy General Staff. Private firms like Mitsubishi, Aichi, Nakajima, and Kawanishi would submit the designs, and after the navy tested prototypes, it would award contracts to those firms coming closest to its requirements. It was under these arrangements that, beginning in 1928, a series of competitions produced some of the world's best reconnaissance aircraft, carrier bombers, and carrier fighters of the 1930s. For its part, the navy, while continuing the design and manufacture of a small number of aircraft types in which it believed that it should take the lead, came to restrict its limited facilities to the testing and modification of aircraft prototypes. Thus, under the new arrangements the navy was to do much of the research, and private enterprise was to undertake most of the production.[13]

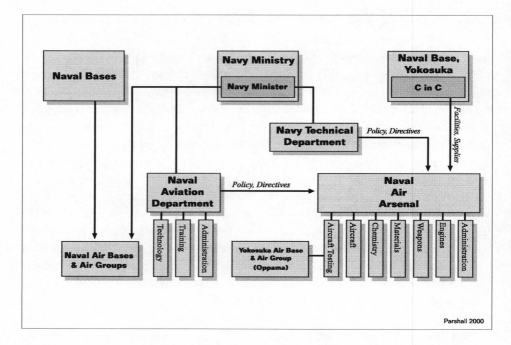

Fig. 2-1. Administrative organization of Japanese naval aviation, 1930s

The development of aviation technology in the Japanese navy was so closely related to the administrative control of naval aviation that I must pause here to say something about the latter. During the early years of naval aviation, its administration was in the hands of the Naval Affairs Bureau of the Navy Ministry, its training was the responsibility of the Naval Education Department, and its technological development was directed by the Navy Technical Department. But with the increase in the scale and complexity of naval aviation, the need for a single administrative organization coordinating these various functions became obvious. For this reason, in 1927 the navy had created the Naval Aviation Department,[14] located in Tokyo, directly responsible to the navy minister but remaining outside the Navy Ministry itself. (Fig. 2-1.) In addition to having responsibility for the development of airframes, engines, ordnance, and equipment relating to naval aviation, the department was given charge of all air training, except for air combat training, which remained in the hands of the various air groups.[15]

Technical research relating to naval aviation took a different route before it too was subsumed under the Naval Aviation Department. In April 1923, in order to consolidate all its research, for both warships and aircraft, the Navy Technical Department founded the Navy Technical Research Institute in Tokyo. This facility was, however, destroyed in the great earthquake of that year, and a new aviation research facility was established at Kasumigaura in 1924. To the Kasumigaura

Branch of the Navy Technical Institute the navy brought most of its aeronautical research and testing equipment, though a number of draftsmen and engineers were left at the Hirō facility. In 1929, however, an aircraft-testing station was also established at the Yokosuka Naval Dockyard, which in 1930 also became a testing center for aircraft engines.[16]

By the London Naval Treaty of 1930, Japan had, with great reluctance and consequent turmoil within its navy's high command, accepted further limitations on its warship construction in relation to that of the British and American navies, most critically in the cruiser category.[17] Now, shorn of its strength in cruisers, which had up to the London Treaty made up for its inferiority in capital ships, the Japanese navy turned to air power to make up for these deficiencies. In view of the increasing potential of air power, at the outset of the 1930s the navy attempted to consolidate its aviation research still further by bringing its technical research facilities together with the tactical training facilities already in existence at Yokosuka. In 1932, construction was begun on a Naval Air Arsenal (Kaigun Kōkūshō, or Kūshō for short), which was completed in 1936 and placed under the command of the Yokosuka Naval Base. The creation of the arsenal brought together for the first time all work in aircraft design and flight testing, as well as the construction of prototypes not under contract with private firms. Though it thus became a center of Japanese naval aviation technology, the arsenal served several masters. While administratively it came under the authority of the Yokosuka Naval Base, for purposes of technological development its management was divided between the Naval Aviation Department and the Navy Technical Department, the former assuming all responsibility for aircraft design and production, the latter having charge of the development and testing of most weapons (except for aerial bombs) and all equipment (cameras, radios, etc.).[18] Within the arsenal was the Flight Testing Department (Hikō Jikkenbu), which carried out flight tests of new prototypes as well as of new models of aircraft already in service. It measured their performance under standard conditions to make sure that they were safe and met the navy's basic performance requirements. If they did, they were passed on to the tactical and training unit, the Yokosuka Air Group (see below), which tested their combat capabilities and suitability for carrier operations. Considering the importance of the large number of aircraft designs that it came to evaluate and the outstanding success of some of these designs by 1937, the establishment of the Naval Air Arsenal as an advanced aviation engineering center marked a giant step forward for Japan as one of the world's leading aircraft producers.[19]

In 1932, as its first order of business, the Naval Air Arsenal improved the system of managed competition for the design and development of naval aircraft that had been in use since the 1920s by the Japanese aircraft industry. The new arrangement, known as the Prototypes System, called for the *pairing* of firms to compete for orders of various types of aircraft that were to be designed and produced according to specifications set forth by the navy. The firm whose prototype successfully met these specifications was awarded the navy contract to put its design into production. But it was far from being a winner-take-all arrangement; the losing firm would be expected to produce its competitor's design, or to produce the engines for the aircraft, as a second-source supplier. This was a significant innovation, one that coaxed the best competitive energies from private industry in order to obtain the best designs for the navy, but that also led, once the best design was selected, to the synthesizing and sharing of the technologies involved. The Prototypes System was a revolutionary step in the way the aircraft industry came to compete, integrate components, and build aircraft. Not only did it provide the guidelines for a series of outstanding naval aircraft, the first wholly designed by Japanese aircraft engineers; it also laid the basis for the military procurement system that exists in Japan to this day. It was a very Japanese approach to procurement in that it did not drive out the losers in design competition. Rather, it served as a recognizable example of Japanese industrial policy from that day to this, one that provided a series of safety nets to protect strategic industries.[20]

These organizational details are important to understanding the direction given to the sudden acceleration in Japanese naval aviation technology that took place in the 1930s. Throughout the previous decade, as we have seen, Japanese aircraft production had been based for the most part on foreign designs manufactured in Japan under licensing agreements. Beginning in 1932, with a decade of apprenticeship and experience in aircraft production behind it, the navy moved decisively to become self-sufficient in aircraft design and manufacture. The establishment of the Naval Air Arsenal had much to do with this, but the driving force behind this new policy came out of the Naval Aviation Department itself. There, in 1932, Rear Adm. Yamamoto Isoroku,[†] chief of the Technical Bureau of the Department from 1930 through 1933 and chief of the department itself, 1935–36, pushed through a plan intended to break the dependence of the navy—and by extension, of the Japanese aircraft industry—on foreign aircraft designs. The plan provided for autonomous production of naval aircraft based essentially on Japanese designs, on the navy's emerging operational needs, and on the mobilization of civilian aircraft companies.

Like most other air power nations, Japan did not, of course, achieve complete independence from foreign aircraft technology. During the rest of the 1930s the Japanese aircraft industry imported various equipment, engines, and even aircraft, largely from the United States, and during the Pacific War it received at least a trickle of such materiel from its Axis allies.[21] Yet Yamamoto's initiative at the Naval Aviation Department, combined with the Naval Air Arsenal's Prototypes System, started a process that was to result in the design, development, and production of some of the finest aircraft in the world.

While the Naval Aviation Department was the source of a good deal of innovative thinking about naval air doctrine and technology, effective aircraft design and production was continually hampered by one of the inherent and critical flaws in the prewar Japanese government: the debilitating and corrosive rivalry between the armed services. The ongoing failure of the army and navy to cooperate, as well as the inadequate organizational integration of the navy itself, eventually led to serious aircraft production problems that could have been avoided had there been more opportunities for inter- and intraservice discussion of critical technological issues. This lack of cooperation also led to a prodigious waste of time and technological resources and, by the end of the Pacific war, produced far too many types of aircraft, a situation that limited the overall number of planes that could be produced.[22]

LAND-BASED AIR POWER
The Naval Air Groups

Even after the Japanese navy had assembled a significant carrier force in the 1930s, it continued to increase its land-based contingents in keeping with its initial strategy of providing a rapid defense of the home islands against the possible westward advance of an American naval offensive. Indeed, it was land-based aircraft that provided the bulk of Japan's naval aviation up to the eve of the Pacific War. In this the Japanese navy was unique among the three major naval powers during the interwar period. In the immediate prewar years the only analogy to Japan's shore-based naval air units were the United States Navy's shore-based patrol squadrons and the two air wings of the United States Marine Corps.

As explained in chapter 1, the creation of land-based naval air contingents had begun in 1916 with the establishment of the Yokosuka Naval Air Group, followed after the end of World War I by the establishment of air groups at Sasebo, Kasumigaura, and Ōmura. Given the navy's concentration on the surface navy, particularly its cruiser force, no similar units were established for the remainder of the 1920s, nor did any comprehensive administrative system exist for land-based naval air power. Then, beginning in 1930, confronted with the restrictions on surface ship construction to which Japan had agreed at the London Naval Conference that year, the navy determined to make up for these restrictions by strengthening its naval air arm. Between 1930 and 1937, under the first two of the navy's "Circle" programs (its shorthand designation for a series of interwar naval expansion programs),[23] air groups were established at nine new air bases around the Japanese home islands and in Korea: Tateyama, Kure, Ōminato, Saeki, Maizuru, Kisarazu, Kanoya, Yokohama, and Chinkai (Chinhae). (Map 2-1.)

By the end of 1937 the navy possessed 563 aircraft based ashore. Added to the 332 aircraft aboard its carrier fleet, it thus had a total of 895 aircraft and 2,711 aircrew (pilots and navigators) in thirty-nine air groups.[24] While Japan's carrier aircraft were considerably fewer in number than the total American naval air strength for the same period, its shore-based naval aircraft were substantially more numerous. This discrepancy in force structure would have been meaningless at the outset of any encounter between the two naval powers in the 1930s. But Japan's substantial land-based air power was to work to its advantage when it went to war in 1937 with a land power, China.

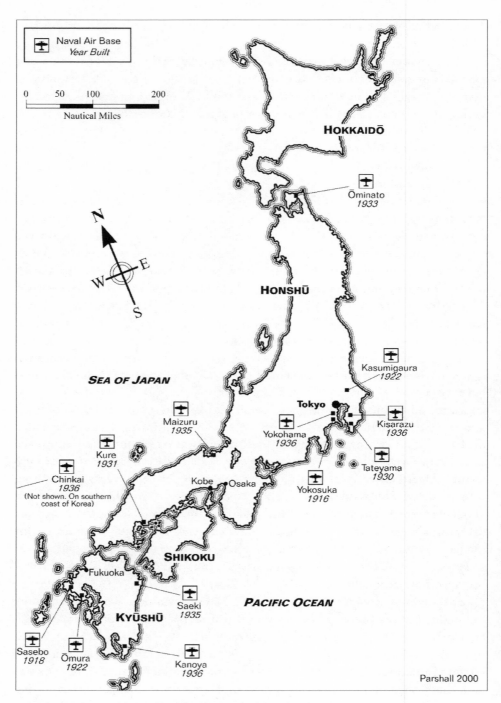

Map 2-1. Japanese naval air bases, home islands, 1916–1937

JAPANESE NAVAL AIR RECRUITMENT AND TRAINING

While production of the aircraft for the new land-based air groups, as well as for the increasing number of carrier-based air groups, strained Japan's aircraft production facilities at the time, the greatest problem was to provide the necessary increase in air and ground crews. This task was made more difficult by the competing demands of the army, as well as by the navy itself, since the navy required that its fleet carriers and floatplane-carrying battleships and cruisers maintain their full complements of aviation personnel.[25] From the earliest days of the Yokosuka Air Group's establishment, Japanese naval aviation, unlike the other branches of the service, mainly used its operational units as training facilities rather than training its personnel in specialized schools. The advantage of this system was that it gave aviation training more flexibility in dealing with the navy's budgetary fluctuations. For example, if it was determined that naval air training should be suddenly expanded, as happened at the outset of the 1930s, it was possible to shift resources (both personnel and equipment) from regular operational units in order to do so.[26] Eventually, in 1930, the Kasumigaura Air Group was designated as the unit for basic flight training for student pilots and aircraft maintenance for student mechanics, while the Yokosuka Air Group was once more designated as a training unit, now specializing in advanced flight training in aerial combat and air reconnaissance. The Yokosuka Air Group was also used, as I shall explain, in the flight-testing of experimental aircraft.

Improved training was predicated, of course, upon an adequate supply of intelligent, healthy, and motivated young recruits. At the beginning, it had been planned that only Naval Academy graduates would become pilots. But it was soon realized that this trainee pool would have to be expanded. Thus, regular training of noncommissioned officer pilots began in 1916, and by about 1921 the number of noncommissioned pilot trainees was already higher than that of officer pilot trainees, and thereafter so remained.[27] Moreover, with the anticipated growth in the number of air groups early in the 1930s, the number of academy graduates volunteering for the naval air service was obviously inadequate, and the lengthy preparation they had received for service in the surface fleet was largely irrelevant to achievement of proficiency in naval aviation.

Two parallel training programs were therefore established that radically expanded the pool of pilot trainees in the naval air service. The first of these, created in 1928, was a program for noncommissioned officers, designated in 1930 as the Pilot Trainee System (Sōjū Renshūsei, or Sōren for short). This program recruited and trained noncommissioned officers drawn from fleet service. The second, established in 1929, was the Flight Reserve Enlisted Trainee System (Hikō Yoka Renshūsei, or Yokaren for short), which drew its candidates directly from civilian life. It provided for the recruitment and training of boys fifteen to seventeen years of age who had finished primary school, who were in excellent physical condition, and who were at the top of their classes. Inducted into the navy, these youngsters were given three years of general education—similar in part to the training at the Naval Academy—that brought them beyond the middle-school level, after which they would be given a short period of training at sea. Then, depending upon their abilities, they would be divided into pilot and observer candidates and given specialized training at one of the air groups. While a small number of trainees still continued to be drawn from commissioned volunteers, the great majority of Japanese naval air pilots and observers up through the Pacific War were produced through either the Sōren or the Yokaren system, an arrangement that made Japanese naval air training markedly different from that in the United States Navy, which largely restricted pilot training to those of commissioned rank.[28]

Beginning in 1934, flight training was also available to a small number of college and university graduates who had majored in oceanography and who were members of the Japanese Student Aviation League. After their admission into the Student Aviation Reserve (Kōkū Yobi Gakusei) program, these students were given about two months of general naval education followed by ten months of pilot training at Kasumigaura. Graduates of this program become reserve ensigns. The first three classes (up to March 1937) specialized in carrier attack aircraft and seaplanes, while later classes were trained in various types of aircraft. After Pearl Harbor this program expanded rapidly, training over ten thousand men in 1943.[29]

While undertaking a complete overhaul of its recruitment system for pilots and observers, the navy took steps to make its flight training both more uniform and more rigorous. Although the Sempill Mission had considerably improved Japanese naval air training in general, for the rest of the 1920s training focused largely on simply improving flying skills, specifically carrier-deck takeoffs and landings. To a certain extent the flight instruction provided by the Sempill Mission had left an inhibiting legacy, in that it had tended to encourage the intuitive abilities of a handful of star pilots while failing to put in place an adequate program of routine practice to improve the skills of the average pilot trainee. One officer who had felt this most keenly was Capt. Yamamoto Isoroku, who had arrived at the Kasumigaura Air Group in September 1924. Several months later he became the group's executive officer, the first assignment in what was to be a close identification with naval air power for the rest of his life. While at Kasumigaura, he underwent flight training and soloed, an unusual initiative in the navy at this time for someone of his rank. Convinced that the navy's single aircraft carrier was useless if only a few skilled pilots were able to land on it, Yamamoto soon cracked down on what he saw as the careless, daredevil elitism of the best of Japan's prospective naval aviators and came to insist on relentless and rigorous drill for the broad mass of trainees at Kasumigaura. Later on, he instituted intensive training in instrument flying of the sort that Lindbergh and Admiral Byrd had pioneered so successfully.[30]

Yamamoto left Kasumigaura at the end of 1925 when he was assigned to Washington, D.C., as naval attaché. But the rigorous training he had insisted upon continued, much of it devoted to carrier takeoffs and landings, practiced both on land and on the deck of the Hōshō. With the addition of the Akagi to the fleet in

Photo. 2-1. Yamamoto Isoroku (1884–1943) in the
rank of captain

1928, the navy formed the First Carrier Division, which made it possible for aircrews to gain experience in flight operations involving more than one carrier. Thus,
while takeoffs and landings still occupied much of the training of carrier pilots, an
increasing amount of time was given over to tactical training once the ships of the
First Carrier Division began to maneuver together.

EMERGENCE OF AIR ATTACK TECHNIQUES

By the 1930s, Japanese naval air doctrine had begun to shift away from an emphasis on aerial scouting and reconnaissance toward the idea of using aircraft to attack
enemy fleet units. Consequently, for much of that decade greater attention was
given to the development of effective tactics and aircraft for attack missions than to

the development of tactics and aircraft for defensive interception of enemy planes. Indeed, the initial combat operations of the naval air service two decades before had been offensive rather than defensive. The navy's first attempt at aerial bombardment against enemy surface units had been the horizontal bombing attack carried out at Tsingtao in the autumn of 1914, an operation undertaken with crude bombsights and almost no training, and thus without any significant results. After the war the Sempill Mission had provided some instruction in horizontal bombing *(suihei bakugeki),* along with some British bombsight technology.

But Japanese interest in this particular tactic had largely been aroused by the publicity surrounding the bombing tests off the Virginia Capes in 1921. The storm of controversy provoked in America by these tests was reported in some detail to the Japanese naval high command by Comdr. Yamamoto Isoroku, then on detached duty for study in the United States.[31] While the conditions for the tests—the bombardment of anchored, unmanned, and undefended vessels—had been controversial and the results inconclusive, air enthusiasts in both Japanese services had insisted in carrying out similar experiments in their own country. The target selected was the undefended, unmanned, and drifting hulk of the coast defense ship *Iwami* (the former Russian battleship *Orel*) off Yokosuka in July 1924. While bombs dropped from an average height of 1,000 meters (3,000 feet) eventually sent the *Iwami* to the bottom, critics noted that it took nearly four hours to do so, that no more than 20 percent of the bombs hit the target (a ratio that nevertheless compared favorably with the American tests), and that it left unresolved the question of how such an attack would have fared against modern battleships under way and defended both by their own antiaircraft guns and by fighter aircraft. Predictably, battleship and air power proponents in the navy argued over the results of this sort of bombing test in the same way that their counterparts disagreed in the United States.[32]

During the remainder of the decade, the navy annually carried out further experiments in horizontal bombing to improve bombing equipment, aiming skills, and bomb release techniques. Practice runs were made at medium heights of between 2,000 and 5,000 meters (7,000 and 16,000 feet), either by single aircraft or by small formations of two or three planes aiming on stationary targets. While the results of these tests were reasonably good, the attempt after 1930 to make the tests more realistic by directing them toward moving targets caused hit percentages to plummet. To make them more effective, bombing runs were lowered to 1,000 and even 100 meters (3,000 and 300 feet), at speeds of not more than 50 knots. Accuracy improved somewhat, though it was recognized that in actual combat, bombing at such low altitudes and speeds would make the attacking aircraft extremely vulnerable to defensive fire. Thus, in the mid-1930s the navy tried an alternative technique: a return to higher bombing runs, now carried out by larger formations of bombing aircraft whose ordnance would create a larger bomb pattern to assure that at least some would score hits on a moving target. But while both techniques improved hit ratios somewhat, the ongoing problems in horizontal bombing were the lack of an accurate bombsight and inadequate training to improve coordination between bomber pilots and bombardiers. Thus, the results achieved were still so unsatisfactory and the probable risks in actual wartime situations so great that voices began to call for a halt to level bombing altogether. It was not until a year before the Pacific War that special team training, initiated to improve coordination between bomber pilots and bombardiers, began to increase substantially the accuracy of bombing runs against stationary targets. Against moving targets, little progress was made, and in consequence the navy developed two other bombing tactics that promised greater and more consistent success: aerial torpedo attacks and dive bombing.[33]

Of these two tactical alternatives, aerial torpedo bombing was the first studied by the naval air arm. The tactic appealed to the Japanese navy because it was technologically feasible; because it was tactically related to surface torpedo warfare; and because it was in keeping with the navy's offensive tradition. Japanese naval interest in aerial torpedo operations had emerged as early as 1912, at the birth of Japanese naval aviation itself. Considerable impetus to the idea had been provided by a series of simulated night attacks, launched by aircraft based at Oppama on Japanese fleet units at Tateyama Bay in Chiba Prefecture during the naval maneuvers of 1916. During these years, moreover, a number of the navy's early aviators had begun to argue the importance of developing what they saw as the enormous potential of the new tactic. Among these were lieutenants Nakajima, Kaneko Yōzō, and Kawazoe Takuo. In 1919, Kawazoe drafted a pioneer study, "On Torpedo Attacks" (Raigeki-ron), which is said to have made a powerful impression on his fellow aviation pioneers.[34]

The principal obstacle to the more rapid advancement of this tactical concept during these years was a lag in the development of the required technology—of the torpedoes themselves, of the aircraft to carry them, and of the mechanisms to assure their steady flight first through the air and then through the water. In particular, the navy possessed no torpedoes sufficiently small to be carried by the lightweight aircraft of the day but sufficiently rugged to withstand the impact of being dropped from any great height above the water, since the impact forces tended to break, bend, or otherwise mutilate the torpedo. The demonstration of aerial torpedo attacks provided to navy pilots by the Sempill Mission at Kasumigaura had used only wooden dummy torpedoes. When real torpedoes were first used in an exercise in Tokyo Bay in 1922, the devices had to be dropped at a height no greater than 5 or 6 feet (1.5 or 2 meters) above the water and at an airspeed of no more than 50 knots in order to assure a successful run against a target. In combat, of course, these limitations would have left attacking aircraft extremely vulnerable to enemy antiaircraft fire and even, in a rough sea, at hazard from the waves.[35]

Over time, these difficulties were surmounted by research along a number of different lines. In 1931, largely through the work of Ordnance Lt. Naruse Seiji,[†] who had studied the relevant technology in Britain and who had successfully designed and tested an experimental model, the navy adopted the Type 91 aerial torpedo.

The Type 91 was a formidable weapon. It had a range of 2,000 meters (7,000 feet), a speed of 42 knots, and an explosive charge of 150 kilograms (331 pounds).[36] It could be launched at an airspeed of 100 knots and heights of 100 meters (300 feet). In these respects it was slightly inferior to the later American torpedo, the Mark XIII, employed at the start of the Pacific War. The Japanese navy's preference was for greater hit probability at short ranges—which necessitated lower release speeds—and the navy gave only secondary consideration to the vulnerability of the aircraft carrying the torpedo. While the Type 91, like all aerial torpedoes, contained a significantly smaller explosive charge than a torpedo fired from surface craft, the Japanese navy was certain that hits by four or five of them would doom a battleship.[37] The Type 91 went through many versions that increased its strength, launch speeds, and explosive power, but it remained the standard aerial torpedo of the Japanese navy from its development to the end of the Pacific War, and its most famous victims were the British capital ships *Repulse* and *Prince of Wales* at the outset of the war.

The problem of impact forces breaking or deforming the torpedo shell was solved by strengthening the body structure. The first efforts involved constructing a thicker hull; subsequently T-bars (and, later, I-bars) inside the hull were added. Later versions of the Type 91 were strong enough that they could survive water entry with launch speeds up to 350 knots.[38] But air-launched torpedoes must have satisfactory aerodynamic characteristics prior to water entry and satisfactory hydrodynamic characteristics after water entry. Resolving the conflicts between these requirements took many years. The problems of entry angle, pitch, yaw, and especially in-flight roll of the torpedo—which affected the course of the torpedo once it entered the water—tested the ingenuity of the engineers at the Naval Air Arsenal. Some of these problems were not completely solved until the eve of the Pacific War. In 1930 the development of a metal coil-spring release mechanism in the aircraft carrying the torpedo helped assure that the torpedo would assume the required angle upon impact with the water. During the 1930s the technical staff recognized that the problems of pitch and yaw during air flight could be reduced by extensions to the fins affixed to the tail assembly of the torpedo. It took more time, however, to solve the combined problem of designing an aerial torpedo with both the aerodynamic characteristics required for launching from any significant height and the hydrodynamic characteristics necessary for the weapon to follow a predetermined course and depth once it entered the water.[39]

The aircraft employed to carry the new torpedo was also the result of many years of development. In 1923 the British aircraft designer Herbert Smith, employed by Mitsubishi, designed an all-around carrier-based attack aircraft to replace the triplane Type 10 (Mitsubishi 1MT1N), whose configuration had proved impractical. After years of testing and several preliminary models, his design was finally adopted by the navy in 1931—an unprecedented lag between design and adoption—as the Type 13-3 carrier attack aircraft (Mitsubishi B1M3),* a single-engine three-seater aircraft that could carry one 45-centimeter (18-inch) torpedo or two 250-kilogram (551-pound) bombs.[40] The next year the Type 13-3 was embarked on the carriers *Hōshō* and *Kaga* and served as the navy's main attack aircraft during the brief aerial combat over Shanghai in 1932.

Along with these advances, there had emerged, as early as the mid-1920s, a coterie of dedicated, skilled torpedo pilots like Lt. Comdr. Kuwabara Torao and lieutenants Kikuchi Tomozō,[†] Maeda Kōsei,[†] and Saitō Masahisa[†] who, through constant practice in day and night attack methods, came to develop aerial torpedo tactics into a powerful offensive system.[41] It is a mark of their capabilities that Kuwabara and Kikuchi were among the handful of naval airmen who came to hold carrier commands in the Japanese navy.

Given the lag in technology and organization, tactical doctrine came slowly, and until 1928 most aerial torpedo practice was carried out by single aircraft. The same lag also allowed the early development of certain tactical concepts that now seem bizarre. One example stemmed from the navy's concern that in the decisive fleet encounter, enemy capital ships would be able to avoid torpedoes launched from Japanese surface destroyer (torpedo) squadrons by turning away. Convinced that only torpedo planes could thwart this maneuver, the navy attempted to work out a scheme for the coordination of surface and air attacks, with torpedo aircraft in a supporting role. In April 1928 the formation of the First Carrier Division, bringing together a number of ships and aircraft, permitted the navy to attempt such a tactical scheme. In annual maneuvers held that summer off Amami Ōshima, the First Fleet, which included the First Carrier Division's *Hōshō,* practiced coordination between the *Hōshō*'s air attack squadron, the fleet's cruiser squadrons, and its surface destroyer flotillas. Because the aircraft and aerial torpedo technology of the day required a low-level, low-speed attack, the tactic called for the torpedo aircraft to orbit on station while waiting for the surface torpedo forces to get into position and then, after the latter had done so, to attack the enemy from the unengaged side.[42] (Fig. 2-2.) By middecade, Japanese torpedo aircrews themselves had become skeptical about the feasibility of such a tactical scheme in actual combat, and commentators today are even less charitable about the idea. A tactical situation suitable to an aerial torpedo attack might take hours to develop, while the window of opportunity for such an attack might be of only a few minutes' duration. It would be quite impractical to launch torpedo aircraft, to have them orbit on station while waiting for destroyers and cruisers to get into position, and, finally, to have the torpedo bombers get into position themselves, all at a time when air-to-air and ship-to-air communications were inadequate. It says volumes about the absence of naval air combat experience and the relative novelty of the use of aircraft at sea, as well as the lag in technology, that this utterly impractical tactic could have persisted as accepted doctrine in the Japanese navy until the mid-1930s.[43]

In any event, the use of aerial attacks by massed aircraft of different types as a potent offensive element lay further on in the decade, when faster and more powerful aircraft would be launched from larger and more numerous carriers. But with the technological advances in torpedoes, not only were speeds and launch heights

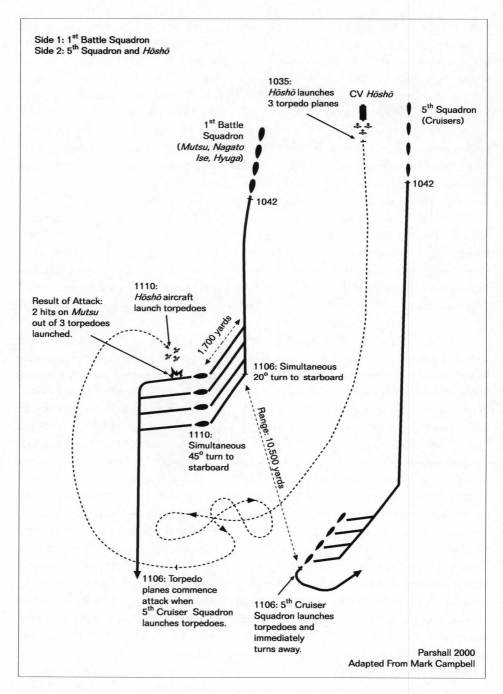

Side 1: 1st Battle Squadron
Side 2: 5th Squadron and *Hōshō*

1035:
Hōshō launches
3 torpedo planes

CV *Hōshō*

5th Squadron
(Cruisers)

1st Battle
Squadron
(*Mutsu, Nagato
Ise, Hyuga*)

1042

1042

1110:
Hōshō aircraft
launch torpedoes

Result of Attack:
2 hits on *Mutsu*
out of 3 torpedoes
launched.

1,700 yards

1106: Simultaneous
20° turn to starboard

Range: 10,500 yards

1110:
Simultaneous
45° turn to
starboard

1106: Torpedo
planes commence
attack when
5th Cruiser Squadron
launches torpedoes.

1106: 5th Cruiser
Squadron launches
torpedoes and
immediately
turns away.

Parshall 2000
Adapted From Mark Campbell

Fig. 2-2. Coordinated exercise in offensive air tactics, Amami Ōshima, 1928

in torpedo attacks increased, but the likelihood of hits against moving targets jumped to 60 percent in 1932 and 88.4 percent in 1933. By about 1935, the navy's torpedo units were regularly scoring hits at a rate of 50 percent under the worst daylight conditions and often 100 percent under the best, so that the navy came to expect an average hit rate of 70–80 percent. Much depended on the weather, of course, and upon the effectiveness of the evasive tactics employed by the target vessels. One reason for the remarkable success in these practice runs was the weakness of naval antiaircraft fire in these years, which meant that few attacking aircraft were judged to have been downed. Nevertheless, when one considers that the calculations necessary in aerial torpedo bombing—the target's course, speed, and anticipated evasive action; the angle between the torpedo and target; the safe release distance (that between the torpedo's point of entry into the water and the point at which its detonator activated); and the distance at which the aircraft had sufficiently closed the target (not more than 1,000 meters [3,000 feet])—all had to be made with the naked eye, the high hit rates achieved by Japanese naval aircrews during these years demonstrated their great skill and spirit. Year by year, word began to spread throughout the navy that carrier-based air power posed an ominous threat to the main surface forces.[44]

The last aerial offensive tactic employed by the navy was a technique only recently developed in the West. Dive bombing had been pioneered by the United States Navy in the mid-1920s, in part because of the difficulties and limitations that had been found to hinder both high-level horizontal and low-level torpedo bombing of warships—particularly small, fast warships—under way. In 1926 a fighter squadron at the naval air station at San Diego had experimented with the idea of "glide bombing." Diving down at land targets in relatively shallow dives and pulling out at about 1,500–1,000 feet (450–300 meters) to release their ordnance, these aircraft had come within a few feet of the target.[45] But the tactic of dive-bombing as it came to be developed as a punishingly effective tactic by the United States Navy was born in October 1926 when a flight of navy fighters, diving almost vertically from 12,000 feet (3,500 meters), carried out a simulated and surprise attack on capital ships sortieing from San Pedro Harbor, San Diego.[46] Over the next five or six years, various tests and experiments conducted by the United States Navy demonstrated that dive bombing at angles of 70 degrees or more could achieve remarkable accuracy even against smaller, faster warships. The advantage of a near-vertical dive was that the horizontal motion of the dive-bombing aircraft was practically negligible, obviating the need for the pilot to adjust his aim for forward motion; all he had to do was to maintain his sight on the target as it moved. Moreover, these tests showed that because of the height at which the aircraft approached their target, the angle of their dive, and their speed in the dive, the tactic made effective response of shipboard antiaircraft defenses very difficult, and nearly impossible if the dive-bombing aircraft approached on different bearings.[47] By the beginning of the 1930s, the main residual problem in the development of dive bombing as a dominating aerial tactic was that there were as yet no suitable dive-bombing aircraft, fighters being too lightweight and structurally inadequate to carry ordnance sufficiently heavy to do real damage to a major warship.

In both the Japanese and American navies the adoption of dive bombing as a major offensive tactic was reflective of a sea change in doctrinal thinking about the role of naval aviation, particularly carrier aviation. The early 1920s had seen carrier aircraft used largely for scouting purposes or for spotting the fall of shell from the battle line. By the end of the decade, the need to control the air above the great gun duel between opposing lines of capital ships—that is, to drive off enemy scouting or spotting aircraft from above the decisive battle area—had become the primary role for carrier aviation and thus had given rise to the carrier fighter, which was seen as playing a defensive role.[48] However, by the beginning of the 1930s, carrier aircraft had come to be viewed as instrumental in attacking capital ships themselves, less in terms of sinking them—since few in either navy saw that as a realistic possibility, given the small bomb loads aircraft of the time were able to carry—than in terms of slowing them down.

Then, in the mid-1930s, Japanese and American naval airmen began to consider that the enemy carriers themselves were logically the principal targets for offensive air operations. Again, the objective of such attacks was not so much to sink the opposing carriers as to cripple their launch and recovery operations by destroying their flight decks at the outset. This, of course, could be accomplished only by aerial attacks of pinpoint accuracy. Sinking carriers could be accomplished, of course, by aerial torpedoes, but not only did such torpedoes continue to exhibit problems of delivery; it was also feared in the Japanese navy that this tactic might well take longer and would thus give the enemy time to fly off his own aircraft. Eventually, as I shall explain in chapter 6, the Japanese navy would work out aerial assault tactics that employed coordinated dive bombing and aerial torpedo runs. In the meantime, dive bombing came to be seen as the best anticarrier tactic in both navies.[49]

Publicity in the United States given to air shows incorporating dive-bombing demonstrations, supplemented by reports by Japanese naval attachés, was undoubtedly the source of Japanese naval interest in the new tactic. In 1929, at the initiative of Vice Adm. Andō Masataka,[†] chief of the Naval Aviation Department, the department began gathering basic data concerning the aerial techniques, training, and aircraft needed to develop dive bombing in the Japanese navy. From 1930 to 1932, fighter aircraft carried out a number of dive-bombing attacks against old warship hulks. In 1930, fighters from the First Carrier Division dive-bombed the old cruiser *Akashi* in Tokyo Bay, using 4-kilogram (8.8-pound) practice bombs, and the next year they attacked the old cruiser *Chitose* in Saiki Bay, using 30-kilogram (66.2-pound) bombs, a test in which several bombing runs achieved 100 percent accuracy in hitting the target. In 1932 the Yokosuka Air Group and the Naval Air Arsenal began a joint study of dive-bombing techniques, using modified British Bulldog fighters in near-vertical dive-bombing runs against the hulk of the cruiser *Aso*.[50]

Okumiya Masatake,[†] who as a young officer pilot aboard the carrier *Ryūjō* was one of the first Japanese naval aviators trained in this new tactic, years later remem-

bered the early difficulties in the development of dive bombing, even against stationary land targets. At first, he recalled, dives were made at an angle of 30 degrees
from an altitude of 1,000 meters (3,000 feet) and about 2,000 meters (7,000 feet)
from the target. A large white cloth was placed on the field and next to it optical
equipment that measured dive angles. The young and inexperienced pilots had
great difficulty in judging the correct angle for their dives, though after about a
month they were able to make dives of 60 degrees. The greatest problem, however,
was wind, since changes in wind direction would throw off the pilots' aim time and
again. In high-level bombing, the bombsight automatically corrected for wind at the
altitude of the aircraft, but in dive bombing, such correction was not possible, since
wind direction was subject to radical change in the midst of a bombing run. Only
with experience were dive-bomber pilots able to effectively correct for wind
changes.[51]

As dive-bombing technique developed, it became typical for pilots to begin their
dives from a height of about 3,000 meters (10,000 feet), adjusting the angle of their
dive, rather than trying to aim, until they were about 1,000 meters (3,000 feet)
above the target, by which time they had attained speeds of 250 to 270 knots.[52] At
that height they adjusted their aiming sights before they reached the release altitude
of about 500 meters (1,500 feet). While similar tests were carried out by other air
groups over the next several years, the First Carrier Division was assigned the task
of translating these attacks by single aircraft on stationary targets into effective tactical doctrine employing coordinated attacks by multiple aircraft against moving
warships. In 1935, at the Kashima bombing range on the coast of Ibaraki
Prefecture, the navy built a full-size mock-up of the U.S. carrier *Saratoga,* complete
from the flight deck down, on which navy aircraft achieved generally good results
in dive-bombing attacks.[53] By 1937 the Japanese navy had developed a highly
skilled cadre of practitioners of the new art, chief among whom was Lt. Egusa
Takashige,[†] destined to be Japan's great dive-bombing ace of the Pacific War.[54]

Despite the fact that in every instance, dive bombing provided greater accuracy
against moving targets than horizontal bombing, it became clear that the stress on
airframes caused by the violent maneuvers during and after a diving run was far
greater than the fighter aircraft, which had been initially used in practice dive-
bombing runs, had been designed to take. In trying to find a suitable aircraft for the
new tactic, the navy also tried out the Type 90 reconnaissance seaplane, modeled on
the American Vought O2U Corsair and adopted for land-based operations, but its
dive speed was insufficient.[55] What was needed, if dive bombing was to become a
standard tactic for the navy, was an aircraft of rugged construction especially
designed for the purpose. Thus, in 1933 the navy issued bids for the design and
development of a carrier dive bomber[56] of exceptional structural integrity and great
maneuverability. The contract award was won by Aichi, which through licensing
arrangements with Heinkel—which had itself begun designing and building dive
bombers—was able to import a Heinkel HE 66 dive bomber. Aichi engineers modified the aircraft to meet the navy's specifications, including the installation of a

Japanese engine and a particularly rugged undercarriage. The result was the Aichi D1A1, a two-man biplane, adopted by the navy in 1934 as the Type 94 carrier bomber. It was soon succeeded by an improved version, the Aichi D1A2, which, as the Type 96 carrier bomber,* was an outstanding aircraft for its day.[57]

But while the Type 94 was a state-of-the-art aircraft for its time, like contemporary Western dive-bombing aircraft it made physical and mental demands on its crew that in some ways seem outlandish by today's standards. Okumiya Masatake, as a young lieutenant, was one of the first to fly the Type 94 off the deck of a carrier, the *Ryūjō*. He has provided us with an understanding of the multiple and often simultaneous tasks required of the crew while on a dive-bombing mission:

> In addition to flying the aircraft, the pilot was responsible for carrying out the dive-bombing attack and for firing the two fixed-forward machine guns. His two feet managed the aircraft's control surfaces, his right hand worked the stick and worked the machine guns; his left managed the engine controls and released the bomb or bombs, all the time looking through the aiming sight. A speaking tube connected to the observer was positioned near his left ear, a radio receiver was positioned at his left and both ears had to constantly monitor the sound of the engine. At his mouth was an oxygen mask, but his nose had to be sensitive to various smells, particularly of gasoline.
>
> For his part, the observer had to handle the radio telegraph, deal with incoming coded messages and decipher them, measure drift, wind speed, and wind direction, calculate the aircraft's actual speed, determine its actual position. When necessary, he also had to fire the flexible rear-firing machine gun, take photographs, drop message bags, use flag or flash signals, and, when in a dive, assist the pilot by reading off the angle of dive.[58]

This is multitasking at its most horrendous!

In any event, with the appearance of the Aichi D1A1, dive bombing came into its own in the Japanese navy.[59] In 1935 the navy had begun to practice formation dive bombing and to experiment with a formula whereby carrier fighters would stay above the dive bombers as a cover force while the latter dove into the attack. But controversy over the superiority of dive bombing as opposed to torpedo bombing, which had begun soon after the formation of the First Carrier Division in 1928, was to grow in intensity during the succeeding decade. The only way to resolve the debate conclusively would have been to study the results of a number of actual combat situations in which each was used. In the absence of such wartime proof, the advocates of each tactic merely made self-serving arguments concerning the great contribution it would make to winning the decisive battle at sea.[60] Eventually, as we shall see, the Japanese navy was to work out a powerful offensive system of coordinated mass assaults by fighter aircraft, dive bombers, and torpedo planes that was practiced repeatedly and with great precision by the navy in the years immediately prior to the Pacific War.

THE ROLE OF THE FIGHTER IN JEOPARDY

In the 1920s the Japanese navy gave little thought to the use of fighter aircraft in an offensive capacity. Given the fact that the fighters of the time had very short ranges and thus seemed to have little use in blue-water operations, and the fact that for most of the decade Japan had only one small carrier to embark them, the navy's indifference is not surprising. It was, however, a marked contrast to the attitude in the Japanese army. Reviewing the lessons of air warfare over the Western Front during World War I, the army air service concluded that fighter aircraft were the main elements of air power. In the 1920s, therefore, it was the Japanese army, rather than the navy, that made the greatest progress in developing air combat tactics. Army airmen studied European fighter tactics extensively in the immediate postwar years, and in 1927 and 1929, instructors from France were invited to give lectures on the subject.[61] In the navy, for the most part, air combat technique during the 1920s did not progress much beyond the introductory training provided by the Sempill Mission at the outset of the decade.

By the end of the decade, with the acquisition of the large carriers *Akagi* and *Kaga,* the navy did begin to undertake a number of efforts to improve the aerial combat skills of its fighter service for advanced training. Lt. Nakano Chūjirō[†] was sent to the army's Air Gunnery School at Akeno and Lt. Kamei Yoshio to Britain. Upon their return, in a series of special training exercises held at the Yokosuka Naval Air Base in December 1929, they undertook to pass on to other pilots the techniques they had mastered. These exercises, which brought together pilots and instructors from the Yokosuka, Ōmura, and Kasumigaura naval air groups, as well as from the carriers *Kaga* and *Hōshō,* included training in aerial gunnery, single aircraft combat, single versus multiple aircraft tactics, aircraft attacks from various approaches, and some formation tactics. Moreover, the Japanese navy still believed that it had much to learn from foreign instruction in air combat skills. In the autumn of 1930, at the navy's invitation, two officers from Britain's Royal Air Force offered a five-month course in fighter tactics, with special emphasis on gunnery. This was followed in 1931 by a six-month training program in aircraft weapons and their maintenance, also provided by RAF personnel.[62]

Over the next two or three years the leading air groups of the naval air service selected their best pilots for participation in frequent and intensified training programs, exercises, and drills in fighter combat, held by the Yokosuka Air Group fighter squadron and largely centered around single plane-to-plane combat. Out of this rigorous and competitive training environment there emerged a number of highly skilled and motivated fighter pilots—officers like Kamei Yoshio, Kobayashi Yoshito,[†] Okamura Motoharu,[†] and Genda Minoru[†]—who by the late 1930s came to shape the navy's fighter doctrine and who eventually commanded some of the navy's best air groups in the Pacific War.[63] Starting about 1932, some gained fame as members of special flight teams that barnstormed the country, demonstrating their acrobatic skills during subscription ceremonies held to raise money for the public donation of aircraft to the nation. A three-man team led by Lieutenant Kobayashi and known as the "Sky Circus" was formed in 1931. In 1932 it expanded to include nine members under the leadership of Lieutenant Genda and became known as the "Genda Circus." Lieutenant Okamura was to form his own "circus" later that year.[64]

The mid-1930s were golden years for the development of fighter tactics at Yokosuka, as these young men took their biplane fighters aloft day after day to pit their skills against each other and to try out new aerial dogfighting techniques. It was about this time that Mochizuki Isamu,[†] a flight petty officer at the time, developed one of the most brilliant of these schemes—the *hineri-komi* (literally, "turning in"), a half loop and roll—with which he time and again bested the famed Genda himself. Essentially it was technique by which a fighter pilot with an enemy on his tail could, by several deft and sudden maneuvers, quickly take a firing position astern of the enemy. To perform it, Mochizuki would pull up into a loop. Just before the apex of the loop he would sideslip out of the loop, cutting down on his turning radius significantly and thus putting himself on the tail of his enemy. (See app. 9 for an illustrated explanation of the maneuver.) The significance of the maneuver, which was to be demonstrated early on in the navy's air war in China, was that it allowed an aircraft of lesser turning ability to make up the difference with an aircraft of superior turning performance. Eventually adopted by all Japanese navy fighter units and by Japanese army fighter pilots as well, it was the only original aerial tactic developed by the Japanese that was not known to foreign pilots before the Pacific War.[65]

Thus, by the mid-1930s the Yokosuka Naval Air Base had become the mecca of fighter pilots and the pioneering center for the development of fighter tactics. More important, the Japanese naval air service as a whole had begun to pull even with the Japanese army in air combat capabilities. Indeed, the growing skill of the navy's pilots was demonstrated in the joint training exercises held by the two air services from 1934 to 1936. Ostensibly the maneuvers were a matter of cooperative training in aerial combat; in practice they were a manifestation of the intense competition born of traditional interservice rivalry and the divergence of tactics, equipment, and training principles. The many dogfights involved in the first exercises, held in 1934 at Yokosuka, produced a draw between the two services. But in the more complex exercises held at Akeno in 1935 and again at Yokosuka in 1936, navy pilots are said by Genda Minoru to have completely outclassed their army counterparts.[66] While the China War forced the termination of these interservice air competitions, by 1937 it was clear that the navy's fighter arm had come of age.

Yet even as the air combat skills of its aircrews were improving in the early 1930s, the navy, and its air service in particular, had begun to doubt the value of its carrier fighter units. In part this was due to the traditional preference in the Japanese navy for offensive operations, for which the bombing plane was admirably suited and the fighter plane, in its defensive role, was not. When Lt. Comdr. Shibata Takeo,[†] a leading fighter pilot, tried to point out to a Navy General

Staff officer the importance of fighters in defending the fleet, the latter shot back a stinging rebuke against defensive tactics: "And you claim to be a Japanese!"[67] Doubts about the viability of fighters were also due to a condition that appears to have been perceived by all the world's air powers during these years: the generally inferior performance of fighter aircraft in relation to bombing planes.[68] First of all, there was no possibility of using fighters in an offensive role, since most carrier fighters of the day had a range of not much more than 100–150 miles. They would be unable to provide cover for carrier bombers, whose average range was over 200 miles. But even in a defensive role, the existing fighter aircraft seemed at a disadvantage vis-à-vis the bomber. Increasingly Japanese pilots came to believe that fighters would have difficulty carrying out the maneuvers necessary to bring down enemy bombers without at least a 30 percent superiority in speed. By this standard, they judged that the fighter aircraft they flew—generally the Nakajima A2N (Type 90) and the Nakajima A4N (Type 95)* carrier fighters,[69] while among the best in the world at the time, were still too slow and underarmed, as demonstrated time and again in gunnery training when targets moved too fast for fighter planes to make many hits.

For these reasons there arose, in about 1934, a general opinion among fighter pilots at Yokosuka that fighters really no longer had an operational role, a sentiment shared by some of the navy's best fliers, including Genda Minoru. This view intensified with the appearance in 1936 of the radically designed twin-engined Mitsubishi G3M (Type 96 "Nell") medium bomber,* whose speed and range surpassed any aircraft Japan had produced up to that point. (See chap. 4.) In air maneuvers in April 1937, a fighter squadron was given the task of defending the Sasebo Naval Base from the attack of a flight of G3M bombers flying in from Kanoya. As it turned out, the raid was judged a complete success, the defending fighters failing to get in a single blow. To many, such events were proof that fighters ought to be abolished and carrier decks given completely over to attack aircraft.[70]

As we have seen, the Japanese navy, like the British and American navies, had given thought in the early 1930s to using fighters as dive bombers for the sake of speed and fuel efficiency, and in 1933 Genda Minoru himself had advocated that serious study be given to this possibility. But at a time when the concept of the decisive surface battle had apparently hardened into dogma and the principal duty of carrier fighters accompanying the main force was seen to be clearing the skies of enemy aircraft over the battle area, the navy concluded that it was not possible to spare fighter aircraft for any other purpose.[71]

Yet there were airmen in the Japanese navy at this time who maintained that the fighter still had a vital role to play in air operations and that its current problems could be solved by changes in tactics, design, and command and communications systems. Lieutenant Commander Shibata, at that time a division officer at the Ōmura Air Group and a bitter rival of Genda Minoru, was one of these. In his view, one of the reasons that skilled fighter pilots at Yokosuka had trouble hitting targets towed at high speed during the training exercises was that exercise rules forbade attacking aircraft from approaching at an angle of less than 20 degrees from the line of flight of the target (for fear of hitting the plane towing the target). This unreasonable and unrealistic restriction, he argued, prevented pilots from attacking from astern and momentarily holding the target in their sights, as could happen in actual combat. Shibata argued, moreover, that current navy air combat manuals presented a false bias in favor of bombing aircraft. The superior speed of bombing aircraft could be overcome, he insisted, by changing tactics, such as attacking from the rear—which would dramatically increase the number of hits—or aiming at the most vulnerable parts of the enemy aircraft: its wing tanks.[72]

Shibata and another officer at Ōmura, Comdr. Ikegami Tsuguo,[†] also concluded that an essential reason for the inferiority of defending fighters to attacking bombers lay in the lack of any early-warning system that would enable defending fighters to spot an approaching enemy first. While this was a universal problem for the fighter commands of all the world's air powers and would not be solved until the perfection of radar, at the time Shibata and Ikegami held that intensive effort needed to be given to improving intelligence, aircraft communications, and command and control aboard Japan's aircraft carriers. In the meantime, much could and should be done to redesign the single-seat fighter. This meant increasing its speed, maneuverability, and armament, to give it a margin of superiority over bombers. Ultimately, of course, Japanese fighter plane designers would be forced to concentrate on only one of these three capabilities in which to achieve outstanding performance.[73]

In early 1933 the testing of the Type 90 carrier fighter and the identification of its defects had provoked what was to become a famous and prolonged debate among the navy's fighter pilots as to the proper emphasis for fighter design: speed or maneuverability. The controversy originated as an argument over the performance and maneuverability of the Type 90, which had proved superior to the Type 3 but inferior in speed to a modified version of the British Bulldog fighter plane. To improve the Type 90, one group of navy pilots had advocated increasing the wing area in order to decrease the wing loading. In a memorandum criticizing the intricate dogfighting tactics of the Yokosuka Air Group, Lt. Comdr. Odawara Toshi-hiko,[†] who had been a test pilot for the Flight Testing Department of the Naval Air Arsenal, opposed this idea, saying that any decrease in wing loading should be accomplished by reevaluating the structural materials of the aircraft in order to lighten it for greater speed. His statement provoked a storm of controversy and a heated response from Comdr. Okamura Motoharu, who had his own "Flying Circus" at Yokosuka. Okamura attacked Odawara's ideas as unsound and insisted that speed and rate of climb were less important factors in the design of a fighter plane than maneuverability. Odawara's counterblast in another memorandum provoked Okamura to challenge him to a mock combat fly-off (which never took place) and split Japanese naval fighter pilots and designers into two camps.[74]

The Yokosuka Air Group was at the center of the controversy, and tests that its pilots ran convinced them of the superior importance of maneuverability. As a result, maneuverability became the supreme design criterion for fighters after 1935, though challenges to this view came forth again during the China War.[75] Lt. Comdr. Sawai Hideo, staff officer of the Naval Aviation Department, and others believed that the Japanese navy failed to produce a superior fighter in the mid-1930s, but they did not blame the emphasis on maneuverability. If anything, they championed it. For them, the lack of distinction in Japanese designs in this period resulted from hasty design and production as well as the General Staff's interference. The urgings of perceptive officers in the Aviation Department like Commander Sawai and the testimony of pilots in the air war over China after July 1937 eventually produced a dramatic improvement in Japanese fighter designs. Their efforts led, as we shall see, to the design and development of Japan's first all-metal monoplane fighter, the Mitsubishi A5M (Type 96) carrier fighter,* an aircraft that gained fame because of its great maneuverability.[76]

RECONNAISSANCE AIRCRAFT

In this assessment of the evolution of Japanese naval air tactics and related technology from their beginnings up to the mid-1930s, it remains only to comment briefly upon the development of the navy's aerial search capabilities.[77] This had been the raison d'être for Japanese naval aviation at its beginning. During World War I, ship-borne (though not ship-launched) reconnaissance seaplanes had been used on a number of search missions, and after the war a number of long-range reconnaissance training flights from Yokosuka to Okinawa and to the Chinkai Naval Base in Korea had demonstrated the potential value of aerial reconnaissance for fleet operations.[78] Japan's first carrier, the Hōshō, had been built with the idea of scouting and reconnaissance very much in mind. Logically, the importance of scouting should have grown with the increasing role for carrier aviation and the imperative of launching a first strike against enemy carriers. Yet, as I shall explain in a later chapter, the Japanese navy failed to develop reconnaissance as a primary function of carrier aviation because its increasing fixation on offensive operations, and attack planes sacrificed the hangar space available for reconnaissance aircraft.

But the navy's dilemma, as it began to assemble a carrier force during the interwar years, was similar to that of the American and British navies in the same period. All three navies were keenly aware of the limited capacity of carriers and were chary of using up precious space on board for anything other than fighters and attack aircraft. Given its emphasis on offensive operations, the Japanese navy was particularly reluctant to do so. Nevertheless, the navy attempted to develop reconnaissance aircraft with sufficient capabilities to warrant a place on carriers. But the models that were produced continually proved inferior in performance to the attack aircraft the navy adopted.[79] The first plane officially designated as a "C" (reconnaissance) aircraft was the C1M1/C1M2 (Type 10) designed for Mitsubishi by the British aircraft engineer Herbert Smith. It was accepted by the navy in 1922 but could not match the performance of the Mitsubishi B1M (Type 13) shipboard attack aircraft (torpedo bomber) when the latter came into service in 1924 and thus was not incorporated into Japanese carrier air groups. The B1M was used not only for torpedo bombing but also for scouting missions. In 1935 the navy tried again and ordered Nakajima to design a specialized reconnaissance aircraft. The result was the Nakajima C3N1, which after carrier trials was actually accepted as the Type 97 shipboard reconnaissance aircraft. But once again, the superior capabilities of an attack aircraft crowded out the reconnaissance aircraft from the navy's carrier decks. The navy's new torpedo bomber, which eventually became the B5N (Type 97) shipboard attack aircraft,* performed comparably to the C3N1, which was dropped by the navy after the building of only two prototype models. As a result, the B5N was given double responsibilities as an attack and reconnaissance aircraft.[80] It was not until the advent of the Nakajima C6N1 "Saiun" in 1942 that the Japanese navy finally had a specially designated reconnaissance aircraft with sufficient performance to justify making room for it in carrier complements.

For comparative purposes it is useful to touch briefly upon the evolution of scouting in the United States Navy.[81] In the United States Navy, floatplanes had been developed for spotting and scouting, and they retained a spotting role on battleships and cruisers. By the late 1920s the scouting role had been turned over to carrier-based aircraft, and eventually specialized carrier aircraft, like the Vought O2U, were developed, though floatplanes were retained on cruisers and battleships for short-range scouting and spotting purposes and flying boats were used for strategic searches ("reconnaissance" not being a term in the U.S. naval lexicon). By 1928, therefore, the United States Navy had formed dedicated scouting squadrons assigned to its carriers. In 1941, with the delivery of the first Douglas SBD Dauntless scout bombers to American carriers, the United States Navy acquired an aircraft that superbly filled the dual role of scouting and bombing. Thus, American carriers entered the Pacific War embarking distinctly designated scouting squadrons, which were principally dive-bombing units and which were identically equipped, except that scout bombers carried lighter ordnance loads.

The Japanese and American navies took different paths, then, in the development of aerial reconnaissance. In the years before the Pacific War, while it recognized that its solutions were less than ideal, for fleet reconnaissance as a whole the Japanese navy came to rely on catapult-launched cruiser floatplanes, which were also used for the purpose of spotting for surface gunnery in the early 1930s. These aircraft had been initially and essentially designed, however, to fill the patrol and scouting requirements of the fleet. For this purpose, the navy acquired a number of excellent single-engine ship-borne floatplanes during the interwar period. In 1927, in an effort to modernize its aerial scouting technology, the navy had developed the Type 90-3 reconnaissance seaplane, one of the first such aircraft with an all-metal fuselage and one of the first designed to be embarked on Japanese warships as permanent equipment. The Type 90-3 was succeeded in 1934 by the Kawanishi E7K1/2 (Type 94),* which was embarked on Japanese cruisers in the mid-1930s. In 1935 a faster, more durable aircraft, the Type 95 reconnaissance seaplane, a single-float biplane designed and produced by Nakajima (as the E8N),* was embarked on most Japanese battleships and heavy cruisers until the end of the decade. By World War II the Japanese navy employed this single-engine floatplane-type scout aircraft in greater numbers aboard its surface units than any other type of floatplane in any of the major navies of the world.[82]

While the Japanese and American navies approached the problem of short-range scouting and reconnaissance for the fleet in different ways, both recognized the need for even longer-range overwater reconnaissance, though given the availability to the Japanese of potential island bases in Micronesia, the need was greater for the Americans. It was for this purpose that both navies developed the large flying boat (supplemented in the Japanese navy by the mid-1930s by land-based twin-engined bombers).[83] The first really successful Japanese aircraft of this kind was the Felix-stowe F.5. It was a twin-engined biplane flying boat of wood and fabric designed by the Short Brothers and built in Japan principally by the Hirō Naval Arsenal. Based at Yokosuka and Sasebo, the F.5, with its range of over 600 nautical miles, was the navy's principal long-range reconnaissance aircraft from 1921 to 1930. In that year, it was replaced by the Hirōshō H1H1 (Type 15), also a twin-engined wood-and-fabric aircraft, but with greater speed and endurance. The H1H1 remained the navy's long-range reconnaissance mainstay until 1938. During the interwar period, these two flying boats provided the navy with excellent opportunities to gain experience in long-range overwater reconnaissance (including an unprecedented round-trip flight by an H1H1 from Yokosuka to Saipan in the Mariana Islands and back). But as these aircraft were performing valuable service, Kawanishi, under navy contract, was developing an even bigger and better flying boat, the H6K1, adopted by the navy early in 1938 as the Type 97,* an aircraft of all-metal construction that was to prove to be of remarkable endurance over the vast reaches of the Pacific. Collectively, these three aircraft set the precedent for superior flying-boat design that made Japan the leader in this type of aircraft by World War II.

Yet the very planes that were to accomplish the reconnaissance mission, the floatplane and the flying boat, were limited in some respects. Floatplanes were usually kept out in the open, on the catapults of cruisers and battleships. Here the planes were subject to wind and salt spray, which over time caused breakdowns at critical moments even with the most conscientious attempts at maintenance. Their retrieval by parent ships was difficult if seas were rough, and they were often damaged in the process. Moreover, recovery required the parent ship to come to a dead stop, causing that ship to lag behind the rest of the fleet and, worse, to invite submarine attack. Flying boats, for their part, were excellent machines for long-range reconnaissance, and while they could operate in somewhat rougher waters than floatplanes, they generally required calm seas to land or take off, unless they could also operate from land, a capability that, unlike the later version of the American PBY "Catalina" amphibian, no Japanese flying boat possessed.

Nevertheless, it was not aircraft that hindered Japanese reconnaissance capabilities but doctrine and training. Because of the priority the naval air service placed on offensive operations, scouting and reconnaissance suffered. Japanese aircrews assigned to reconnaissance were too often ill trained, inexperienced, and careless. Aerial reconnaissance would continue to be a problem in the Japanese navy through the interwar period and into the Pacific War. As it is a complicated problem, I shall return to it in chapter 6.

SHANGHAI, 1932
The Navy's First Experience in Aerial Combat

Because it is related to the development of the Japanese navy's air combat skills rather than to naval war per se, I conclude this chapter with a brief discussion of the first real test of the navy's aerial warfare capabilities: the Shanghai "Incident" of early 1932. While the origins of that conflict need not detain us here, the eighty years since have made it clear that the fighting in Shanghai was triggered when elements of the Japanese Naval Landing Force, permanently stationed there, were dispatched to evict regular Chinese forces from a contested sector in the city.

Once the fighting had begun, the commander of those elements of the Japanese Third Fleet anchored in the Whangpoo River called in seaplanes from the seaplane tender *Notoro* anchored on the Yangtze and directed them to attack enemy positions in the city. On 29 January several seaplanes carried out low-level attacks (about 300 feet [90 meters] from the ground) on Chinese military positions in Chapei (the old Chinese sector of Shanghai), on artillery batteries outside the city, and on an armored train at the Shanghai North Railway Station. These operations caused a heavy loss of civilian lives and property. Japanese accounts at the time, as well as several Japanese operational histories since, maintained that Japanese aircrews involved in these attacks not only made every attempt to stay clear of the city's International Settlement but also took care to confirm their targets and to aim their bombs. But on this first day of operations, mist and drizzle so obscured the airmen's targets, it is said, that they had to drop flares and to request the Naval Landing Force to light bonfires to mark their approaches to certain targets. When one adds to this assertion the crudities of contemporary bombing techniques and mechanisms, it is not surprising that the ten missions conducted that day also wrought major damage to civilian property and caused a significant number of civilian deaths.[84]

With the arrival of the carrier *Kaga* off the Chinese coast the next day and the carrier *Hōshō* two days later, the Japanese navy was in a position to put nearly eighty aircraft—mostly Nakajima A1N2 carrier fighters and Mitsubishi B1M3 carrier bombers—in the air over the Shanghai combat zone. Air-to-air clashes took place over the city on 5 February between five aircraft from the *Hōshō* and a total of nine Chinese fighter planes, and again on 19 February, also involving aircraft from the *Hōshō*. The most memorable encounter occurred on 22 February, when three A1N2 carrier fighters escorting three B1M3 carrier bombers from the *Kaga* achieved Japan's first aerial kill, the shooting down of a Boeing fighter (piloted by an American volunteer). Then, after reviewing intelligence that the Chinese air forces were preparing a counteroffensive, the Third Fleet decided to launch a series of bombing raids along the central China coast, concentrating against Chinese airfields at Su-chou and Hang-chou. These attacks were carried out from 23 to 26 February. After returning from the particularly devastating raid on the Hang-chou airfield, six A1N2 carrier fighters from the *Hōshō,* escorting nine bombers from the same carrier, tangled with five enemy aircraft, shooting down three of them.[85]

Compared with the scale of air combat in the China and Pacific wars, the navy's air operations over Shanghai in February 1932 were insignificant skirmishes. Yet they were not without instructive value. Even though the A1N2 fighter proved inferior in performance to the Boeing Model 218 fighter,[86] the brief air campaign demonstrated the above-average flying skills of the navy's pilots, and the relative precision of the navy's bombing techniques when the weather was clear. A postwar Japanese naval air history refers, for example, to the near annihilation of Chinese air units at the Hang-chou airfield on 26 February as a textbook operation.[87] (The attack was orchestrated, it should be noted, by the Third Fleet air officer, Comdr. Ōnishi Takijirō, later admiral and father of the kamikaze concept at the end of the Pacific War.)

In any event, the activity of Japanese air units over the Shanghai area represented the first significant aerial operations in East Asia. The bombardment of Chapei was the most destructive aerial attack on an urban center until the Condor Legion's assault on Guernica five years later. For the Japanese naval air service, the fighting over Shanghai marked its first combat operations from carrier decks. But the navy's air service would not face its real test until a second conflict with China five years later. The navy's determination to play a leading role in that conflict would plunge its aircrews and aircraft deep into the continent's mountainous interior, flying hazardous missions of unprecedented length and endurance, but for objectives of dubious value to the navy.

3

FLIGHT DECKS

Japanese Carriers and Carrier Doctrine, 1920–1941

It is important to understand that the various naval air tactics and technologies outlined in the last chapter had a symbiotic relationship to the composition of the Japanese carrier fleet.[1] The construction of that fleet began at a time when carrier design in the three major navies was being shaped not only by the universal problems of propulsion, hull structure, seakeeping, crew accommodation, and compatibility with shore facilities, but also by the growing recognition of the ways in which the embarkation and flight operations of aircraft enormously complicated the task of naval architects. Above and beyond the matter of appropriately proportioned flight decks for air operations—takeoffs and landings—there were problems of the proper siting of control centers for such operations, provision of adequate aircraft storage, the location of maintenance facilities and magazines for aircraft ordnance, and the arrangement of storage and delivery systems for large quantities of aviation fuel, along with the distribution of physical safeguards to minimize the resultant hazards of fire and explosion. In addition to these new challenges, the naval limitation treaties signed after World War I restricted the displacement tonnage of individual carriers to 23,000 tons, although in the case of the Japanese and American navies it allowed the conversion of certain capital ships to carriers (the *Akagi* and *Kaga* and the *Lexington* and *Saratoga*).[2]

But two problems in particular bedeviled carrier design in this period. The first was rapidly changing aircraft technology, particularly the increasing weight and wing loading of aircraft, which required longer flight decks for takeoff. The second was the still uncertain function of the carrier and its place relative to the battle line. These were ambiguities that, for a while at least, seemed to argue for the installation of heavy surface weapons on carriers for defense against cruisers and destroyers. Given these problems, it is not surprising that carrier design in these years was a matter of trial and error, and that in all three major navies the design of the first warships of this type included certain features that proved impractical in the long run.

JAPANESE CARRIER DESIGN IN THE TREATY ERA

These matters relate particularly to the design and construction of the *Hōshō*, Japan's first and essentially experimental aircraft carrier.[3] Viewed from the perspective of later carrier design, the *Hōshō*, at less than 8,000 standard tons displacement, with a flight deck of only 168 meters (552 feet) was a very small carrier. The design also incorporated certain features that demonstrated the uncertainties of her designers in confronting problems involved in flight operations. As completed in 1922, the *Hōshō* was fitted with a rudimentary island-type bridge, on the starboard side of the flight deck about 45 meters (150 feet) from the bow, from which the ship was conned and flight operations controlled. Just aft of the island were the carrier's three stacks, which were hinged so as to fold over into a horizontal position during flight operations. Forward of the island, the flight deck itself was inclined slightly downward. Two small aircraft elevators, one forward and one aft, led down to the single narrow hangar deck that began forward of the island bridge, widened amidships, and at the fantail took up the full beam of the ship.[4]

After repeated experimentation in launching and recovering aircraft in the year after the *Hōshō* was commissioned, the navy decided to remodel the ship. Because the island superstructure, its mast, and the three stacks reduced the 23-meter (75-foot) flight deck and to some extent obscured the pilot's visibility, they were all removed or rearranged in 1924. With the removal of the island bridge and its mast, the *Hōshō* became a flush-deck carrier. Flight operations were controlled from an operations platform beside the flight deck, a decision that influenced Japanese carrier design for over a decade. But the positioning of the carrier's boiler uptakes proved to be troublesome. Even in their horizontal position, the three stacks caused smoke and stack gas to drift across the path of flight operations, and the stack wells encroached too far into the already narrow flight deck. For this reason, in 1934 they were permanently fixed at an angle downward over the ship's side. In 1931 the lengthwise arresting gear, which had proved inadequate and had thus contributed to a number of landing accidents, was replaced by a system of transverse cables across the deck.[5]

As originally designed, the *Hōshō* could carry approximately twenty aircraft. The first types embarked after the ship was commissioned were Mitsubishi 1MF1-5 (Navy Type 10) carrier fighters and Mitsubishi B1M1 (Navy Type 13) torpedo

planes, some of which were used for reconnaissance.[6] During its first decade, the
Hōshō's small size posed no limit to her usefulness, given the slow speeds and light
naval aircraft of the day. But by the late 1930s, as larger and faster attack aircraft
were developed, the *Hōshō* could accommodate only half her original complement.
For this reason, for the rest of her period of service she was used for training or, at
best, defensive cover for the fleet. She was relegated to auxiliary status by the end
of the Pacific War and was one of the two operable carriers left to the Japanese navy
at the end of that conflict. Yet long before that, the *Hōshō* had proved of value as
a laboratory for carrier design, construction, and flight operations.[7]

If the small size and modest aircraft complement of the *Hōshō* prevented her
from being a significant element in the navy's strategic planning in the 1920s, the
completion of the fleet carriers *Akagi* and *Kaga*,[8] and the more than 120 aircraft they
added to the offensive capability of the fleet, did indeed create new strategic as well
as tactical possibilities for the navy. Yet their initial design incorporated features that
demonstrated continued uncertainties about the function of carriers and an under-
estimation of the rapidity of change in both the technology and the tactics of naval
aviation. The *Akagi* was begun as a battle cruiser whose construction was halted
because of the capital ship limitations imposed on all signatories by the Washington
Naval Treaty. While the essential battle cruiser hull structure was retained, the warship's new function as a carrier and her consequent need for hangar space necessitated a number of modifications. The armor belt was lowered and reduced in thick-
ness, and the torpedo bulges were modified. Both modifications improved stability
and helped compensate for the topside weight of the double hangar deck.[9] A major
design problem in both the *Akagi* and the *Kaga* was the disposal of boiler exhaust.
In the *Akagi* this was done by trunking the boiler uptakes over to starboard, so that
the exhaust was vented through one large funnel that was canted downward and
through a small upward funnel immediately abaft of it.

At the time of her initial construction in 1923, the *Akagi* was a flush-deck carrier (i.e., she had no island bridge). Her most unusual feature was the multiple-
flight-deck arrangement—somewhat similar to that of the British carrier *Furious*
and the *Courageous*-class carriers constructed several years earlier—which was
thought to accelerate flight operations by making it possible to launch and retrieve
aircraft simultaneously. For this purpose, the *Akagi* had three separated, vertically
arranged flight decks. An upper flight deck, 190 meters (624 feet) in length, was the
longest and was slightly sloped from a point amidships toward the bow and toward
the stern to facilitate landings and takeoffs for the underpowered aircraft of the
day. Beneath it was a middle and very short (18-meter [60-foot]) takeoff deck for
the smallest and lightest of the carrier's aircraft. Beneath that, on the main deck,
was a somewhat longer (49-meter [160-foot]) flight deck for launching torpedo
bombers. The sixty aircraft that the carrier was originally designed to embark were
housed in three hangars. As originally completed, there were two long hangar decks
at the same levels as the middle and lower flight decks, both of which were used for
operational aircraft. There was a third short hangar deck aft and below the two

longer hangar decks. The aft elevator serviced the upper flight deck and all three
hangar decks. To transport these planes to and from the hangars, the upper flight
deck incorporated two elevators, one toward the bow and a smaller one toward the
stern.[10]

Just as these flight-deck and hangar arrangements in the *Akagi* represented
assumptions about the limitations of aircraft performance at the time that she was
designed, the carrier's armament, like that of the American carriers *Lexington* and
Saratoga, reflected contemporary and ultimately mistaken ideas about the heavy
surface weapons installed on carriers for use in possible gun action with enemy warships.[11] The *Akagi* carried ten 8-inch (20.3-centimeter) guns, four in twin turrets on
each side of the middle flight deck, roughly amidships, and three in single mountings in casemates on each side of the ship. While this firepower was numerically
superior to that of the *Lexington* and *Saratoga,* the placement of the *Akagi*'s main
batteries actually put her at a comparative disadvantage, since the American carriers mounted their eight 8-inch guns in twin turrets fore and aft of their island
superstructures, allowing them to bring all eight guns to broadside, while the *Akagi*
could bring a maximum of only five guns to bear on any single target.

It can be argued that the arming of carriers with heavy surface weapons was logical at the time, considering the tactical and technological situation of the mid-
1920s, when carriers had to operate close to the battle line (because of the limited
radius of their aircraft) and thus within the range of enemy surface guns.[12] Time
and a change of opinion by strategists and designers in all the major naval powers
were to indicate both the futility and the redundancy of such heavy armament: the
vulnerability to shellfire of any aircraft carrier, particularly the flight deck, would
make it suicidal for such a ship to participate in a gun action; the ship's greatest
defensive protection came to be seen as the offensive capabilities of her own attack
aircraft.[13]

The layout of the *Akagi*'s contemporary, the *Kaga,* was similar to that of the
Akagi in many respects. But because the *Kaga* was originally laid down as a battleship rather than a battle cruiser and thus had a shorter and broader hull, her upper
flight deck was 19.5 meters (64 feet) shorter and slightly wider than that of the
Akagi. The main flight deck was perfectly horizontal for its entire length. Her
propulsion system was smaller and thus allowed a slower maximum speed (a little
over 27 knots). Boiler exhausts were vented through two tubes 30 meters (100 feet)
long on each side of the ship, an arrangement quite similar to that of the British
Furious. These tubes extended horizontally toward the stern, where the funnel
mouths were canted downward and outward.

Within half a dozen years of the commissioning of the *Akagi* and *Kaga,* advances
in naval aircraft, changes in naval opinion, and actual operational experience had led
to the need to make drastic alterations in some of their most innovative features as
conceived early in the 1920s. By the early 1930s the considerable increase in the size
and power of naval aircraft required far more distance for takeoff than that provided
by the two lower flight decks on both ships. Surface armament was now viewed as

Photo. 3-1. The aircraft carrier *Kaga* transiting the Cossol Passage, Palau,
Caroline Islands, July 1933
Source: Fukui, *Shashin Nihon kaigun zen kantei shi,* 1:337.

less important for a carrier than the size of her air group. A flush deck may have been
preferred by some carrier pilots, but not by others, who considered islands to be useful reference points during landing operations, and certainly not by those who had
to conn the ship or control her flight operations. And finally, the funnel arrangements for the *Kaga,* hotly disputed at the time of their design by naval architects,
proved unworkable, since hot gases and smoke still obstructed or disturbed flight
operations at the stern of the ship.[14]

For all these reasons, the two carriers underwent reconstruction during the mid-
1930s at the Sasebo Naval Yard.[15] Because of her slower speed, impractical funnel
configuration, smaller flight deck, and thus general inferiority to her sister ship, the
Kaga was the first to be modernized, even though she had been commissioned a
year later than the *Akagi.* Her extensive reconstruction was completed in one year,
from June 1934 to June 1935, while modifications for the *Akagi,* though far less
extensive, took three years, largely because of budgetary delays.[16]

The single most important modification for both ships was the elimination of
the three-stage flight-deck arrangement and its replacement by a single extended
upper flight deck that projected over the stern and almost to the bow. This alter-
ation made possible far greater hangar space and thus a considerable increase in
aircraft capacity: ninety-one for the *Akagi* and ninety for the *Kaga.* The two longer
hangar decks—which formerly had also been flight decks—were now extended forward almost to the bow, and the lowest hangar deck was enlarged. The original elevators remained in place and serviced the flight deck and hangar decks as in the
ships' original layout, but a third elevator was added forward and serviced the flight
deck and the two long hangar decks. Navigation and control of flight operations
were now conducted from a modestly scaled island bridge, constructed on the port

side of the flight deck for the *Akagi* about halfway along the flight deck, and on the starboard side for the *Kaga*.[17]

The difference in the location of the island superstructures of these two carriers needs some explanation. Along with the carrier *Hiryū* (see below), then under construction with her sister ship *Sōryū*, the *Akagi* was one of only two aircraft carriers in the world to have an island on the port side. Initially it had been intended that the bridge on both the *Akagi*, then undergoing modernization, and the *Hiryū*, then building, would be located on the starboard side of the flight deck toward the bow. A study issued by the Naval Aviation Department, however, suggested that this particular configuration would produce an unacceptable amount of turbulence for flight operations, and thus the island superstructure should be placed amidships. But because the boiler uptakes on the *Akagi* and *Hiryū* were located at that spot on the starboard side, it was necessary to shift the bridge to the port side, an arrangement that had the advantage of helping to provide a counterweight to the funnel. Pilots, however, complained that the air turbulence over the deck was actually worse with this arrangement, and they prevailed to the extent that subsequent Japanese carriers had their islands on the starboard side. The *Akagi* and *Hiryū* were not modified, probably because there was insufficient evidence that their island configurations caused a significant problem.[18]

Other modifications common to both the *Akagi* and the *Kaga* were the substitution of completely oil-fired for coal-fired and mixed-firing boilers, a substantial increase in fuel oil bunkerage, the trunking of the boiler uptakes into a single funnel that projected downward over the starboard side, the removal of the twin forward 8-inch turrets (in order to extend the single flight deck), and an increase in antiaircraft armament. The *Kaga*, however, required specific additional improvements: the lengthening of the hull to improve the ship's drag coefficient, the addition of a new propulsion system of four sets of Kampon equal-pressure geared turbines and new propellers, and the raising of the ship's metacenter—as part of a wide-ranging effort to correct the serious instability of a significant number of Japanese warships that was diagnosed in the mid-1930s—by adding an additional torpedo bulge that increased the beam. In the *Akagi* the twin 8-inch turrets were removed, leaving the remaining six 8-inch guns in casemates as the main armament, three on each side abaft the bridge; in the *Kaga* the four guns were moved to casemates, so that all ten 8-inch guns were retained. This last arrangement demonstrated the continuing contemporary uncertainty surrounding the function and place of carriers in combat. Okada Heiichirō, who as an engineering lieutenant helped draft the plans for the modernization of both the *Kaga* and the *Akagi*, tells us that the plans, particularly those concerning the removal of the forward turrets, created a heated debate within the navy. Led by Adm. Yamamoto Isoroku, the Naval Aviation Department, wishing to transform the two ships from functional hybrids into true carriers, urged removal of *all* the main batteries. The Navy Technical Department, dominated by gunnery-minded officers, argued that removal of such armament would leave the carriers vulnerable in any surface engagement.

The compromise seems to have been reached by simply removing the forward turrets so as to conform to the new flight-deck arrangements.[19]

Soon after the *Akagi* and *Kaga* went into service in the late 1920s, fleet maneuvers made obvious the offensive potential of carrier aviation. Staff college war-gaming further underscored the possibilities of the carrier weapon, as did well-publicized advances in American carrier aviation. Thus, Japanese navy leaders became convinced of the need for more carriers. But budgetary limitations, and the fact that the construction of the *Akagi* and *Kaga* had already used nearly 54,000 of the 81,000 tons allocated to Japan for carriers by the Washington Treaty, meant that only one or two fleet carriers could be constructed within the remaining 27,000 tons. Accordingly, the navy attempted to build an effective carrier at less than 10,000 tons, in order to have it exempted, along with the *Hōshō*, in the calculation of Japan's allowed carrier tonnage. These considerations governed the design of the *Ryūjō*, the navy's third-generation carrier and the second Japanese carrier originally designed as such.[20] Her designers, determined to keep her displacement under 10,000 standard tons, drew up plans that originally called for an 8,000-ton ship. Such size limitations resulted in the design of a flush-deck carrier with boiler uptakes trunked over the starboard side, no heavy surface armament, almost no armor protection, and provision for only one hangar, capable of housing twenty-four aircraft.[21]

But even while the design was on the drawing boards, various studies had determined that such a small number of aircraft would comprise the effectiveness of the air group. For this reason, the design was altered to include a second hangar deck above the first, so that forty-eight aircraft could be embarked. This addition increased the *Ryūjō*'s displacement to almost 12,500 standard tons—a fact kept secret at the time—and, what was worse, added too much weight above the waterline, making her less stable. A year after her launching in 1933, a well-publicized capsizing incident in the navy, involving the torpedo boat *Tomozuru*, brought home the danger posed by this defect.[22] The *Ryūjō* was therefore brought into the Kure dockyard for the required modifications, which included incorporation of new hull bulges, the addition of a heavy ballast keel, and removal of some antiaircraft batteries. But even these modifications proved insufficient to improve the ship's seaworthiness. Caught in the great storm that battered the Fourth Fleet off the coast of Honshū in 1935, the *Ryūjō* shipped huge amounts of water in the heavy seas because of her low forecastle, a fact that again raised questions about her stability.[23] Once more the *Ryūjō* entered drydock, this time to have the front of her bridge reshaped to lower wind resistance and to have her forecastle deck raised by adding an extra deck.[24] While these changes did little to improve the overall efficiency of this "minimum carrier" (the words are Norman Friedman's), her defects of size did provide salutary experience for the design of the navy's next set of carriers.

The two ships of the *Sōryū* class had their origin in the desire of the Navy General Staff to circumvent, legally, the treaty limitations on total carrier construction. Taking advantage of the definition of an aircraft carrier as a warship designed primarily for aircraft operations, the staff conceived of a hybrid warship that was as much a cruiser as it was a carrier, thus not to be counted in the total carrier tonnage allocated to Japan. Drawn up in 1931–32, the initial designs for this class had therefore incorporated not only a flight deck but also cruiser-class (6-inch [15.2-centimeter]) armament mounted in barbettes forward of the flight deck.[25]

But even as these plans were being drafted, Japan had begun to consider withdrawal from the treaty system by the end of 1936. As Japanese renunciation of the treaties would make irrelevant the question of keeping naval tonnage within any limitations, the question of the 81,000-ton limit on carrier construction would become moot. On this assumption, the Navy General Staff set forth its requirements for two new carriers, using the general hull configuration and flight-deck arrangement of the hybrid design, but eliminating the cruiser armament.[26] The *Sōryū*, laid down in 1934 and completed in 1937, met most of these requirements, and though she exceeded the planned displacement by 5,000 standard tons, her hull was very light for a ship of her size. Her powerful cruiser propulsion system provided an extraordinary maximum speed of 35 knots. The *Sōryū*'s design retained the double-deck hangar system capable of accommodating sixty-eight aircraft (fifty-one operational and seventeen reserve), but the lower and shorter of the two hangars was placed well within the hull for greater stability than afforded by the *Ryūjō*'s layout. The ship was provided with three elevators, one forward and two smaller elevators amidships and aft. In what was becoming a trademark of Japanese carriers, the boiler uptakes were trunked over the starboard side amidships in two downward-venting funnels. Just forward of these, on the starboard side, was located a small island superstructure.[27]

In July 1936, six months after the *Sōryū*'s launching, the keel was laid for her sister ship, the *Hiryū*. But by this time experience and research seemed to argue for some fairly basic changes in the design of the class. Taking a cue from the near disaster that had threatened the Fourth Fleet in the great storm of 1935, the *Hiryū*'s design was modified by strengthening the hull, raising the forecastle, and increasing the beam for greater stability. Additional armor was contributed to the ship's main belt (though the horizontal protection was the same as the *Sōryū*), and the antiaircraft battery was redistributed.[28] Although she normally operated sixty-four aircraft during the interwar period, the *Hiryū*'s maximum aircraft capacity, seventy-three, was slightly larger than that of the *Sōryū*. The *Hiryū*'s island superstructure was located, like the *Akagi*'s, on the port side of the ship, just forward of the starboard side funnels, an arrangement that, again as with the *Akagi*, was eventually found to be troublesome for flight operations.

By the end of the treaty era, therefore, the Japanese navy had completed four aircraft carriers and had two more building. From their specific characteristics and capabilities, it is possible to trace the evolution of Japanese carrier design, operating doctrine, and operating efficiency for the period from the end of World War I to about 1937. The *Hōshō*, as we have seen, had been an experimental ship whose design had been influenced by British experience during World War I, but whose small size restricted the number of aircraft she could embark and thus limited her offensive potential. But the fourfold jump in displacement from the *Hōshō* to the *Akagi* and *Kaga* had less to do with Japanese perceptions of the need to increase aircraft capacity than with the fact that the Japanese navy had available capital ship hulls on which work had been suspended as a result of the naval agreements at Washington in 1922. Indeed, as several studies have suggested, in the mid-1920s the Japanese navy, like the American navy, believed that small carriers—10,000 tons or less—in larger numbers would provide greater aircraft operating capacity. Given the vulnerability of carriers, such a dispersal of carrier air power would lessen the impact of the loss of any single carrier.[29] If true, this belief may have been nearly as much a factor in the design of the small carrier *Ryūjō* as the desire to keep her displacement under 10,000 tons and thus exempt her from the Washington Treaty limits. Yet the Japanese and American navies later came independently to the conclusion that a carrier of 10,000 tons was ineffective as a combat unit because it could not operate enough aircraft. In the 1930s, other factors were to favor the increased construction of larger and faster carriers, including the continuing need for longer flight decks to allow the takeoffs of larger and heavier aircraft.[30]

CARRIER CONSTRUCTION IN THE POST-TREATY ERA

The end of the naval arms limitations treaties in December 1936 allowed Japan to build ships of all classes, including aircraft carriers of unprecedented size and performance. During the five years between the end of the treaty era and the onset of the Pacific War, the navy added the two finest carriers it ever built: the *Shōkaku* and *Zuikaku*. Indeed, some have argued that they were the two most successful warships ever built for the navy. Ordered in 1937 under the "Circle Three" construction program to counter growing U.S. carrier strength, the *Shōkaku* class was conceived as part of a fast carrier group capable of operating with the monster *Yamato*-class battleships; such missions called for large, fast carriers, capable of embarking a powerful aerial strike force and able to defend themselves effectively. The General Staff specifications called for the same aircraft complement as the remodeled *Akagi* and *Kaga* (seventy-two aircraft, with twenty-four in reserve); the same speed (34 knots) as the *Sōryū;* a greater radius of action (9,700 nautical miles at 18 knots) than any of their predecessors; and hull armor to withstand an 8-inch (20.3-centimeter) shell fired at 12,000–20,000 meters (13,000–22,000 yards) or an 800-kilogram (1,764-pound) bomb launched from a high-level bomber.[31]

As the two ships were almost identical, were laid down within six months of each other, and were completed a month apart, a discussion of the arrangements for the namesake of the class is appropriate for both carriers. Designed with the experience gained in operating the navy's four other large fleet carriers, the *Shōkaku*, in a number of respects, particularly in profile, was a bigger and more heavily armed and armored version of the *Sōryū*. Though her flight deck was planked and unarmored, she was 10,000 tons heavier than the *Sōryū* because of the armor on her main deck above her machinery, magazines, and aviation gas. Nevertheless, flooding calculations made at the time of her construction ensured that she had the stability equal to that of battleships of the day. Her island, like the *Sōryū*'s, was well forward on the starboard side; abaft on that side were two funnels trunked downward. Three elevators brought the aircraft up from her two hangar decks to her flight deck. All three decks were equipped with fueling stations, so that aircraft could be refueled on all three decks. Her closed-in hangars presented the same fire hazards, however, as those of other Japanese carriers (see below). Her armament—eight twin 5-inch (12.7-centimeter) dual-purpose gun mounts controlled by four directors, as well as a light battery of forty-two 25-millimeter antiaircraft guns in triple mounts—was certainly more formidable than that of the *Sōryū*. Her engines, which delivered 160,000 horsepower, 10,000 more than even the *Yamato*, were the most powerful ever installed in a Japanese warship. By the time of her participation in the Hawai'i strike, the *Shōkaku*, though embarking slightly fewer aircraft than demanded in the specifications, provided a formidable offensive capability: twenty-seven Aichi D3A dive bombers, twenty-seven B5N torpedo bombers, and eighteen Zero fighters, seventy-two aircraft in all (not counting the twelve reserve aircraft).[32]

The *Shōkaku* and *Zuikaku* were critical additions to the Japanese carrier fleet. In performance and capability they exceeded all American carriers until the wartime appearance of the *Essex*-class carriers. So valuable were these two warships that the decision to mount the Pearl Harbor strike was based in part on their availability to the mobile task force organized for that operation.[33] Certainly their service record lived up to the care that went into their design and construction; on the American side their battle honors were matched only by the *Enterprise*. By the time they met their ends in 1944, they had participated in every carrier battle except Midway, where their absence may have been the margin between victory and defeat.[34] Indeed, their ubiquity, performance, and durability in more than two years of fierce combat in the Pacific led Admiral Nimitz to aver with some heat that the happiest day in his life would be when "those two ships" were finally sunk.[35] It can be said that when that time came, their destruction spelled the end of the Japanese carrier fleet.

Before leaving this discussion of the design and construction of Japan's carrier fleet, I should touch upon the navy's effort to supplement its publicly announced carrier construction programs by the creation of a "shadow fleet" of auxiliary and merchant vessels that could be quickly converted into carriers in case of a wartime emergency.

Two practical considerations shaped this effort. The first of these had to do with the tonnage restrictions imposed by international agreements. After laying down the *Sōryū* and *Hiryū*, Japan had reached (and indeed exceeded) the carrier tonnage that it could build under the terms of the Washington Treaty. The second consideration anticipated the prospect of an unrestricted building program in a post-treaty era, the navy recognizing that the nation had limited shipyard capacity for keel-up naval construction.

For these reasons, early in the interwar period the Japanese navy, sometimes assisting and subsidizing private shipbuilding firms, began to design and construct both naval auxiliaries and merchant vessels suitable for easy conversion to light fleet carriers. The navy had begun this "shadow" building program even before the London Naval Treaty.[36] In the late 1920s it worked with the Nihon Yūsen Kaisha on the design of three fast passenger vessels subsidized by the Ministry of Transportation and built to navy specifications for easy conversion to carrier configuration. In the event, these particular ships were launched and completed but were never actually converted into aircraft carriers.

The first ship of this "shadow fleet" that was built and actually converted to a carrier (during the Pacific War) was the 10,000-standard-ton submarine tender *Taigei,* on which conversion work was secretly started in 1941 and completed in November 1942, when she was renamed the carrier *Ryūhō.* But her small flight deck, insufficient hull strength, and inadequate diesel propulsion system (later replaced by destroyer turbines) prevented her from ever becoming an effective fleet unit. In 1934, under the "Circle Two" naval construction program, the navy ordered four auxiliary vessels that could be converted into submarine tenders, fast oil tankers, or light fleet carriers, as needed. The *Tsurugisaki,* the first of these ships laid down, was completed as a submarine tender in 1939 but converted into a carrier in late 1941 and renamed *Shōhō.* Her sister ship, the *Takasaki,* laid down in early 1935, was commissioned as the carrier *Zuihō* in 1940. The other two vessels, the *Chitose* and *Chiyoda,* were laid down as seaplane carriers and converted to flush-deck carrier configuration during the Pacific War. As a group, these conversions, though quickly completed for the most part, were largely unsuccessful because of their low speed, small aircraft capacity, and inadequate protection. The *Zuihō,* with her destroyer-type turbines, was probably the best of the lot and was the only one of this group that had joined the fleet when the war began, serving in five of the major carrier operations of the Pacific War.[37]

It remains only to mention in passing those aircraft carriers under construction as hostilities began in December 1941. None proved to be a durable asset to the navy in the coming struggle, but the most promising of the group was the 30,000-ton *Taihō,* laid down in July 1941 and launched in April 1943, the first Japanese carrier with an armored flight deck. To that extent, she appears to have been patterned on the British *Illustrious,* which she closely resembled. One of the last big fleet carriers to join the Japanese fleet, in her short life the *Taihō* was never to have the opportunity to test her flight deck against aerial bombs. Completed in March 1944, she was sunk by a submarine three months later.[38]

Conversion work on the hulls of two new 27,000-ton luxury liners of the Nihon Yūsen Kaisha began in October 1940, and they were launched in June 1941 as the *Hiyō* and *Jun'yō,* joining the fleet in the summer of 1942. But their hybrid propulsion system of destroyer-type boilers mated to turbines designed for mercantile use provided inadequate power and thus made them too slow for fully effective fleet operations and subject to frequent breakdowns. The *Taiyō* was another carrier converted from an NYK liner under construction in the months immediately prior to the Pacific War. Intended as a convoy escort carrier, she was to prove inadequate to the task after she joined the fleet. Her sisters, the *Chūyō* and *Un'yō*, converted after the war began from NYK liners already in service, proved similarly ineffective.[39]

IMPLICATIONS OF JAPANESE CARRIER DESIGN

The single greatest factor affecting the difference in the design and operation of Japanese and American carriers during this period was the method of calculating maximum aircraft capacity. In the Japanese navy, as in the Royal Navy, aircraft capacity was determined by the size of the hangar rather than by the size of the flight deck. While from the beginning American carriers normally parked most of their aircraft on the flight deck and used the hangars below only for aircraft repair and maintenance, Japanese carriers used their hangars as their main storage area, as well as for servicing, refueling, and reloading ordnance (although rearmament of dive bombers was often performed on the flight deck). Such an arrangement had important implications for both aircraft capacity and flight operations. As flight-deck storage provides considerably more aircraft space, Japanese carriers of roughly the same displacement as American carriers usually had significantly smaller air groups. Considering the numerical disadvantage that the Japanese thus imposed upon themselves, it may seem odd that Japanese aircraft designers did not place more emphasis on folding wings for their carrier aircraft. Of the three main types of Japanese carrier aircraft at the time of Pearl Harbor, only one, with a considerable wingspan, the Nakajima B5N carrier attack aircraft, had folding wings. The other two—the Aichi D3A carrier bomber and the Mitsubishi A6M2 carrier fighter—had wings that folded only at the tips, an arrangement made out of a concern for keeping the wingspan within the dimensions of the elevators, not out of a concern for saving hangar space. (Fig. 3-1.) The incorporation of folding mechanisms into the wing structure was believed to add too much weight and thus to represent an unacceptable sacrifice in performance.[40]

Yet if Japanese aircraft carriers built in the 1920s and early 1930s differed from American carriers in their arrangements for aircraft storage, they shared with their American counterparts the common characteristic that their design sacrificed defensive protection for the ships themselves in order to maximize the offensive potential of their aircraft. While it is true that the *Akagi* and *Kaga* retained some of their original capital ship armor, it was drastically reduced during their conversion. On the *Sōryū* and *Hiryū*, armor was limited to modest protection over machinery, magazines, and aviation gasoline tanks, while on the *Ryūjō* it was practically nil. As in the case of American carriers, the flight decks were superimposed upon the hull rather than constituting a strength deck that formed an integral part of the hull, as in the carriers of the Royal Navy of the period.[41] Because their designers were unwilling to make the sacrifices of speed, weight, or space that substantial horizontal protection would have required, the flight decks of prewar Japanese carriers

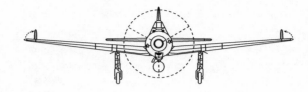

Mitsubishi A6M (Type 0 Carrier Fighter)

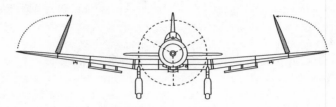

Aichi D3A (Type 99 Carrier Bomber)

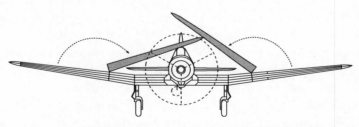

Nakajima B5N (Type 97 Carrier Attack Bomber)

Parshall 2000

Fig. 3-1. Wing-folding arrangements for Japanese carrier aircraft

consisted of wooden planking laid lengthwise over thin steel decks (U.S. carriers had their deck planking athwartships). Nor were the hangars of prewar Japanese carriers armored, though they were enclosed by storerooms, so that their aircraft and ready crews were shielded from wind and weather. (Fig. 3-2.)

Such arrangements entailed operational consequences that ranged from inconvenient to outright dangerous. Because of ventilation problems, aircraft could not normally be warmed up in the hangars. Much worse, as evidenced by the damage suffered by Japanese carriers during the Pacific War, when enemy bombs penetrated the unarmored flight decks and exploded in the hangars, the effects of the resultant blast pressures could be disastrous: the flight deck blown apart and the hangar sides buckled. Enclosed hangars also prevented the easy disposal of fuel and ordnance over the side in the event of a hangar fire, and effectively prevented fighting such a fire with hoses from any screening ships that might be in a position to act as fireboats. Moreover, as the hangars were neither vapor-tight nor flash-tight, they were vulnerable to explosions from ordnance or aviation fuel.[42]

Japanese aviation fuel arrangements were also suspect. While even early-war carrier aviation gas tanks were surrounded by spaces filled with inert carbon dioxide gas, the tanks themselves were incorporated into the structure of the vessel.[43] This meant that shock stresses imparted to the hull could be directly transmitted to the tanks, causing them to crack and leak, sometimes disastrously. Late-war carriers attempted to remedy this problem by filling the void spaces with reinforced concrete, but this measure was only partly successful. Furthermore, there is no indication that early-war Japanese carriers were capable of filling their fuel lines with carbon dioxide, as became American practice soon after the outbreak of hostilities.[44]

In addition, while Japanese carriers incorporated elaborate firefighting equipment, including fireproof curtains, banks of foam dischargers, flooding systems, and armored damage-control stations throughout the hangar decks, the very nature of enclosed hangars and the vulnerable fueling system design meant that the damage mitigation measures were largely doomed from the start.[45] This fact, combined with a mediocre level of damage-control training and organization (see chap. 6), meant that Japanese carriers were unduly prone to aviation fuel fires, a defect that contributed in one degree or another to the loss of the four carriers at Midway as well as to the later sinkings of the *Taihō* and *Shōkaku*.[46]

From the beginning of carrier aviation, it was important in the Japanese navy, as it was in its American and British counterparts, to control the movement of aircraft, particularly landing aircraft, across carrier flight decks. The first necessity was to bring landing aircraft to a secure stop, a function they were unable to perform entirely on their own. Early in the 1920s the Japanese navy adopted the British system of longitudinal wires across the flight deck to slow incoming aircraft, but this system too often failed to stop aircraft attempting to land. By the 1930s, Japanese carriers switched to the far more effective French system of transverse wires to engage the arrester hooks of landing aircraft.[47] As in the U.S. and Royal navies, Japanese carriers also made use of a crash-barrier system to prevent aircraft that

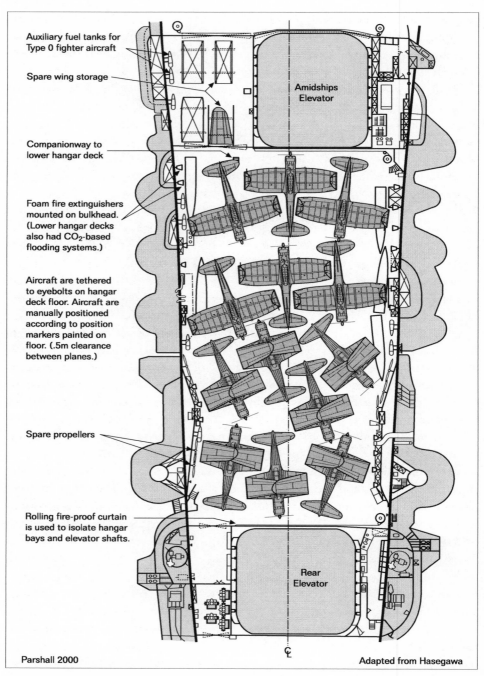

Auxiliary fuel tanks for
Type 0 fighter aircraft

Spare wing storage

Amidships
Elevator

Companionway to
lower hangar deck

Foam fire extinguishers
mounted on bulkhead.
(Lower hangar decks
also had CO_2-based
flooding systems.)

Aircraft are tethered
to eyebolts on hangar
deck floor. Aircraft are
manually positioned
according to position
markers painted on
floor. (.5m clearance
between planes.)

Spare propellers

Rolling fire-proof curtain
is used to isolate hangar
bays and elevator shafts.

Rear
Elevator

Parshall 2000

Ç
Ł

Adapted from Hasegawa

Fig. 3-2. Interior of the *Hiryū*'s upper hangar deck, aft

missed or failed to be restrained by the arresting gear from smashing into aircraft spotted forward. This system consisted of a set of three wires (in later carriers, two sets) about 2 meters (6 feet) high, strung one above the other across the deck between supports on either side of the flight deck, each of which was attached to a hydraulically operated sliding restraint. When an errant aircraft hit the wires, they were pulled forward and were ultimately stopped by the hydraulic mechanism, taking up the shock and stopping the aircraft. If aircraft were to be parked forward of the barrier, it could be lowered for each incoming aircraft and reset for the next.[48] Arresting gear was fitted both fore and aft, indicating that just as in U.S. practice, Japanese fleet carriers were equipped to conduct emergency landing operations over the bow with the ship going astern.[49]

CARRIER FLIGHT OPERATIONS

As Hugh Popham has written in his fine study of British naval aviation, all carrier flight operations are governed by two determinants: space and time.[50] These determinants were particularly severe in the days of cyclic flight operations before the "flex deck" operations of the post–World War II era, when carriers came to have ready decks for both landings and takeoffs. Popham's additional point that in a carrier space is organized vertically, rather than horizontally, was truer of the British and Japanese navies than of the American navy because the British and Japanese tended to store most of their aircraft below, on the hangar deck, and to do most of the servicing of aircraft in hangars rather than on the flight deck. This arrangement thus made elevators more central to the spotting, maintenance, and storage of the carrier's aircraft than on American carriers—which parked most of their aircraft on the flight deck—and thus had a greater impact on the duration of flight cycles. In preparation for a flight cycle, aircraft in the hangars had to be manhandled onto the elevators, off them, and then pushed or pulled down the deck, where they were properly spotted for launch. The laborious process—tricky and even dangerous in foul weather—was reversed when, at the end of a recovery cycle, landed aircraft at the forward end of the flight deck were struck below.

Flight operations on Japanese carriers were directed from a platform located on the rear of the island bridge by an air operations officer *(hikōchō)*. A launch began with the carrier headed into the wind,[51] and aircraft to be used on a particular mission properly spotted on the deck with engines run up and chocks still under the wheels. The air operations officer checked the wind-over-deck determined from a speed indicator at his side, and when the wind speed was judged sufficient—14 meters per second, or approximately 27 knots—he would have a white flag with a large black ball hoisted. (In low-light conditions, as during the launching of the first attack wave from the *Akagi* at the Battle of Midway, the procedure may have involved a lamp.) The air operations officer would then give a signal to a flight-deck officer, who would wave away the chocks; the deck crew would drag the chocks from the wheels and scurry to the sides of the flight deck. The air operations officer would then raise a white flag from the bridge as a signal for launch, and the first aircraft would move up the deck. The pilot judged wind direction during takeoff by means of a steam jet trailing vapor at the forward end of the flight deck. As long as the white flag flew from the bridge, aircraft took off at twenty- to thirty-second intervals.[52] A minimum takeoff length of 70 meters (230 feet) was required by the Zero fighter plane; heavier aircraft required nearly twice as much takeoff distance.[53] Catapults, while used to launch floatplanes from other aircraft-carrying vessels, were never installed on any Japanese carriers.[54]

In general, the Japanese did not use a landing signals officer ("Paddles," in the U.S. and Royal navies) to recover aircraft, though a crewman *(seibiin)* under the supervision of the air operations officer was stationed aft to signal to the aircraft as required. The air operations officer would hoist a red flag in case of a fouled deck to signal a wave-off. A set of standardized signals was developed to communicate with incoming aircraft. Carrier identities themselves were indicated by a large "kana" symbol painted on their flight decks (usually on the port quarter, but sometimes on the port bow). By day, a black ball with two numerical flags under it was hoisted, indicating that the carrier was ready to receive aircraft and giving the wind velocity over the deck in meters per second. Wind direction was indicated by the steam jet at the front of the flight deck. A red flag from the *seibiin* signaled that the pilot should go around again; a white flag with an *H* meant that the aircraft's hook was not lowered.[55]

At night these signals were replicated via a series of colored lights. A white light in the center of the landing array could be used to blink messages to the incoming pilot. A line of red, blue, and white lights aligned fore and aft just abaft the island were used to indicate relative wind over the deck. The outline and centerline of the flight deck were illuminated in white lights, while crash barriers and the aft edge of the deck were indicated by transverse rows of red lights. Each bank of lights could be dimmed independently by rheostats.[56]

Aircraft waiting to land formed a group to starboard of the ship, circling to the right. When it was time to land, the next aircraft in the cycle would break left, circle the ship across the bow and down the port side, then turn in to the left and line up approximately 700 meters (2,000 feet) astern at approximately 200 meters' (700 feet) altitude.[57] Each pilot would establish his glidepath by lining up his incoming aircraft with a series of adjustable and differently positioned red and green lights (*chakkan shidōtō*, "landing guidance lights") on either side of the deck, an arrangement similar to the "call the ball" system later developed by the British and used on American carriers. (Fig. 3-3.) Each pilot flying in astern of the carrier with wheels, flaps, and arrester hook down would have to adjust his flight path until he had both pairs of lights in his sight, a perfect horizontal lineup for landing. To determine the correct height for his approach to the carrier's deck, he adjusted his glide angle according to the correct vertical position of the colored lights in his sight. A perfect glide slope would have the green light positioned immediately above the red. If he could see only the red light, he was below the perfect slope, and if the

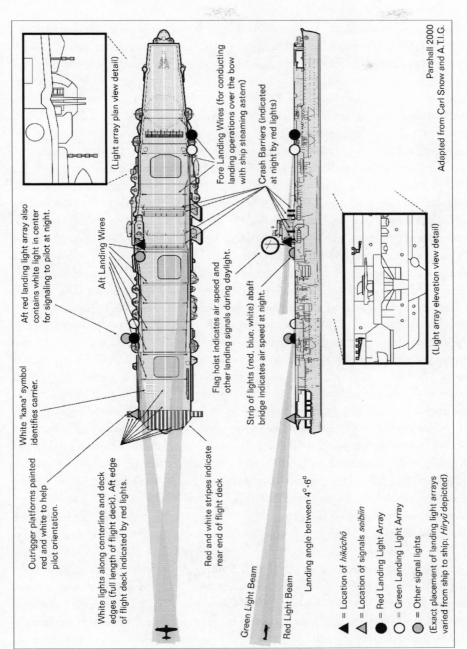

Outrigger platforms painted red and white to help pilot orientation.

White "kana" symbol identifies carrier.

Aft red landing light array also contains white light in center for signaling to pilot at night.

(Light array plan view detail)

Fore Landing Wires (for conducting landing operations over the bow with ship steaming astern)

Crash Barriers (indicated at night by red lights)

Aft Landing Wires

White lights along centerline and deck edges (full length of flight deck). Aft edge of flight deck indicated by red lights.

Flag hoist indicates air speed and other landing signals during daylight.

Strip of lights (red, blue, white) abaft bridge indicates air speed at night.

Red and white stripes indicate rear end of flight deck

(Light array elevation view detail)

Green Light Beam

Red Light Beam

Landing angle between 4°-6°

▲ = Location of *hikōchō*

△ = Location of signals *seibiin*

● = Red Landing Light Array

○ = Green Landing Light Array

◉ = Other signal lights

(Exact placement of landing light arrays varied from ship to ship: *Hiryū* depicted)

Parshall 2000
Adapted from Carl Snow and A.T.I.G.

Fig. 3-3. Japanese carrier landing operations

red light was over the green, he was coming in so low that he would smash into the carrier's stern if he didn't pull up. If the green light was positioned far above the red, the pilot was coming in too high and risked missing the arresting gear and hitting the crash barrier, or worse.[58] He was further aided in this process by the white-painted outrigger platforms near the aft end of the flight deck. These platforms helped him gauge the orientation of the flight deck even if the deck itself was obscured by the nose of the aircraft.[59]

The pilot aimed to maintain an airspeed of approximately 10 knots above stall speed, which typically translated to 70–75 knots.[60] Assuming he had kept the lights lined up properly, just prior to crossing the after end of the flight deck the pilot would cut his engine, and gliding in, his hook would catch the arrester wire and stop the aircraft. He would then release the hook and taxi forward.[61] The crash barriers would be lowered,[62] the aircraft moved to the forward end of the flight deck, and the barriers reset for the next aircraft.

This technique of "continuous stowage" *(renzoku shūyō)*—the recovery of landing aircraft in quick succession by respotting the just-landed planes forward of the crash barriers—was regularly practiced aboard Japanese carriers by the mid-1930s. By the Pacific War, Japanese carriers could land aircraft every twenty-five to forty-five seconds. When necessary, they were pushed back from the forward end of the flight deck to the after end and serviced there in preparation for the next launch.[63] But in most cases, once a recovery cycle had been completed, the aircraft were struck below, to be serviced and armed. It was this procedure, governed by elevator cycles,[64] that kept Japanese carrier flight operations at a slower pace than those of their American opposites, who in general performed most refueling and rearming functions on the flight deck. This slower pace, combined with all the hazards brought about by the proximity, in a confined space, of highly combustible fuels and ordnance, held a potential for disaster. There was always the possibility that in urgent combat situations, the delay implicit in the slower flight cycles of Japanese carriers might cause proper rearming procedures to be cast aside in favor of greater speed in rearming and refueling. Again, the often-told loss of the *Akagi* and *Kaga* at Midway is testimony to this ominous problem.[65]

As in the other two carrier navies, the hazards of operations on and off a Japanese carrier were considerable and crashes too frequent an occurrence. Okumiya Masatake, who learned to fly off carriers aboard the *Ryūjō*, recalled in later years how very small the carrier looked coming in to land, and how easily a pilot could misjudge his approach despite the best guidance systems. It was difficult but essential, for example, to compensate instantly for the slightest deviation between the carrier's heading and the wind direction as indicated by the steam jet on the flight deck. In a side wind of 10 meters (33 feet) per second, a second of inattention by a pilot approaching the carrier's stern would cause the aircraft to be blown 10 meters sideways. With the *Ryūjō*'s deck only 23 meters (76 feet) wide, this would mean that one of the aircraft's wheels would miss the flight deck, and the plane would plummet into the ocean. Only the selection of carrier pilots with

Photo. 3-2. The aircraft carrier *Sōryū* landing a B3Y1 Type 92 carrier attack bomber in December 1937, near Saeki Bay. Note the steam jet on the flight deck to indicate wind direction.
Source: Fukui, *Shashin Nihon kaigun zen kantei shi*, 1:345.

instant reflexes and great enthusiasm, near perfect teamwork between air and deck crews, and constant and rigorous training kept the occasional crackups on deck and splashes into the sea from becoming a chain of disasters.[66] Of course, in flight operations there were always a few aircraft that went over or completely missed the deck and fell into the ocean. To minimize personnel losses in this event, Japanese carriers engaged in flight operations, like their American counterparts, always trailed one or two guard destroyers astern, ready to rescue downed aircrew.

EMERGENCE OF JAPANESE CARRIER DOCTRINE

In the early days of carrier aviation, the justifications for building carriers were speculative and the designs for constructing them were necessarily experimental. The variety of carriers produced by the Japanese navy in this period is ample testimony to these conditions. As in the U.S. and Royal navies, carrier doctrine was quite tentative. It developed sporadically on the basis of both the demands of the Navy General Staff for superior warships and the practical results of Japanese carrier operations in these years.

When the *Hōshō* was first added to the Japanese fleet and the *Akagi* and *Kaga* were being constructed as carriers, the principal functions of naval aviation were spotting, reconnaissance, and antisubmarine patrol. There was as yet little thought given to the use of carrier aircraft as important components in offensive operations, and thus little consideration of carrier doctrine. With the formation of the First Carrier Division in 1928 and with the availability of more than one carrier, serious consideration began of the study of the role and place of carriers in a fleet engagement.[67] Yet even then, carrier aviation was seen as a force multiplier, not as a decisive element of sea power on its own. The chief function of carrier aircraft was still tactical and defensive in nature: to secure "command of the air" over the surface battle area, increasing the effectiveness of friendly battleships over their enemy counterparts. Of course, at this point there was little possibility of carriers operating in a long-range strategic role, largely because of the limited effective range of carrier aircraft, which in the late 1920s was not much more than 100 miles.[68]

In the early 1930s, therefore, the navy still placed emphasis on the tactical use of carrier air power, particularly in support of the main battle force. For example, a principal function of carrier attack aircraft during this period was cooperation with the surface batteries of the main force and the laying down of aerial smoke screens for supra–smoke screen fire by battleship main batteries, a role that reflected the continuing "big-gun" priorities of the navy. Moreover, in the fleet maneuvers from 1928 to 1935, which always pitted a "Red Fleet" representing the Americans against a "Blue Fleet" representing Japan, carrier fighters were employed mainly in repelling enemy spotter aircraft and in protecting friendly target observation planes. Japanese naval tacticians had come to believe that for one side or the other to prevail in such a contest, a major air engagement would have to be waged for control of the air over the opposing fleets, a duel that would precede the showdown surface battle. Because their performance was so limited at this time, carrier fighters were conceived of only as defensive aircraft over the fleet, but always in direct support of fleet units engaged with the enemy's main surface forces. Not unreasonably, therefore, by the early 1930s naval aviators, for their part, came to see the enemy's carriers as the main target of carrier offensive air power, whereas the navy's capital ship gunnery staffs continued to believe that carrier strikes should have enemy battleships as their priority targets.[69]

Thus, early in the 1930s there was as yet no unified doctrine in the Japanese navy as to how carriers were to be used in a fleet action. The Battle Instructions *(Kaisen yōmurei)* of the navy,[70] which had governed fleet operations since roughly 1900, were ambivalent on this issue even as late as the 1930s, though they appeared to lean toward the "battleship first" principle, as before. They declared that "attacks on the enemy main force [his battle line] should be timed at the opportunity for the decisive fleet engagement," and they urged "attacks on enemy carriers at the outset of such an encounter so as to immobilize them in the ensuing [surface] battle." Such equivocation was part of a larger ambiguity of the instructions concerning the role of air power in naval warfare. Because they eventually became so out-of-date in relation to air power, in 1933 the Navy General Staff set up a committee to study the problem of revision of the instructions. Its members were so divided over the issue of air power that the committee made little progress. Eventually, since the whole matter had become controversial, what emerged from the committee in 1934 was a set of vacillating and far narrower guidelines, "Draft Instructions for Air Combat" *(Kōkūsen yōmu sōan)*, which satisfied no one and was regarded with contempt by the navy's air officers.[71]

With every increase in the range and power of carrier aircraft, the most salient characteristic of carrier air power came to be seen as its ability to reach out beyond the range of existing surface weapons. It was inevitable, therefore, that Japanese gunnery staffs as well as naval airmen should begin to argue that the reconnaissance capabilities of naval air power should be combined with its growing offensive potential to perfect the concept of a preemptive aerial strike at the enemy's aircraft carriers.[72] It was only by the elimination of the enemy's carriers that Japanese forces could achieve air superiority over the area of the surface battle. Beginning about 1932–33, therefore, the Japanese navy began to shift its initial aerial targets from the enemy's battleships to his carriers, and by middecade, with the heightened performance of bombing aircraft, particularly the dive bomber, the destruction of the enemy carrier force became the focus of intensified research and practice by the naval air forces. As I shall demonstrate in a later chapter, the navy's increasing tactical skill in offensive air operations in the late 1930s was to turn its confidence in naval aviation into an article of faith. But what is important to understand here is that by the mid-1930s, among navy airmen the proper exercise of air power was seen to be less in the direct support of surface forces than in seeking its own opportunities to destroy an enemy who might be over the horizon.[73] In 1937 the navy worked out a scheme of air operations against the U.S. Pacific

Fleet that included the following principle: air operations were to take place before the decisive battle, and such operations would have as their objectives both the command of air space over the battle zone *and* the destruction of the enemy's carriers *and* battleships.[74]

The essential condition for that destruction was that Japanese naval air forces be able to strike first, before Japan's carriers came within range of the enemy's carriers. That in turn depended on the Japanese ability to "outrange" the enemy in the air, just as Japanese surface forces were hoping to do by shell and torpedo on and below the ocean's surface. This meant that the Japanese navy would have to develop attack aircraft that could "outrange" those of the United States Navy. It was for this reason that throughout the 1930s the Japanese navy came to emphasize range in its specifications when calling for bids for aircraft design. This emphasis was driven home in the design of Japan's front-line carrier attack aircraft in service as the Pacific War opened, and it continued throughout that conflict. Because of their lighter construction, Japanese carrier attack aircraft could indeed search and attack at greater ranges than their American opposite numbers. During the Pacific War, U.S. searches were generally limited to 325–360 miles, while Japanese naval aircraft often searched to ranges of 560 miles. American carrier aircraft could attack to about 200–250 miles, whereas their Japanese counterparts could strike up to about 300–350 miles. Yet as Eric Bergerud has pointed out, during the war both sides learned from experience that in flying any given aircraft in combat, it was essential to allow for a large margin of error rather than flying to its combat radius (the maximum distance the aircraft could fly, perform its mission, and return to base with sufficient fuel to land safely).[75]

The realization of "outranging" enemy naval air power thus gave substance to the concept of preemptive mass aerial attack. This in turn meant the freeing of Japanese carriers from having to provide direct support to the main battle force. Now they might operate in the vanguard of the fleet as a means of strengthening the fleet's reconnaissance capabilities, acting either independently or in cooperation with cruiser forces.[76] Yet as I noted earlier and shall discuss again in a later chapter, one difficulty with this concept was that Japan's carrier forces themselves did not devote adequate training and attention to the reconnaissance mission.[77]

Moreover, the concept gave rise to a difficult problem that was to take a good number of years to solve: whether to concentrate or to disperse the fleet's carriers in battle, an issue highlighted by Japan's continuing numerical inferiority under the unfavorable ratios that had been imposed by treaty limitations. The nub of the problem lay in the fact that while carriers possessed great striking power, they were also extremely vulnerable. Unlike a battleship, a carrier did not need to be sunk in order to be eliminated as a fighting unit. Since the flight decks of both Japanese and American carriers were unarmored, destruction of these decks would essentially neutralize these warships. True, intensive navy studies in the 1930s pointed to the difficulty of judging at what point bomb damage would neutralize a carrier beyond

repair. Yet it is hard to see how a carrier could remain effective if its aircraft elevators were put out of action.[78]

Although their offensive potential was best realized by concentrating them in
order to launch devastating mass aerial attacks, by the same token, should all the
carriers be surprised and struck, they could be annihilated at one blow, a possibility that was enormously increased in the second half of the decade with the advent
of dive bombing. On the other hand, if carriers were dispersed in order to minimize
the impact of any one enemy aerial assault, not only would the ability of individual
carriers to defend themselves be lessened, but their weaker formations of attack aircraft would be more likely to fall to enemy fighters, and because of factors of time
and fuel, their attacks would be more sporadic. It was difficult, moreover, to concentrate aircraft groups from carriers not within sight of one another. In the early
1930s, when the navy had only two fleet carriers, it was impossible to test the relative merits of concentration and dispersal in fleet maneuvers, so that much theo-
rizing was tested in the form of table-top war-gaming. By 1936, however, on the
basis of fleet maneuvers that year, as well as of map exercises, most Japanese tacticians had come to favor the doctrine of carrier dispersal, so that a numerically superior foe could not destroy all the Japanese carriers at once, even though they recognized the disadvantages that this dispersal might bring.[79] Yet as I shall explain in
chapter 6, the doctrine of carrier dispersal, as the Japanese navy conceived it in
1936, gave scant attention to the problem of fleet air defense. Given the meager
offensive power of carrier aircraft in the mid-1930s, this may have been under-
standable, but fleet air defense continued to be a fundamental weakness for
Japanese carrier formations straight into the Pacific War.

Contemporary Japanese tactical thinking concerning the optimum employment
of dispersed carrier air power was set forth in a Staff College study in November
1936. The study proposed that smaller Japanese carriers were to steam in a dispersed formation, and large fleet carriers were to operate alone. Dispersed formations were to be deployed so as to encircle the enemy, enabling individual carriers
to concentrate their attacks on the enemy fleet without themselves becoming a
massed target. Yet with Japanese carriers so far out in front of their own main battle force, serious losses were to be expected by the most advanced units. In the
words of the study, the leading Japanese carrier "must be prepared to be impaled
as it impales the enemy" (gūshi suru no kakugo aru o yō su). Air attacks against the
enemy fleet were to be launched at a range of 350 miles, and all attack aircraft were
to be committed by the time Japanese carriers were 250 miles from the enemy. The
study argued that if Japanese attack aircraft at the time of hostilities had no better
range than their American opposites, their bomb loads were to be reduced, and
midair-refueling (kūchū nenryō hokyū) techniques were to be developed in order to
give them the edge. (There is no evidence that the Japanese navy ever actually practiced such techniques.) The key to success was to be mass attacks, delivered pre-
emptively because of the advantages of surprise and of "outranging" the enemy.

Given the Japanese navy's limited confidence in the ability of fighter aircraft to defend fleet units against the assaults of enemy torpedo and dive bombers, it is not surprising that the study said almost nothing about the maintenance of combat air patrols over Japanese carriers. On the other hand, if the enemy's offensive carrier power was destroyed at the outset, air defenses would be unnecessary. In any event, until the advent of radar and its contribution to efficient vectoring of defending aircraft, carrier-borne fighters could not hope to defend their carriers effectively against incoming enemy air attacks.[80]

The general composition of Japanese carrier air groups during these years reflected these ideas. It is difficult to be precise about the composition of such air groups, in part because individual carrier hangar configurations changed with the modernization and refitting of individual carriers, and in part because postwar reference works on Japanese naval aviation often tabulate significantly different data concerning air groups. Nevertheless, two principles in the composition of Japanese carrier air groups seem to be constant throughout the period.

First, in keeping with the offensive priorities of Japanese carrier doctrine, carrier air groups were weighted in favor of attack aircraft—dive bombers and torpedo bombers—over fighter planes for defense. Second, in the mid-1930s, between attack aircraft, priority was given to torpedo over dive bombers, unlike the composition of carrier air groups in the United States Navy, where the emphasis was reversed. For example, the composition of the air groups of the two largest carriers reflected these preferences. As modernized in 1935 and 1938 respectively, the *Kaga* embarked forty-five torpedo bombers, thirty dive bombers, and sixteen fighters, and the *Akagi* carried fifty-one torpedo bombers, twenty-four dive bombers, and sixteen fighters. In comparison, typical U.S. carrier air groups of the 1938–41 period included one fighter, one torpedo, and two dive-bomber squadrons, with each squadron consisting of twenty-one aircraft, eighteen operational and three spares.[81]

This Japanese preference undoubtedly reflected a traditional faith in torpedo warfare and the belief that torpedoes simply had greater explosive power than the ordnance that dive bombers were capable of carrying. With the demonstrations of the effectiveness of dive bombing late in the 1930s, the emphasis shifted, however, so that by early 1941 most Japanese carriers embarked roughly equal numbers of torpedo and dive bombers, though still far fewer fighter aircraft. Although torpedo planes and dive bombers together greatly outnumbered fighters on Japanese carriers, fighters still accounted for a higher proportion of the total (about one-third) than on U.S. carriers. The comparable figure in the United States Navy was one-fourth; only after the Pacific War began did the proportion of fighters on U.S. carriers increase.[82]

4

SOARING

Japanese Naval Aircraft and the
Japanese Aircraft Industry, 1937–1941

I have been discussing the controversies that took place in the 1920s and 1930s over specific technologies, armaments, and tactics on the way to the creation of a modern air service within the Japanese navy. But it is important to keep in mind that during the interwar period these arguments took place against the background of a broader and intensifying debate within the navy as to the appropriate place of aviation in naval warfare generally. As in the United States Navy, the lines in this debate were drawn between the majority of officers in the fleet and the high command who held that the main batteries of the battle line remained the final arbiter of victory at sea, and the much smaller group of air power enthusiasts who argued that the range, speed, and destructive capability of the airplane had overturned the supremacy of the battleship. In charting this debate and its influence on the development of Japanese naval aviation, two facts must be kept in mind. The first point has been mentioned earlier in this study: In Japan, as in other nations, the capacities of air weaponry were consistently exaggerated by its advocates during this period. In particular, governments assumed bomb-delivery capabilities by aircraft that were not to exist until World War II. In its initial phase, therefore, the aircraft-versus-gun debate was between visionaries who claimed for the airplane all the things it could not yet do, and realists who noted the enormous disparity in capabilities between air and surface units.

Photo. 4-1. The aircraft carrier *Akagi* entering Ōsaka Bay, 15 October 1934, with Mitsubishi B1M1 (Type 13) and Mitsubishi B2M1 (Type 89) carrier attack aircraft aboard
Source: Fukui, *Shashin Nihon kaigun zen kantei shi*, 1:328.

The second point to note is that in its later phase, the debate was not between a blindly obdurate battleship faction and a small clutch of airmen struggling to find at least some naval role for aviation. Rather, it involved an argument between a battleship-oriented naval orthodoxy now sensitized to the potential of air power and a group of air power radicals who believed that all future naval warfare would be decided by aviation. The former held that the offensive power that aviation had by then acquired should be exploited to ensure victory by the surface fleet. The latter, centering their vision largely on the range and striking power of land-based heavy aircraft, advanced "the theory of air power omnipotence" *(kōkū bannō ron)*, which called for the scrapping of all capital ships.

THE NAVAL AVIATION CONTROVERSY

In a sense, the opening shot in the argument had been fired at the very dawn of Japanese naval aviation when, in 1915, Nakajima Chikuhei, then a young engineer lieutenant, had written the air power declaration outlined in the first chapter. Yet as I have shown, in 1914 the prodigious technological gap between air power theory and air power fact made Nakajima's manifesto the statement of a visionary, not a realist. Over a decade later, this gap still hampered aviation proponents. Speaking at the Kasumigaura Naval Air Base in 1927 before a group of General Staff officers, Lt. Comdr. Kusaka Ryūnosuke,[†] destined to be one of Japanese naval aviation's most important figures, ticked off some of the advantages provided by aircraft in naval combat. Aircraft could operate over a wider combat area in a shorter period of time than surface craft. Aviators had a wide range of vision. Aircraft were difficult to shoot down because of their small size and speed. Aircraft in the attack were capable of dealing out psychological as well as physical damage. Yet, admitted Kusaka, the limitations of most aircraft in naval warfare were obvious: they could not stay in the air for long periods of time, they had difficulty operating with the fleet over great distances, their operations were at the mercy of the weather, and their bomb-carrying capacity was too limited to cause substantial damage to an enemy fleet.[1]

To an extent, of course, the development of carriers and their aircraft solved some of these problems, but at a time when the Japanese government and armed services were concerned about the possibility of an enemy bringing *his* aircraft carriers close to Japanese shores, the range of those land-based aircraft then in service seemed insufficient. Writing in the naval journal *Yūshū* early in 1930, Comdr. Matsunaga Toshio,[†] then executive officer on board the *Akagi,* argued for a larger land-based attack aircraft that could seek out and destroy an approaching enemy fleet while it was still far out at sea. Had Japan such bombers, capable of ranges of several thousand miles, possessing greatly increased bomb loads, based at strategic locations around the home islands, and supplemented by two or three aircraft carriers, these could prevent any enemy invasion force, even enemy carriers, from getting through, Matsunaga insisted.[2]

Rear Adm. Yamamoto Isoroku, who had become head of the Technology Bureau of the Naval Aviation Department in 1930, voiced similar arguments about the necessity of developing a new long-range capability for naval aviation. Yamamoto now had both the vision and the influence not only to make land-based air defense of the home islands a reality but to push it out into the far reaches of the Pacific. At the time, the small carrier aircraft possessed by both the Japanese and American navies were generally equal in the ranges at which they could seek and attack an enemy. Yamamoto, looking ahead to the day when Japan would be able to use its then demilitarized islands in Micronesia to create a chain of bases across the central Pacific, saw the tremendous "outranging" advantage of a long-range attack aircraft operating from those bases. Shifting from one island base to another, such a flexible bomber attack would upgrade the Japanese navy's attrition strategy against the larger westward-moving American fleet. The Navy General Staff had also recognized the increasing value of Micronesia as a base for operations against the United States Navy and had ordered the design of the largest flying boats for use in the islands. But judging from the results of aeronautical engineering research, it became clear that land-based bombers were more likely to satisfy the navy's operational needs than flying boats.[3]

With this concept in mind, Yamamoto initiated plans for the design of a land-based all-metal twin-engined monoplane with a range of 2,000 nautical miles and a 907-kilogram (2-ton) bomb load. Because of its experience in developing large all-metal flying boats, the Hirō Naval Arsenal was given the responsibility for developing the aircraft. The result was the Hirōshō G2H1, the largest naval aircraft of the time that was designed from the beginning as a land-based bomber. Mounting two water-cooled engines that were the most powerful available, the G2H1 was completed in April 1933 and, in Yamamoto's presence, made its first flight over Yokosuka that May. Further tests at Kasumigaura made it clear that in many respects the aircraft's capabilities fulfilled the Naval Aviation Department's requirements, and in 1936 it was adopted by the navy as the Type 95 land-based attack aircraft. But in the meantime, continued evaluation had demonstrated that the aircraft's engines were unreliable and actually underpowered for its size, and that its massively strutted fixed landing gear made it slow and cumbersome. Only eight G2H1s were therefore produced, and it was always regarded as a second-line aircraft.[4]

Yet the concept of a long-range land bomber inherent in production of the G2H1 did not die; indeed, Yamamoto was casting around for the development of another aircraft even as the G2H1 was being tested. As luck would have it, the army had also been experimenting with all-metal multiengined aircraft and had brought engineers from the Junkers firm in Germany to work with Japanese designers at Mitsubishi in developing a line of such aircraft that would incorporate the latest design features. Yamamoto recognized that the pool of technical skill now available at Mitsubishi was unrivaled anywhere else in Japan. He used his relentless energy and determination to press for assigning to Mitsubishi, on a noncompetitive basis, a contract for designing and developing a new reconnaissance plane. It would be capable of long overwater flights to determine American fleet movements in the Philippines and the Hawai'ian Islands. The aircraft was to surpass the G2H1 in performance but to be generally based on its airframe and engine type. In April 1934 Mitsubishi completed a single prototype of such an aircraft, the Ka.9, retroactively designated the G1M1. Its capabilities—an astounding range of 3,265 miles and a maximum speed of 165 knots, made possible by more powerful water-cooled engines (replaced, in later models, with radial engines) and a retractable undercarriage (the first in any Japanese aircraft)—delighted Yamamoto, who personally went up in the aircraft after its preliminary test flight. Further testing indicated that, more than being just a defensive long-range reconnaissance aircraft, the G1M1, if further developed as an offensive long-range bomber, had the capacity to give reality to the vision of Yamamoto and other air power advocates. Thus was born the first of the land-based twin-engined bombers, which led to the development of the G3M (see below).[5]

If the appearance in the mid-1930s of the land-based long-range bomber strengthened the arguments of the air power supremacists in the Japanese navy, their expectations were paralleled by the hopes that the navy's so-called *teppō-ya* ("gun club") placed on plans for the super-battleships *Yamato* and *Musashi*. It was the conjunction at middecade of these two opposing weapons systems—neither one was yet operational—that fueled the sudden aircraft-versus-gun debate in the Japanese navy, a controversy that was little reported in the West at the time and has been largely overlooked by Western naval historians in the decades since.[6] The debate was the result of two proposed solutions to the same problem: the numerical inferiority of the Japanese battle fleet in comparison with that of the United States. Japanese naval war games and maneuvers during these years had confirmed once again the inevitable victory of superior numbers in a collision between forces of similar composition. The solution of the "gun club" to this tactical dilemma was the construction of capital ships far more powerfully armed and armored than those of the enemy. The solution of the air power advocates, on the other hand, was to change drastically the composition of Japanese naval forces by making carriers the navy's main force, so as to circumvent and render irrelevant Japan's inferiority in capital ships.[7]

Among the first of the naval air staff to seize upon the appearance of the large land-based bomber as the harbinger of air power supremacy was Capt. Ōnishi Takijirō,[†] destined to become one of the navy's most forceful air power advocates, a prewar confidant of Yamamoto Isoroku, and the architect of the navy's desperate kamikaze strategy at the end of the Pacific War. Beginning with an assignment to the seaplane carrier *Wakamiya* about the time of Nakajima's circular letter on naval air power, which Ōnishi seems to have read with great enthusiasm, his early career had been mainly devoted to naval aviation, both as a line and a staff officer. In 1930, as a member of the Training Bureau of the Naval Aviation Department, he had written a memorandum calling for a drastic overhaul in the navy's aviation

Photo. 4-2. Capt. Ōnishi Takijirō (1891–1945)

structure and policies, including, among other things, an expansion of the number of land-based air groups. Now, four years later, as executive officer of the Yokosuka Air Group, Captain Ōnishi drafted an essay on naval air power that was far more strident. It called for the scrapping of all capital ships and a placing of the navy's offensive capabilities mainly on aircraft. Repeating the arguments that Nakajima had used nearly twenty years before, Ōnishi inveighed against the stupidity of the rumored General Staff plans to construct super-battleships, claiming that the cost of one such monster could pay for a thousand top-of-the-line fighter planes. Conversely, Ōnishi applauded the advent of the new land-based bomber, declaring with more enthusiasm than evidence, "It is already dangerous for surface units to enter within the range of such a bomber group. Because battleships are fragile under enemy attack, it is wrong to make them the navy's main force. For our naval armament we should shift from battleships to land-based air power."[8]

Other, younger, air power advocates, restless under the battleship orthodoxy of the navy's high command, began to weigh in with similar opinions. Asked to write on "Naval Armament Essential for the Effective Prosecution of War with the United States" as part of his study at the Naval Staff College, Lt. Comdr. Genda Minoru drafted an essay that proposed that the navy center its efforts on land- and carrier-based aircraft, with cruisers, destroyers, and submarines to be used in a supporting role. As for battleships, Genda wrote that they should be either scrapped or used as hulks for jetties. As he had been warned by Ōnishi when both were assigned to the Yokosuka Air Group, such ideas provoked a storm of criticism from gunnery and torpedo officers, and word went around the Staff College that Genda was a little crazy.[9]

For his part, Yamamoto regarded the plans for the projected battleships as the height of folly. At first he confined his opposition to sarcastic references to battleship orthodoxy in conversations with his colleagues and subordinates in naval aviation. About 1934, when he commanded the First Carrier Division, he remarked to a group of young pilots, "Even though the thick-headed *teppō-ya* have modified their outlook somewhat, they still don't grasp the realities of air power, so you young men will have to renew your efforts in training and study [in order to convince them]."[10] The next year, as head of the Naval Aviation Department, he disparaged the "big-gun" dogma with even greater ridicule:

> As you know [he told a group of naval aviators at the Yokosuka Air Group], it is the custom for wealthy families to display splendid art objects in their living rooms. Such objects have no practical value, yet such households derive a certain prestige from them. Similarly, the practical value of battleships has declined, but the world's navies still set great store upon them and they retain their symbolism as an indicator of naval power. You young airmen shouldn't insist on the abolition of the battleship, but rather you should think of it as a decoration for our [navy's] living room.[11]

But by this time the super-battleship project was under serious discussion as part of the "Circle Three" program. For that reason Yamamoto attempted to take the case for air power directly to the project's powerful backers in the navy's upper echelons. At the talks preliminary to the London Naval Conference of 1930, despite his misgivings, Yamamoto had followed his instructions and insisted upon parity in cruiser tonnage for Japan. But upon his return from London, he had met with Vice Adm. Koga Mineichi,† chief of the General Staff's Intelligence Division, to register his objections to the plans for the construction of the super-battleships. Koga had earnestly defended the project, noting the apparent lesson of recent French naval policy. France had been one of the first major naval powers to start building aircraft and submarines in lieu of capital ships, Koga pointed out, but once it started doing so, France had dropped to a second-rate naval power.[12] In vain Yamamoto tried to convince Capt. Fukuda Keiji of the Navy Technical Department, who had been given the responsibility for coordinating the design plans for the monster battleships, of the ultimate vulnerability and obsolescence of such warships. Despite his admiration for Yamamoto, Fukuda, fired by the technological challenge involved in designing ships of this unprecedented size, countered with explanations of their planned impregnability. Yamamoto ran into even more adamant resistance in his arguments with Vice Adm. Nakamura Ryōzō, chief of the Navy Technical Department and one of the super-battleship project's most determined architects. Fruitlessly Yamamoto sought to demonstrate with detailed figures that the navy would gain far greater offensive power by spending the same amount of money on naval aviation.[13]

To an extent, of course, the resistance of the navy's high command to criticisms of its super-battleship program reflected an irritation at having its collective wisdom challenged. When Adm. Takahashi Sankichi, commander of the Combined Fleet and before that commander of the First Carrier Division, stepped around to the General Staff and the Navy Ministry to express the view that perhaps the navy should concentrate on building its air power rather than building bigger battleships, his suggestion met with exasperation. "When Suetsugu Nobumasa held your command," he was told, "he wanted us to emphasize submarines because he was a submarine man. Now, because you used to be head of a carrier division, you want us to plump for more aircraft. We simply can't have Combined Fleet commanders giving vent to such personal biases." Despite Takahashi's lofty command and the fact that he still had an open mind on the air power–versus–sea power issue, his opinions cost him the trust of those overseeing the planning and construction of the super-battleships. From that time on he was cut off by the General Staff from further information about the project, an example of the arrogance of the navy's bureaucratic fiefdoms.[14]

But the high command's rejection of the arguments of Yamamoto and the other air power advocates was not just a matter of upper-echelon hubris. "Gun-club" officers believed that there were solid criticisms to be made of the concept of "air power omnipotence." As they pointed out, aircraft were still unreliable machines, affected as they were by weather. Moreover, aerial attack had as yet failed to sink a battleship under way. Conversely, they pointed out, both the offensive and defensive power of capital ships had increased: new techniques in spotting the fall of shot had supposedly doubled the accuracy of battleship main batteries; and the number and effectiveness of ship-borne antiaircraft weapons had increased substantially.

It is, of course, the responsibility of military professionals not only to assay what is tactically necessary today but also to give thought to what may be tactically possible tomorrow. The state of technology and the rapidity of its progress are the variables in their capacity to do so rationally. These serve to set the military visionary of yesterday apart from the clear-headed military prognosticator of today. When Nakajima Chikuhei sent around his circular in 1915, the feeble capacities of aircraft lent an air of fantasy to his ideas. We can now see that by the mid-1930s, when

Yamamoto Isoroku argued for the primacy of air power, the gap between air power theory and technological reality was closing with a rush.

Nevertheless, by the evidence available at middecade, the navy's battleship orthodoxy seemed to have the greater logic in the controversy. The problem with Yamamoto's arguments was that in the mid-1930s they still comprised prediction, not fact. Dive-bombing techniques and aerial torpedo tactics were still being worked out, and the new twin-engined bomber had yet to be tested in any sort of combat, let alone employed to attack moving targets. Moreover, compared with the radical theories of air power advocates like Ōnishi and Genda, who wanted to scrap all capital ships, the mainstream view, which argued for a balance of air and surface forces, seemed to the high command to be more rational. The mainstream view also seemed clearly confirmed by the adherence of the British and American navies to such a balanced force structure and doctrine. In any event, the weight of the high command was behind the plans to construct the super-battleships *Yamato* and *Musashi*. Thus, air power advocates like Yamamoto were unable to halt the project or to divert the same resources to strengthening the navy's air power. In the years ahead, Japanese naval airmen would argue with increasing confidence for the primacy of air power, and a few even demanded its complete independence from the two established services.

The issue of an independent, unified air force had been raised as far back as the early 1920s, largely at the initiative of army airmen. A joint army-navy committee had been established at that time to look into the merits of creating such a force. Nothing came of the concept because both services remained essentially opposed to it, but in the mid-1930s, with the great strides occurring in aircraft capabilities, with the increasingly vocal claims being made in each service for the primacy of air power, and with the emergence of independent air arms in major European countries to serve as a model, the idea was brought up once again, initially by advocates in the army. The concept created such a storm of controversy in the navy that the Naval Aviation Department established another committee to look into the matter. In July 1937 the report of the committee, drafted by Ōnishi Takijirō, concluded that the idea was essentially unsound, and the scheme was dropped. Essentially, the navy's opposition was based on two grounds: first, the suspicion that any unified air force would be dominated by army personnel and by army tactical considerations, and second, the belief that an independent air force would substantially weaken the navy's own air power, seen as critical to the navy's surface operations. The latter supposition seemed to be confirmed by the example of the weakening of the British navy's air service after the creation of the Royal Air Force.[15] So Japan, like the United States, entered World War II with its aviation divided between its two major services. Of course, the United States Army Air Forces came to acquire far greater autonomy than its Japanese army counterpart, and the large land-based air fleets of the Japanese navy (see chaps. 6 and 7) became more autonomous than American naval air forces, tethered as the latter were (except for Marine Corps air units) to their carriers.

Japanese Naval Aircraft Development
on the Eve of the China War

As we have seen, the development of an effective land-based long-range bomber
had been the first of Yamamoto's priorities. The impressive capabilities of the
Mitsubishi G1M1 aircraft had provided a real basis for Yamamoto's conception of
such a bomber. Completed at Mitsubishi's Nagoya plant as a shore-based reconnaissance aircraft, it had been tested at the Mitsubishi airfield at Kagamigahara in
April 1934. The results, surpassing the navy's performance requirements, had created a sensation in Japanese naval air circles. As a result, the navy issued specifications for a new long-range attack aircraft. Mitsubishi tested the first prototype in
July 1935, and after a series of modifications, the Navy Air Arsenal finally adopted
it in June 1936 as the Navy Type 96 attack plane, G3M1 (known to Allied air
forces during the Pacific War as the "Nell"). The Japanese dubbed it *chūkō,* a contraction of an unofficial designation for the plane, *chūgata kōgeki-ki,* which meant
"medium attack plane." The plane was also called *rikkō,* from a contraction of a
part of its official title, *rikujō kōgeki-ki,* "land-based attack plane." It was a sleek,
all-metal monoplane medium bomber whose slender shape was retained by exclud-
ing any internal bomb bays from the design, its 800 kilograms (1,764 pounds) of
bombs or a single torpedo being slung from racks fitted beneath the fuselage.[16]
Powered by two air-cooled radial engines, the *chūkō* was armed with two machine
guns mounted in dorsal turrets and one in a ventral turret.[17]

Once the *chūkō* had been accepted, the Japanese navy had to train a far greater
number of aircrews (pilots, observers, and radio operators) and ground crews, since
the new bomber required more personnel to man and maintain than any previous
navy land- or carrier-based aircraft. The Tateyama Air Group was the first unit to
receive the new airplane, and distribution to the Kisarazu and Kanoya naval air
groups soon followed. When the G3M1 first went into service, the navy made it a
practice to draw its crews from the most skilled and experienced of those who flew
its carrier attack planes, men with seven to ten years in the navy and over a thousand hours of flight time with the fleet. In the coming first months of Japan's air
war in China, these airmen were to constitute the vital cadre of the navy's medium-
bomber forces on the continent. All through the spring of 1937, *chūkō* crews operating from these bases undertook intensive training in long-distance operations
during flights to the Bonins, Saipan, and other overwater destinations.[18] In range,
speed, payload, service ceiling, and state-of-the-art radio equipment, the G3M1 was
an unprecedented Japanese aircraft. When it appeared over Chinese skies in the late
summer of 1937, it took international aviation circles by surprise and led some foreign observers to assume that it was simply a Japanese version of the German
Junkers 86 bomber. In fact, the G3M1 was superior to the Junkers in every respect
and at the time was surpassed only by the prototype of one of the greatest heavy
attack planes ever built, the Boeing B-17. The skill of the aircrews who flew it,
when added to the superb performance of the aircraft itself, created crack air

groups possessed of tremendous morale and energy, convinced of their capacity to wreak horrific destruction, and unshaken in their belief that no fighter plane could touch them. In time the *chūkō* would prove to be a flawed aircraft, but its near-fatal defects—absence of protective armor, inadequate defensive armament, and unprotected fuel tanks—would not be revealed until it had been tested in the fire of combat over China.[19] Even before the war, its crews worried about the fuel tanks catching fire, and from the first day of the raids on China their suspicions were confirmed, the bomber bursting into flames almost every time it was hit. While it must be remembered that at this time few military aircraft in the West had significant armor protection or were equipped with self-sealing gas tanks, it is testimony to the obduracy of the Japanese navy's air leaders, or to their willingness to sacrifice aircrews, that these problems persisted in later navy bomber designs.

The appearance of the G3M1 medium bomber in the spring of 1937 coincided with the apogee of antifighter sentiment in the Japanese navy. The new bomber's performance, particularly its speed relative to all operational Japanese fighter aircraft, seemed to underscore the impotence of the latter in the face of such capabilities. Bomber advocates like Lt. Comdr. Nitta Shin'ichi[†] believed that the fighter plane was no longer effective as either a defensive or an offensive aircraft. In his opinion it had become useless in an interceptor role because it could not maintain a superiority in speed, and it was of little use as an attack escort because it did not have the range to accompany the larger type of bomber.[20]

Yet in the months just prior to the China War, a revolutionary carrier fighter was coming on line that would restore the balance between fighters and bombers. Its origin lay in the search, early in 1934, for a new single-seat aircraft to replace the Nakajima A4N (Type 95) carrier fighter, a biplane that had from its inception been regarded as only a stopgap design. Even at a time when great strides were being made in aviation technology—in increased engine power and more streamlined configuration—the design of carrier aircraft posed particularly difficult problems, largely due to the inherent restrictions imposed by carrier flight-deck operations (including problems of visibility, landing speed, and the need to conform to the dimensions of the flight elevators). Given these restrictions, the design of a successful carrier fighter required a careful selection of performance priorities within the specifications set forth by the navy for any particular aircraft. Prepared by Lt. Comdr. Sawai Hideo of the Department of Engineering at the Naval Air Arsenal, the specifications for the new carrier fighter called for high speed, low weight, and excellent control.[21]

While air combat in China was to exercise an important influence in the design and development of certain aircraft, the specifications issued by the navy for its aircraft were nevertheless largely determined by the evolution of its missions at sea. This was especially true of fighter aircraft. Until about the time of the China War, the navy's needs for carrier fighters had been limited to those of fleet air defense against enemy spotter planes and attack aircraft (a problem to be discussed in chap. 6). But around 1935–36, as part of its emerging concept of a preemptive strike against enemy carriers, the navy began to consider the use of fighter escort for such an operation. About that time, therefore, the performance requirements for the navy's carrier fighters were significantly raised. Fighters no longer had only to drive off enemy reconnaissance craft but had to oppose enemy fighters, and this required a new level of performance. It was from this consideration, as much as from combat experience in China, that the navy's two most successful fighters were designed and developed in the years immediately preceding the Pacific War.[22]

At Mitsubishi, one of the two firms selected to enter the design competition, Horikoshi Jirō, an experienced aeronautical engineer who ultimately gained a world reputation, was named to head the design team. While trying to meet all the navy's requirements for the new aircraft, the Horikoshi group decided to place particular emphasis on speed and rate of climb. To maximize these, the team devoted intensive study to designing an aircraft with the minimum amount of air drag. Completed in January 1935, the product of this yearlong effort was a waspish-looking all-metal open-cockpit monoplane powered by a 500-horsepower radial engine and armed with two 7.7-millimeter machine guns mounted in the nearly elliptical wings. The careful design and smooth contouring of the aluminum monocoque construction of the fuselage, which included the use of flush rivets, made Horikoshi so confident that the aircraft would create the minimum amount of air resistance that he retained the use of fixed landing gear. While the retractable undercarriage was a recent feature favored among aircraft designers abroad, Horikoshi wished to avoid the extra weight and complex mechanisms it required.[23]

In flight tests at Kagamigahara in February 1935 the finished aircraft superbly justified the intensive effort the Horikoshi team had put into it. Attaining a speed of 243 knots, it exceeded navy specifications by 54 knots, and whereas the navy had required a time of climb to 5,000 meters (16,000 feet) of six and a half minutes, the Mitsubishi plane did that in five minutes, forty-five seconds. Since the tests also revealed some deficiencies in maneuverability, the incorporation of split flaps in the next prototype provided the sort of precise pilot control needed for dogfighting. Once out of Mitsubishi's hands, the aircraft was given rigorous trials and evaluations by the test pilots of both the Naval Air Arsenal and the Yokosuka Air Group. By the time further modifications of wing and tail configurations were finished, the A5M, as the plane was designated, was an aircraft of unprecedented speed and maneuverability. In the fall of 1935, in a mock air battle carried out by the pilots of the "Genda Circus," the A5M was tested against the latest models of various existing Japanese and foreign fighter planes and bested them in nearly all performance categories and tactical situations. In the autumn of 1936, the navy finally adopted the A5M as the Type 96 carrier fighter.[24]

The appearance of the A5M put a damper on the anti-fighter-plane sentiment within the Japanese navy. Even Capt. Ōnishi Takijirō, then chief of the Training Bureau of the Naval Aviation Department and the leading bomber enthusiast within the navy, spoke of deferring any decision on the utility of fighters until the A5M had been thoroughly evaluated. Its superb maneuverability, moreover, underscored the emphasis the navy seemed to have placed on dogfighting, as opposed to reliance on pure speed and firepower. This issue had been at the center of a heated controversy among the navy's top fighter pilots in the first half of the decade, as discussed earlier. But most important, the appearance of the A5M carrier fighter, along with that of the G3M medium bomber, marked the culmination of Yamamoto Isoroku's ambitious program of aircraft reequipment for the navy and signaled the entry of Japanese aviation into an era of self-sufficiency. In design, structure, and performance, the A5M was among the best fighters, and certainly the best carrier fighter, in the world at the time, and it gave Japanese aeronautical engineers the confidence that they could meet the highest standards.[25]

After the A5M was encountered by American pilots flying with the Chinese in their war with Japan (chap. 5), the fact that it was a Japanese-designed and Japanese-produced aircraft impressed American intelligence officers as much as the plane's performance. Reporting to Washington, Claire Chennault wrote that flight tests against various Western aircraft confirmed that the A5M was "one of the best up-to-date pursuit airplanes in the world." But, he emphasized, "the most striking significance about the Japanese Type 96 pursuit airplane is that not only is the airplane designed and constructed in Japan, but the motor, the metal sheets and tubing, the propeller, the instruments are made in Japan either under license or from their own designs." He concluded, "Japan is self-supporting and independent in building airplanes."[26]

Japanese Naval Air Technology in the Post-Treaty Era

Such was the accelerating advance of aviation technology that even as the A5M fighter was being distributed to the navy's carrier- and land-based units in the spring of 1937, the Naval Aviation Department was initiating plans for a fighter design that would surpass it in performance. The specifications for the aircraft had been drafted by Lieutenant Commander Sawai of the Naval Air Arsenal, and the preliminary planning document for the aircraft had been drawn up in May after meetings between officials of the Aviation Department and representatives of the aircraft industry. But requirements for the new plane were afterward significantly shaped by the conditions of air combat in the first two months of the China War. In the opinion of the navy's front-line pilots in that conflict, the navy needed a fighter with the speed and firepower to destroy an enemy bomber, the range and endurance to escort the navy's G3M bomber on long-range missions, and the maneuverability to deal with any fighters it might meet on the way.

Based on these general requirements, the Naval Aviation Department issued to Mitsubishi and Nakajima specifications of unprecedented difficulty for a carrier fighter: a maximum level speed of 270 knots at 4,000 meters (13,000 feet), but a landing speed of less than 58 knots; a takeoff distance of less than 70 meters (230 feet); maneuverability equal that of the A5M fighter, but an armament of two 20-millimeter cannon in addition to two 7.7-millimeter machine guns. In any single category these requirements either surpassed or were the equal of those of the world's outstanding fighter aircraft of the time. But what made the task of combining all these specifications within one aircraft so difficult was not the individual requirements but the fact that most of them were mutually incompatible. In particular, the obligation to incorporate a number of features, such as extra fuel capacity and heavy armament, for range and firepower, would inevitably increase the aircraft's weight, while at the same time unprecedented speed and maneuverability were still required. Faced with these seemingly insoluble difficulties, the Nakajima company judged the specifications impossible and withdrew from the design competition.[27]

Not surprisingly, the Mitsubishi design team was headed by Horikoshi Jirō, who quickly realized that the basic problem was that the range and armament requirements called for a large and heavy aircraft, whereas the speed and maneuverability requirements argued for a small and light airplane driven by a light and powerful engine. Obliged to use existing Japanese power plant technology (and initially settling on an 870-horsepower Mitsubishi Zuisei engine), Horikoshi concluded that the solution to the problem lay principally in a relentless effort toward weight reduction, uncompromised success in aerodynamic design, and the inclusion of such innovations as would contribute significantly to satisfying any one requirement without materially affecting the others. Over the course of a year and a half, the Horikoshi team, meeting frequently with navy pilots, company representatives, and officials of the Naval Aviation Department, struggled to meet these objectives.

At one of these meetings, in January 1938, at the Yokosuka Air Arsenal, an intense argument broke out between two navy pilots with experience in air combat in China. The issue was the controversy over the priorities in fighter plane design described in chapter 2. Lt. Comdr. Genda Minoru argued that the most important capability for a fighter plane was its maneuverability and consequent close-in dogfighting ability. Lt. Comdr. Shibata Takeo countered that inadequate maneuverability could always be made up by pilot skill and that Japanese bomber losses over China made clear the need for escort by fast, long-range fighters. Although the Horikoshi team, in designing the new aircraft, attempted to satisfy both these priorities, judging from the structure and configuration of the final design the navy appears to have sided with Genda.[28]

The Horikoshi team solved the seeming incompatibilities in the design of the new aircraft one by one. A reevaluation of the standard Japanese navy stress tables dictating the strength of the structural components to be used in any aircraft led to the conclusion that the safety factors could be downgraded in certain instances and lighter-than-usual components substituted. In doing so, the team was aided by the fortuitous appearance of "Super Ultra Duralumin," a new zinc-aluminum alloy recently developed by Sumitomo Metals that possessed far greater strength than existing copper-aluminum alloys. Air drag was reduced by streamlining the all-metal monocoque construction through the use of flush riveting, the adoption of retractable landing gear, the incorporation of a cockpit canopy, and the use of a "washout" configuration of the wings—a subtle downward twist at the wing tips. To bridge the incompatibilities of increased range and increased speed, the design incorporated the use of a detachable and aerodynamically shaped auxiliary fuel tank that could be carried beneath the fuselage and quickly dropped in combat, one of the first such devices in any air force. Generous wing area, large ailerons, and the adoption of a constant-speed variable-pitch propeller promised exceptional maneuverability and pilot control, and the wing mounting of two 20-millimeter cannon and two fuselage-mounted 7.7-millimeter machine guns provided formidable armament for a fighter plane of that time.[29]

The result of all these innovations by Horikoshi and his colleagues was a sleek and nimble-looking aircraft that was completed in March 1939 at the Mitsubishi plant at Nagoya. It was run through its company paces at Kagamigahara, where it surpassed all the standards the navy had set for it. After a few adjustments had been made, including minor changes in the wing design and the substitution of a more powerful Sakae 12 engine, the aircraft was turned over to the Naval Air Arsenal and the Yokosuka Air Group for navy flight trials that began in December 1939 and lasted nearly six months. In June 1940, impelled by the exigencies of the China War, the navy assigned fifteen of the new aircraft to the Twelfth Air Group already in China at the same time that the airplane's carrier trials at sea were taking place aboard the *Kaga*. At the end of July, once the reports of the *Kaga* tests and the final conclusions from the Yokosuka test centers were in, the navy formally accepted the new aircraft as the Mitsubishi A6M (Type 0) Carrier Fighter.•[30]

The Mitsubishi Zero, as it came to be known worldwide, was undoubtedly one of the most ingeniously designed fighter planes in aviation history. While its configuration undoubtedly drew upon recent technological developments of the West, particularly those in the United States, there is no clear evidence that its overall design did not originate with the Horikoshi team.[31] At the time of its appearance it was an aircraft of incomparable speed and phenomenal range (the latter being three times that of contemporary British and German fighters). Its low wing loading enabled it to turn inside any fighter plane then in production, and its large ailerons enabled its pilots to fly rapid rolls. The 950-horsepower Sakae engine with which the later models were equipped and the plane's innovative wing design made it able to climb faster and steeper than any contemporary aircraft.[32]

At the time that it first entered combat, the serious flaws of the aircraft were not yet obvious, though in some cases they were the result of design trade-offs and were thus the obverse of its superior qualities.[33] Like the design of a warship, the design of a combat aircraft represents a series of trade-offs between weight, speed, ceiling, range, maneuverability, armor, armament, and a number of other variables. Other defects were due to the restrictions imposed by Japan's limited industrial base and inadequate strategic resources.

To begin with, its lightness, indeed its near fragility of structure, which helped to give the aircraft unprecedented maneuverability, meant that it contained too many single-point failure points (points at which structural failure would cause destruction of the entire aircraft), a weakness compounded by the fact that it possessed virtually no armor protection for either its pilot or its fuel tanks. While its rate and angle of climb were unprecedented for the time when the aircraft first took flight, its lightness meant that its diving speed was relatively slow, a defect that later in the Pacific War was to put it at a terrible disadvantage with respect to heavier and faster Allied fighter planes. While the Zero was a marvel of maneuverability below 4,500 meters (15,000 feet), its performance fell off sharply above that altitude, even though it had a flight ceiling of 10,000 meters (33,000 feet). Moreover, while the Model 21, the production model at the opening of the Pacific War, had a cruising speed of 180 knots and a maximum speed of 288 knots around 4,500 meters, at any speed above 260 knots the large ailerons of the A6M stiffened and the plane became incredibly sluggish and, here again, lost its deadly maneuverability.

There is no doubt that Horikoshi Jirō produced a fighter plane of outstanding performance, even though the Navy General Staff had presented him with an almost impossibly conflicting set of requirements and specifications. Yet after the war Horikoshi admitted that these deficiencies in performance—poor diving speed, poor handling capabilities at high altitude, and a comparatively low maximum speed—were all due to the aircraft's small engine.[34] This last imperative Horikoshi could do nothing about, since by the late 1930s Japan was restricted in its access to the strategic alloys essential to the production of high-tensile steel used in the larger American engines that were being developed.[35] Moreover, a much larger engine would simply have shaken the Zero apart, given its structural fragility.

One last serious imperfection of the Zero should be mentioned: its armament. While its two 20-millimeter cannons in addition to its two 7.7-millimeter machine guns appeared to give it tremendous punch, this armament was to prove less than ideal for a fighter aircraft. In the first place, the cannon's rate of fire and initial muzzle velocity were both low, which made it more difficult to hit a target than was the case with machine guns. Not only did the weight of the cannon and its heavier ammunition add significantly to the weight of the aircraft and thus affect its performance; the weight of the cannon ammunition meant that fewer rounds could be carried than machine-gun ammunition. As for its rifle-caliber machine guns, these were unlikely to inflict fatal damage on a heavily armored enemy, be it a bomber or a fighter plane. With twenty-twenty hindsight it is possible to argue that pilots of the A6M would have been better served if their aircraft had been armed entirely with heavy (.50-caliber) machine guns, as were most of the Allied enemies that it was to encounter in the Pacific War.

But during its appearance in the China War these ominous defects lay relatively far in the future, undetected by the Chinese and Russian pilots who flew the decidedly inferior planes that the Zero would encounter in the skies over the continent. During the Pacific War, later models of the aircraft were successfully modified to correct a number of these deficiencies, but midway through that conflict the heavy casualties

Photo. 4-3. Mitsubishi A6M3 (Type 0) Model 22 carrier fighters
Source: Kōkūshō Kankōkai, *Kaigun no tsubasa,* 3:26.

among experienced Zero pilots, combined with the great increase in the performance of Allied fighter aircraft, rendered these improvements irrelevant in combat.[36]

In the more than sixty years since the Zero entered combat, its reputation has gone through cycles of admiration and condemnation. The object of popular awe and dread during the Pacific War, in postwar decades it wrongly came to be seen among publics in Western nations as a stereotypically flimsy product of inferior Japanese workmanship. By and large, pilots who came up against it in combat had a much more measured view of its strengths and weaknesses, and aviation historians in recent years have come to reinforce that middle view. But in any long-range assessment of the Zero, one thing must certainly be kept in mind: from its earliest conception, both its designers and the Japanese navy intended that at some point it was to be replaced by an aircraft of even greater all-around performance.

It was the profound misfortune of the navy and the nation that this never came to be. During the war the navy worked on several designs that could have replaced the Zero. The N1K2-J Shiden ("Violet Lightning") was one of the best aircraft in the Pacific War and, by default, became the "successor" to the Zero, since the intended successor, the A7M Reppū ("Hurricane"), was not even designed until 1944. There was indeed a superlative aircraft that did, in a sense, "succeed" the Zero, the Mitsubishi J2M Raiden ("Thunderbolt"), a single-engined fighter provided with powerful armament and significant protection.[37] The problem with all these aircraft was that they took too long to design, develop, and produce. By the time they came on line during the Pacific War, the tide of the conflict was running so violently against Japan that their appearance made little difference. The Raiden was a case in point. Developed by the overworked Horikoshi team, the aircraft was delayed by a series of design problems. Had it been available to meet the arrival of the second-generation Allied fighters in the southwestern Pacific in early 1943, it might have made some difference in that otherwise disastrous air campaign. As it was, the aircraft did not see serious combat until late 1944, and then only in small numbers.[38]

In any event, from 1937 to 1941 the navy developed not only outstanding carrier fighters but some of the best carrier attack aircraft of these years as well. The China War was to provide their first combat tests. In the fourth and fifth years of the navy's involvement in that conflict, it introduced two excellent new bombers into its aerial operations on the continent: the Aichi D3A dive bomber and the Nakajima B5N attack plane.

The first of these had been conceived in the summer of 1936 as a replacement for the aging Aichi D1A2 (Type 96) carrier (dive) bomber. The specifications for the design competition had called for a two-seat monoplane design with speed and range capabilities equal to those that would become available in the Mitsubishi A5M carrier fighter. The winning entry by Aichi Tokei Denki turned out to be a rugged aircraft. Its design had been influenced to a great extent by contemporary dive-bomber designs of the German Luftwaffe. From the Heinkel HE 70, Goake Tokuichirō, Aichi's chief engineer for the project, took the aircraft's large elliptical wing, and from the Junkers JU 87, the famed Stuka dive bomber, he borrowed the configuration of dive-brakes under each wing to assist in control of the aircraft on dives and pullouts. Though Goake and his team were concerned with efforts to reduce drag, a consideration of the inevitable complexity and weight of retractable landing gear led to their decision to retain a fixed undercarriage. The original power plant, a 710-horsepower Nakajima Hikari radial, was deemed insufficient and was eventually replaced by a 1,000-horsepower Mitsubishi Kinsei 43 radial. In competitive trials with an aircraft of Aichi's one rival for the contract, Nakajima, the Aichi plane proved far superior. Following service trials and numerous minor airframe changes, the Aichi D3A1 was accepted by the navy as the Type 99 carrier dive bomber Model 11.*[39]

The Type 99 was put through carrier qualification trials aboard the *Kaga* and *Akagi* in 1940, and in that year and the next it saw limited combat, operating from land bases in China and northern French Indochina. Roughly contemporaneous with the Stuka and the Douglas Dauntless, the D3A1 was essentially the equal of both in structural integrity, maneuverability, and speed, though in bomb load, range, and diving ability it was inferior to the Dauntless. Its early combat results were outstanding. Participating in all major Japanese carrier operations in the first year of the Pacific War, the Type 99 was to sink more Allied warships than any other type of Axis aircraft, but this may have been a function more of the outstanding aircrews who flew and fought in it than of the inherent superiority of the aircraft. In any case, the glory days of the Type 99 were brief. As early as the fall of 1942 the slow speed and poor armament of the aircraft made it shockingly vulnerable to Allied fighters, and its use in the land-based air war in the southwestern Pacific could only be termed suicidal.[40]

Even before the advent of the D3A1 dive bomber in 1940, the navy had issued specifications for a new carrier torpedo bomber, since none of the prototypes for such an aircraft developed in the early 1930s had proved satisfactory. An interim aircraft, the Yokosuka B4Y1 (Type 96),* the last fabric-covered biplane torpedo bomber in Japanese naval service, had played an active role in the China War. A more modern aircraft, with performance equal to the latest fighters, was obviously needed. Specifications had been issued as early as 1935, calling for a three-seat single-radial-engined aircraft of monoplane design, capable of a speed of 180 knots at 2,000 meters (about 7,000 feet), able to carry an 800-kilogram (1,764-pound) torpedo or an equivalent bomb load, and an endurance of four hours when carrying its full payload, or of seven hours for unarmed reconnaissance missions. Nakajima's entry, the B5N, which eventually beat its Mitsubishi competitor for the navy contract, was a cleanly designed aircraft. It was equipped with such novelties as a variable-pitch propeller, a retractable undercarriage, and a hydraulically operated mechanism that folded the wings up and inward at approximately their halfway point for storage aboard a carrier. Completed in 1936, the Nakajima B5N1 made its first flight in January 1937, finished first in the competitive trials in November of that year, and was soon after adopted by the navy as the Type 97 carrier bomber.[41]

Though it almost immediately went into carrier service, the B5N was also allocated to the navy's land-based air groups for operations in China, where, escorted by A5M carrier fighters, it performed well in support of ground forces. Combat experience in China and normal technological evolution led to a new version of the aircraft, the B5N2, driven by a more powerful engine (the 1,000-horsepower Nakajima Sakae 11). The B5N2 went into production early in 1940 as the Type 97 Model 12 and by 1941 had replaced the earlier version as the navy's front-line carrier attack bomber. (A successor aircraft, the Nakajima B6N, was on the drawing boards in 1941 but was awaiting its flight trials when the Pacific War broke out.) At the time of Pearl Harbor, where it helped to destroy the American battleship force, the B5N2 was undoubtedly the world's best carrier torpedo bomber, far superior to either the American Douglas Devastator or the ancient British Fairey Swordfish. But eventually, like the Aichi D3A1, its slow speed and paltry armament relative to U.S. fighter aircraft led to its wholesale destruction in the skies over the southwestern Pacific.[42]

Two other aircraft developed for the navy prior to the Pacific War—the Mitsubishi G4M medium bomber and the Kawanishi H8K1 flying boat—rounded out the family of aircraft that provided the material edge of the navy's offensive air power on the eve of the Pacific War.

The Mitsubishi G4M had its origins in the navy's desire for a replacement for the G3M bomber (even as the G3M was first entering combat in China), about the same time that the navy sought an eventual replacement for the A5M fighter.[43] Not surprisingly, the navy wanted a bomber superior in performance to the G3M: a plane with increased engine power, greater speed, range, and payload, and better armament (which the slender configuration of the G3M could not accommodate).

Development of such an aircraft by Mitsubishi—which in this case obtained the navy contract without going through the normal competitive process—took time, and it was not until September 1939 that a prototype was ready for flight-testing at Kagamigahara airfield. The twin-engined bomber that first flew in late October of that year was a cigar-shaped aircraft—indeed, the Japanese dubbed it the *Hamaki* ("Cigar")—with an airframe that would be easy to manufacture and that would accommodate an internal bomb bay and more effective defensive armament: four machine guns, in the nose, the port and starboard waist positions, and the dorsal blister, as well as a cannon in the tail. Satisfied with its performance, Mitsubishi turned the plane over to the Yokosuka Air Group for its service trials in January 1940, following which the navy accepted the G4M as the Type 1 land-based attack plane Model 11.*[44]

Nevertheless, nearly a year was to pass before production of the new bomber was authorized, in large part because the navy wasted time in attempting to employ a modified version of the aircraft as a more heavily armed escort for the navy's medium bombers. At the time, the G3M bombers were suffering comparatively heavy losses in the skies over China because the A5M fighter had insufficient range for long-range bombing operations and because the A6M fighter had not yet come on line. But the G6M1 Type 1 "wing tip escort aircraft" *(yokutan engoki)* proved to be a failure for three reasons: it handled poorly because the reconfiguration of the aircraft to accommodate increased cannon armament caused a shift in the aircraft's center of gravity; the addition of partial protection for the wing tanks caused a reduction in fuel capacity and thus a reduction in range; and the eventual appearance of the Zero in the same month that the first two G4M1s were completed eliminated the need for such an escort bomber. For all these reasons, the production of the G6M1 was canceled.[45]

At last, in the spring of 1941, the G4M in a bomber configuration was allocated to the Takao Air Group in China. If the G4M was an improved version of the long-range bomber that Yamamoto Isoroku had envisioned early in the 1930s, it was, like its predecessor, an aircraft whose serious flaws would become apparent only in combat. Its two Mitsubishi Kasei radial engines, of approximately 1,400 horsepower each at cruising speed, helped to give it the range the navy desired for its land-based medium-bomber force—in theory, 3,700 miles. To achieve that phenomenal range, greater than that of the American B-17, Mitsubishi, again under navy pressure, sacrificed ruggedness, armor, and armament. Despite improvements in armament and an effort to include fuel tanks that were in part self-sealing, the G4M was an aircraft so lacking in armor and thus so vulnerable to explosion under enemy fire that in the Pacific War it was to earn the grim sobriquet "The One-Shot Lighter" among its crews and the dismissive nickname "Zippo" among American fighter pilots.

In this sense the G4M was a flying contradiction. Designed to work in tandem with the Zero fighter as escort, its maximum range was too far for even the Zero, though admittedly bombers with greater ranges than fighters comprised, of course, a worldwide phenomenon for much of World War II. Facing an enemy target unprotected by adequate fighter defense or employed against a target area first cleared by Zero escorts, the G4M was able to achieve some remarkable bombing runs. The bombing of Chungking and other missions deep into central and southern China in the spring and summer of 1941, the destruction of the battleships *Repulse* and *Prince of Wales* at the outset of the Pacific War, and the long-range attack on Port Darwin, Australia, in the spring of 1942 are all testimony to the extraordinary reach of the G4M. But without fighter escort it was a flying firetrap, and in the air war in the southwestern Pacific this frailty eventually forced its pilots to make bombing runs at altitudes that were sufficient to reduce enemy fighter attacks but also made bombing accuracy almost impossible.

By the years of the Pacific War, seaplanes—both flying boats and floatplanes—came to occupy a significant place in Japanese plans for amphibious operations in the southern Pacific. Advance seaplane bases to supply reconnaissance and air cover for invasion convoys were seen as easy to establish, given the large number of quiet lagoons and sheltered harbors of the tropical Pacific.[46] For great distances, the flying boat was still the navy's principal reconnaissance aircraft, and the navy continued to depend on Kawanishi to produce this type. The Kawanishi H6K had proved to be an outstanding aircraft, but in 1938 the navy was already thinking of a successor and therefore issued to Kawanishi specifications for a flying boat superior in performance to the British and American equivalents of the H6K, the Short Sunderland and Sikorsky XPBS: a cruising speed of 240 knots and a range of 3,900 nautical miles. Beginning in August 1938, Kawanishi began testing models of the projected design in wind tunnels and water tanks. These experiments led to the development of the H8K1, a clean but sturdy-looking high-wing monoplane with cantilevered wings that held four Mitsubishi Kasei engines of 1,530 horsepower, the navy's most powerful and reliable power plants. Contrasted with the navy's land-based bombers, the H8K1 was a stoutly protected and defended aircraft, equipped with extensive armor protection and armed with 20-millimeter cannon in the dorsal and tail turrets and 7.7-millimeter machine guns in the two beam blisters, the ventral and cockpit hatches, and the bow turret. A prototype had undertaken its maiden flight in January 1941, and after successful service trials late that year the navy accepted the aircraft as the Type 2 flying boat, Model 11.* The Kawanishi H8K1 had been conceived as a reconnaissance aircraft, but its speed and range led the navy to use it also, like its predecessor, as a transport and, on several occasions during the Pacific War, as a bombing aircraft. It was, in any event, an outstanding representative of its type. Because of its rugged construction and excellent armor and armament, Allied fighter pilots considered it the most difficult Japanese aircraft to bring down. For all these reasons, it was probably the finest flying boat of World War II.[47]

For shorter-range reconnaissance, as well as operations, the navy came to acquire two workhorse floatplanes for the fleet. Despite its obsolete configuration, the singular maneuverability of the Mitsubishi F1M1/2 Type 0 ("Pete") observation seaplane,* a single-engined two-seat single-float biplane that went into production in 1940, led to its use not only as a catapult-launched aircraft aboard battleships and cruisers but also as an interceptor, a dive bomber, and a coastal patrol aircraft.[48] Similarly useful was the Aichi E13A1 Type 0 ("Jake") reconnaissance seaplane,* a single-engined three-seat twin-float monoplane that went into production in 1940. Operating from cruisers and seaplane tenders, it saw service in 1941 both in attacks along the China coast and in reconnaissance over Hawai'i.[49]

In this survey of Japanese naval aircraft developed from the mid-1930s to the opening of the Pacific War, it remains only to mention two attack aircraft that were in various stages of development by the opening of the Pacific War but that played significant roles later in the conflict: the Nakajima B6N (Tenzan), a three-seat single-engined carrier attack plane intended to replace the Nakajima B5N, but which proved to be only marginally better; and the Yokosuka D4Y (Suisei) dive bomber, with the only in-line engine ever used aboard Japanese carriers. Intended to replace the Aichi D3A, the D4Y ran into major technical problems, and it did not come into widespread service, either as a reconnaissance aircraft or as a dive bomber, until midway through the Pacific War.[50]

THE JAPANESE AIRCRAFT INDUSTRY

If the industry that produced these aircraft was "unimpressive," in the dismissive view of a postwar American survey of the wartime Japanese economy and technology,[51] it was only in comparison to the scale and progress of the aircraft industry in the United States during these same years. From 1937 onward, the growth in Japanese aircraft production was remarkable even as management of the industry was increasingly directed by the government.

The two largest manufacturers, Mitsubishi and its nearest rival, Nakajima, were the only companies that designed and produced aircraft for both armed services. By 1937, Nakajima was beginning to edge up on Mitsubishi as the nation's largest airplane manufacturer. The next two competitors produced aircraft exclusively for the Japanese army and were trailed distantly by Aichi and Kawanishi. Whereas Japanese industry made a little over eleven hundred aircraft deliveries to the two military services in 1936, it delivered more than five thousand in 1941.[52] By 1941, Nakajima's airframe plant at Ōta and engine factory at Musashi were enormous, and Mitsubishi's airframe plant in Nagoya was the second largest in the world.

The first half of the 1930s had seen the Japanese aircraft industry move out from a period of importation and imitation of foreign models toward domestic design as well as production of airframes and engines. As we have seen, the Japanese navy had taken the lead in the development of an independent Japanese aircraft industry with the establishment of the Naval Air Arsenal at Yokosuka in 1932. The arsenal soon began designing and manufacturing its own aircraft in competition with civil manufacturers, as well providing guidance to these same manufacturers in the production of aircraft under contract to the navy.[53]

By the end of the 1930s, therefore, except for its use of imported machine tools and presses and residual foreign design influences, the industry was almost entirely domestic in character. Yet the industry's relationship with government—or, more exactly, with the two military services—was essentially still as it had been earlier: the army and navy awarded contracts to aircraft manufacturers in accordance with service needs but otherwise exerted little control over, and provided no material support for, these same contractors. The Japanese army left both engineering research and trial production of aircraft in the hands of private aircraft contractors. The navy, however, conducted the necessary research in its own laboratories, which after 1932 were located at the Naval Air Arsenal at Yokosuka. Though it contracted with civil manufacturers for the production of most of its aircraft, the navy also adopted some aircraft designed and manufactured by the Yokosuka Air Arsenal. On their part, Japan's civil aircraft manufacturers were responsible for procuring their own labor and materials but were free to expand or contract on the basis of the volume of business they carried.[54]

Then, with the onset of the China War, the industry came under increasingly tight government control. In 1938 a new law compelled all aircraft companies of a certain capitalization to be controlled as to equipment, techniques and production plans. In the years that followed, the government, while not directly providing capital, did offer numerous incentives for the aircraft industry to expand, including loans made through industrial banks, leasing of government-owned machine tools, and other indirect forms of assistance.[55]

In return, by the spring of 1941 the two military services came to control all aspects of management over favored aircraft plants, establishing standards for acceptance of aircraft, setting up inspection procedures, and stationing their technical representatives and inspectors in the factories so that quality standards were maintained. By the end of that year, as the availability of certain strategic materials necessary for the manufacture of aircraft, particularly aircraft engines, became even more restricted, each of the services organized its own control of these raw materials, which it allotted to the aircraft manufacturers handling its contracts.

The positive qualities in the design and manufacture of the navy's aircraft demonstrate the skill of a significant segment of the Japanese engineering community—near brilliant in the case of the Zero—and the reasonably effective overall planning and production methods of prewar Japanese airframe and engine plants. Yet as wartime pressures and exigencies were to reveal, there existed serious inherent problems in the Japanese aircraft industry on the eve of war, difficulties that were to become worse as the war went on.

There was, first of all, the problem of the limited pool of scientific and technical expertise in Japan and the modest scale of the research facilities that could augment that expertise. This situation would not have become so critical had Japan maintained access to scientific and technical developments in the West, particularly in the United States, during the prewar decade. As it was, this access increasingly narrowed during the 1930s, and Japanese industry, particularly its aircraft-manufacturing segment, was largely ignorant of the scale and progress of aircraft design and manufacture in the United States.[56]

The excessively paternalistic relationship between the Japanese government also aggravated the adverse consequences of this technological isolation. Without foreign competition, there was little incentive for technological innovation. Instead of the sort of price competition that existed in the West, the Japanese aircraft industry was characterized by price-fixing and excessive government patronage. In this hothouse atmosphere the industry failed to make breakthrough technological progress, and competition often halted at the development of an aircraft prototype, with subsequent industry efforts being placed largely on production.[57]

Japan's technological isolation also compounded the problems caused by the nature of the aircraft industry's workforce. While there existed a small grouping of experts like Horikoshi Jirō at the top of the Japanese industrial scale, for the most part the industrial workforce at the lower levels had less than a generation of mechanical experience behind it. This meant that there was a significant discrepancy in the relative efficiency of Japanese and American aircraft workers in their respective industries, with the average Japanese worker producing about one-third of the output of his American counterpart. There were several explanations for this discrepancy other than lesser mechanical experience, of course: the fact that half of all riveting and one-third of all sheet-metal processing in the Japanese aircraft industry was done by hand; the existence of bottlenecks caused by inadequate machine tools, which were sometimes worn, poorly designed, inadequately cast, or low in speed of operation.[58]

The Japanese government also created a serious bottleneck when, in 1938, it insisted that a significant percentage of aircraft manufacture be carried out by sub-contractors, many of which were quite small and not that efficient, since they in turn often used home industry. This sometimes led to a lack of precision and standardization of parts, imperfections that could hamper final assembly efforts at the plant and handicap maintenance operations on aircraft in the field. For the most part, such subcontracting slowed the speed of production. In a large aircraft of 100,000 to 150,000 parts, this could become a serious problem, but it also manifested itself in the manufacture of the advanced design of the Mitsubishi Zero, which made it difficult and time-consuming to produce, since much hand labor was involved.[59]

Finally, the Japanese aircraft industry was seriously hampered by the standoff relations between its two military masters. Across a range of functions and activities, the army and navy demonstrated their inability or unwillingness to cooperate in the development of combat aircraft. Both services carried out aviation design and production research and development in their arsenals and depots, but neither shared the results with the other. Each service saw to it that particular aircraft were designed and produced only for that service. In the months immediately prior to the Pacific War, when a shortage in strategic raw materials necessary to engine and airframe production became critical, each service developed its own sources of supply for such resources with little thought to the needs of the other service.[60]

An example of the obdurate nature of such interservice suspicion and hostility was provided by Germany's wartime naval attaché to Tokyo, Capt. Paul Wennacker. After the war Wennacker recalled that during a tour of the Nakajima aircraft plant he was first guided by several naval officers around the navy's development and manufacturing division of the plant. At the conclusion of the tour, the navy men opened a door that had been kept tightly closed. Here the naval officers bade him good-bye, and on the other side of the door a group of army officers took him on a tour of their section of the plant, an area to which the navy officers had no access.[61]

During the immediate pre–Pacific War years, none of these defects within the Japanese aircraft industry was of major consequence, and collectively they were more than balanced by the significant growth of the industry and the quality of aircraft it produced. Yet even at the opening of the war, the navy possessed an imperfectly armed air service. The carriers of the Combined Fleet had all the first-line aircraft they could embark, but many of the land-based naval air groups had too few of the latest-model fighters and medium bombers.[62] Once the Pacific War turned into a grinding conflict of attrition, the Japanese aircraft industry was so riven by the widening fissures I have described that it had little hope of matching the output of its enormous rival across the Pacific.

5

ATTACKING
— *a* —
CONTINENT

The Navy's Air War in China, 1937–1941

The outbreak of Japan's war in China in the summer of 1937 caught the Japanese navy unprepared to deal with a major continental war and interrupted its plans for an orderly expansion of naval aviation. Aircraft production and aircraft-related construction under the "Circle Three" program were just in their first year, and most of the expansion planned under the "Circle Two" program was behind schedule. Only half of the projected land-based air groups had been completed by the end of 1936, and the construction of additional aircraft carriers and seaplane carriers had been delayed. Moreover, all the navy's operational front-line aircraft—the Nakajima A1N (Type 90) and Nakajima A4N (Type 95) fighters, the Aichi D1A (Type 94) dive bomber, and the Mitsubishi B2M (Type 89)• and Yokosuka B3Y (Type 92)• torpedo planes—were of vintage biplane design: metal airframes covered with fabric. These were adequate aircraft when they first went into service but were obsolescent in terms of speed and combat durability by the time the China War broke out. What was to save the day for the Japanese air campaign in the first months of the conflict was the introduction of the new generation of naval aircraft—all-metal in construction, monoplane in design, and unprecedented in performance—discussed in the previous chapter.[1]

The Navy Begins an Air War in China, 1937–1938

The way in which Japanese naval air power came to be used against China can be explained both by the vagaries of circumstance and by the navy's insistence that if a war was to be waged on the continent, the navy should share in the acclaim, the resources, and the budgetary spoils that would surely follow.[2] Despite the belligerence with which Japan entered the war with China in the summer of 1937, and the ferocity and destructiveness with which it conducted the conflict over the next eight years, it is clear that the opening of hostilities caught both its armed services unprepared for the scale of operations that soon took place. The initial clash between Chinese and Japanese ground forces early in July at the Marco Polo Bridge outside Peking had involved only a handful of troops on either side. Had the conflict been restricted to northern China, an area seen (from the Japanese perspective) as falling within the army's sphere of interest, the "China Incident," as the Japanese termed it, might not have erupted into full-scale war. But the rising tide of Chinese popular anger, the Japanese concern over the large number of Japanese civilians in the Yangtze river delta, and the hair-trigger opportunism of the staff of the Japanese Third Fleet, headquartered at Shanghai, quickly spread the crisis into central China, an area traditionally seen as falling within the navy's strategic horizons. Early in August a minor but reckless provocation by a junior Japanese naval officer in Shanghai ignited an explosion of fighting in the city. On 13 August hostilities broke out between the twenty-five-hundred-man Naval Landing Force in Shanghai and Chinese troops in the city, and the next day Chinese planes attacked Third Fleet warships anchored in the Huang-p'u (Whangpoo) River, even as the Japanese army was rushing five divisions to the scene. By midmonth, therefore, Japan and China were locked in an ever-expanding conflict.[3]

While the two Japanese services had, on 11 July, already reached agreement on operational jurisdictions in the event of full-scale war—the army taking responsibility for northern China, the navy for central and southern China—it was clear from the beginning that surface naval forces would have only a restricted role in what would become essentially a land war. As the navy's shore forces were limited to the small Naval Landing Force in Shanghai, it was also obvious that air power would be the navy's most effective contribution to the conduct of operations on the Asian mainland. Initially the navy's air units in China had two principal missions: the primary task of destroying Chinese air units and their bases and, secondarily, support for the army's ground operations. In these tasks their performance outmatched that of the army's air units in China. In the fall of 1937, much to the irritation of his staff, Gen. Matsui Iwane, the army's overall theater commander in central China, remarked to a newly arrived staff officer of the Third Fleet that the support given his ground forces by the army air service was worthless, and that he largely relied on the navy for air operations.[4]

At the time of the Marco Polo Bridge incident, however, Japanese naval air power in the projected theater of operations consisted of the air groups of three carriers on station in the East China Sea—the *Kaga, Ryūjō,* and *Hōshō*—whose temporarily reduced air complements totaled a little more than eighty aircraft, plus a few floatplanes aboard cruisers anchored in the Huang-p'u. While these carrier planes could and would be used for operations in the Shanghai area and at other points along the China coast, their limited range and the navy's initial lack of air bases ashore made it very difficult to use ship-borne aircraft against more distant inland targets. Indeed, had it been against a different enemy, the Japanese navy would not have considered risking its precious carriers so close to land-based air power. As it was, the navy dismissed the operational abilities of Chinese air forces to launch attacks against fast-moving naval units.[5]

It was fortuitous for the navy, however, that it now had two land-based air groups in the home islands—one at Kisarazu just southeast of Tokyo and another at Kanoya in southern Kyūshū—recently equipped with the new G3M twin-engined medium bombers. In mid-July, with the threat of a wider conflict increasing daily, the two groups had been placed under a joint command, the First Combined Air Group, and brought closer to China. The twenty-four G3Ms of the Kisarazu Air Group were sent to Ōmura in western Kyūshū and later to Cheju Island (Saishu-tō, Quelpart Island) south of the Korean Peninsula, and the eighteen G3Ms of the Kanoya Air Group were flown to Taihoku (Taipei) on Taiwan. Another combined air group, the Second, comprising the Twelfth Air Group at Saeki on northeastern Kyūshū and the Thirteenth at Ōmura, both composed mostly of carrier fighters and bombers, was also formed and moved near Dairen (Ta-lien) in Japan's Kwantung Leased Territory on the Liaotung Peninsula, to wait on standby in case it should be needed in northern China.[6] (Map 5-1.)

These new units came under the control of the Third Fleet, commanded by Vice Adm. Hasegawa Kiyoshi. Aboard his flagship, the old cruiser *Izumo,* anchored in the Huang-p'u next to the Japanese Consulate General, Admiral Hasegawa decided on his own authority to expand the war by exploiting the navy's new strategic reach. Twenty-four hours after the initial eruption of fighting in Shanghai, he ordered strikes at points along the coast from Japanese carriers stationed in the China Sea. For the next several months Japanese carrier aircraft were to become heavily engaged in short-range operations against Chinese air units and air bases in central China. But it was the long-range, overocean bombing missions of the medium bombers of the First Combined Air Group that took the world by surprise. Flying from Taihoku on Taiwan and Ōmura in Kyūshū against Chinese bases 400–500 miles inland, the G3Ms of the First Combined Air Group delivered not only bombs on Chinese targets but shocks to Western complacency about Japanese progress in air power. Indeed, so dramatic was this accomplishment by the navy's land-based air units that Gen. Ishiwara Kanji, chief of the Operations Division of the Army General Staff, is supposed to have remarked that it might be just as well if the army air service was turned over to the navy.[7]

Yet if the reach of the navy's air arm was now breathtaking, these first efforts at

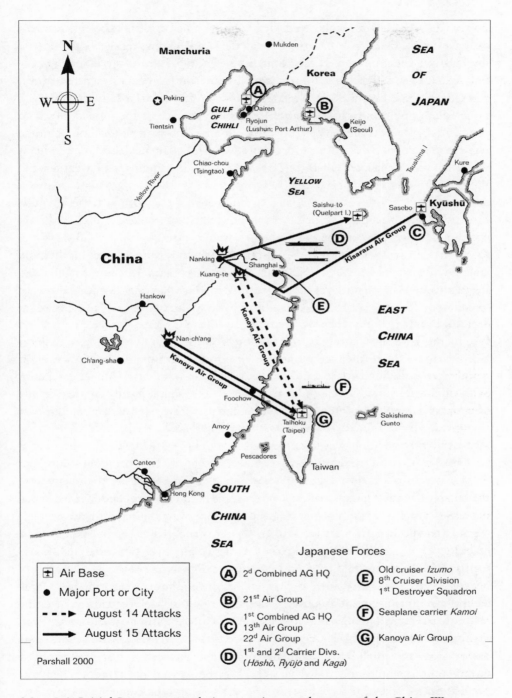

Japanese Forces

Ⓐ 2d Combined AG HQ	Ⓔ Old cruiser *Izumo* 8th Cruiser Division 1st Destroyer Squadron
Ⓑ 21st Air Group	
Ⓒ 1st Combined AG HQ 13th Air Group 22d Air Group	Ⓕ Seaplane carrier *Kamoi*
Ⓓ 1st and 2d Carrier Divs. (*Hōshō, Ryūjō* and *Kaga*)	Ⓖ Kanoya Air Group

Legend:

⊞ Air Base

● Major Port or City

- - -▶ August 14 Attacks

———▶ August 15 Attacks

Parshall 2000

Map 5-1. Initial Japanese naval air operations at the start of the China War,
August 1937

strategic bombardment encountered a host of difficulties, not the least of which was treacherous weather. On 14 August, the day the bomber crews received their orders, the edge of a typhoon in the East China Sea began to cover the target area in central China. High winds made it impossible for aircraft to get off the carrier decks, and the land-based bombers at Ōmura had to stand down. From Taihoku, however, the medium bombers of the Kanoya Air Group flew across the Taiwan Strait to attack Kuang-te and the Chinese Air Force flying school at Hang-chou. Chinese fighters shot down three of them, one more was badly damaged, and the results of the attack were meager. On the next day, despite continuing bad weather, the Kanoya Air Group put all fourteen of its operational G3Ms in the air for an attack on Chinese air facilities at Nan-ch'ang. Its bombers flew toward the target in murk and turbulence, had great difficulty in locating their objectives, and caused only minimal damage, but returned to Taihoku without loss. The twenty G3Ms of the Kisarazu Air Group that took off from Ōmura were not so fortunate. Battling the violent weather on their way to Nanking, they were set upon by Chinese fighter aircraft en route—and again over the target. In attacking Nanking, the bombers were forced to make low-level runs because of the heavy cloud cover, and upon heading back up into the clouds, they were jumped by Chinese fighters, which shot down four of the Japanese aircraft before the force could reach its temporary base on Cheju Island. On 16 August the Kanoya Air Group lost more aircraft in a raid on Yang-chou, including that of the flight leader, Lt. Comdr. Nitta Shin'ichi, a victim of the fighter aircraft that he had considered so technologically inferior in his debates with fighter plane advocates. Within the first three days of combat, the First Combined Air Group had lost half of its bombing force.[8]

Particularly ominous was the proven flammability of the new G3M bomber, a vulnerability that was never really corrected on either the G3M or its successor, the G4M. Two episodes taken from different campaigns during the air war over China graphically demonstrate the consequences of this fatal weakness in design and construction. The first took place during the first long-range mission on 15 August, when twenty G3Ms of the Kisarazu Air Group struck Chinese air bases around Nanking. During their bombing run the Japanese planes were attacked by Chinese Curtiss Hawk fighters. Sgt. Hosokawa Hajime, riding in one of the bombers, years later recalled seeing the fourth aircraft in the formation explode into flame after having been hit in one of the wing tanks. Flying alongside the stricken aircraft, Hosokawa watched in horror as its crew pushed into the front cabin to escape the searing flames that began to consume the fuselage. So intense was the heat that, in desperation, the pilot flung open the top hatch. The rest of the crew pushed through the opening and stood jammed together above the flames. Then fire belched out of the cabin window, and Hosokawa and his compatriots watched helplessly as the plane fell to earth. Then the third aircraft in the formation was also hit in the wing tanks, and it too was wrapped in fire, and again the crew members crowded into the front cabin and stood packed together in the open hatch. The plane captain was seen to put his arms around his fellow crew members when

Photo. 5-1. Mitsubishi G3M (Type 96) medium bombers flying over mountainous Szechwan Province on their way to Chungking
Source: Nihon Kaigun Kōkūshi Hensan Iinkai, *Nihon kaigun kōkūshi,* 4: front photographs.

suddenly the conflagration roared up through the hatch, and the aircraft hurtled earthward.[9]

In an attack on T'ai-ping-ssu airfield outside Cheng-tu later in the war, seventy-two G3Ms were on a bombing run over the field when they were struck by Soviet-built Polikarpov I-15 and I-16 fighters. Lt. Takeda Hachirō, flying in a rear-guard echelon below the main formation, was to remember how the enemy fighters swept past him to concentrate their fire on the lead bomber. Fire quickly broke out at the wing root of that aircraft, and it began to sink. Takeda recalled that the aircraft assumed an almost vertical dive as flames streamed along its side, and at 2,000 meters (7,000 feet) both wings tore off the fuselage and the plane plunged to earth, looking to Takeda like a pencil being thrown to the ground.[10]

One may ask why, in each of these examples, the aircrews did not simply bail out of their stricken aircraft, since there seems to have been sufficient time to do so. The answer appears to be that while Japanese medium-bomber crews wore parachutes on routine or training flights, they did not wear them on flights in which there was real combat risk over enemy territory. Apparently it was a point of honor

Photo. 5-2. Mitsubishi G3M (Type 96) bomber crews returning from a bombing run over central China
Source: Mainichi Shimbun, *Nihon no senshi, 4: Nitchū sensō,* 2:138.

among these crews that if their plane was hit over enemy territory, they sealed their fate with their plane to avoid the disgrace of being captured. Moreover, if the plane was somehow able to crash-land or ditch on the way home without death to the crew, it would be safer for its members to stick together.[11]

While the navy's land-based medium bombers were engaged in fierce struggles over China's cities and bases, its carrier aircraft stormed up and down the coast of central China. On 22 August the *Ryūjō*'s fighter squadron undertook a fierce battle with Chinese fighters over Pao-shan in Kiangsu Province. At the end of September both the *Ryūjō* and the *Hōshō* were engaged in operations along the south China coast. By early October, with the acquisition of bases in the Shanghai area, the air groups of both carriers were temporarily based at Kunda airfield, outside Shanghai.[12]

Over the last two weeks of August 1937, the navy's medium-bomber units pressed home their attacks against Chinese air bases in the Yangtze river valley, where they encountered fierce resistance. Unescorted by fighter planes—because the navy believed that the *rikkō* units didn't need such escorts, and because long-range fighter escort was not available anyway—they were destroyed in alarming numbers. The losses among the slower carrier attack aircraft employed in separate attacks were, if anything, worse. The available planes, particularly the slow Mitsubishi B2M2 (Type 89) carrier attack bomber, were all too often chopped out of the sky by the more nimble Curtiss Hawk fighters flown by the Chinese.[13]

Chinese antiaircraft batteries also began to take a toll of Japanese aircraft. Indeed, it has been estimated that during the course of the air war in China, antiaircraft fire accounted for approximately half of the navy's air combat losses and Chinese fighters for the other half (proportions that prefigured Japanese aircraft losses in the southwestern Pacific during World War II).[14]

In the first weeks of the war, therefore, Japanese inexperience in long-range bombing operations under actual combat conditions made such operations highly dangerous and quite costly in relation to the modest damage they inflicted on Chinese aircraft and airfields. In part this was due to the small number of bombers the Japanese navy initially employed in its air strikes. There were several reasons for this: the inflated expectations concerning the potential of the land-based bombers, which led the navy to believe that a flight of only three such aircraft could wreak decisive destruction; the initial failure of the navy to recognize that attacks on targets on land (unlike discrete targets at sea) required mass formations; and the necessity to rotate the limited number of trained bomber aircrews over the course of day and night raids in order to prevent their physical exhaustion. Eventually these early lessons caused a change in the composition of the navy's long-range bombing formations: while early-daylight bombing raids were undertaken by an average of nine to eighteen aircraft, strikes later in the autumn of 1937 comprised twenty-seven to thirty-six bombers.[15]

Another problem for the Japanese navy lay in the scheduling of the daylight raids on inland targets. Most of these were timed for midmorning, since at dawn, targets in the Yangtze river valley tended to be obscured by mist. But this scheduling eliminated any surprise, since Chinese fighter units, alerted by observers on the coast over which the Japanese attackers had to pass, were often able to catch the bomber formations on their return flight, if not before.[16]

Still another difficulty was the fact that the early Japanese bomber formations lacked the cohesion that could have provided them with greater defensive firepower. Frequent bad weather and initial losses over the target made it difficult to keep the formations closed up. Initially there was a poor fit between the administrative, training, and operational organization of the medium-bomber units involved. The navy's land-based air groups usually comprised eighteen to twenty-seven aircraft, but for training purposes these had been divided into subunits of six aircraft each. The operational air attacks on naval targets had called for still a third formation, the *shōtai*, of two to three aircraft. Thus, Japanese bomber aircrews were not used to flying in larger formations of the sort that would have given them greater and more coordinated defensive firepower. The situation worsened when, because of combat losses, the organization of bomber formations began to break up and it became necessary to cobble together odd-lot formations. Because of insufficient training, Japanese bomber units that attacked their targets in small *shōtai* formations had trouble reforming after their attacks into larger groupings for mutual protection. This meant that on their return flight they frequently suffered appreciable losses when they were jumped by enemy fighters.[17]

Yet the most important reason for Japanese bomber losses in the early weeks of the war was the lack of fighter protection. For the most part this was due to the navy's assumption that bombing aircraft could always outperform fighter planes and therefore could usually dispense with fighter escort. But even had the need for fighter protection been recognized at the outset of the war, the only available navy fighter planes—the Type 90 and Type 95 carrier fighters—were approaching obsolescence. They were, moreover, short-range aircraft, and a significant number of them were needed to provide air cover for carriers on station off the China coast.

For all these reasons, in the first two weeks of the war the Japanese navy suffered the loss of thirty-three carrier and land-based aircraft, twenty of them to enemy fighters.[18] Despite the world's amazement at the revelation of Japan's long-range strategic capability, as far as the navy was concerned, these losses cast a shadow of uncertainty over the future of long-range bombing. Indeed, the transoceanic bombing program of unescorted daylight raids over Nanking was shut down by late August 1937 until solutions could be found to the loss problem.[19] Over time, experience and improvements in training and tactics would increase Japanese bombing efficiency and reduce loss rates.

In reflecting upon the heavy losses and extreme difficulties suffered by Japanese bombers in these first weeks of combat, we must remember, of course, that the Japanese naval air units were really only the first among the world's air forces to learn the lesson of bombers' vulnerability to interceptors. No amount of proper organization and formation flying could have prevented such losses. The same lesson was learned in December 1939 by British Wellington bombers at the hands of Luftwaffe fighters in the Battle of Heligoland Bight and by Luftwaffe bomber crews at the hands of the RAF Fighter Command in the Battle of Britain, when fighter air defense became truly formidable with the aid of radar.

In any event, it was becoming clear to Japanese naval leaders that the key to success in bombing raids was fighter support, and such support would require improved fighter design. After the initial air battles of mid-August 1937, the commander of the Second Combined Air Group submitted a report pointing out the necessity for fighter escort. The report provided specific recommendations for new fighter specifications, which included a monocoque construction, heavier weapons, and the extension of the operational range of fighters. Plans for such an aircraft—which was to become the famed Zero fighter—were under way by October of that same year. But the design, construction, testing, and allocation of any aircraft, particularly of an aircraft that posed the design and construction challenges of the Zero, were the work of years, not months. Indeed, it would be nearly three years before the first Zeros became operational.[20]

In the meantime, however, a new carrier fighter just coming on line did much to solve some, though not all, of the navy's operational problems. Though designed and built before the China conflict, the A5M carrier fighter was of such advanced performance that it gave great encouragement to Japanese commanders. In late September 1937 the first of the new aircraft flew off the decks of the three carriers on station that had been recently equipped with them. About this time, moreover, Japanese victories on the ground around Shanghai made available a number of air bases where the fighters could be stationed. As the Shanghai area with its remaining Chinese air power posed a slightly greater risk to Japanese carriers, it made sense to disembark some carrier air groups and to station them at these land bases.[21] Inevitably, given the high performance of the A5M, it was soon employed to escort Japanese bombers. As it came into action in increasing numbers, the Japanese navy began to establish air superiority.

Though the A5M was fast and very maneuverable for a monoplane, it had a rival in the Curtiss Hawk III biplane, the main fighter employed by the Chinese. The Curtiss Hawk was capable of acrobatics that the A5M could not match. What provided the margin of victory for the Japanese in the aerial duels over China was the skill of the Japanese pilots, who employed, among other tactics, the *hineri-komi,* which allowed them to cut inside the tight turns of these Chinese aircraft. Moreover, the A5M showed an ability to absorb battle damage despite its light airframe. The durability of the A5M fighter was manifested on at least two dramatic occasions. In early December 1937, in an air battle over Nan-ch'ang, one of the Mitsubishi fighters, piloted by Aviation Petty Officer Kashimura Kan'ichi,[†] lost a third of its right wing after having been rammed by a Chinese Curtiss Hawk, but was nevertheless able to return the 200 miles to its base without further mishap. (See photo. 5-3.) In late May of the next year, almost the same thing happened over Hankow to another A5M pilot who also flew home safely.[22]

With the advance of Japanese ground forces in the Shanghai area and the capture of Chinese airfields there, the navy was able to base a number of its fighter groups ashore. With the arrival in September of the A5M, the skies over Shanghai were cleared of Chinese fighters. The Second Combined Air Group (comprising the Twelfth and Thirteenth air groups) was moved to the China mainland, after which it began a campaign to annihilate Nationalist air units around Nanking. The combination of one of the world's best fighter aircraft and the navy's best pilots proved devastating. The campaign opened with a major air battle over Nanking on 19 September, during which twelve A5M fighters, accompanying carrier bombers and reconnaissance seaplanes, tangled with an assortment of over twenty enemy fighter planes. In this encounter the Chinese defenders were completely outclassed by the A5M, whose greater speed and rate of climb gave it an enormous advantage, and by the tactics of the Japanese pilots who flew it. Lt. (and later Comdr.) Yokoyama Tamotsu[†] was to recall decades later that "the reason for the superiority of the Type 96 (A5M) fighters which raided Nanking was that, aside from [the aircraft's] own good performance, at the time, all the pilots in the Thirteenth Air Group had mastered the *hineri-komi* maneuver."[23] For whatever reason, the result was a clear Japanese victory: the attackers shot down between seven and twelve Chinese aircraft with no loss to themselves (though several Japanese reconnaissance and bombing aircraft serving as decoys were destroyed).[24]

The next day a flight of A5Ms approaching Nanking sighted Chinese opposi-

Photo. 5-3. Aviation Petty Officer Kashimura Kan'ichi returning to base at
Hankow in his Mitsubishi A5M (Type 96) carrier fighter after a midair collision
over Nan-ch'ang, 9 December 1937
Source: Kōkūshō Kankōkai, *Kaigun no tsubasa,* 1:11.

tion, but the latter fled the scene almost immediately. On 22 September the skies
above Nanking were clear of Chinese defenders, and early in October the navy
again began sending G3Ms to attack Nanking. At the same time, Japanese carrier
units were also assigned to provide tactical support to Japanese army ground forces
in their drive on the Chinese capital. Japanese carrier pilots, whether flying fighters,
dive bombers, or attack planes, soon found themselves engaged in close support
missions—low-level reconnaissance of enemy positions, strafing enemy mobile
units, and bombing enemy supply columns—for which they had scant training or
experience but which they performed with exceptional skill, a testament to the general quality of Japanese naval aircrews.[25]

Japanese bomber operations recommenced against Nanking in October and
continued through the autumn of 1937, with little serious Chinese opposition. As
the Japanese army closed in on Nanking, the navy's air units continued the campaign against the Chinese Nationalist Air Force elsewhere in central China. In two
major air battles over Nan-ch'ang, on 9 and 22 December, the Japanese claimed to
have destroyed fifty-four enemy aircraft: twenty-nine in the air and twenty-five on
the ground.[26] In such combat, a number of the navy's leading fighter pilots like Lt.
Comdr. Nangō Mochifumi[†] gained Japanese public acclaim through their heroic
exploits and the number of kills they chalked up.[27]

While Japanese navy pilots had their successes, one of the real problems in the development of fighter tactics was the tradition of personal combat that went back to Japan's middle ages. In aerial warfare, this tradition was manifested in the Japanese penchant for dogfighting. It was difficult for Japanese navy pilots to forgo the opportunity for personal glory in the individual dogfight for the sake of the teamwork demanded by formation flying. Yet they also had a rationale for seeking out Chinese pilots in individual combat. They recognized that the bombing of Chinese airfields usually resulted in the destruction of enemy planes, whereas a Japanese victory in the air eliminated the enemy pilot as well. More than once, however, Japanese bomber crews were disconcerted by the failure of the escorting A5M pilots to continue their close support because they had abandoned the bomber formations in order to begin dogfighting with enemy fighters.[28]

There were other reasons for the failure of Japanese close fighter support for bomber formations, of course. One was the lack of oxygen equipment in the A5M fighters. Even more critical was the absence of adequate aircraft-to-aircraft communication. In the years before Japanese aircraft were uniformly equipped with radio telephone systems, it was difficult to achieve command and control in formation flying. Yet as the bomber campaign in China evolved and the number of bombers increased, the number of fighters assigned to protect them also increased. This made inevitable the need for formation flying and fighting, a tactic new to the great majority of Japanese pilots. Gradually, in dozens of encounters, Japanese navy pilots got better at flying and fighting together. It was thanks to their combat experience early in the China War that the navy's fighter pilots achieved greater flexibility with the *shōtai*, the three-plane formation developed before 1932 from the tight RAF "vic" and also used by the navy's bombers. In the hands of the navy's best fighter pilots, the looser *shōtai* eventually became the standard formation for air-to-air combat.[29]

By the autumn of 1937 it had become apparent to the Japanese high command that significant amounts of military hardware, particularly aircraft and aircraft parts, were being supplied to the Chinese Nationalist government by the Soviet Union, and that the main entry point for such weapons and supplies was Lan-chou in Kansu Province. Clearly it was important for the Japanese military to destroy the Lan-chou base and interdict this supply route. Normally, since Lan-chou was outside the navy's theater of operations, the task would have fallen to the Japanese army. But with its Type 97 heavy bomber still being tested, the army had no aircraft of sufficient range, and the mission was given to the G3M bombers of the Kisarazu Air Group, then based at Saishū-to (Cheju Island). Moving up to an advance base at Nan-yuan, just outside Peking, the bombers launched a series of raids against Lan-chou beginning in November. It is an indication of the unpreparedness of the Japanese military for the war into which they had stumbled that the bomber crews flew to Lan-chou using a map copied from a popular boys' magazine, there being no adequate military maps of this part of China available. This may have been the reason that the navy initially failed to appreciate the high elevation of the terrain along the route. Forced to fly most of the way at 4,000–4,500 meters (13,000–15,000 feet) without oxygen, the bomber crews suffered severe headaches and nausea on these missions. The resistance of Chinese interceptors was fierce, and a number of returning crews were convinced that Soviet fliers filled some of the cockpits. In any event, the attacks only temporarily halted the flow of Russian assistance, and Japanese bombers were obliged to return to Lan-chou frequently over the next several years.[30]

With the fall of Nanking at the end of 1937, Japanese ground forces began a slow and bloody offensive toward Hankow, now the temporary seat of the Chinese government, some 300 miles west of Shanghai. Hankow was beyond the radius of fighter aircraft, but the Second Combined Air Group acted upon the recommendation of Lt. Comdr. Genda Minoru, its air staff officer, that a series of lightly defended air bases be established between Shanghai and the areas to which the enemy had now retreated. Into these forward bases Japanese transport aircraft flew fuel, ammunition, and mechanics. Fighter planes escorting the longer-range bombers could stop for rest and refueling on their way to and from their targets. This forward-base strategy proved eminently successful and took the Chinese by surprise.[31] Now operating from bases around Nanking, Japanese naval air units waged a six-month aerial offensive against this and other inland centers of Chinese resistance in central China. But they now discovered that the Nationalist Air Force had been substantially strengthened by Soviet aircraft like the I-15 and I-16, and apparently by Soviet pilots as well. This new infusion of air power prevented the annihilation of the Nationalist Air Force and enabled the Chinese to mount a desperate resistance against the Japanese air offensive.

As one traces the course of air combat across China, one of the major difficulties in analyzing the conflict is the problem of arriving at an accurate assessment of combat losses on both sides. A case in point is the epic air battle over Hankow on 29 April 1938, the biggest in the war up to that time. The Japanese raided the city with approximately eighteen G3M bombers, escorted by approximately thirty A5M fighters. They were opposed by between sixty and eighty Soviet-built aircraft, some of which were flown by Chinese pilots and more by Soviet personnel. Upon sighting the approaching Japanese, the Chinese fighter pilots tore into the Japanese bomber formation, probably causing some Japanese losses, but were themselves attacked by Japanese A5M fighters, apparently with major losses. As the Japanese headed home following their bombing mission over the city, they were attacked by enemy aircraft supposedly flown by Soviet pilots, and a wild melee ensued. According to Japanese records, it was an annihilating victory for the invaders: a bag of fifty-one Chinese aircraft. On the other hand, one Chinese semiofficial account claims a total of twenty-one Japanese aircraft destroyed. Another English-language account, apparently based on Chinese sources, speaks of a crushing Japanese defeat: the destruction of every Japanese fighter plane and all but three of the Japanese bombers.[32]

It is difficult to reconcile such dramatically conflicting accounts as these. Exaggerated assertions of aircraft kills in the air forces of all nations have usually been caused by the confusion of rapid and violent combat, the emotional intensity of the moment, and the inadvertent duplication of claims concerning enemy aircraft shot down. Moreover, in the case of the Japanese navy there was no regular system of after-action interviews conducted by intelligence officers to attempt to arrive at an accurate assessment of results. The Japanese navy had gun cameras but used them only for training and did not install them in combat aircraft because of the effect of the extra weight on aircraft performance. The Chinese air service may have had even more serious shortcomings in making valid combat assessments. It is nevertheless possible to arrive at an approximation of what really happened in an air battle by using, as an accurate count, the losses admitted by each side. For example, in the action of 29 April 1938, Chinese authorities recorded that twelve of their aircraft were lost; the Japanese navy admitted losing two bombers and two fighters. The high numerical claims made by each side after the battle indicate its ferocity, but not its actual loss count. Using the admitted-losses formula, the revised figures suggest that the battle was a significant Japanese victory, though not on the grand scale that the navy asserted.[33]

While these aerial battles were being fought in the skies over China, the Japanese bombing campaign against Chinese cities and air bases continued. In the land drive on Hankow, Japanese naval air units were ordered to soften up enemy air defenses in central China.[34] For this purpose, various land-based air groups, including the newly organized Fifteenth Air Group, built around a nucleus of carrier attack and dive bomber squadrons flown ashore from the Sōryū, as well as the twin-engined bomber units of the Second Combined Air Group, were thrown into the campaign. The Japanese became increasingly bold in their attacks on Chinese airfields, bombing and strafing planes and facilities from increasingly lower altitudes. In one notable raid on the airfields at Nan-ch'ang in July 1938, a group of three aircraft from the Fifteenth Air Group actually landed on the ground, where the Japanese pilots methodically shot up barracks, hangars, and personnel and torched aircraft parked on the field before taking off unscathed. This practice was repeated on several occasions.[35]

THE NAVY'S LONG-RANGE AIR OPERATIONS OVER CHINA, 1939–1941

In October 1938, Hankow fell to the invaders. But contrary to Japanese expectations, this did not bring about the collapse of the Nationalist regime. The capital was moved yet again, this time to Chungking, far into the mountainous interior of Szechwan Province, approximately 470 air miles from Hankow. The new capital was thus at a distance too far and in terrain too rugged to be reached by Japanese ground forces. By the end of 1938, therefore, the war had become stalemated, and Imperial General Headquarters in Tokyo had come to the belief that this isolated Chinese government could only be forced to surrender after its population had been terrorized by aerial bombing and its supply and communication routes to the outside world had been interdicted.

Thus began the second phase of the navy's air war in China, a campaign now concentrated on two efforts: a ceaseless air bombardment of China's remaining urban centers, particularly of its wartime capital, and the direction of continuous attacks on the ports, roads, and railways of southern China. (Map 5-2.) In planning these operations, the Japanese high command, unlike those in America and Britain that directed the Allied strategic air offensives against Germany and Japan in World War II, did not include industrial targets among their major objectives. The reason was simple: Chinese industrial facilities were so limited and so widely scattered as to render ineffective any attempt to destroy them.[36]

The first of these efforts, the terror-bombing of Chinese cities, had already begun. In one raid on Canton in May 1938, for example, a flight of G3M bombers had killed six hundred civilians and had injured an additional nine hundred. Raids against that city, by G3M2 bombers of the Mihoro Air Group flying from bases in Taiwan across the South China Sea, had continued throughout the summer of 1938.[37] Now the navy placed priority on forcing the collapse of the Chiang Kai-shek government by bombing its wartime capital into rubble.[38]

In carrying out raids against coastal cities in central China, the navy had some help from the army, which eventually contributed its new Mitsubishi Type 97 heavy-bomber units to the aerial offensive. But by and large the smaller bomb capacities of most army bombing aircraft—and, more important, the smaller number of bombers overall and the absence of adequate strategic bombardment doctrine in the army—meant that the army could at best play only a supporting role in the air offensives over central China, and none at all in southern China. This situation was a source of both satisfaction and irritation within the navy. On the one hand, it appeared to demonstrate that the navy had made far greater progress in the doctrinal and technological development of air power than its sister service and thus deserved a larger share of the government's material support. On the other, the ongoing diversion of naval air power toward support of army ground operations and away from the navy's original and primary function—the destruction of enemy air and surface forces at sea—was a source of continuing irritation and concern to many in the navy. In an attempt to maintain its constant readiness against a third-country naval power, the navy kept the bulk of its air units with the Combined Fleet, detaching them as needed for service on the continent. From time to time it pulled these bomber units out from China for training and exercises with fleet units at sea.[39]

In the spring of 1939 the navy decided to launch its first long-range aerial offensive into the Chinese interior, undertaking a series of raids against Chungking and other cities in southern and central China. On these operations the bombers had to fly without fighter escort. For all its superior combat assets, the A5M fighter, even with drop tanks and operation from forward bases, simply did not have the range to furnish protection to the navy's bombing units. Even without fighter escort, however, the G3M bomber groups created havoc. The first attack on the capital by twenty-seven bombers in May 1939 was an incendiary raid that created huge fires

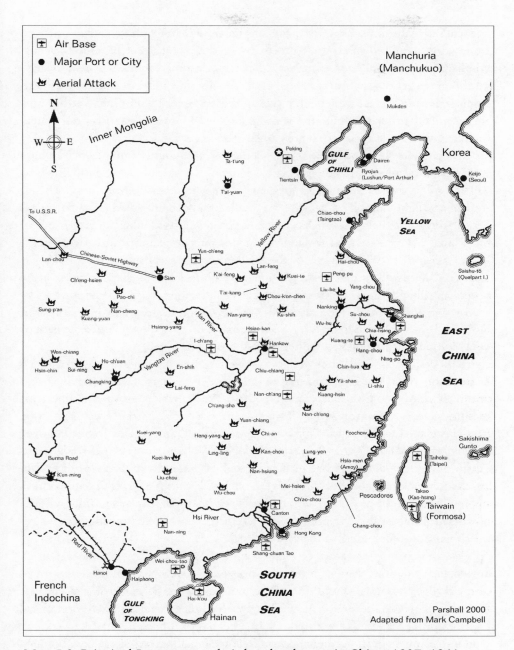

Map 5-2. Principal Japanese naval air bombardments in China, 1937–1941

and caused enormous casualties. For the next two years these terror raids on Chungking mounted in size and intensity, so that the capital became the most bombed city in China, and because of the compact arrangement of the city, the devastation created was enormous.[40] In 1939 the number of navy bombing aircraft employed against these targets on a typical mission over the interior was between eighteen and thirty-six, but in the summer of 1940 between fifty and ninety bombers were being regularly sent against cities in central China.[41]

In September the key airfield on the Chinese supply route from the Soviet Union was back in business, and Soviet aircraft, some of them again apparently flown by Russian pilots, were once more appearing in the skies over central China. The air staff of the First Combined Air Group—anticipating the navy's annual personnel and organizational change in December, which would undoubtedly take it out of the China theater—decided to launch a major air campaign against the Chinese base. "Operation 100" was one of the few major air operations of the China War in which the navy's air units were joined by units from its sister service, navy observers riding in army bombers and vice versa. In the face of stiff opposition by enemy fighters, the early-December raids succeeded in destroying Chinese aircraft both on the ground and in the air but were unable to close down either the base or the continuing supply of Soviet aircraft to the Chinese.[42]

In the spring of 1940, after the usual winter hiatus, the navy decided to launch "Operation 101," the greatest aerial offensive of the war to date. In April of that year 120 G3Ms from the First Combined Air Group (the Kanoya and Takao air groups), under Adm. Yamaguchi Tamon,[†] and the Second Combined Air Group (the Thirteenth and Fifteenth air groups), under Rear Adm. Ōnishi Takijirō, moved to new bases at Hankow and nearby Hsiao-kan. The operation was designed to knock out enemy air bases in Szechwan Province generally and military facilities around Chungking in particular. It began in mid-May with a series of night attacks by the First Combined Air Group on various barracks, arsenals, and military supply depots around Chungking, as well as on emergency airfields and airstrips within a 100-nautical-mile radius of the capital.[43]

Given the primitive nature of night-bombing techniques and technology in all air forces at the time, it is doubtful that these strikes were very effective. But most of the daylight attacks, whose immediate purposes were sheer terror and destruction of civilian life and property, quickly achieved these objectives. Using detailed photographs of Chungking provided by the navy's photointelligence services, Japanese planners of the Combined Attack Force headquarters at Hankow divided the city into five sectors. Over the next several months the Second Combined Air Group, supported on occasion by the army's heavy-bomber units, attacked each of these sectors in turn. In each raid, 50–100 tons (45–90 metric tons) of bombs (either incendiary or high-explosive bombs) were dropped on Chungking in an operation so routine in its first stages that it became known as the *chunkin teikei* (figuratively, the "Chungking Milk Run").[44]

But these raids, which earned the condemnation of Anglo-American nations at the time and of historians in the decades since, were physically and mentally exhausting for the flight crews involved, particularly as the Chinese began to strengthen their air defenses around their wartime capital. Departing from airfields around Hankow, the aircrews faced a seven-hour round-trip run to Chungking, three of which had to be spent on oxygen when the aircraft flew at greater heights to avoid Chinese antiaircraft fire along the route. At these heights, temperatures in the aircraft were well below freezing. Near the target, the bombers began to be buffeted by antiaircraft bursts, and in the later stages of Operation 101 the final fifteen minutes of the bombers' approach were spent under attack from Chinese fighter planes defending the city. Day after day the campaign went on, some aircrews in action for six or seven days in a row, returning to base each day in the heat and humidity of the central China summer.[45]

Through June 1940, Chinese fighters protecting Chungking had not ascended to attack the Japanese bombers at the latter's service ceiling of 9,000 meters (30,000 feet), but about mid-July, Japanese aircrews began to find Chinese interceptors, mostly Soviet-made I-15s and I-16s, awaiting them there. Now the navy's G3M bomber groups began to pay the price for not having a long-range fighter available to escort them. As in the early days of the China war, the ensuing combat once again began to cause rising losses of Japanese aircraft and personnel, as the Chinese defenders fought doggedly to break up the attacking formations. In this desperate combat both sides resorted to novel tactics to gain the advantage. With questionable success, for example, Chinese fighter aircraft dropped time-delay parachute bombs above and in front of the Japanese bomber formations. For their part, the Japanese took to sending special reconnaissance aircraft on ahead of the regular formations to report on Chinese air movements over Chungking and to provoke Chinese fighter formations to rise to attack them, whereupon these Japanese aircraft would flee the air space.[46] The bombers would then attempt to time their attacks while the enemy interceptors were back on the ground refueling.[47]

Then, in the late summer of 1940, the advent of the Zero (A6M) completely changed the tactical situation over the skies of central China, though it seemed at first that the Zero was punching against empty air. Lt. Yokoyama Tamotsu[†] had been one of the first to fly the Zero in an operational unit that June. At that point the Zero was so new that a manual had not yet been written for it, and all Yokoyama and his fellow pilots of the Twelfth Air Group had to go by were the records of its test flights made by the Navy Air Arsenal and the Yokosuka Air Group.[48] On 19 August, Yokoyama, leading a flight of twelve Zeros and escorting fifty-four G3M bombers, took off from Hankow and, staging through I-ch'ang, headed toward Chungking. Naval air intelligence reported that thirty Chinese fighters were awaiting them over the city. Eager to avenge earlier losses among the bombing units and confident of the new aircraft they flew, Yokoyama and his comrades slipped in over the city at 6,000 meters (20,000 feet), but to their dismay not a single Chinese fighter rose to meet them. Yokoyama lowered the altitude of his flight and continued to search but still found no trace of the enemy. The bombers dropped their ordnance on Chungking, but Yokoyama and his Zeros returned to Hankow empty-handed. Most probably Chinese intelligence had learned in advance of the presence of the Zeros at Hankow, and the defending air units had simply been withdrawn from the city until the Zeros had left. In early September, Yokoyama led his flight in a second effort to catch the defending force of Chinese fighters over Chungking, and again the Chinese pilots kept their distance and refused to rise to the challenge.[49]

Outwitted in August by the Chinese air units defending Chungking, the Japanese now planned a ruse of their own. On 13 September Lt. Shindō Saburō[†] and Ens. Shirane Ayao[†]—both of whom were to become outstanding fighter pilots in the Pacific War—led a flight of Zeros escorting G3M bombers on the thirty-fifth raid against Chungking. Once again the skies over the city were empty, and after the Japanese bombers had dumped their loads and headed back to base, the flight of Zeros apparently went with them. But left behind was a reconnaissance aircraft, which radioed Shindō that approximately twenty-seven Chinese aircraft were returning to their airfields near the city. Back swept Shindō and Shirane and their compatriots, and diving out of the sun, they slashed into the Chinese formations. After thirty minutes the skies had been cleared of Chinese opposition, and the Japanese were to claim that all the enemy aircraft had been destroyed without the loss of even one of their own, though it seems more likely that the number of Japanese kills was somewhere between thirteen and twenty-four. In any event, the salient victory demonstrated what devastation could be wrought by superb pilots flying one of the world's best fighter aircraft.[50]

Over the next several months, the dazzling new fighter plane swept all Chinese opposition from the skies.[51] By the end of autumn 1940 the headquarters of the Combined Air Attack Force claimed fifty Chinese aircraft shot down in air combat and another sixty-three destroyed on the ground. But the material advantage the Japanese navy came to enjoy in the air war over China in the last years of the navy's involvement there was not limited to the Zero fighter. In September, Chungking was also being successfully attacked by the new Aichi D3A (Type 99) dive bomber and the Nakajima B5N (Type 97) carrier attack plane, flying from the navy's forward air base at I-ch'ang.[52] Collectively, the victories scored by these three aircraft marked the dawn of the brief era of Japanese air power dominance in East Asia and the Pacific.

Yet by summer's end 1940, Operation 101 had been closed down. It had involved 3,715 sorties, comprising 182 raids (168 of them in daylight and 14 at night), only several of which, at the end of the campaign, had involved fighter escort. Over 2,000 tons (1,800 metric tons) of bombs had been dropped on Chungking and its environs at a cost of nine Japanese aircraft lost and nearly three hundred damaged. By the end of the operation, Chungking had been turned into rubble, and the Chinese government and a considerable portion of the city's population had been forced to burrow into the hillsides to seek refuge from the daily avalanche of bombs. Yet strategically, Operation 101 accomplished very little. Indeed,

the meager results were collectively an advance notice of the limitations on strategic air bombardment campaigns, particularly those directed against civilian popu-
lations of the sort waged over Europe from 1940 through 1945. Though the physical effects of the terror-bombing of China's wartime capital were so horrendous as
to cause the Nationalist government to censor reports coming out of Chungking,
the destruction soon became meaningless, as additional bombs simply churned up
the rubble. Most important, the campaign utterly failed to bring the Nationalist
regime to the negotiating table. Given these facts, the mounting of another bombing offensive, "Operation 102," in which the navy once again sent its twin-engined
bombers in large numbers over Chungking during the spring and summer of 1941,
was a mark of the bankruptcy of Japan's strategy in China and of the inability of
the Japanese high command to think of other means to bring about victory on the
continent.[53]

The other major effort of the navy's air arm over China, the severance of China's
communication and supply routes to the outside world, was already well under
way. By the autumn of 1938 most of the important junctions on the Chinese rail
lines had been occupied by the Japanese army, leaving China with only a frag-
mented rail system. Moreover, in the summer of 1939 all the major ports on the
Chinese coast, with the exception of Hong Kong, were in Japanese hands. As of
1940, therefore, except for horse-cart and coastal junk traffic, China had only three
links to the outside world: the Lan-chou Road through Szechwan and Kansu
provinces to the Soviet Union in the northwest; the railway running southeast from
K'un-ming to Hanoi in French Indochina; and the Burma Road running southwest
from Yunnan Province to Lashio.[54]

To the destruction of each of these links, in turn, Japanese naval air units turned
their attention. Operation 100 in late 1939 had been only partly successful in reducing the flow of military hardware from the Soviet Union, and so the route was once
more subjected to Japanese aerial assault. But the drop in Soviet military assistance
to China was less the result of Japanese air bombardment than of the reordering of
Soviet military priorities in light of the increasingly taut situation on Russia's western military frontiers. By the spring of 1940, certainly, what little military assistance
was reaching China came from the United States, and that by way of southern
China along the road and rail links connecting the region with Burma and French
Indochina.

Because Chinese air power was so much weaker in southern than in central
China, the scale of Japanese air operations there was considerably smaller. In the
summer of 1939, after the establishment that April of a Japanese naval air base at
Hai-k'ou on Hainan Island, carrier-based air units, cooperating with G3M bomber
units, most notably the Takao and Fourteenth naval air groups, began to launch aerial attacks on Chinese communications in the coastal regions of Kwangtung and
Kwangsi provinces, particularly targeting Chinese freight congestion near the border
with French Indochina. Aircraft of the Fourteenth Air Group—eventually including
the new Aichi D3A dive bombers—repeatedly attacked rail traffic running between

Nan-ning, Liu-chou, Kuei-lin, and Kuei-yang, while seaplanes shot up coastal ship traffic off the south China coast. By February 1940, having blocked numerous tunnels and bridges in southern China that would take a long time to repair, the Japanese navy had effectively cut the Chinese link with French Indochina. Then, in the summer of 1940, after the French collapse in Europe, Japan was able to pressure the French colonial government in Indochina into closing its side of the railway to Chinese use.[55]

After the Japanese occupation of northern French Indochina that summer, the navy was able to base the G3M bomber of the Takao Air Group at airfields around Hanoi, from which it began to launch attacks on the Burma Road in October. The air offensive against the Burma Road was dangerous and demanding. Because of frequent bad weather and treacherous air currents over the rugged terrain through which the road passed, the bombing of the vital bridges along the road with any degree of accuracy proved extremely difficult, and even when damaged, the bridges would be feverishly repaired by Chinese hand labor. After the Takao Air Group returned to Japan in March 1941, its work was taken over by the Fourteenth Air Group. Over the course of several months, in relentless attacks on the road, the Fourteenth dealt these bridges some crippling blows, and by June 1941 the Burma Road was closed.[56]

Yet even as the Japanese navy had extended the range of its aerial operations in China, the portion of its land- and sea-based units devoted to the China conflict had begun to be reduced. As the danger of conflict with the United States increased, naval air units had to be redirected for training and service with the fleet. These reductions had started as early as 1939. The number of naval aircraft actually based in China had been slashed from over three hundred to less than half that, and while the main strength of the navy's air power devoted to the China theater was still centered on three combined air groups, the major components of these units were based in either Japan or Taiwan and only stationed temporarily in China for each operation. By the end of 1940 only two naval air groups, the Twelfth and the Fourteenth (composed essentially of land-based carrier aircraft), remained on the continent. The carriers were also withdrawn from station off the China coast, leaving only a seaplane tender or two on station (though one or more carriers were occasionally sent on temporary patrol off southern China). By the early autumn of 1941, as planning for the drive into Southeast Asia and eventual hostilities with the Allied powers quickened in pace, only eleven Japanese naval aircraft were left in China, the navy having turned over to the army all its air operations on the China mainland.

THE MEANING AND LEGACY OF THE NAVY'S AIR WAR IN CHINA

The Imperial Japanese Navy's air war in China from 1937 through 1941 is replete with ambiguities and contradictions. There is, to begin with, the question of the cost of the war in terms of aircraft and personnel. As noted earlier, this has been an issue of wide dispute and will continue to be so in the absence of verification and comparison of the best Japanese and Chinese records available. In the meantime, relying solely on the official history of the Japanese naval air service, it appears that in roughly four years of air combat over China the Japanese navy lost 828 men (680 aircrew and 148 ground crew) and 1,169 aircraft (554 destroyed and 615 badly damaged). The greatest losses were suffered in 1937, during the first four and a half months of the war (285 men killed in action and 229 aircraft destroyed or badly damaged), but the numbers dropped sharply in 1941 as the Japanese won the war in the air (27 men killed in action, 166 aircraft lost or damaged). As in the case of the Allied air offensive against Germany during World War II, it was the bomber crews who suffered the greatest losses (379 bomber personnel killed in action out of 680 casualties in all categories of aircrew).[57]

Just what the Japanese air offensives against China accomplished from 1937 to 1941 is an even more slippery question. It can never really be answered unless and until historians are able to collect sufficient military, economic, political, and social and psychological data in China relevant to these war years and to subject it to the sort of comprehensive and exhaustive analysis found in the U.S. Strategic Bombing Surveys conducted in Germany and Japan after World War II. Yet in the sense that Japan's air war in China failed to bring about victory, or at least substantial military advantage for Japan in its conflict with the Nationalist regime, it prefigured the problems faced by all the strategic bombing campaigns of World War II. The view of some in the Japanese naval air service prior to 1937 that strategic bombers were decisive and could dispense with fighters was not unlike the contemporary British conviction that "the bomber will always get through." Unfortunately, Westerners did not learn from Japan's experience in the China War how erroneous was that assumption. This may have been due to Eurocentrism and professional dogma, but it was also due to the fact that Japanese xenophobia and paranoia as to "Western spies" made it difficult for Western nations to gather reliable military intelligence in Japan and Japanese-controlled China.

In any event, the same question may be asked of the Japanese air war on the Asian continent that has been asked of the British and American strategic bombing missions in Europe: Why, "in the face of great expense, lack of combat experience, strategic confusion and tactical ignorance,"[58] did the Japanese embark on a strategic bombing campaign in China in the first place? As I have indicated, there seems to have been no more rational explanation for air campaigns like Operations 101 and 102 than the fact that after the ground war had reached a stalemate, the Japanese navy and army could think of few other alternatives.

There were only two marginal advantages gained by the navy in its China air campaigns. The first was that its interdiction of China's communications to the outside world did reduce the flow of strategic materiel to China and thus, for a time, eased Japanese military operations in the central and southern parts of the country. The second was the fact that despite the sharp reverses it suffered at the outset of the conflict, the Japanese navy maintained control of the skies over central and southern China for the four years of its involvement in the China War. Its relentless attacks, employing better-trained and more disciplined aircrews, as well as far better weapons, crushed the Chinese Nationalist Air Force, which by itself never again posed a threat to Japanese air dominance on the continent, even after the start of the Pacific War.[59] It can be argued, of course, that after 1941 the Chinese, in cooperation with American units like the Flying Tigers, fought Japanese *army* aircraft to a standstill on certain occasions. But concerning the whole course of the navy's air war in China, the assertion of its supremacy remains valid.

In any event, it is not the impact of the air war on China that concerns us but rather its impact on the development of Japanese naval air power and on Japanese naval thinking prior to the Pacific War. To begin with, despite the deeply rooted fixation of the Imperial Japanese Navy on warships as the decisive weapons of naval war, the navy's air war in China brought home to nearly all its leadership the tremendous offensive potential of aerial weapons. In this sense the war greatly altered the navy's assumptions concerning the use of air power. Whereas before the war, aircraft had been seen largely in terms of their use in various tactical roles, the ability of the navy's land-based bombers to attack distant targets had demonstrated their strategic value. Even fighter aircraft, which had been envisioned as being limited to a purely defensive role, came to be seen as offensive air weapons, particularly after the appearance of the Mitsubishi Zero.[60] Just as important, the China War was of tremendous value to the Japanese navy in demonstrating the way in which aviation could contribute to the projection of naval power ashore. It is not too much to say that the air power assembled early in the war from the carriers *Kaga, Ryūjō,* and *Hōshō,* along with that of the land-based air groups in Kyūshū and Taiwan, prefigured, on a modest scale, the concentration of air power four and a half years later by the semi-independent carrier task group that undertook the Hawai'i operation.

A corollary to the navy's recognition of the enormous potential, if not the primacy, of air power was the effect on navy thinking of the sudden increase in the scale of aerial warfare. The air operations over China showed the tactical advantage of employing considerably larger units than had been contemplated before the conflict. Specifically, the navy came to learn that because of Chinese fighter plane and antiaircraft defenses, the only way in which air strikes could be made effective was to send up large formations of attack aircraft covered by a strong fighter force. Granted that air operations over land were different from operations at sea, the results of a concentration of air power were not all that different in the two situations. If anything, air operations could be even more decisive at sea, where the destruction of a carrier was a permanent loss, whereas the crippling of an air base might be only temporary. Thus, the navy came to recognize the effectiveness of scale: the air group system had increasingly given way to the formation of combined air groups, and combined air groups brought about the concept of air fleets, with which the navy was able to launch the massive hammer blows against Allied naval forces and facilities in the first months of the Pacific War.[61]

As a result of the air war over China, moreover, aircraft technology steadily improved as the lessons of air combat were effectively incorporated into aircraft design, through either the improvement of existing service models or the development of new types of aircraft. The design of the Zero was a case in point, as we have seen. But the coordination and integration of air combat experience with the capabilities of aircraft designers and production facilities would not have been possible without the existence of the effective centralized institutions for research and development discussed earlier: the Naval Aviation Department, the Naval Air Arsenal, and the Yokosuka Air Group. In the prosecution of the war, these central command organizations and research and testing units were greatly expanded, and an improved system of combat supply and repair initiated.[62]

Vital, too, was the tactical proficiency that the navy's fighter pilots gained during the China War. Before the conflict, the navy's air service was an organization without practical experience in air combat. As one veteran of the air war later pointed out, the exploits of individual fighter pilots during the Shanghai Incident of 1932 were colorful, but they really belonged to the Richthofen age of air duels rather than to the age of modern air fighting.[63] Even the exercises of the Yokosuka Air Group and the tactical experiments and innovations of veteran pilots like Genda Minoru and Shibata Takeo in the mid-1930s could not begin to match in value the experience of furious combat over China. Moreover, the Japanese naval air service had pioneered new roles for fighter aircraft. It was the world's first air force to use fighter planes as escorts on long-range bombing missions, a role not assumed by Allied fighter aircraft until 1943. During the first several years of the China War, the navy's fighter pilots began to improve their air discipline and to perfect their basic three-aircraft combat formation, the *shōtai*. It was the skill of Japanese fighter pilots honed in air combat over China, 1937 to 1941, as much as the excellence of Japanese air weapons, such as the Mitsubishi Zero, that provided the confidence behind the aggressive Japanese air operations in the first six months of the Pacific War.[64] Yet the navy's great concern, despite the boost in confidence the China War gave to its fighter pilots, was the fact that these pilots still knew very little about the skills of their most likely opponents in the future, the carrier fighter pilots of the United States Navy.

The value of the navy's experience in China was not limited to fighter plane air-to-air combat. Carrier fighter units, trained for operations at sea, demonstrated their tactical value in use against military targets on the ground, a capability the navy began to consider exploiting for use in maritime combat as well. Out of the China War experience of shooting up enemy aircraft and airfield installations on the ground, the navy began to experiment with the use of fighters to strafe surface targets at sea, particularly the bridges of enemy ships, so as to create confusion in the enemy command while carrier dive and torpedo bombers attacked hulls, decks, and main batteries.[65]

The most singular progress in operational efficiency during the China War was made by the navy's land-based air groups. As a result of their missions deep into the interior of the continent, the G3M bomber units gained confidence in long-range operations and demonstrated that the navy had a strategic as well as a tactical air arm, one capable of striking an enemy far behind the front lines on land or several hundred miles out at sea. Before the war, moreover, the navy's air power had been intended to sink enemy warships exclusively. After the first year of the conflict, however, proficiency in knocking out enemy air bases and other land targets became an important gauge of the navy's combat-readiness.[66]

But the China War also revealed a fatal weakness in Japan's strategic posture. Even though the China War was a continental conflict, it was the Japanese navy rather than the army that was forced to carry the major burden of the air war over China for four years. This fact, which threatened a balanced Japanese strategic posture, also revealed a shocking lack of peacetime cooperation between the two services in the development of air doctrine and the promotion of operational skills. Indeed, it was symptomatic of the wider problem of interservice rivalry and distrust that was to be an important cause of Japan's defeat in the Pacific War.[67]

More specifically, the China War posed impediments to the development of Japanese naval air power. In the widest sense, it diverted the Japanese navy from its primary mission, the destruction of its American counterpart. Practice in air operations with the Combined Fleet had been halted or delayed. Except for air-to-air combat, few of the operations of the China air war—cooperation with army ground forces, bombardment of military and air facilities, interdiction of transportation and supply routes—involved missions that the navy had viewed as priorities. The maritime value of naval air groups in China began to decline as the capabilities of their aircrews diverged from their original mission. This was particularly true of the G3M bomber units, since level bombing of land targets—particularly the random terror-bombing of cities—did not demand the same kind of accuracy necessary in bombing ship targets at sea. Moreover, though the navy periodically recycled most of its air groups back to service with the Combined Fleet during the China War, training in ocean reconnaissance, carrier flight-deck operations, and attacks on surface vessels actually declined during this period. Finally, the sudden expansion of naval air power forced the navy to spread both its budget and its instructor cadres over a greater number of naval air groups. For that reason, realistic training in carrier warfare—such as exercises in the concentration of carriers and their aircraft—was impeded for a number of years. Thus, as the navy began to wind down its aerial operations on the continent in 1940 and 1941, the Combined Fleet had to train furiously to recover its naval air capabilities at sea.[68]

Most serious of all, despite the confidence that the navy's air combat over China may have provided to naval fighter pilots and bomber crews, it shaped Japanese attitudes toward aerial tactics, aircraft design, and aviation logistics in ways that were to prove disastrous in the Pacific War. One does not have to accept entirely Eric Bergerud's recent statement that the air war over China was a "tactical wasteland" to agree with him that it led the navy into some dangerous oversights and assumptions concerning air combat in other skies and against other opponents. In the first place, Chinese opposition to the navy's aerial offensives was limited in quality and quantity. In the face of generally inferior Chinese fighter aircraft, the light and nimble A5Ms and later A6Ms were usually able to sweep the skies clear for the advance of the navy's medium bombers (the G3Ms and the later G4Ms) and its carrier attack bombers (the B5Ns and D3As) against Chinese cities. Satisfied in the range and speed of its bombing aircraft, which with virtual impunity had been able to lay waste to large areas of Chinese cities by the end of the navy's bombing campaign, the navy devoted scant effort to the development of a heavily armed and armored bomber that could repel all but the most powerful fighter attacks. Similarly, in the absence of any such bomber in the hands of its Chinese enemy, the navy was under no great pressure to develop fighter aircraft of sufficient armament and structural ruggedness to attack a heavy bomber like the Flying Fortress, which the United States Army Air Corps was acquiring in these same years.[69]

The absence of powerful aerial opposition in the China air war also allowed Japanese fighter pilots to persist in their continuing predilection for acrobatics and one-on-one dogfights, even when assigned the mission of bomber escort. In part this was because the navy's tactical rules for fighter protection for bomber formations called for only "indirect cover" *(kansetsu engo)*, according to which fighters flew above and at a distance from the bomber force they were to protect. This left them relatively free to maneuver and to leave the formation at will to pursue enemy fighters, no matter how distant. Despite complaints from bomber pilots that fighters consequently often left them unprotected, this arrangement worked fairly well in China, where enemy fighters were inferior in numbers, tactical skills, and performance. In the Pacific War, as the Japanese were to learn to their cost, such loose fighter protection in the face of ferocious and numerous enemy interceptor attacks quickly led to the destruction of a Japanese bomber force.[70]

Moreover, as Bergerud has pointed out, theatrical maneuvers like the *hineri-komi* worked well in the low-altitude combat of the China skies, where the configuration and power plant of the Zero gave it an enormous advantage over any enemy aircraft foolish enough to challenge it in the combat environment its pilots preferred. But as a fighter plane doctrine, dogfighting was largely a thing of the past for most Western air services. Halfway around the world, the German Luftwaffe was already demonstrating that high-speed hit-and-run tactics exploiting superior altitude and aircraft speed were far more likely to bring down an enemy than tail-chasing maneuvers. But this would require aircraft heavier and faster than the Zero, a stark reality brought home to Japanese pilots in the skies over the southwestern Pacific.

The China War also permitted Japanese naval air units to form bad habits concerning air base construction. Since the Chinese Nationalist Air Force had few bombing aircraft with which to launch sudden mass raids on Japanese advance airfields, Japan's naval air service was under little pressure to hasten air base construction behind the front lines through the acquisition of modern earth-moving equipment or to prepare adequate antiaircraft protection and sophisticated networks of taxiways and aircraft revetments. In fact, on at least two occasions Japanese air units at Hankow were caught in surprise bombing raids by the Chinese and suffered heavy casualties. Still no corrective measures were taken to prevent such damage. The navy would pay dearly for this leisurely, primitive, and haphazard approach to air base construction when it encountered an enemy able to move its air bases rapidly forward and from them to attack the advance bases the Japanese were able to develop only with great difficulty.[71]

Looking at the Japanese naval air service in the summer of 1941, there is no doubt that in technology, fighting capabilities, and organizational efficiency, it was a far better combat arm than it had been four years before. The question was whether it was now prepared to overcome, by sudden and furious assault, an enemy whose forward defenses were slender but whose latent strength was enormous.

6

FORGING
— *the* —
THUNDERBOLT

Japanese Naval Air Power as an Offensive System,
1937–1941

The first several years after the collapse of the international naval limitations in the mid-1930s, the evolution of naval aviation in all three major navies depended upon the studies, research, and exercises internal to each navy, supplemented by whatever intelligence could be gleaned regarding the tactical and technological developments of the other two. Assessments of the viability of specific aircraft, ships, weapons, and tactics of naval air war were for the most part still a matter of educated guess-work in each navy.

The general conception of the role of naval aviation in a fleet action was remarkably similar in all three navies. While each held to the primacy of the heavy surface gun as the final arbiter of naval combat, none viewed such combat as simply a replay of Jutland. Rather, all saw the future clash between capital ships as being decisively affected by the introduction of naval air power, either through damage to the enemy's battle line (*after* the destruction of his air power) or through the disruption of his gunnery. The top brass in all three navies had confidence in the ability of heavily armored capital ships to withstand all but the heaviest attacks by land- or carrier-based aircraft and had doubts that carriers could long survive unprotected in a clash with battleships. Their opinions were based not on the blind obduracy of "battleship admirals" but on a range of detailed studies and practical experiments. These showed that the bomb loads of most naval aircraft were inadequate to destroy a capital ship under way and took into account the meager protective armor on aircraft carriers.

The outbreak of the war in Europe in 1939, and the active involvement of the Royal Navy's Fleet Air Arm in the subsequent naval combat in the North Sea, the Atlantic, and the Mediterranean, seemed to promise a more realistic gauge against which to measure the validity of such speculation. Yet if the first two years of the war failed to confirm the primacy of the capital ship, they hardly confirmed that the aircraft carrier had taken its place. Within the first eight months of the war, the Royal Navy had lost two of its carriers—one to the guns of capital ships—with only the destruction of a German light cruiser to show for it. While it is true that during the next year, British carrier aircraft sank three battleships (French and Italian) and damaged two others, all were in port and at anchor. Indeed, the first dramatic sinking of a capital ship under way in which naval aircraft played a significant role did not occur until the spring of 1941, with the sinking of the German *Bismarck*. She was crippled by British carrier-borne torpedo bombers, and they demonstrated that she could not operate in the face of enemy air superiority, but her actual destruction was wrought by heavy British surface units.

Moreover, with one exception—the British attack on the Italian fleet at Taranto, November 1940—the nature of the conflict waged by the Royal Navy during 1939–41 seemed to have limited relevance for Japan as its naval high command contemplated possible conflict with the United States. To begin with, neither of Britain's enemies in those years, Germany and Italy, possessed a carrier force that posed a threat to the British fleet or Britain's naval facilities. The Royal Navy thus lacked the tactical or technological impetus to develop carrier warfare. Also, hampered by budgetary limitations and struggling with the Royal Air Force over the control of naval aviation, the Royal Navy was bound to lag somewhat behind the Japanese and American navies in developing carrier forces, particularly carrier aircraft. Finally, the nature of naval operations in the Atlantic provided little opportunity to develop carrier warfare. The range of uses to which the Royal Navy was obliged to put its carrier forces—tracking and destroying enemy surface raiders, providing convoy escort, ferrying land-based aircraft to critical combat theaters, and the like—seemed to have little relevance to the Japanese navy. As the Japanese had given scant thought to trade protection, the attention the Royal Navy devoted to escort carriers, catapult-armed merchantmen, and other innovations stirred little interest on the part of the Japanese Navy General Staff. For the Japanese navy, the guiding objective that drove the training of its aircrews, the development of the aircraft they were to fly, the design of the carriers from which those aircraft were to operate, and the positions those carriers were to take in any fleet action remained the midocean destruction of the U.S. carrier forces and battle fleet.

THE PROMISE AND PERILS OF JAPANESE NAVAL AIR TRAINING

We have seen how the China War proved to be instrumental in furthering the tactical confidence and developing the tactical doctrines of the Japanese naval air service, as well as in increasing the number of its operational units. But the expansion of the service and an effort to upgrade the qualifications of its personnel had begun even before the China conflict erupted. In May 1937, in order to increase the caliber of navy pilots, particularly those who would be section leaders, the Flight Reserve Enlisted Trainee (Yokaren) course system was expanded to place an emphasis on the recruitment of youngsters who had the equivalent of a U.S. high-school education, not just middle-school education, as before.[1] This latest training category enabled the Japanese naval air service to draw upon a new pool of young men who could be more rapidly trained. It complemented the older sources of pilot recruits: the small number of Naval Academy graduates who volunteered for flight training; the slightly larger number of pilot trainees drawn from enlisted ratings under twenty-four years of age (who might reach the rank of warrant officer or special-duty ensign or lieutenant, junior grade); and the large number of candidates drawn directly from civilian life into the original Yokaren program. This expanding system of pilot procurement further enforced the tendency for fliers in the Japanese navy to be enlisted men rather than officers.

But the very high ratio of enlisted men in the cockpits of Japanese naval aircraft—about 90 percent—was not only the result of the recruiting avenues that had been established. It was also due to the particular conditions of Japanese naval aviation and to the navy's promotion system. During the years when the greater portion of Japanese naval aviation was carrier-based, there was little incentive for junior officers to volunteer for flight training. Future command prospects for naval aviators were limited.

Junior officers in the naval air service could not count on their pilot training as a ticket to rapid advancement, in part because of the rigid seniority system of the Japanese navy, and in part because carrier and air group commands were not limited to those officers who were naval aviators. Thus, as late as the Pacific War most of these commands were held by naval officers who were not air-qualified, because there were too few pilots of sufficient seniority to occupy them. On its part, the United States Navy dealt effectively with this problem in two ways: first, by making it the rule that all such commands could be held only by aviators; and second, by giving a number of nonaviator senior officers sufficient flight training to qualify them for these aviation commands.[2] The rapid expansion of the land-based component of the Japanese navy's air arm during the China War to some extent opened up the prospects for naval aviators to assume aviation commands, and admittedly, three of the six carrier captains in the Pearl Harbor operation had gone through flight training at Kasumigaura. Yet the generally lesser influence of Japanese naval aviators over the conduct of operations in their own service was to have important repercussions on a number of occasions during the Pacific War.[3]

Initially, all basic flight training was conducted at the Yokosuka Naval Air Base, but in the late 1930s it was moved to Tsuchiura, where in November 1940 a training air group was established to carry out this function. As the navy expanded its recruitment for the Yokaren courses, other training air groups up and down the Japanese home islands were established to handle the increase in personnel.[4] After graduating from these units with approximately three hundred hours' flying time, future fighter pilots were sent on for further training at one of three operational air groups: Ōmura or Ōita on Kyūshū, or Tokushima on Shikoku. There they mastered carrier flight operations, acrobatics, formation flying, and air combat maneuvers. After this, they were posted to combat units, either to a carrier or to a land-based air group for another year of intensive training. The best pilots, with an average of about eight hundred flying hours, were attached to carriers. Squadron commanders had even more experience.[5]

Not all aviators were trained to fly fighter planes, of course. A program for Special Flight Training Students (Tokushūka Kōkūjutsu Renshūsei) was revived in November 1938 to provide nine months of intensive instruction in bombing, observation, and communications, particularly for those officers who would be assigned to bombers. The training of these student candidates in horizontal bombardment was to be particularly important, since the greatly increased accuracy they achieved in practice (against stationary targets) was to be of prime importance in the opening hours of the Pacific War. No less important was the training, given to certain land-based naval air groups, in aerial torpedo attacks on warships under way. Here too the training was to pay off thunderously at the outset of the war. The Japanese navy was far more assiduous in training navigators, bombardiers, and gunners than the army, and by 1941 its training units had turned out some twenty-five hundred such aircrews.[6]

A particular feature of advanced Japanese naval air training in the interwar period was a tactical training process called *sengi*. "Combat skills" comes perhaps closest to an English translation of the word, and it referred to a series of tests undergone by individual aircrews and judged by fellow fliers. Established in the 1920s but not made official until the mid-1930s, it was holistic in that it included training not just in aerial tactics but also in leadership, aircraft maintenance, communications, and various other elements that contributed to successful air combat, and for this reason the training included not just aircrews but also ground crews. It was both a top-down and a bottom-up system in that it was the product of intense interaction between the Naval Aviation Department (which controlled all naval air training, not the Naval Education Department, as was the case for the rest of the navy) and the actual air groups (which were the actual training units). It thus integrated the practical experience of the navy's aviators—and, during the China air war, the results of actual air combat—with the wider-ranging perspectives of headquarters. For that reason *sengi* training allowed an unusual amount of input from junior officers. Normally, after annual training exercises in the Japanese navy, there would be a postexercise review at which a few senior officers would speak, following which the meeting would be concluded. But in the Japanese naval air service, the views of the junior officers who had the most active role in the exercise would be sought out. In this way, a thorough airing was given to innovations across a wide spectrum of practical issues: fleet air defense, air-to-ship radio communications, night air combat, quick landing and storage aboard carriers, and related matters.[7]

There is little doubt that *sengi* training contributed significantly to the combat proficiency of Japanese naval air groups in the decade before the war. But Japanese naval air training faced impediments, both internal and external. One problem was that, like many bureaucratic initiatives, *sengi* training tended, in the years immediately prior to the war, to become formalized and routinized and thus lost some of its earlier spontaneity and ability to challenge accepted doctrine. As it did so, there was an increasing tendency, particularly among the navy's fighter pilots, to ignore some of the more important tactical principles it had established, such as formation flying and combat, and to revert to their predilection for the individual heroics of dogfighting.[8]

But Japanese naval air training also faced the ongoing shortage of naval fuels that had confronted the Japanese navy since its switch from coal to oil after World War I. Training in carrier flight operations in particular suffered from this deficiency. Carriers steamed at high speeds to provide the wind-over-deck needed to get aircraft aloft, and in the process they consumed huge amounts of oil. The First Carrier Division, long the core of the navy's carrier forces, always exceeded its fuel allotment in training and was thus resented by other fleet elements. For this reason, aircraft were generally sent ashore for general flight training and for both bombing and torpedo practice. Training in carrier flight operations was thus undoubtedly more restricted than in the United States Navy, which had abundant petroleum stocks.[9]

The Japanese naval air service's most marked difference from its American counterpart was that up to the last year or so before the Pacific War, it had no concept of mass training for its pilots, largely because of the Japanese navy's obsession with quality over quantity. The navy's most internationally known fighter ace to survive the war, Sakai Saburō,[†] was to recall in his memoirs that pilot training in the 1930s was selective in the extreme: only the most physically and academically qualified young men in the entire nation could hope to be considered for basic flight training. (Sakai himself was one of seventy trainees selected from more than fifteen hundred applicants.) Once selected, students in the seven to nine months of naval flight training—increased to a year after 1940—faced a ferocious test of physical and mental skill. Sakai recalled that his training at Tsuchiura was a constant and exhausting series of demands on the body and mind: obstacle courses, diving, acrobatics for balance and muscular coordination, exercises to develop peripheral vision, and tests to speed reaction time. "During the 1930s," Sakai wrote, "the Japanese Navy trained approximately one hundred fliers a year. The rigid screening and expulsion practices reduced the many hundreds of qualified students to the ridiculously low total of a hundred or fewer graduated pilots."[10] Those few who mastered these rigorous challenges proceeded to advanced training with carrier- or land-based air groups, and from there to combat with operational units in China. By 1941, in training and experience, the navy's fighter pilots as a whole were among the best in the world, and its carrier pilots were probably *the* best among the world's three leading carrier forces. But there was a fundamental defect in the rigorous training program, a defect that stemmed from the navy's basic assumption concerning the nature of a U.S.-Japanese conflict and the conviction that quality was more important than quantity. On the basis of these two premises, the Japanese navy had adopted a training program that produced a much smaller pool of aviators than its American counterpart.

Different assumptions concerning the length of a U.S.-Japanese war and a consequent difference in aircrew training policies in the immediate prewar years were fundamental to this quantitative discrepancy. The Japanese gambled on the clash being brief and therefore placed priority on having at hand a small core of superb aircrews who, flying superior aircraft with superior skill, could decimate their enemy counterparts in a lightning conflict. For that reason, in December 1941 there were just a little over five hundred Japanese naval aircraft dedicated to training purposes. While the navy issued a plan in 1941 for the training of some fifteen thousand pilots annually, the war overtook this effort to build an adequate reserve of qualified aircrews. The navy was thus forced to enter the war with only its cadre of first-line pilots. Should attrition in combat take its toll, there would be no reserve of trained airmen to take the place of those who were lost.[11]

The assumptions and policies of the United States Navy were quite different. Convinced that any conflict with Japan would be prolonged, it gave priority to building up a large reserve of qualified aircrews. Some three years before the Pacific War, the United States Navy made a basic decision to expand pilot training and the production of training aircraft, even if, at the time, this meant limiting the number of combat aircraft and personnel in operational air units.[12] Thus, on the eve of the Pacific War the number of proficient pilots in the United States Navy constituted a relatively large pool of about eight thousand or so. In contrast, while the annual number of graduated pilots increased substantially as the Pacific War approached, in late 1941 the Japanese navy had on hand probably not much more than nine hundred *outstanding* pilots—mostly on carriers—out of a total pilot pool of around thirty-five hundred.[13]

EVOLUTION OF JAPANESE FIGHTER TACTICS

But the consequences of these flaws in Japanese naval air training lay in the future. In the four years between the end of the treaty era and the outbreak of the Pacific War, that training, combined with the experience of air combat over China and the accelerated efforts to prepare for the possibility of air and surface operations against the United States Navy, intensified the development of the Japanese navy's air combat tactics.[14]

It was during the China War, as we have seen, that the navy's fighter and bomber squadrons perfected the basic tactical formation, the three-aircraft *shōtai* composed of a leader and two wingmen.[15] When not actually engaged, the three aircraft usually formed an equilateral triangle with about a 50-meter (160-foot) interval between the section leader and his wingmen with all three flying at the same altitude. When anticipating combat, Japanese navy pilots usually adopted a looser formation, with much greater intervals between the section leader and the wingmen in order to provide for greater flexibility. Often this formation took the shape of a rough scalene triangle (much like the United States Navy's A-B-C formation), with one aircraft trailing the leader at about 200 meters (650 feet) higher altitude and the third flying about 300 meters (1,000 feet) higher than the leader to provide top cover.[16] (Fig. 6-1.) From this basic formation a section leader could deploy his aircraft into a line astern for successive firing passes against a target or into a line abreast in order to box a target in with alternate passes from each of the two wingmen while he remained above and astern for protective cover.

Success for these formation tactics in the wild chaos of combat required an aircraft of exceptional maneuverability, which the navy had in the Mitsubishi Zero, and pilots of consummate skill whose teamwork was the result of hours of relentless training and practice. The coherence of the *shōtai* formation and the impressive gunnery runs achieved by the navy pilots who maintained it in the midst of the most violent aerial acrobatics are testimony that in the years immediately prior to the Pacific War, the navy's fighter squadrons were composed of highly disciplined aviators and enjoyed high unit cohesion. Their coordinated hit-and-run tactics took them away from their natural inclination for dogfighting, in which pilots clung tenaciously, if unimaginatively, to the tail of an enemy aircraft. Indeed, so familiar with each other's combat tactics were the fliers in a three-man *shōtai* that some navy pilots claimed to have developed an almost sixth sense *(ishin denshin)* by which they could communicate with their two comrades flying with them. Apparently this coordination of thought and action could sometimes be extended to the nine-man *chūtai* (a vee of three *shōtai*), but in air combat involving really large formations, such as the eighteen-man *daitai,* it was impossible to maintain such tight control.[17] (Fig. 6-1.)

Postwar interviews with surviving Japanese navy pilots have indicated that such mental telepathy did exist. On the other hand, famed pilot Sakai Saburō recalled that he saw very little of such empathy between officer and noncommissioned officer pilots because of the strict status distinction between the two. It is possible that this telepathic sense existed at the opening of the war even between noncom and officer fighter pilots who had trained constantly together in a cohesive unit, only to be lost later on under the impact of attrition and the constant replacement of pilots.[18]

In any event, this nearly automatic pilot-to-pilot coordination, if it existed, depended upon pilots of long training and experience. Tactical control of aircrews of less elite status would be more dependent upon airborne radio communications. Here it must be noted that air-to-air and air-to-ground communications were a problem for the air services of all nations during these years. Crystal-controlled equipment—which comprised all four types of radio sets in the Japanese navy—

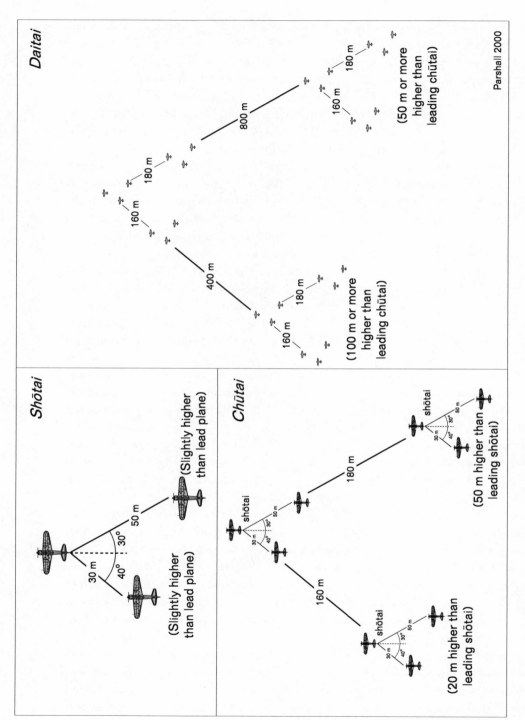

Fig. 6-1. Tactical formations for Japanese navy fighters

operated at only a few frequencies, though it maintained those frequencies accurately. Analog-tuned equipment, on the other hand, covered relatively broad frequency bands but drifted because of vibration and the idiosyncrasies of electronics. Japanese radio (as distinct from radar) appears to have been nearly the equal in performance of U.S. equipment prior to the Pacific War. Eventually, of course, the enormous effort the United States put into electronics, developing superior radio equipment at an unprecedented rate and supplying it promptly to American combat forces, proved impossible for the Japanese to match.[19]

In the late 1920s the Japanese navy had begun the first serious attempts to develop radio communications in its aircraft, an effort accelerated by the unfortunate incident of the 1929 annual naval maneuvers, when several aircraft from the *Akagi* were lost in bad weather because they could not communicate with the carrier.[20] That same year the first Japanese-designed radio equipment was produced, and a communications section and a communications officer were added to each air group. But the greatest difficulties in transmission among the radio devices placed aboard Japanese naval aircraft in these years were posed by radio telephone systems. Radio telegraph (using Morse code) existed and was used effectively in bombers and reconnaissance aircraft, but it was obviously impractical for communication between fighter aircraft engaged in split-second combat maneuvers. The Japanese Type 96 radio telephone was developed in 1936 but was not installed in Japanese naval aircraft until early in the Pacific War. The quality of shipborne radio telephones was adequate, but at this stage of Japanese radio technology, comparable quality was not available in airborne systems: transmission was too often obscured by interference and static, and reception of voices was therefore too often fuzzy.[21] It was for these reasons that fighter pilots usually had to rely on a variety of visual signals: wagging the wings, hand semaphores, prearranged signal flares, or on such mental-telepathic communication as appeared possible after months of intensive practice and training.

On the eve of the Pacific War, Gordon Prange tells us, radio communications were a serious problem for those planning the Pearl Harbor operation, since only radio telegraph would carry the 250–300–mile distance from the carriers to the target. For that reason, the pilots participating in the operation, including the fighter pilots, had to master Morse code in the months previous to the attack. For much of the Pacific War, this communications handicap, in combination with the lag in Japanese development of an effective radar system, was to pose a critical disadvantage for Japanese fighter units.[22]

Yet it is clear that in the years 1937–41 the aircraft and pilots of the navy's fighter squadrons had come into their own, both defensively and offensively. Great hopes were placed on the Zero's 20-millimeter cannon for protecting the navy's ships and bases from enemy bombers. The latter were to be opposed by fighter formations that would concentrate, if possible, on the lead bomber. To cover its carriers, the Combined Fleet devised an elaborate system of fighter patrols (discussed below).[23] But though fighter aircraft now comprised the core element in fleet air defense, their place in the navy's growing offensive power was even more valued. While the idea of using fighters as bombers had not proved to be practical, the China War had demonstrated that the range and firepower of the Zero appeared to make it a formidable adjunct to any bombing force the navy could assemble. This belief was apparently confirmed by the success achieved by Zero fighters in the first offensive operations of the Pacific War. Indeed, it can be argued that after the Japanese air victories over Pearl Harbor, Port Darwin, Colombo, and Trincomalee, the Japanese navy's estimation of the value of fighter aircraft in a primarily offensive role became seriously exaggerated. In this view, the insistence of Japanese air officers—Genda Minoru among them—that the bulk of the Midway task force fighter aircraft be used as escorts for bombers against Midway Island, rather than for the maintenance of an adequate combat air patrol (CAP) over the Japanese carriers, was a decision that contributed to the ultimate Japanese disaster in that campaign.[24]

COMING OF AGE
The Navy's Air Attack Tactics

Of the navy's various methods of aerial bombardment, it was horizontal bombing that was given the most extensive trial during the China War. The navy's long-range high-altitude bombing missions over China gave its air units useful experience in various aspects of such operations, but given their emphasis on saturation bombing, they did little to improve the bombing *accuracy* of the navy's land-based bomber groups. At the same time, from its studies on the possible effects of the high-altitude horizontal bombing of maritime targets, the navy expected that it would be difficult to destroy a heavily armored capital ship by a few aircraft carrying small bombs. Only large bombs dropped by numerous aircraft had any real chance of success, the navy believed. Indeed, its research on the subject led the navy to conclude that use of the largest available ordnance, if modified (see below) and if dropped from a high altitude, could penetrate warship armor and thus accelerate the destruction of enemy surface units. But the problems seemed insurmountable: there were too few aircrews sufficiently skilled to attempt attacks against ships under way; moreover, the navy's medium bombers could carry only one 800-kilogram (1,764-pound) bomb. Thus, from its bombing experiments at sea and from its actual bombing campaigns in China, the Japanese navy came to recognize a frustrating paradox. On the one hand, hits against a target at sea were far more likely to result in the permanent elimination of that target—its sinking—than hits directed against an air base or city quarter, which could often be repaired or reconstructed. On the other hand, the destruction of a moving target at sea by high-level bombing was much more difficult, if not impossible, to accomplish.[25]

By 1941, therefore, the navy's experiments in high-level horizontal bombing were so discouraging that it was on the verge of abandoning the effort entirely and relying instead on torpedo and dive-bombing tactics.[26] It was an accepted belief that in a surface engagement, twelve to sixteen direct hits from the largest shells could destroy any warship afloat. While it would require the total striking power of six *Akagi*-class carriers to accomplish the same result by high-level bombardment, it was held that the same number of torpedo bombers could probably sink more than ten capital ships.[27] But in planning the Pearl Harbor strike the Japanese navy concluded that it could not rely on torpedo attacks or dive bombing by themselves. As Gordon Prange has recounted in his study of that operation, the Japanese assumed that not only would any battleships anchored next to Ford Island be protected by torpedo nets, but the standard American double mooring of warships would mean that only the outer battleships would be vulnerable to torpedo attack. Moreover, the lighter ordnance carried by the Japanese carrier dive bombers could not be expected to do fatal damage to the heavily armored decks of the U.S. battleships.[28] Thus, horizontal bombardment was left as the only means of dealing with the "battleship row" at Pearl Harbor. But the navy's efforts in horizontal bombing had proved a major disappointment for most of the 1930s.

By his own account, at least, it appears to have been Lt. Okumiya Masatake, an instructor at the Yokosuka Naval Air Base, 1938–39, who first suggested one of the means to improve the accuracy of the navy's horizontal bombardment. After arriving at Yokosuka in 1938, Okumiya made a careful study of basic flight-school test scores. He concluded that the fundamental problem was one of aptitude. There were many good pilots in the navy, but few good bombardiers, largely because the best graduates of flight school became fighter or attack aircraft pilots. Because they were not trained as bombardiers, attack aircraft pilots simply became drivers, with bombardiers sitting in the back seat. Okumiya argued that some of the best pilot graduates of flight school should be given intensive bombardier training and then teamed up with the most skillful bombardiers in a permanent unit, working together until they functioned almost as one man. Okumiya's proposals were soon taken up by the navy, and at his recommendation, Ens. Furukawa Izumi, one of the best pilots in the Yokosuka Air Group, was given special training in horizontal bombardment. It was Furukawa who then became a central figure among the navy's bombing experts and, as a member of the *Akagi*'s attack squadron, took the lead in training carrier aircrews in horizontal bombardment. With energy and determination, Furukawa molded the *Akagi*'s Nakajima B5N bomber crews into a precision instrument.[29]

The next step to improve horizontal bombing was to reduce the drop altitude for such operations from 4,000 meters (13,000 feet) to 3,000 meters (10,000 feet). This was the minimum height from which armor-piercing bombs could develop sufficient momentum to penetrate deck armor (though the planes risked more intense antiaircraft fire in bombing from this altitude). That having been decided, a new bombing formation was developed, which was smaller and thus concentrated more bombing units against a target. These efforts led to an improvement in accuracy from 10 percent to 33 percent and later, after further intensive practice at Kagoshima in the summer of 1941, to even better results.[30]

The solution to the particular problems posed by the U.S. battleship anchorage at Pearl Harbor was to modify the available ordnance to be used. On the eve of the Pacific War, the Japanese navy had three types of bombs in its inventory: a 250-kilogram, a 500-kilogram, and an 800-kilogram (551-, 1,103-, and 1,764-pound) bomb. Only the last of these, the Type 99, was suitable for use against the armored decks of capital ships. The Type 99 was actually an AP naval shell, which the navy now decided to convert by equipping it with an aluminum shock-absorbing plug placed ahead of the charge to protect it from impact detonation, so that the shell would explode after penetration, not upon impact. (Fig. 6-2.) The navy's ordnance experts judged that it would be able to penetrate 15 centimeters (5.9 inches) of horizontal armor, which was the thickest deck protection of even the newest battleships.[31]

In the attack on moored warships at Pearl Harbor, the improved tactics and technology in Japanese horizontal bombing were to pay off thunderously. The most dramatic hit, of course, was scored on the battleship *Arizona* by a Type 99 bomb, which in striking alongside the ship's no. 2 turret caused the massive explosion—made famous by motion-picture film footage—that instantly destroyed her.[32] Though horizontal bombing was used frequently later by both the Japanese and American navies in the Pacific War, it never again achieved such success, and in any event no major surface unit under way was ever sunk during World War II by high-altitude horizontal bombardment.

While dive bombers had been used with some effect by the navy in the latter stages of the China War, particularly against communication routes in southern China, as a whole, dive-bombing techniques were not noticeably advanced by that conflict. Except for roads and bridges, the navy's targets in China did not call for the same sort of pinpoint accuracy necessary to attack a warship under way. Thus, it was largely in naval exercises and practice runs at sea during these years that the navy's dive-bomber crews perfected their skills. Building on experiments in the mid-1930s that combined dive bombers for the attack and carrier fighters for top cover, and exploiting the advanced capabilities of the Aichi D3A dive bomber, the navy began to work out a powerful formula for surprise attack on enemy fleet units.[33]

Perfected by Lt. Takahashi Sadamu[†] in 1940–41, the tactic called for the dive bombers to approach on a course opposite to the target, in one of a number of possible formations, beginning their attack at an altitude of probably 3,000 meters (10,000 feet) and about 20–30 nautical miles from the target. At that point, forming in echelon, the bombing aircraft would go into a shallow dive of about 10 degrees at full throttle. In succession, the aircraft would plunge in a dive of about 65 degrees, aiming at a point in advance of the target's intended course and releasing their bombs at a height of 600 meters (2,000 feet) above the target.[34] After releasing its payload at the bottom of its dive, each aircraft would retract its air brakes, pull sharply up, and, at low altitude, use all possible speed to avoid anti-aircraft fire and get away. In certain circumstances the lead dive bombers were to be sacrificed in an attempt to suppress such fire with their own bombs. The navy

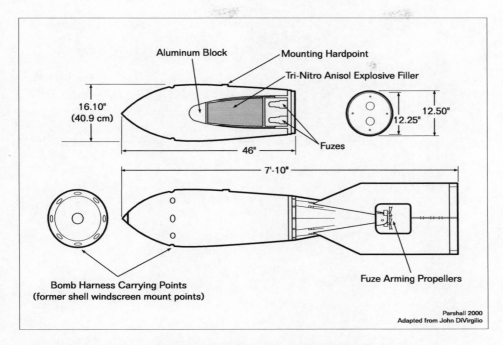

Fig. 6-2. Schematic of Type 99 Model 80 heavy armor-piercing bomb

anticipated that losses would be severe among dive-bombing squadrons in such operations. During the Pacific War the navy estimated that to make five or six direct hits on a major ship, eighteen planes would be required, of which eight would probably be shot down.[35]

Japanese dive-bombing doctrine called for bombing runs to be made from either the bow or the stern (with bow-on attacks the most preferred) if the wind was negligible, but if the wind speed was greater than 15 meters per second (30 knots), standard procedure (during the Pacific War, at least) called for the dive to be made with the wind at the tail of the plane in order to minimize wind drift errors. When several dive-bombing formations attacked at once, they would come in from different directions. (Fig. 6-3.)[36]

Repeated practice in these techniques in the years before the war gradually improved the percentage of hits in bombing runs. In the Combined Fleet exercises of 1939, navy dive bombers of several types achieved a 53.7 percentage of hits; and two years later, in the First Fleet training exercises, using Aichi D3A aircraft exclusively, dive-bombing units attained a high of 55 percent. By 1940, therefore, the navy had adopted the Takahashi tactic as its standard dive-bombing practice. In the first year of the Pacific War it achieved dramatic results: the sinking in the Indian Ocean of the British cruisers *Cornwall* and *Dorsetshire*—on which 90 percent of the bombs struck home—and the small carrier *Hermes* in April 1942.[37]

The Japanese navy had traditionally considered the torpedo the most lethal

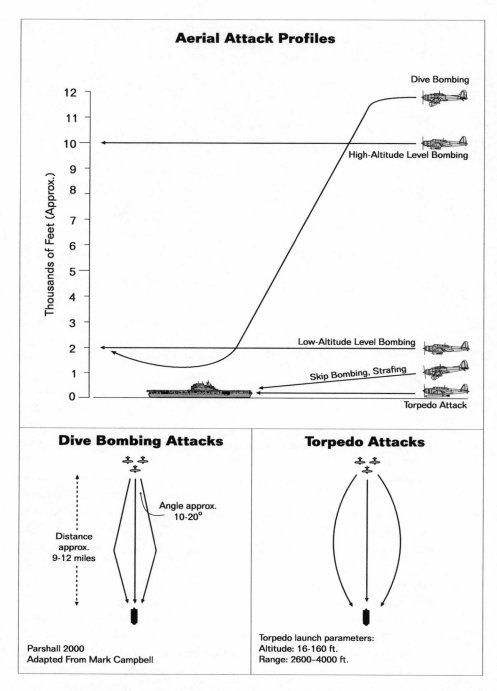

Fig. 6-3. Japanese navy aerial attack methods

weapon for use against ships, and during the interwar years it conducted an extensive torpedo research program. By the beginning of the Pacific War, therefore, the navy was armed with powerful torpedoes of unrivaled speed and range. The configuration of the Type 91 aerial torpedo, when it was first developed in 1931, had enabled the navy's torpedo bombers to launch from a height of 100 meters (330 feet) while maintaining an airspeed of 100 knots.[38] For lack of targets, torpedo bombing was the one aerial assault tactic that played no part in the China War. Through constant practice at sea and the acquisition of larger and more powerful aircraft, however, the navy was able to improve upon the performance of its torpedo bomber units. By 1937, navy torpedo bombers were able to release their torpedoes at heights of up to 200 meters (660 feet) and speeds of up to 120 knots. By 1938, Japanese tactical doctrine called for releasing them at approximately 1,000 meters (3,300 feet) from the target. Advances were also made in massed attack, and beginning in 1939, the Combined Fleet undertook research and training to coordinate carrier- and land-based torpedo operations. By that year too, night torpedo attacks, first attempted in 1934, were being carried out behind flare-dropping pathfinder units. Given these advances, to some navy men it seemed as if aerial torpedo operations were irresistible.[39]

On the other hand, real problems remained. To begin with, there was the question of shipboard antiaircraft fire. Many held the view that in an actual combat situation, defensive fire, particularly from battleships, would be so intense that the hit ratios would be only one-third of those achieved in peacetime training and that, conversely, losses among air attack units would be unacceptably high. Under these conditions it was an open question whether such tactics were worth the sacrifices involved, and whether aerial torpedo attacks should therefore be abandoned altogether. Furthermore, the Combined Fleet exercises that attempted to coordinate attacks by carrier- and land-based torpedo aircraft soon created dangerous complications. The hair-raising proximity of attacking bombers crowded into a relatively confined air space, all trying to get in a hit while taking evasive action from antiaircraft fire, demonstrated the extreme danger of midair collisions unless some restrictions were imposed on target approaches. This led to instructions that torpedoes were to be dropped from greater heights and distances, which in turn provoked a heated controversy over the future of aerial torpedo tactics. Some, particularly in the Yokosuka Air Group, complained that the new safety limitations meant that torpedoes would be launched at such a distance that even the smallest miscalculations in aim would cause the torpedo to miss the target. Moreover, the distant-launching doctrine violated the *nikuhaku-hitchū* ("press closely, strike home") tradition of the Japanese navy, hallowed ever since the small-craft surface actions of the Sino-Japanese war of 1894–95.[40]

Ultimately, the adoption of the improved Type 91 aerial torpedo and certain changes in tactical formations improved the hit percentages and reduced the hazards in training. The matter of losses to defensive fire remained a nagging worry, however. In any event, the safety limitations seem to have remained in force, since the standard approach for the navy's torpedo planes by the time of the Pacific War was at an altitude of between 1,000 meters (3,300 feet) and 3,000 meters (9,800) feet, depending upon atmospheric and target conditions. The torpedo squadrons, usually running on an opposite course to the target, would often divide some 10-12 nautical miles from the target, approaching it from two sides. (Fig. 6-3.) As in Japanese dive-bombing doctrine, the final run was generally made in a loose string (or in a line abreast if facing intense antiaircraft fire). The aircraft would then drop their torpedoes at an altitude of 50–100 meters (160–330 feet), some 800–1,200 meters (2,600–4,000 feet) from the target, at an airspeed of 140–162 knots.[41] In this way the torpedo aircraft would carry out a "hammer and anvil" attack: no matter which direction the target turned, it would always present a broadside to one group of attackers.

Before turning to the relationship of all these offensive schemes to the development of Japanese carrier doctrine in the last years before the Pacific War, I should mention one other aerial torpedo tactic that was to play a decisive role in the opening hours of that conflict: the shallow-water attack.

Much is made of the fact that the perfection of shallow-water attack was an important part of the preparations of the Combined Fleet in the summer and autumn of 1941 for the Pearl Harbor operation, and of the fact that the inspiration for the tactic derived from the example of the British attack on Italian fleet units at Taranto in November 1940.[42] In fact, consideration of shallow-water attack had begun as early as 1939, and not with Pearl Harbor specifically in mind. In that year, during the fleet's annual exercises, torpedo planes dispatched from Yokosuka had "attacked" warships anchored in the shallow waters of Saeki Bay, Kyūshū. Because the shallow depth defeated an otherwise well-executed attempt, the navy determined to study the problem, largely at the initiative of Lt. Comdr. Aikō Fumio,[†] the chief torpedo instructor of the Yokosuka Air Group. That autumn, Aikō begun studying naval charts of Manila, Singapore, Hong Kong, and Vladivostok, as well as Pearl Harbor, all of which were found to have an average depth of 15–25 meters (50–80 feet). To be effective in attacking anchored ships in such circumstances, Aikō realized, an air-launched torpedo could not be allowed to dive more than 12 meters (39 feet) below the surface, a requirement that would demand a change in tactics and, even more important, some difficult and innovative changes in torpedo design. Aikō worked on the problem for some time, and while he himself did not solve it, he made a major contribution to an understanding of its parameters in a report to the Naval Aviation Department that incorporated his research as well as the navy's experience in torpedo attacks.[43]

As was explained in chapter 2, the problems of impact forces breaking or deforming the hull of an aerial torpedo had been solved by the early 1930s. But good performance for a torpedo launched from the air required different fluid dynamic configurations for air and water flight. The difficulties of pitch and yaw during air flight were solved, as they were somewhat later by the United States Navy, by the addition of frangible wooden extensions to the fins at the rear tail

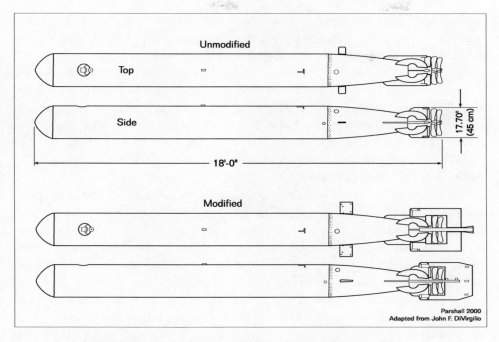

Fig. 6-4. Type 91 aerial torpedoes for normal and shallow-water use

assembly. A solution to the roll problem had been attempted by affixing small steel gyro-controlled contrarotating fins (sometimes called flippers) to the torpedo at the forward end of the tail cone. The initial attempts used fins that were inadequate to control roll during air flight. Yet larger fins would have degraded the subsurface performance of the weapon. The solution, reached in 1941, was, again, the addition of frangible wooden extensions to the fins that would break off upon the torpedo's entry into the water and thus leave the clean configuration necessary for the hydrodynamic performance of the weapon. (Fig. 6-4.)[44]

As the last technological problems of aerial torpedoes were being overcome, the tactical aspects of shallow-water torpedo attack were studied and practiced by the torpedo squadron of the Yokosuka Air Group under the leadership of Lt. Comdr. Murata Shigeharu,[†] the navy's leading aerial torpedo specialist. When he became commander of the *Akagi*'s torpedo squadron in the summer of 1941, Murata led the development of shallow-water attack in the First Air Fleet, then being readied for war. During the autumn of 1941 Murata took his torpedo pilots to Kyūshū to practice over the shallow waters of Kagoshima Bay. Over the next four months, experimenting with various speeds, approaches, drop heights, and torpedo configurations, Murata and his pilots perfected the torpedo weapons and tactics that so stunningly opened the Pacific War.[45]

But carrier torpedo bombers were not the only aircraft employed in perfecting the navy's proficiency in aerial torpedo attacks. In the years immediately prior to the Pacific War, certain land-based air groups equipped with twin-engined bombers began aerial torpedo training. One of these was the Kanoya Air Group, whose G3Ms had participated in the opening of the air war over China. In the years that followed, this unit usually undertook bombing missions over China during the summer months, but from December through April it participated in the annual exercises of the Combined Fleet, practicing torpedo runs against surface units. In particular, it practiced torpedo drops against ships steaming at high speed and, in theory, defended by fighter cover. By late 1941, relentless training by the Kanoya Air Group, now newly equipped with G4Ms, had made it a formidable weapon for use against enemy surface units.[46]

By 1939 the Japanese navy had begun to devote a good deal of study and practice to melding all the air attack systems discussed here—horizontal bombing, dive bombing, torpedo bombing, and fighter attacks—into a single system of massed aerial assault.[47] In part the idea stemmed from the conclusion that surface targets under way and taking evasive action would be far harder to hit by a single type of air attack than by a combination of different types. By adroit handling, for example, a warship under attack might be able to comb the wakes of a number of torpedoes launched from one direction, but a simultaneous attack from another quarter would greatly reduce the chance of successful evasion, and an air assault that combined attacks by both torpedo bombers and dive bombers would make it difficult for the target to avoid being hit.

Out of the research devoted to the problem of coordinating massed air attacks by carrier aircraft there emerged an air doctrine that called for closely phased operations by various types of aircraft. In the scheme that the navy began to work out, the attack would be launched about 200 miles from the enemy. As it approached the target, the strike force, organized into vanguard and rear elements, would divide. Some fighters would provide direct cover for the attack groups racing in to hit their targets from predetermined altitudes. Others would sweep the enemy's combat air patrols from the sky. Still others would strafe the bridges and decks of enemy carriers, an idea that derived from the experience of navy fighter pilots in ground attacks in China. The fighters would have barely swept past when high-level horizontal bombing attacks would be delivered from a 3,000–4,000-meter (10,000–13,000-foot) altitude, to be immediately followed by dive-bombing sorties that would be launched from about 3,000 meters, the dive bombers racing down at angles of 50–70 degrees and releasing their bombs about 500 meters (1,600 feet) above their targets. Almost simultaneously, a succession of torpedo attacks would be delivered, presumably 50–100 meters (160–330 feet) above the waves.[48]

The conduct of an operation of such complexity, precision timing, and risk required an expanded tactical organization, meticulous planning, rigorous training, skilled aircrews, and bold leadership to keep it from suffering a series of disastrous miscues. All of these ingredients were essential, of course, to the preparations for the single greatest occasion up to that time in which this system of diverse but massed aerial assault would be realized: the attack on Pearl Harbor. But such an operation involving massed aircraft could not have been even contemplated had not the navy first developed a system of massing its aircraft carriers.

JAPANESE CARRIER DOCTRINE

The dramatic advances in naval aviation in the 1930s widened the gap between reality and the navy's formal tactical principles—its Battle Instructions, which were concerned almost exclusively with surface engagements. The revision of the instructions was a complicated and time-consuming process. By 1939, however, with the emergence of the concept of the decisive air battle, the rapid growth in Japanese naval air strength, and the development, in effect, of a naval air force with its own tactical priorities, the navy had come to recognize that the creation of an overall naval air doctrine could be achieved only by a major reorganization of the formal principles of Japanese naval thought. To this end, the Naval Staff College drafted a "Supplement to the Battle Instructions: Air Operations" *(Kaisen yōmurei zokuhen: kōkūsen-bu),* later distributed by the Navy General Staff to all units and stations. This statement, which served as an intermediate step on the way to a formal revision of the Battle Instructions, stressed the importance of preemptive attacks; a shift in target priorities for air attacks from the enemy's battle line to his carriers; decisive air combat as a necessary prelude to victory by surface units; and the identification of land-based air groups as one of the principal elements of naval power. Measures to transform these principles into a formal revision of the Battle Instructions were incomplete at the opening of the Pacific War.[49]

The idea of a preemptive tactical strike directed at the enemy's carriers as priority targets supposed, of course, a concentration of massed aircraft. As discussed earlier, the preemptive-strike concept had provoked a question of considerable difficulty and controversy within the navy: whether to concentrate or disperse the navy's carrier forces in combat. This dilemma stemmed from a number of questions: Would the apparent advantages of a preemptive strike from a concentration of carriers be offset by the disadvantage of risking all one's own carriers to a similar strike by the enemy? Or conversely, how would individually dispersed carriers provide for defense in case they were caught by a numerically superior enemy?

At the time of the China War, fleet maneuvers and table-top war games had led the navy to favor the doctrine of dispersal. For that reason, in 1937 the training and maneuvers of the navy's two carrier divisions—the First (comprising the small carriers *Hōshō* and *Ryūjō*) and the Second (comprising the *Kaga* and *Akagi*)—were conducted separately. Therefore, the employment of Japan's carrier forces en masse did not at this point extend beyond the table-top war-game stage.[50] But the first years of the China War had revealed an increase in the combat capabilities of fighter aircraft, as well as the importance of massing attack aircraft, both for bombing impact and for defense against fighters. These years also saw the modification of the navy's dispersal doctrine for carrier operations. As we have seen, small formations of attack aircraft were unable to do much damage to their targets and were

vulnerable to Chinese fighters if unescorted. These conditions had soon led the navy
to recognize that bombers were effective only if they were massed and protected by
substantial fighter cover. Extending these realities to air war at sea slowly but
inevitably led to the conclusion that carrier forces should be concentrated.[51]

The impetus for a shift to a doctrine of carrier concentration came from another
quarter as well. In 1937, at the urging of Capt. Ōnishi Takijirō, the air power
enthusiast, the navy had established an "Air Power Research Committee" (Kūchū
Heiryoku Iryoku Kenkyūkai, or Kūi-ken for short)—a small study group ostensibly formed to assist in the development of operational and armaments planning,
but in reality set up by the navy's mainstream to keep the heterodox views of Ōnishi
and the like-minded within carefully monitored channels. While the Kūi-ken never
led a charge on the navy's battleship orthodoxy, it gathered data on the effects of
various kinds of ordnance under differing operational conditions, data that would
be useful in pondering the effectiveness of an attack by massed carrier aircraft, as
indeed it was so used in planning the Hawai'i operation.[52]

Actual training and practice also illuminated the problem. The 1939–40 fleet
exercises centered on the effectiveness of coordinated air attacks by massed formations of dive bombers, torpedo bombers, and protecting fighters. In doing so, they
highlighted even more clearly the problems of coordinating such attacks from
dispersed carriers. Radioed instructions to dispersed carriers, for example, would
sacrifice surprise, and preliminary concentration of air groups from widely dispersed carriers would needlessly consume precious aviation fuel.[53]

The solution to this dilemma, it has been claimed, came suddenly in 1940 to
Genda Minoru, then serving as assistant naval attaché in London. As he later told
it, he was sitting in a London movie theater and watching a newsreel that showed
a concentration of American carriers steaming together in a box formation. It
immediately occurred to him that not only could carriers operate together in a single formation in order to mass air groups for offensive operations, but the risk of
discovery and subsequent attack on such a formation would be more than offset by
the ability of the concentrated carriers to launch a larger combat air patrol.[54] It also
meant that massed carriers should be able to throw up a greater concentration of
antiaircraft fire than could be achieved by any single carrier, though this left open
the doctrinal question of fleet air defense, specifically the question of whether or not
carriers would maneuver together and screening escorts would remain close to the
carriers (see below).

As it turned out, in the year before the outbreak of the Pacific War the navy
opted for a compromise between concentration and dispersal. In its plans for action
against an enemy fleet, specifically in a carrier-versus-carrier engagement, the two
carriers of each carrier division were concentrated, but the divisions themselves
were to be widely dispersed, forming an enormous vee with the open side toward
the enemy in order to make his encirclement possible.[55] In fact, there was no opportunity to practice this formation, and it was never used during the war. What *was*
practiced and employed early in the war was the box formation, in which Japan's

Photo. 6-1. Comdr. Genda Minoru (1904–89)

six fleet carriers were dispersed in a rectangular formation, 7,000 meters (23,000 feet) separating one from the next. (Fig. 6-5.)[56]

Yet Genda Minoru's doctrinal discovery, if such it was,[57] induced the Combined Fleet to undertake a number of operational experiments in the concentration of carriers. Early in 1941 the *Kaga, Sōryū,* and *Hiryū* combined to form a temporary training unit to perfect such operations. While these trials had some success, the absence of an overall carrier commander and the lack of a standardized training program for the fleet's carrier divisions pointed up the need for a permanent carrier command.[58] Up to that point, the navy's carriers, as they were placed in commission, had been assigned to carrier divisions—generally two or three carriers to a division—and these divisions allotted to different fleets. Not only did both fleets and carrier divisions change from time to time, but there was little effort to work

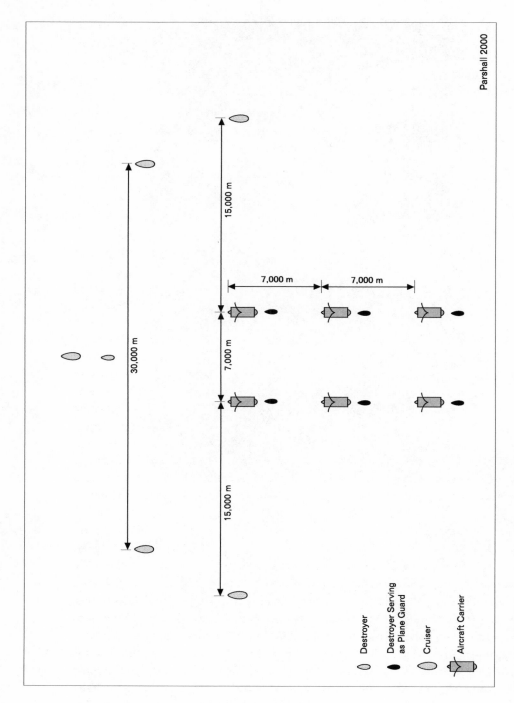

30,000 m

15,000 m

15,000 m

7,000 m

7,000 m

7,000 m

Parshall 2000

Destroyer

Destroyer Serving
as Plane Guard

Cruiser

Aircraft Carrier

Fig. 6-5. The Japanese "box formation" for carriers, 1941
Source: Genda, *Shinjuwan sakusen,* 63.

them together. Generally, fleet commanders—most of them in the battleship tradition—and even carrier division commanders were content with this arrangement,
one that left carriers to function as important, but strictly adjunct, components of
the battle line.

But the commander of the First Carrier Division, Rear Adm. Ozawa Jisaburō,[†]
saw in the potential of the navy's scattered carriers a revolutionary means to achieve
formidable offensive power. While not himself an aviator, Ozawa was well
instructed in naval aviation matters, including carrier operations, by his subordinates, particularly Lt. Comdr. Fuchida Mitsuo.[†] Fuchida, the air group commander
on the *Akagi,* continually preached to him the importance of carrier concentration
and urged that the First and Second carrier divisions should train and operate
together. Thus, Ozawa himself came to see the need not only to reorganize the carrier divisions but to harness all the navy's air power under a single command. To
that end, Ozawa had twice urged Yamamoto, now commander of the Combined
Fleet, to authorize the formation of an "air fleet" within the Combined Fleet, so
that all its air units—both carrier- and land-based—would come under a unified
command, in order to train and fight together. Yamamoto, while undoubtedly recognizing the profound strategic implications of such a tactical concentration, twice
deflected Ozawa's recommendation, realizing, one supposes, that time would be
needed to overcome traditionalists within the Combined Fleet itself. In June 1940,
however, Ozawa took the risk of forcing Yamamoto's hand by writing directly to
the navy minister, outlining his ideas for an air fleet. Conscious of Japan's accelerating drift toward war, Ozawa warned that such a force had to be organized while
the nation was still at peace. Standardized training at all levels and practice in coordinating the movements of large carriers would have to be mastered in peacetime if
the new force was to be effective in war. Yamamoto was understandably nettled by
Ozawa's going over his head with the air fleet concept, one that provoked heated
discussion at the highest navy levels. But in December 1940 he authorized its imple-
mentation, thus ending the remaining opposition within the navy.[59]

The new organizational system retained carrier divisions but abolished combined air groups in favor of air flotillas, which were to be the land-based equivalent
of carrier divisions (and in fact they had the same designation, *kōkū sentai,* in
Japanese).[60] The air fleet system itself started with the organization of the Eleventh
Air Fleet, which was activated in January 1941 and consisted of three air flotillas,
comprising eight land-based air groups. In the coming conflict this force was to
spearhead the navy's thrust into Southeast Asia in the winter of 1941–42. But the
real concentration of naval air power came in April 1941 with the creation of the
First Air Fleet, headed by Vice Adm. Nagumo Chūichi[†] and composed of the First,
Second, and Third carrier divisions, plus two seaplane carrier divisions and ten
destroyers. (Later, that September, with the commissioning of the two new carriers
Shōkaku and *Zuikaku,* the Fifth Carrier Division was added, and the Third, comprising the small carriers *Hōshō* and *Ryūjō,* was detached from the First Air Fleet
to provide cover for the main battleship force.)[61]

At the time it was formed, the First Air Fleet was the single most powerful agglomeration of naval air power in the world, specifically including the U.S. Pacific Fleet, comprising as it did all seven of Japan's fleet carriers in commission and 464 aircraft: 137 fighters, 144 dive bombers, and 183 torpedo planes (figures that include reserve aircraft). One must understand, of course, that activation of the First Air Fleet was not a total break with the traditional mission or force structure of the Japanese navy. If one looks at both its organization and its command structure, it is clear that it was still a fleet created to participate in a decisive engagement whose main contestants would be opposing battleships—a scheme in which the Japanese navy persisted through 1943—and that it was not an independent tactical formation capable of undertaking a naval operation on its own. Indeed, it was to form only one component, though the single most important one, of the mobile task force *(kidō butai)* that Yamamoto sent across the Pacific for the Pearl Harbor strike. Nevertheless, I have to agree with Gordon Prange's assessment that the First Air Fleet, in its massing of carriers, was revolutionary in strategic concept. I also agree that while it does not appear to have been created with the Hawai'ian operation specifically in mind, it is hard to see how that operation could have been conceived, let alone executed, without its existence.[62]

In important ways, the formation of the First Air Fleet, and the tactical arrangements derived from it, turned out to be paradoxical. The First Air Fleet was essentially a carrier force that had been formed to deliver a preemptive strike against enemy carriers. Yet for the first five months of the Pacific War the Japanese carrier fleet was unchallenged by a significant Allied carrier force, and thus it was largely directed against objectives on shore: Pearl Harbor, Port Darwin, Trincomalee, Colombo, and the installations at Midway.[63]

In considering the evolution of Japanese carrier doctrine in its final prewar form, it must be understood that as late as Midway, the Japanese navy still did not regard the carrier as the prime combat element of the fleet. Indeed, the main force at Midway was taken to be the battleship division built around Admiral Yamamoto's monster flagship, the *Yamato*. It would not be until March 1944 that the Japanese navy would create the First Mobile Fleet, an approximation of the American carrier task force, to which other accompanying fleet units, including battleships, were subordinate. But like the First Air Fleet, it was designed as a quick strike force and had no mobile supply train for continuing offensive operations. In any event, by that time the Japanese navy lacked sufficient carrier strength and sufficient numbers of trained aircrew to match the true carrier task forces that were ranged against them.

Before leaving this discussion of the Japanese navy's concern with concentrated carrier air power, it is important to touch briefly upon the larger offensive purposes to which such a concentration would be directed and upon the tactical problems it raised. In attacks against land-based air power, Japanese carrier doctrine held that a carrier's mobility made the chance of a successful surprise attack considerable. But while carriers might be able to launch a burst of air power, their vulnerability made it particularly important to keep their intentions concealed. For that reason it was planned that upon entering a zone within reach of enemy patrols, a carrier formation should approach the target at a minimum of 25 knots, launch its strike at dawn and at a distance of 200–250 miles from the target, and then, in a majority of cases, retire at high speed. Should there be no danger from a counterstrike, a second strike could be ordered up.[64]

The problems posed by mounting a preemptive attack on an enemy carrier force were obviously greater, given the mobility of naval units, the vulnerability of aircraft carriers—one's own and the enemy's—and the need to knock out the enemy's air power before he could launch his own attack. As early as 1939, various Combined Fleet maneuvers had demonstrated that success in preemptive attack was usually a matter of only a few minutes' advantage. In this, much depended not only upon the time required for carriers to launch their attack squadrons but, even before that, upon finding the enemy first.[65]

AIR RECONNAISSANCE REVISITED

The problem of a preemptive strike brings us once again to the issue of reconnaissance, an activity about which there is sharp disagreement in postwar commentary on the navy's conduct of the Pacific War. On the one hand, after the war Genda Minoru claimed that it was a defect so pronounced in the offensive capabilities of the Japanese naval air arm that it was "the vital cause of our defeat in the Pacific War."[66] Yet David Dickson, a student of the Battle of the Philippine Sea, June 1944, has argued that after Midway, "reconnaissance was the only area of carrier operations in which the Japanese remained superior to their American counterparts right up to the end of the war."[67]

Genda surely exaggerated both the deficiencies of the navy's air reconnaissance capabilities and their consequences. Yet there were severe limitations on those capabilities at the outset of the Pacific War, several of which were pointed out in chapter 2: an unwillingness to sacrifice offensive aircraft in order to embark reconnaissance aircraft on board carriers; an overdependence in blue-ocean operations on shipborne floatplanes that were not always reliable; and the weak training of reconnaissance aircrews.

The official history of Japanese naval aviation has identified other problems in Japanese naval air searches.[68] Among these was the paucity of reconnaissance aircraft types that were fit for operations at sea—that is, capable of water landings—and that at the same time were sufficiently armed to ward off enemy fighter aircraft. That work cites as well the fact that aircrews in patrol aircraft were often worked to the limit of their endurance, increasing the probability that after two or three days of patrol duty, they would miss an enemy through fatigue and inattention.

In this view, the effectiveness of personnel assigned to reconnaissance also continued to be a problem. Great reliance was placed on the tactical judgment of such aircrews, but since the Japanese navy was obsessed with offensive operations, they ere insufficiently trained to make sound decisions regarding aerial searches. This as particularly true of personnel who manned torpedo planes that doubled as :connaissance aircraft. Their lack of concern with the reconnaissance mission was equaled by their lack of skill in navigation and communications.

Indeed, communications remained a vexing problem. As we have seen, the radio systems with which Japanese attack and reconnaissance aircraft were equipped before the Pacific War were generally radio telegraphs, rather than radio telephones. Among aircrews there emerged a considerable spread in radio telegraph transmission skills, depending upon the type of mission for which they had been specifically trained. The skills of aircrews regularly assigned to reconnaissance aircraft were generally good (such crews could transmit approximately seventy to seventy-five Japanese phonetic symbols per minute, on average); those aircrews in attack planes assigned to reconnaissance missions on an ad hoc basis were generally unskilled, except for those in the lead aircraft, who had been given advanced training.

Yet if Japanese naval air searches had deficiencies, one must not conclude that they were ineffective. To begin with, reconnaissance was certainly not neglected in the prewar Japanese naval air service. The navy had carefully worked out a reconnaissance doctrine that, on the face of it, was fairly sound. Just before the war the standard search method was a single-phase radial pattern out to 300–350 miles when the surface fleet was steaming under alert but not expecting an attack. The more demanding parallel-search pattern was a common variation. The ideal altitude for spotting the enemy on the horizon was judged to be 300–400 meters (1,000–1,300 feet) above the ocean's surface, which limited vision to 30–35 miles. For maximum results, however, the standard altitude maintained was between 1,500 and 3,000 meters (5,000 and 10,000 feet).[69]

There is, as well, the mixed record of Japanese naval air reconnaissance in the Pacific War. Early in the war some outstanding successes were achieved by land-based reconnaissance units and flying boats, especially in relation to the Japanese invasions of Malaya and the Philippines. But the Japanese navy was to pay a terrible price for the neglect of rigorous air search procedures in the late spring of 1942. Certainly the mistaking of the U.S. oiler *Neosho* for a carrier during the battle of the Coral Sea was a costly error. But the allegedly spectacular reconnaissance lapse at Midway, often cited as one of the major elements in the Japanese disaster in that battle, has been strikingly reevaluated of late and the causes of the debacle located elsewhere.[70] For his part, Eric Bergerud believes that a far more energetic reconnaissance effort by Japanese floatplanes and seaplane tenders stationed in the Solomons in the summer of 1942 might have alerted the navy to the U.S. movement toward those islands. As it was, the Japanese were taken completely by surprise when the American invasion fleet arrived off Guadalcanal and Tulagi on 7 August.[71]

Yet one cannot think of a major Japanese naval air search failure for the rest of the war. In his grand account of the Battle of the Philippine Sea, Samuel Eliot

Morison wrote that air search by both land- and carrier-based patrol craft was the one technique in which the Americans fell far short of perfection, but he specifically cited Admiral Ozawa's air reconnaissance as one of the two redeeming features of the otherwise disastrous operation.[72]

FLEET AIR DEFENSE

The problem of a preemptive strike by carrier air power on an enemy carrier force also raised questions of fleet air defense. In considering such a strike, Japanese tacticians had to assume that the two strikes—one's own and the enemy's—would be launched about the same time. This being the case, considerable study on the eve of the Pacific War was devoted to two questions: first, how to preserve part of the strike force to finish off the enemy after reciprocal aerial attacks had caused reciprocal losses, and second, how to increase the defensive capabilities of one's own carrier force to deal not only with the enemy's first strike but also with his second.[73] Because the Japanese navy was still wrestling with these questions as it plunged into war, it is important to comment briefly on the navy's doctrine and capabilities in fleet air defense.

Although important consideration was ultimately given by the staff of the Combined Fleet to the problem of fleet air defense, too many years had been wasted in ignoring the problem to work out an effective air defense in the short time remaining before hostilities began.[74] There were a number of reasons for this neglect. First among these was the practical difficulty involved in the detection of the approach of enemy fighters and in the organization of effective fighter direction in the years before the advent of radar. Among the navy's air tacticians, these problems led to a consensus, based on the working out of the Fleet Problems of the 1930s, that it would be impossible to defeat completely an air strike launched against one's own fleet. In addition, the importance of an effective fleet air defense was given little serious study in the 1920s and 1930s because the navy's traditional obsession with offensive operations blinded it to all other considerations.

The inadequate provision for the air defense of its carrier task forces was an example of the Japanese navy's failure to think through the issues of fleet air defense as a whole. At the outset of the Pacific War, the effective air defense of any carrier task force, Japanese or American, involved five critical elements: early identification of the attacking aircraft (their direction, altitude, speed, and strength); the proper vectoring of the force's combat air patrol of fighter planes; effective antiaircraft defense to knock down whatever planes managed to slip past the patrol; evasive but coordinated movements by the carriers and their escorting warships to escape bombs and torpedoes yet keep their antiaircraft fire coordinated; and effective damage control to minimize bomb damage. Taken as a whole, it must be said that the Japanese navy's tactics, technology, and organization were deficient in all five areas in varying degrees.

To begin with, any Japanese carrier group began the war with a critical technological disadvantage in confronting a similar American force. Whereas the United States Navy had begun installing service models of air search radar on ships in the summer of 1940, the Japanese navy only began testing shipborne radar before the Battle of Midway.[75] Without this electronic means of early warning, a carrier task force had to depend upon distant surface units acting as pickets and on float-planes orbiting at 20–40 miles. Yet there were usually too few of these to cover each direction from which an air strike could be made, and during the Pacific War, by luck or clever exploitation of cloud cover, American aircraft were sometimes able to approach a Japanese carrier formation within a few miles before being detected. This being the case, a Japanese carrier group would be obliged to depend on its next line of defense, the combat air patrol put up by the carriers themselves.

On the eve of the Pacific War, a Japanese fleet carrier usually embarked about eighteen Zero fighters. These were divided into two groups: nine fighters to provide escort to the outgoing carrier attack aircraft, and nine to stay above the Japanese carrier and thus contribute to the combat air patrol. But this number of patrolling fighters was far too small to provide for an adequate defense in all directions. Without radar, moreover, those directing the carrier group's air defense in combat were obliged to work out a system of standing patrols with only a few planes in the air at a time: one three-plane *shōtai* aloft per carrier; another spotted for launch; and a third in a lesser state of readiness. Standard duration of a patrol was about two hours. If during that time an enemy flight was detected approaching the carrier group, the remaining six aircraft could be scrambled to join the CAP. Each individual fighter pilot was responsible for a sector of air space adjacent to his carrier, and theoretically other aircraft in the patrol could be vectored to any threatened sector.[76]

But there were serious drawbacks to these arrangements. First, the poor quality of the navy's voice radio made it almost impossible to control CAP aircraft already aloft. Second, on the eve of the Pacific War, Japanese navy carriers carried no radar and thus were dependent on visual sightings of their combat air patrol and on whatever radio intercepts of any air activities they might happen to catch. Third, there were serious organizational problems in Japanese fleet air defense. Chief among these was the fact that responsibility for this activity was invariably divided among a number of officers aboard one of the carriers. The position of air defense officer was not permanent; rather, it was assigned on an ad hoc basis to any one of a number of carrier pilots who were otherwise unoccupied. Moreover, relay of urgent intelligence to those acting as air defense officers was often delayed because standing instructions required that such intelligence be passed through air group commanders.[77] As a result of these deficiencies in fighter control, the navy was unable to use its limited CAP assets to maximum effect. More important, as the Pacific War opened, these weaknesses meant that the navy was poorly positioned to take the next step in fleet air defense: the installation of a central coordinating system like the American combat information center that would integrate information coming into a carrier from all sources—radio, radar, and visual sightings—and thus serve as a central point for the coordination of the combat air patrol.

One must also add that the Zero fighters themselves posed certain problems for a heavily engaged combat air patrol. While they were formidably armed with their powerful 20-millimeter cannon, the number of 20-millimeter shells they carried— sixty rounds per gun until later in the war—was too small for the kind of extended combat in which they sometimes found themselves. For that reason, too often they were forced to break off in the midst of air combat to return to their carriers for ammunition.

Japanese antiaircraft defenses also left a great deal to be desired.[78] At the outbreak of World War II, this was true of all the world's navies, of course. But the Japanese navy possessed antiaircraft ordnance that made it particularly difficult to adapt to the quickly emerging threat of aerial attack. The standard Japanese heavy antiaircraft weapon, the 5-inch (12.7-centimeter) Type 89 AA gun, was introduced in 1941 and was serviceable enough. But the fire-control system associated with the weapon, the Type 94 *kōsha sochi,* was inadequate in a number of respects, including its overreliance on manual inputs and control and thus its inability to track fast-moving targets and to develop a solution quickly. Most important, the navy never developed any antiaircraft ordnance equipped with a proximity fuze (see next chapter), which proved to be devastating to Japanese air attacks in the latter stages of the Pacific War. Both in numbers and in effectiveness, therefore, the Japanese navy's antiaircraft defenses were overwhelmed by Allied air attacks during the latter stages of the Pacific War.[79]

The navy was even more deficient in light antiaircraft ordnance. The standard light AA weapon, the .60-caliber 25-millimeter Type 96 gun, had been developed from a French Hotchkiss design. While it possessed satisfactory ballistic properties, it was badly hampered by slow training and elevation speeds in its double- and triple-barreled mountings. Worse, it was hampered by a loading arrangement that required constant changing of magazines, dropping its maximum rate of fire from a theoretical 220 rounds per minute to an actual rate of approximately half that. It was, in sum, an unfortunate design that lacked the high sustained rate of fire of a good light AA weapon, such as the Swiss 20-millimeter Oerlikon or the great range and hitting power of the heavier 40-millimeter Bofors gun, both of which were used by the Allies in great numbers. Unable to upgrade its AA weaponry and pitted against rugged American aircraft, the Japanese navy was forced to conduct its antiaircraft defenses with weapons that were increasingly shown to be ineffective.

Japanese naval doctrine was particularly deficient in creating an effective role for surface units in fleet defense against air attack. Japanese antiaircraft doctrine called for zones of responsibility for antiaircraft batteries, and when no friendly fighters were available for air defense, antiaircraft fire was to be opened at maximum effective range, barrage fire being used against dive bombers and strafing aircraft. It must be noted that Japanese doctrine apparently devoted too little attention to the role of screening units in fleet air defense. When an air attack was anticipated, doctrine called for the adoption of a circular formation around the carriers, but with the carriers free to carry out independent maneuvers and escorting ships free to carry out evasive maneuvers that would allow them, somehow, to follow the carriers.[80] During the Pacific War, U.S. Navy pilots were to report that rather than taking station on the carriers and making the carriers' defense the purpose of their existence, Japanese escorts tended to maneuver independently and become so spread apart from their charges that their antiaircraft defense was ineffective in protecting the carriers.[81] As for the carriers themselves, their maneuvers consisted primarily of putting on hard port or starboard rudder and maintaining a maximum-rate turn, which was sometimes effective against dive bombers, much less so against torpedo aircraft.[82] In combat, the navy learned to its loss that such radical maneuvering inevitably pried apart Japanese formations and degraded the performance of fire-control systems over the course of an enemy air attack. Nowhere was this more disastrously illustrated than in the Battle of Midway, where the escorts for Nagumo's carrier strike force contributed little to the defense of the fleet's most precious assets.

Finally, there was the fact that Japanese carriers were ill prepared to survive the damage inflicted upon them. Chapter 3 dealt with the design flaws of Japanese carriers in this regard. But one cannot discuss the issue of the vulnerability of Japanese carriers to fire and explosion without touching upon the absence of an adequate system of damage control throughout the Japanese navy as a whole. During the Pacific War that defect directly contributed to the loss of a number of Japanese carriers, not only those at Midway but more inexcusably, in 1944, the heavily armored *Taihō*, struck by a single submarine torpedo that inflicted initially minimal damage.[83] The torpedo explosion jammed the ship's forward elevator and ruptured some fuel oil and aviation gas lines and tanks, but at first there was no significant loss of speed or impairment of the carrier's overall fighting ability. There followed, however, several fatal mistakes by the ship's damage-control parties. The first was a decision to open the ship's ventilator ducts to dissipate the gasoline fumes, a decision that merely served to spread them throughout the ship. Then efforts to pump the aviation gas from the ruptured tanks over the side resulted in large spillage of gasoline within the ship. Not surprisingly, a single spark set off a frightful explosion that blew out the sides of the enclosed hangar, demolished the flight deck, and holed the hull in several places, causing the foundering of the carrier.

Part of the problem of faulty damage control on Japanese carriers had to do with training. Unlike its American counterpart, the Japanese navy had slight training in this task and almost no training in emergency flight-deck repairs, though the Japanese were able to obtain a copy of the American navy's damage-control manual early in the 1930s.[84] Then again, the Japanese navy failed to provide clear overall responsibility for damage control aboard its warships, in contrast to the American navy, where the assistant engineering officer was responsible for damage control for the entire ship. Until 1944 there were two damage-control officers on larger Japanese ships. The chief engineering officer was responsible for all damage control in engineering spaces. Topside, all other damage-control efforts were directed by the deck officer, whose damage-control teams were not highly trained because they were composed of men usually assigned other duties. Moreover, the relative status and rank of the damage-control officers worked against smooth cooperation with other officers of the ship. The deck officer was sometimes a mere lieutenant, whereas the engineering officer was usually a commander, an arrangement that made it difficult for the former to demand actions (such as the generation of power) from the latter, a superior officer. Finally, the physical arrangements in Japanese ships often worked against effective damage control. There was usually only a single fire-extinguishing system, so that if the main pump was damaged, as happened on the *Akagi* at Midway, there was no more water supply for the entire ship. Nor was there any provision, as there was on U.S. carriers, for flushing aviation gas lines with carbon dioxide in case of emergency. Moreover, Japanese warships had fewer watertight compartments than did American vessels, and watertight integrity was a problem in many ways.[85]

In sum, the overall impression one gains from an examination of the air defenses of the navy's carrier forces is one of salient vulnerability. By failing to address fleet air defense in aggregate, the Japanese navy created a situation in which multiple deficiencies interacted to aggravate the worst attributes of its ships, aircraft, weapons, and doctrine. The consequence was the creation of a force that was splendid in projecting power at great distance but significantly inferior to its American counterpart in warding off an enemy counterstrike. In effect, a Japanese carrier force had a "glass jaw": it could throw a punch but couldn't take one. This meant that the Japanese navy entered the Pacific War with a powerful combat formation—the carrier strike force—but one that could be shattered in brief span of time.

INOUE SHIGEYOSHI AND THE CALL FOR AN AIR POWER NAVY

I asserted earlier that for all its striking power, the First Air Fleet was still not regarded by the Japanese naval leadership as the main element of the Combined Fleet, a position reserved in Japanese naval orthodoxy for "big ships and big guns." The completion of the super-battleship *Yamato* on the eve of the Pacific War, the launching of her sister ship *Musashi* almost a year before, and plans for the construction of still more and bigger super-battleships confirmed this line of thought in the Navy General Staff.

There were those in the navy high command who had spoken against this mindset, but none more forcefully than Vice Adm. Inoue Shigeyoshi,[†] chief of the Naval Aviation Department from October 1940 to August 1941. In January 1941, attacking what he considered to be the outmoded and unimaginative assumptions underlying the staff's plans for the continued construction of super-battleships, Admiral Inoue argued that such schemes constituted a blind, unthinking response to American building plans rather than a rational preparation for the kind of war Japan would have to wage.

David Evans and I have outlined Inoue's range of arguments for a revised Japanese strategy in our coauthored study of the Japanese navy.[86] The following

Photo. 6-2. Adm. Inoue Shigeyoshi (1899–1975)

remarks are confined to Inoue's observations on the importance of air power. Central to his thinking was his belief—obvious to everyone today, but not to all naval establishments in his time—that with the advent of aircraft and submarines, command of the sea involved three dimensions, not just two. More than this, he argued, surface control of the oceans was dependent upon domination of the vertical dimension, particularly upon control of the air. For this reason, rapid dominance over the western Pacific in the event of war with the United States must first be obtained by aircraft, *then* by surface warships. For a navy man, this was doctrinal heterodoxy indeed, but Inoue went even further. He insisted that even the context of command of the air had changed in recent years: whereas the aircraft carrier had until recently been considered a prime element in naval air power, with their rapid development, land-based bombers and flying boats had become the navy's most potent air weapons. Thus, in Inoue's view, control of the air could be seized by aircraft alone without the involvement of any surface units, specifically including carriers.

In short, Inoue was calling for control of the air by an air force independent of naval ships. This was air power doctrine in its purest form, akin to the arguments of "Billy" Mitchell and Alexander de Seversky but delivered by a naval officer. With hindsight one can see that some of Inoue's radical assumptions about the course of technology were simplistic and mistaken, particularly his dismissal of the carrier as obsolescent and his advocacy of the land-based bomber as omnipotent. Yet one wonders how the course of the Pacific War might have been different if the Japanese navy—or the army, for that matter—had had at its command substantial numbers of strategic bombers of the range, bomb load, speed, and armor of the American B-29 or even of the B-17.

JAPANESE NAVAL AIR POWER ON THE EVE OF THE PACIFIC WAR

While the Japanese navy did not, at the outset of the Pacific War, have at hand the strategic air force that Admiral Inoue would have wished, by the late autumn of 1941 the Japanese naval air arm constituted the most potent offensive force of any of the three major navies. By the first week in December 1941, this naval air power was deployed in deadly array. (Fig. 6-6.) There were over three thousand aircraft (operational and reserve) in the navy. Of these, about eighteen hundred were combat planes that were among the world's finest and could, with important exceptions, fly faster and farther than and generally outperform their American counterparts. The crews manning these aircraft were resolute, intelligent, highly motivated, rigorously trained, and, to a substantial degree, blooded in war. The navy's thirty-seven land-based air groups were distributed at bases deployed from the Kuriles to French Indochina to the Marshall Islands. (Map 6-1.) On paper, the Japanese carrier forces were superior to either the U.S. or the British: ten Japanese carriers (counting the Hōshō) to the American six (the Hornet was working up but not yet operational). Certainly, they were better organized for working together.

The navy's greatest single concentration of air power—over 350 dive bombers, attack bombers, and Zero fighters—was embarked on the six carriers of the Hawai'i Strike Force, steaming toward the waters northwest of Oahu. From there it would launch the thunderbolt that would change the course of naval history. In Southeast Asia, because the operation against the U.S. Pacific Fleet at Pearl Harbor used all of Japan's largest carriers, the navy was obliged to rely on land-based air power and three small carriers to spearhead its projected offensives. To these were added the 526 aircraft of the Twenty-first and Twenty-third air flotillas of the Eleventh Air Fleet, operating from several bases on Taiwan and poised to eliminate American air power in the Philippines before the army's invasion of the islands. Their G3M and G4M bombers were to attack and destroy the bomber base at

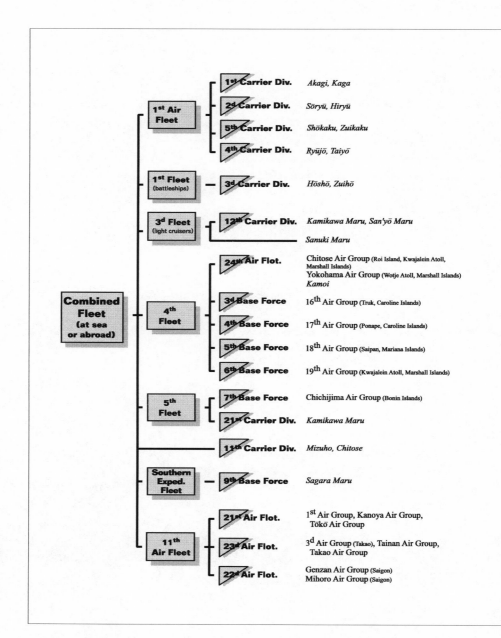

Fig. 6-6. Air organization of the Combined Fleet and air units in the home islands, 8 December 1941

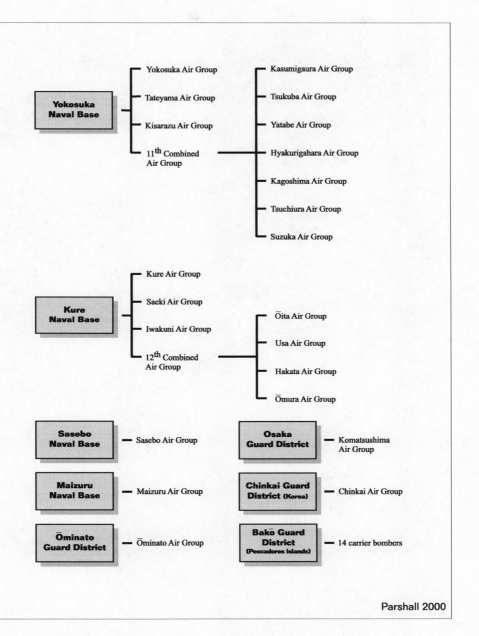

Yokosuka Naval Base
- Yokosuka Air Group
- Tateyama Air Group
- Kisarazu Air Group
- 11th Combined Air Group
  - Kasumigaura Air Group
  - Tsukuba Air Group
  - Yatabe Air Group
  - Hyakurigahara Air Group
  - Kagoshima Air Group
  - Tsuchiura Air Group
  - Suzuka Air Group

Kure Naval Base
- Kure Air Group
- Saeki Air Group
- Iwakuni Air Group
- 12th Combined Air Group
  - Ōita Air Group
  - Usa Air Group
  - Hakata Air Group
  - Ōmura Air Group

Sasebo Naval Base
- Sasebo Air Group

Maizuru Naval Base
- Maizuru Air Group

Ōminato Guard District
- Ōminato Air Group

Osaka Guard District
- Komatsushima Air Group

Chinkai Guard District (Korea)
- Chinkai Air Group

Bako Guard District (Pescadores Islands)
- 14 carrier bombers

Parshall 2000

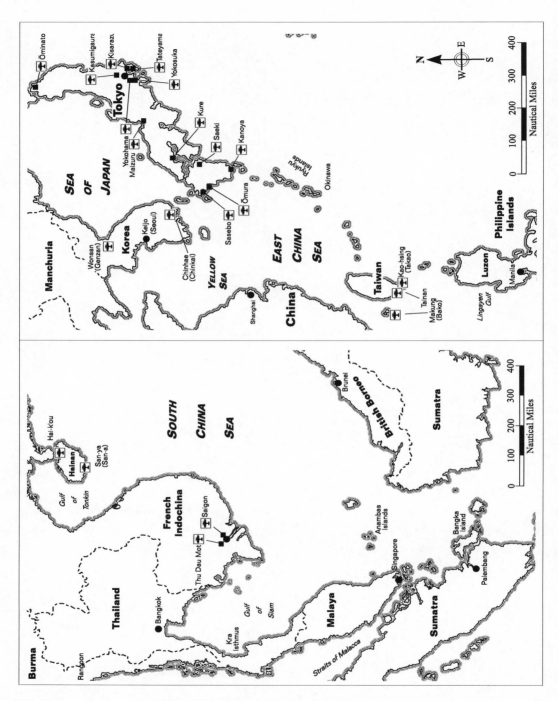

Map 6-1. Major Japanese naval air bases, December 1941

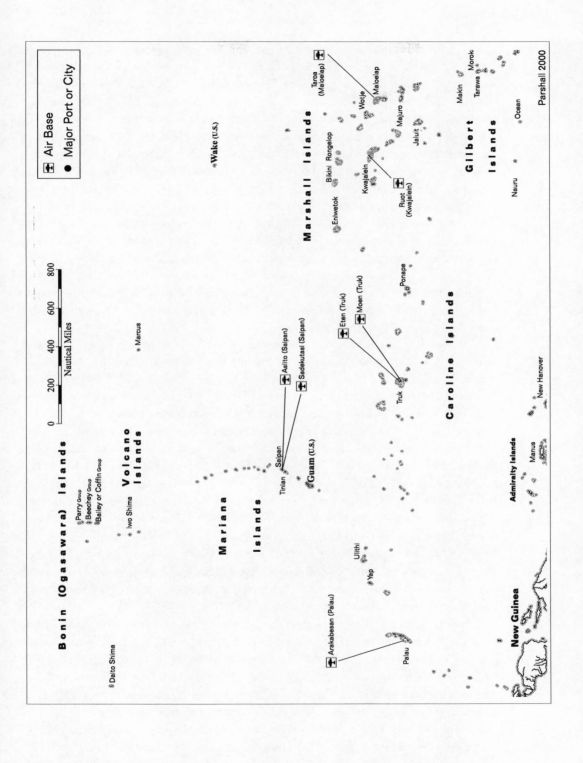

Parshall 2000

Clark Field and the small auxiliary field at Iba, on the coast west of Clark, which at the last moment was substituted for the fighter base at Nichols Field. Ninety Zero fighters, constituting most of the Zeros not embarked on the six carriers of the Hawai'i Strike Force, were to race out ahead across the China Sea to eliminate any enemy aircraft in northern Luzon and to strafe enemy ground targets there. To enable them to make this operation of unprecedented distance for fighter aircraft, the already phenomenal range of the Zero had been extended by various adjustments to engine and propeller speeds and to fuel mixtures.[87] From Palau in the western Caroline Islands, the *Ryūjō,* escorting a small convoy, pushed westward to cover the Japanese landings on Legaspi, on the tip of southeastern Luzon. Much further to the west, G3M and G4M bombers of the Twenty-second Air Flotilla of the Eleventh Air Fleet, along with a handful of Zeros, lifting off from various bases in Japanese-occupied French Indochina, began to patrol the South China Sea as flank guards to the Japanese invasion fleets heading toward Malaya. In the Japanese-held Marshall Islands far to the east, thirty-seven G3M bombers and twenty-four flying boats of the Twenty-fourth Air Flotilla stood ready to attack isolated Allied outposts in the western Pacific.

But the glittering potency of this offensive array shielded a number of weaknesses that would eventually prove disastrous in an extended conflict. Nearly all were connected in one way or another to the Japanese assumption that the coming war would be swift and decisive.[88] Most of the types of combat aircraft had certain fatal defects, largely those of inadequate defensive protection for their fuel tanks and their aircrews. This meant that in an air war of any length, the attrition rates for Japanese aircraft would be severe. In a struggle with a naval enemy backed by the wealth of industrial resources available to the United States, there were too few of them for anything but a short conflict. As late as the summer of 1941, Admiral Inoue had drawn the attention of ranking Navy Ministry and General Staff personnel to material shortages in aircraft, particularly land-based bombers and flying boats. The navy's plans called for the production of seven thousand aircraft by April 1942. Yet in the summer of 1941 the current production of aircraft for the navy of all types was only 162 planes a month. Inoue also took note of shortages in machine guns, ammunition, most types of bombs, and Type 91 aerial torpedoes, as well as inadequate stocks of aviation fuel.[89]

There was, as well, the problem of inadequate numbers of trained personnel and inadequate training organization, facilities, and equipment. In 1937 the navy had planned to have five thousand thoroughly trained aircrew in place by 1941, but the China War forced both a modification of those numbers (down to forty-one hundred) and a reduction in the duration of training cycles. Then, in the several years immediately prior to the Pacific War, the accelerated buildup in naval air organization, weapons, and equipment aggravated an already serious personnel problem. By the time of Pearl Harbor, half of the Japanese naval air service was, by its own reckoning, insufficiently trained, a situation that led to the widespread allocation of inexperienced aircrews. Because the carrier units demanded the highest level of training, they could be supplied only at the sacrifice of the quality of many of the land-based air groups. At the opening of the Pacific War, for example, the table of organization for the first-line air groups was nearly complete, but if one looks at their composition, particularly those of the Eleventh Air Fleet, it is clear that they contained a fairly high percentage of aircrews assigned before their training was finished. In part this was a consequence of the recent commissioning of the carriers *Shōkaku* and *Zuikaku,* which borrowed a number of the best air group leaders for their participation in the Hawai'i operation.[90]

Finally, in the onrush of Japanese naval air expansion, little attention was given to the unglamorous but critical problem of logistics. It was a neglect that was navy-wide, and again it stemmed from the navy's assumption that it would fight a short and victorious war. It manifested itself in an insufficient number of transport aircraft;[91] in a paucity of spare parts, from magnetos to machine guns; in an inadequately developed system of combat theater maintenance and repair; in a failure to recognize that a larger land-based air force would require more air bases, particularly in wartime, and a consequent failure to see that more bases would require adequate civilian engineering facilities and equipment to construct them.[92] Worse, by the navy's own estimates, aviation fuels and lubricants were sufficient for only a year and a half of combat operations.[93] In the opening months of the war, as the navy's aircraft swept the feeble Allied air defenses from the skies of the western Pacific and Southeast Asia, none of these shortages were to count for much. But poor logistics were to become a terrible throttlehold on Japanese naval air power once its advances were halted on the far perimeters of Japanese conquests.

Strategically, on 7/8 December 1941, the navy's aircraft were lifting off of carrier decks and from land bases for offensives of breathtaking distance and risk. In the central Pacific, the carrier strike force was approaching the Hawai'ian Islands; in the western Pacific, flocks of medium bombers lifted off the coral airstrips of the navy's bases in Micronesia to attack American Pacific outposts; on Taiwan, navy fighters and bombers streaked southward toward Luzon, even as carrier aircraft flew westward to attack Mindanao; medium bombers thundered up and over the palm-fringed air bases outside Saigon to spearhead the assault on British Malaya. In Japanese plans, these great aerial movements were aimed to achieve a vast empire of conquest in Asia and the Pacific, which, once occupied, would be held against the enemy in great part by Japanese naval air power.

7

DESCENDING
— *in* —
FLAME

Japanese Naval Air Power Destroyed

In the first six months of the Pacific War, naval air power spearheaded the offensive operations undertaken by Japan. In the early hours of 7 December 1941, the first wave of aircraft from Admiral Nagumo's strike force streaked toward the green hills of Oahu.[1] By ten o'clock that morning, as the second wave departed the skies over Pearl Harbor, the American battle line at Ford Island had been shattered, and the aircraft at Hickam, Wheeler, and Bellows airfields and those at Kaneohe Naval Air Station lay in shambles. Historians will endlessly debate the wisdom or folly of Nagumo's decision not to follow up with a third attack, given that the two American carriers based at Pearl Harbor were at sea and that the oil storage tanks and submarine force at Pearl were left virtually unscathed. Yet there is little doubt that these targets *could* have been destroyed by Nagumo's force. And, for our purposes in this study, the important issue is not the strategic decisions involved but the dramatic demonstration of naval air power with which Japan was able to open the war.

A few days later and 7,000 miles westward, Japanese naval air power delivered a stunning blow at sea by sinking the battleship *Prince of Wales* and the battle cruiser *Repulse* off the coast of Malaya in the opening days of the war. Because it followed aerial assault tactics that the navy had perfected in the years prior to hostilities and because it was the dramatic land-based counterpart to the carrier-based destruction of the American battle line at Pearl Harbor, it is worth pausing to reflect on the nature of this outstanding success by Japanese naval air units.[2]

As noted earlier, the Kanoya Air Group had become the navy's crack land-based torpedo force. Immediately upon learning of the arrival of the *Repulse* and *Prince of Wales* at Singapore, the navy had rushed the Kanoya's twenty-six G4M1 bombers to join the Genzan and Mihoro naval air groups of the Twenty-second Air Flotilla stationed near Saigon since October. The Twenty-second was already a solid outfit, its bomber crews having trained and fought together for several years, though their experience had largely been bombing land targets in China rather than ships at sea. Against the two British ships, the navy planned to use both bombs and torpedoes. Conforming to standard navy doctrine, the attack would open with a high-level bombing attack. The Japanese did not expect to sink either ship with this tactic, because the bombers carried no armor-piercing bombs of the type used to destroy the *Arizona,* all of them having been allocated to the Hawai'i operation.[3] Rather, the purpose of the bombing attack was to smash the upper works of the enemy ships and to distract the gun crews from the approaching torpedo bombers that were to deliver the *coup de grâce.*

The original plan had called for simultaneous attacks by all three air groups. But the groups were given a "search-and-attack" mission in which the elements of each group flew on independent search arcs assigned to them, and they did not all receive information concerning the position of the enemy fleet at once. For these reasons, they arrived over it at different times. Once in position, however, the air-crews conducted their attacks with skill, discipline, and determination despite the furious antiaircraft defense put up by the two warships. No special instructions had been given to the aircrews upon taking off; they simply followed the tactics in which they had trained. The horizontal bombers of each squadron came in at a height of about 1,500 meters (5,000 feet) and dropped their bombs in a close tri-angular pattern. The torpedo bombers came in at right angles to their targets, launching their torpedoes at about 900–1,800 meters (1,000–2,000 yards) from the ships and about 30 meters (100 feet) above the water. While the horizontal bombers of the Mihoro and Genzan air groups scored some hits, it was the dev-astating torpedo assaults by the Kanoya Air Group that finished off both British ships.[4] The last of the air groups to locate the British fleet, the Kanoya aircrews had arrived on the scene after six hours of continuous flying and had been within five minutes of having to return to base because of fuel limitations. But neither these conditions nor the loss of three bombers to British defensive fire in any way lessened the efficiency of the Japanese attack. The captain of the *Repulse,* who sur-vived the sinking, later attested, "The enemy attacks were without doubt magnif-icently carried out and pressed well home. The high level bombers kept tight for-mation and appeared not to jink."[5]

The sinking of the *Repulse* and *Prince of Wales* marked the first time in the his-tory of naval warfare that capital ships under way were sunk by an attack carried out exclusively by aircraft. It convinced even those in the Japanese naval high command who had scoffed that the battleships sunk a few days before at Pearl Harbor had been "sitting ducks" for aerial attack. It was argued at the time—and has been argued again in the more than half a century since—that the contest was hardly equal, since the British ships had been without air cover. But one of the Japanese torpedo squadron commanders insisted after the war that air protection would have made little difference. For one thing, he insisted, Japanese navy training for attacks on surface units had always assumed heavy fighter defense, and, for another, the obsolescent Brewster Buffaloes, the only fighters available to the British, would have been quickly destroyed.[6]

The morale and skill of these Japanese aircrews give credit to his statement. These are assets that are usually best honed by constant and rigorous training, something the three Japanese air groups, particularly the Kanoya, had in abundance. With the onset of actual combat operations, when there is often very little time for training, the precise aim and timing of air attack units begin to fall off. The *Repulse* and *Prince of Wales* went down under the bombs and torpedoes of aviators whose skills were at their peak.[7]

AT THE CUTTING EDGE OF WAR
Air Power in the Japanese Conquest of Southeast Asia

Elsewhere in Southeast Asia, salutary lessons in the destructive capacities of naval air power were also delivered by Japanese naval air units.[8] (Map 7-1.) Early on the afternoon of 8 December (7 December east of the International Date Line), after a harrowing delay caused by fog over the airfields on Taiwan, G3M and G4M bombers of the Kanoya, Takao, and First air groups, accompanied by Zero fighters of the Third and Tainan air groups, lifted off to attack American air bases in the Philippines. Completely surprising the enemy, the Japanese formations destroyed much of the American heavy bomber force at Clark Field and had shot up fighter aircraft at Iba and Del Carmen. These opening raids, employing the strafing tactics perfected in China, seriously reduced Allied air power as a significant factor in the western Pacific for the next six months of the war. To the south, on Mindanao, fighter and bomber aircraft from the *Ryūjō* attacked the naval base at Davao. One of the most spectacular Japanese operations was accomplished some weeks later when twenty-four Zero fighters of the Tainan Air Group based on Taiwan were dispatched on a mass nonstop flight of 1,200 nautical miles to occupy the airfield at Jolo Island at the southern end of the Sulu Sea, an unprecedented mission for single-seat fighters and proof of the amazing reach of the Zero.

For the next two months Japanese naval aircraft raced out in front of Japanese landings in Malaya, the Philippines, and the Netherlands East Indies, blasting Allied military and naval facilities, crippling Allied naval units, and shooting up the remnants of Allied air defenses, composed too often of planes that were inferior in both performance and numbers and flown by pilots whose combat doctrine was not equal to their courage. It was during these early months of the war that the myth

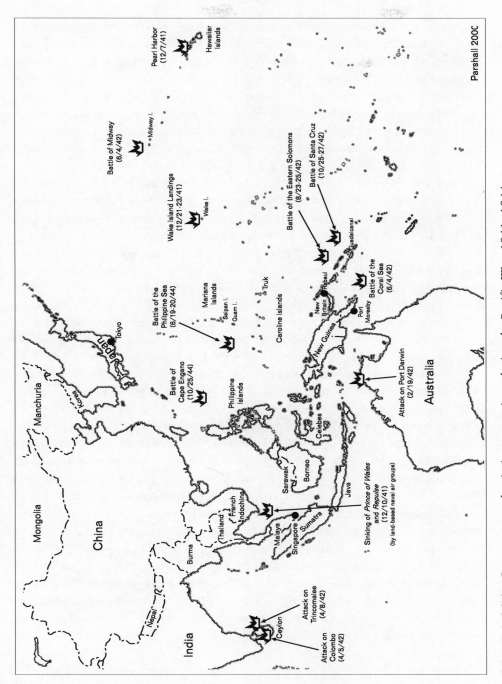

Map 7-1. Major Japanese naval aviation operations during the Pacific War, 1941–1944

Pearl Harbor
(12/7/41)
Hawaiian
Islands

Battle of Midway
(6/4/42)
Midway I.

Wake Island Landings
(12/21-23/41)
Wake I.

Battle of the Eastern Solomons
(8/23-25/42)
Battle of Santa Cruz
(10/25-27/42)
Guadalcanal

Battle of the
Philippine Sea
(6/19-20/44)
Mariana
Islands
Saipan I.
Guam I.
Truk
Caroline Islands

New
Britain
Rabaul
Battle of the
Coral Sea
(6/4/42)
Port
Moresby

Japan
Tokyo
Korea

Battle of
Cape Engano
(10/25/44)

Philippine
Islands

New Guinea

Attack on Port Darwin
(2/19/42)

Manchuria

China

Mongolia

Celebes

Sarawak
Borneo
Java

Australia

Burma

Thailand
French
Indochina

Malaya
Singapore
Sumatra

Sinking of Prince of Wales
and Repulse
(12/10/41)
(by land-based naval air groups)

India

Nepal

Ceylon

Attack on Trincomalee
(4/8/42)

Attack on
Colombo
(4/5/42)

Parshall 200C

of the near invincibility of the Zero was born in the minds of Allied pilots. Trying vainly to match the Zero turn for turn and finding themselves in the aerial environment where the A6M performed best—relatively low-speed low-altitude dogfighting—they found themselves at the mercy of Japanese navy pilots who jinked about the tropical skies, flaunting their acrobatic skills like rapiers.[9]

This equation would change dramatically within a year, but in these first chaotic months of the war, the fighter pilots of the Japanese navy flew and fought in unchallenged triumph in advance of the near-unchecked progress of their nation's ships and men. By February 1942, Malaya was gone, Singapore on the verge of surrender, and Java the only major Allied foothold left in the East Indies. Then it too fell to the Japanese in early March. The Japanese carrier force then launched a series of offensive operations that were unrivaled in their speed, force, and technical excellence until the American fast carrier operations of 1944–45. On 19 February, Admiral Nagumo's four carriers slipped through the Banda Sea, and joining forces with land-based bombers that had advanced to Kendari in the southern Celebes, their aircraft struck at Darwin on the Australian north coast. At that port, their destruction of ships, aircraft, airfields, and valuable stores damaged a vital link in the lifeline between Australia and the dwindling Allied position in Southeast Asia.

From the East Indies, Nagumo's force, now five carriers, bolstered by a number of battleships and cruisers, burst into the Indian Ocean in April 1942 with the twin objectives of sinking the British Eastern Fleet and annihilating British air forces on the western shores of the Bay of Bengal. While Nagumo failed to achieve either objective, aerial assaults in April against British naval units, naval bases, and shipping achieved major success. Under relentless attack by Nagumo's carrier attack aircraft, principally Aichi D3A1 dive bombers, the Royal Navy lost one carrier, two heavy cruisers, and two destroyers. A separate sortie by a force centered around the carrier *Ryūjō* sank various transports and merchant vessels in the Bay of Bengal. The total cost of these operations to the Japanese was seventeen aircraft.

Through the early spring of 1942, therefore, Japanese naval air power, like a sword of finely tempered steel, had slashed away everything that stood in its way. In the Pacific and Southeast Asia, Japanese land- and carrier-based air groups, equipped with superior aircraft, manned by experienced, highly trained, and motivated aircrews, and directed by a well-coordinated strategy, had surprised, outfought, and outflown the ragtag collection of Allied air units, which had been inferior in everything but bravery. An American intelligence report midway through the war had this to say about Japanese naval aircrews in early 1942:

> They were seasoned and experienced products of a thorough training program extending over several years. They were a distinct credit to the Navy's long preparation for the Pacific War. Aggressive and resourceful, they knew the capabilities and advantages of their own aircraft and they flew them with skill and daring. They were quick to change their methods to meet new situations and to counter successfully the changes, modifications, and designs

Photo. 7-1. The aircraft carrier *Akagi* off Kendari, the Celebes, 26 March 1942, followed by the carriers *Sōryū* and *Hiryū*, four battleships, and the carriers *Shōkaku* and *Zuikaku*

Source: Fukui, *Shashin Nihon kaigun zen kantei shi*, 1:331.

of Allied aircraft. They were alert and quick to take advantage of any evident weaknesses. Disabled aircraft, jammed or disabled guns and stragglers were sure to receive their concentrated fire.[10]

Japanese naval air forces suffered only slightly in these engagements, but it is a telling commentary on Japanese training policies and the consequently limited number of aircrews that even these light losses had already begun to impair the combat-effectiveness of certain Japanese naval air groups.[11]

THE BATTLES OF CORAL SEA AND MIDWAY, MAY–JUNE 1942

Then, in May, in the Coral Sea, Japanese naval air forces met their match. The opposing strategies and operations that led to the Japanese reverse do not concern us here and, in any case, have been covered in other studies. But what is clear is that by the time of the Battle of the Coral Sea, American carrier pilots had begun to learn how to deal with the combat methods of their enemy. While Japanese aerial assault tactics against warships continued to prove their worth, as demonstrated by the destruction of the carrier *Lexington,* American carrier fighter pilots took the measure of the Zero and learned how to fight it on their own terms—diving hit-and-run attacks from a superior altitude rather than the tail-chasing dogfights that were a Japanese specialty. The result was that the Japanese lost about sixty-nine planes and ninety pilots and other aircrews in addition to the light carrier *Shōhō.* The casualties among aviators from the fleet carrier *Zuikaku* were such that the ship was left with insufficient aircrews to participate in the subsequent epochal conflict at Midway a month later, since replacements took months to train.[12]

At Midway, of course, the scale of combat, the stakes, and the consequences were far greater.[13] While there were multiple causes of the Japanese defeat, Japanese failures in intelligence and aerial reconnaissance prior to the engagement were critical. In the techniques of aerial combat, the United States Navy's fighter pilots now fought their Japanese counterparts on a basis of equality, and sometimes superiority. Using new tactics, such as the Thach Weave, which exploited the weaknesses of the Zero, they began to hold their own against that vaunted aircraft.[14]

Again, I pass over the details and strategic context of battle to focus on the operational, tactical, and organizational implications of Midway for Japanese naval air power. First, it must be said that the nature of the Japanese defeat in that encounter has been frequently misunderstood. In strategic terms, there is little doubt that it was a momentous reversal in the tide of Japanese conquest in the Pacific, but it was not the "Battle that Doomed Japan." In material terms, the destruction of four fleet carriers—the *Akagi, Kaga, Soryū,* and *Hiryū*—was, of course, a stunning loss, but other carrier hulls were on the slipways or being completed. One estimate is that the navy lost some 228 aircraft at Midway,[15] but at this point in the war the navy was not suffering severe shortfalls in aircraft production.

Nor is it apparent that the defeat caused catastrophic losses to trained aircrews, the most precious element in Japanese naval aviation. Some generalized accounts of the battle imply that most of the Japanese aircrews participating in the battle were killed, and the conventional wisdom is that Midway therefore spelled the end of the navy's highly trained carrier pilots. For years it was hard to dispute these conclusions, in part because surviving aircrews had been so scattered among the remaining warships after the battle that it had been impossible to make an accurate head count, and in part because the navy had taken such extreme measures to conceal the scale of its defeat from the Japanese public in the months and years following the battle.[16]

But careful sifting of the evidence in recent years has shown that in fact only about 110 Japanese fliers died at Midway (most of them from the *Hiryū*), no more than a quarter of the carrier aircrews the navy had at the start of the battle. American aircrew losses were actually greater than those of the Japanese, if Marine Corps aviators from Midway Island itself are included in the tally.[17] Surprisingly, moreover, the morale of Japanese pilots seems to have been higher than ever after the battle. They were unimpressed by the combat skills of their American adversaries, and the superiority of their own skills seemed confirmed by the fact that they had crippled an American carrier. Nor did Japanese aircrew performance fall off sharply after Midway. In interviews after the war, Japanese navy men contended that the high quality of the navy's air arm continued through at least the fall of 1942. In fact, the really serious aviation personnel losses at Midway were those of skilled aircraft maintenance crews, who accounted for perhaps twenty-six hundred of the three thousand shipboard personnel who went down with the four carriers.[18]

Four critical operational lessons were brought home to the Japanese navy after Midway. The first was the importance of a carrier fleet completely shaped for carrier war—that is, a fleet capable of operating independently and providing for its own air defense. Yamamoto attempted this force structure after the battle by his creation of the Third Fleet, centered on two fleet carriers, the *Shōkaku* and *Zuikaku,* for offensive missions and a light carrier, the *Zuihō,* for fleet air defense. Yet the Third Fleet represented a doctrinal compromise between the age of carrier warfare and traditional battleship doctrine. While its force structure was built around the carriers, its purpose was to contribute to the decisive surface engagement by controlling the air space over the projected battle area. It would be several years before the navy absorbed this lesson of Midway completely and formed a carrier force shaped purely by the needs of an air campaign.[19]

Second, in following current doctrine, the First Air Fleet's concentration of carriers had proved disastrous. Expecting a straightforward attack against American base facilities on Midway and ignorant of the proximity of American carriers, the Japanese had no time to disperse their carriers before they were struck by American carrier aircraft. Three of the four Japanese fleet carriers involved in the operation were lost immediately. The *Hiryū,* the fourth carrier, which was separated from the others, was so badly damaged that she went down the day after she was struck. After Midway, Japanese carrier doctrine turned back to the compromise between

ιtration and dispersal. The navy's surviving and newly commissioned carriers
ιow concentrated in divisions of three carriers each, but with each division
y separated from the others.[20]

hird, the battle forced the Japanese navy to rethink the composition of its carrier air groups. The emphasis on attack over fighter aircraft had meant that there had been inadequate numbers of the latter both for combat air patrol and as escort for carrier air strikes. For that reason, the complement of fighter aircraft for Japanese fleet carriers was significantly increased. Since the major objective of Japanese naval air power was to destroy the combat-effectiveness of enemy carriers, great efforts were made to improve the accuracy of Japanese bombing operations and to increase the number of dive bombers at the expense of reconnaissance planes and torpedo bombers.[21]

Fourth, the navy was forced to rethink not only the design and construction of its carriers to provide greater protection for carrier flight decks, aircraft hangars, and fuel storage areas, but also the processes and procedures for refueling and rearming aircraft. The former was attempted in the design of the *Taihō*-class carriers and the latter by post-Midway deck evolutions. Hangar-deck fueling and ammunition loading were forbidden, and all refueling and reloading were now to be carried out on the flight deck and in the shortest possible time. All wooden structures were eliminated, and soap-solution fire-extinguishing systems were made standard equipment in Japanese carriers following the Midway debacle.[22]

ATTRITION IN THE SOUTHWESTERN PACIFIC, 1942–1943

Yet if the Japanese navy had suffered stunning reverses at sea, its position ashore on the southwestern rim of the Pacific seemed eminently advantageous. Rabaul, situated on the eastern end of New Britain, was captured in late January 1942. That April, exploiting the strategic position of Rabaul, the navy sent in the newly formed Twenty-fifth Air Flotilla, which included both the Fourth Air Group, with its squadron of G4M bombers, and the Tainan Air Group, one of the best fighter units in the Japanese naval air service. The Japanese soon extended their control over New Britain and New Ireland, along the coast of eastern New Guinea (and could and should have easily seized Port Moresby on the southeastern coast), before moving down to the northern Solomon Islands. These occupations gave them complete air and naval control over the Bismarck Archipelago and thus provided a springboard for further advances toward Australia or, conversely, a potential barrier ranged on interior lines against Allied counteroffensives toward Southeast Asia. In the spring and early summer of 1942, Japanese naval air power in the southwestern Pacific was at its zenith. Not only was it strategically positioned; its qualitative and quantitative superiority in aircraft and personnel was never again so great. In May 1942, operating from bases at Rabaul and advance fields in Papua New Guinea and in the Solomons, the Twenty-fifth Air Flotilla concentrated its operations over eastern New Guinea in support of the belated attempt

Photo. 7-2. Mitsubishi G4M bombers of the Misawa Air Group over Rabaul
Harbor, 28 September 1942
Source: Kōkūshō Kankōkai, *Kaigun no tsubasa,* 2:91.

to take Port Moresby, an effort that initiated the air war in the southwestern
Pacific.

But in a strategic oversight of major consequence, the Japanese had done little
to capitalize on their advantageous position in the southwestern Pacific by strengthening it. For the next five months, while Japanese naval air forces ranged far into
the Pacific and Indian oceans, not a single full-service air base was established
south of Rabaul. Then, in the summer of 1942, to protect the flank of the U.S.-
Australia lifeline, the United States took the initiative in the region, by landings on
Guadalcanal and Tulagi in the Solomons. These moves set off a six-month struggle
for the Solomons that would eventually not only grind down Japanese surface
forces but also lead to the destruction of the remainder of the navy's first-line land-
based air groups.[23] Slow to recognize the new American threat to Rabaul and the
Bismarcks barrier, the navy now redirected the operations of the Rabaul air forces
to Guadalcanal in order to neutralize American defenses on the island and to isolate its garrison.[24]

Yet early in the Solomons air campaign, a critical problem faced by the Rabaul ase air force, as it tried to throw in more units to face the growing numbers of American aircraft, was the fact it had too few airfields from which to operate. This could have been rectified even at this point if the navy had been able to dispatch adequate construction resources to the area. But base construction had never been a long suit in the Japanese navy, and the few construction units that existed worked with picks, shovels, and wicker baskets rather than the modern equipment—bulldozers, steam shovels, and metal matting—that could quickly turn a patch of jungle into an airstrip.[25] The immediate consequence of this inability to build air bases rapidly was that in the initial critical weeks of the Solomons air campaign, the navy was hampered in the effective use of all the air power it had drawn down from other theaters in Southeast Asia and the southwestern Pacific. It simply had too few places to put it.

Thus, while the American toehold on Guadalcanal and its abandoned Japanese airstrip was still precarious, the Rabaul base air force was unable to get the decisive upper hand in the air campaign. Although on paper it soon had more than enough aircraft to do so, only the Japanese bases at Rabaul on New Britain and Kavieng on New Ireland could accommodate the additional air units that had been flown in, and these bases were far to the northwest of the air combat theater. The advance airfields that the navy did manage to carve out from the jungles between the Bismarcks and the American base at Henderson Field on Guadalcanal were used mainly as refueling stops, and then only when these airfields were sufficiently supplied. Buin, Buka, Kahili, and Shortland Island were eventually developed for offensive operations, but the airfields at Munda and Vila were mostly dirt strips for emergency uses. (Map 7-2.) By the time the navy was able to commit additional base construction resources to the central Solomons, particularly toward the establishment of a major base at Munda, it was too late to save the air campaign, particularly since Japanese air units at Rabaul and Kavieng had to battle U.S. Army and Australian air units operating out of northern Australia and Papua New Guinea.[26]

Now, in the early autumn of 1942, the Japanese navy made another critical miscalculation. Instead of throwing in both the major surface and air elements of the Combined Fleet to augment the available land-based forces of the Eleventh Air Fleet and to crush the American advance position in the southwestern Pacific at the outset, the navy sent in only its best land-based air units, and those in piecemeal fashion. It soon became apparent, however, that the navy had underestimated American air strength in the Solomons area. In order to deal with the enemy seizure of Guadalcanal, the navy was eventually forced to throw in most of the assets of the Eleventh Air Fleet, which were strung across the length and breadth of Southeast Asia. From the Indian Ocean front the navy pulled in the Twenty-first Air Flotilla; from the East Indies front facing northern Australia, elements of the Twenty-third Air Flotilla were diverted to the Solomons; and from the Marshall Islands far to the east came both flying boats and fighters. The medium bombers of the newly constituted Twenty-sixth Air Flotilla—comprising the veteran Kisarazu Air Group and

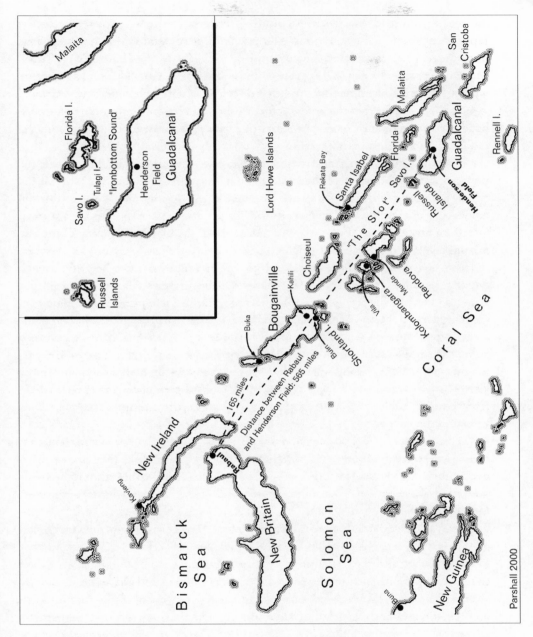

Map 7-2. The Solomon Islands air combat theater, 1942–1943

Parshall 2000

ecently formed Misawa Air Group—were also brought in to reinforce the
nese position in the Solomons. All these units were eventually consumed in the
cious combat with increasingly powerful air units of the United States Navy,
arine Corps, and Army Air Forces. By the end of 1942, Guadalcanal had become
what an American commander on the scene called a "sink hole" for Japanese naval
aviation.[27] Moreover, in the navy's effort to shore up its position in the Solomons,
huge gaps were opened in other sectors of Japan's air defense perimeter, from the
Indian Ocean to the central Pacific.[28]

Out at sea, two carrier air battles that were an integral part of the struggle for
the Solomons—the Battle of the Eastern Solomons in August and the Battle of the
Santa Cruz Islands in late October—resulted in the decimation of the last of the
navy's core of elite carrier aircrews. At the Battle of the Eastern Solomons, the navy
lost the carrier *Ryūjō* and sixty-one airmen. At the Battle of Santa Cruz, the
Japanese suffered the greatest single loss of carrier aircrews to date, 148 aviators.
Indeed, the death ride of the carrier air groups at Santa Cruz can be said to mark
the demise of the prewar carrier air cadres. Of the aircrews who were lost in that
Japanese Pyrrhic victory, twenty-three were section leaders or above or squadron
commanders, including Murata Shigeharu, the famed torpedo plane pilot.[29] Thus,
in four great carrier battles in the first year of the war, Coral Sea, Midway, Eastern
Solomons, and Santa Cruz, it is estimated that the Japanese lost a total of 409 carrier airmen, the navy's best—more than half of the 765 who had participated in the
Pearl Harbor operation.[30] The Americans too had suffered heavily in these engagements, and for that reason it was nearly two years before another carrier duel was
waged in the Pacific.

The consequence of too few advance air bases in the Solomon Islands was that
the Japanese navy—there were few Japanese army air units in the southwestern
Pacific until the last stage of the Solomons air combat—was obliged to fight an air
campaign of attrition at long range, whereas the American enemy based his aircraft
literally at the front. The distance between Rabaul and Guadalcanal was 565 nautical miles, some 60 miles further than the distance the Zero fighters on Taiwan had
been called upon to fly to the Philippines at the opening of the war. At the time that
the navy swept into the Solomons in the spring of 1942, the Combined Fleet had
considered the construction of an air base between Rabaul and Guadalcanal, but by
the time the Americans arrived, only an emergency air field on Buka Island, north
of Bougainville, had been built. Thus, the fighter pilots of the elite Tainan Air
Group had to fly three hours to the combat theater, endure the sudden and violent
pressures of no more than fifteen minutes of air combat over Guadalcanal, followed
by a three-hour return flight home with the possibility of an emergency landing at
Buka. (Only the Model 21 version of the A6M, the workhorse of the navy in the
first year of the war, could fly all the way to Guadalcanal. The succeeding model,
the 32, could not, since its larger engine and added magazines forced a sacrifice in
fuel capacity and thus a reduction in tactical radius.) These exhausting operations
of more than six hours and 1,000 miles quickly took their physical toll on the

fighter pilots who survived the fierce air combat over Guadalcanal and thus accelerated the erosion of the tactical efficiency of the Japanese air campaign. In strategic terms, the failure to establish locally controlled, self-sufficient air bases at the front meant that the navy was unable to provide flexible, responsive air support to Japanese ground and surface forces on or near Guadalcanal, which had come under increasing attack by the Allied enemy. Tactically, it prevented the use of single-engined, land-based bombers whose operational range, with ordnance, did not permit them the round trip from Rabaul to Guadalcanal and back.[31]

Another difficulty faced by Japanese aircrews in the Solomon Islands air campaign was the slender chance for recovery if their planes were downed or crippled. For the most part, if American aircraft were shot down and their crews able to bail out, they could generally count on parachuting into friendly territory. There was at least a fair possibility, moreover, that they could be picked up by American PBYs detailed for search-and-rescue duty. For Japanese pilots who ran into trouble over the Solomons, the prospects were far more ominous. To begin with, land-based Zero units, unlike their carrier counterparts, were not equipped with radio receivers or transmitters. Their pilots, considering them unreliable and too heavy to justify their installation, chose instead to rely on hand signals. Not only did this arrangement sometimes have serious consequences in combat, it also clearly made it difficult to locate and rescue any pilot who might have crash-landed.[32] Most of the Solomon Islands was hostile territory, and while the navy's flying boats, submarines, destroyers, and patrol craft were always on the lookout for downed aviators, air-sea rescue was far less organized than in the American armed forces. Finally, of course, the Japanese military ethos did not permit capture, and for Japanese pilots, crashing one's aircraft into an enemy ship, aircraft, or ground facility was preferable to the disgrace of being made prisoner. Such circumstances added to the mounting Japanese attrition rates in the air war over the Solomons.[33]

Thus, as serious as were the casualties among experienced Japanese navy fliers at the Coral Sea and Midway, it was the air combat over the Solomons that, by the summer of 1943, finally destroyed the combat-effectiveness of Japanese naval aviation as it had developed before the war. The losses suffered by the Tainan Air Group, which included the greatest number of the navy's fighter aces, among them the famed Sakai Saburō, exemplified this situation. By the time it was ordered back to Japan in November 1942, the Tainan Air Group had been reduced to twenty pilots and ground crew.[34]

But losses among aircrews did not constitute the only attrition suffered by Japanese naval aviation personnel in the air campaign in the southwestern Pacific. Okumiya Masatake, in the 1930s a pilot aboard the *Ryūjō*, and in 1943 a lieutenant commander and air staff officer of the Second Carrier Division supporting the air defense of Rabaul, years later recalled his somber impression of the dreadful deterioration of the morale and teamwork of the staffs of the land-based air flotillas (the Twenty-fifth and Twenty-sixth) assigned to defend the base. Exhausted by overwork, drained constantly of officers for combat aircrews, the land-based air

s in the southwestern Pacific began to disintegrate by late 1943. The capabili-
of the air base maintenance personnel also began to shrink severely under the
alling conditions of heat, humidity, poor food, worse medical treatment, and
elve- to twenty-hour workdays, seven days a week. While the navy's high command attempted to give some attention to the increasingly intractable problem of
aircrew attrition, it never came to grips with the increasing enfeeblement of its forward base staff and ground crews.[35]

The Japanese naval air units also lost the intelligence war in the Solomon Islands
air campaign. The Allied intelligence net, composed in varying proportions of
radar, communications intelligence, aerial reconnaissance, and ground observation,
effectively covered New Britain and the Solomons. For that reason, most offensive
operations by Japanese naval air units were reported ahead of time to Allied air
forces. Radar and Allied traffic analysis of Japanese radio communications provided some of the information, and the reconnaissance of Allied B-17s and
Catalinas, scouting Japanese naval air bases, made more air intelligence available.
Particularly harmful to the Japanese cause, however, was the information on their
air operations provided by Australian coast-watchers scattered throughout the
islands. These observers were often able to radio intelligence to American fighter
units several hours in advance of a raid. The Japanese navy had few such assets.[36]

Under the increasing attrition of the navy's fighter units, the escort doctrine for
Japanese bombers began to unravel. As was described in chapter 5, under the doctrine developed during the China War, the navy's fighter pilots assigned to escort
duty for bomber formations generally flew indirect cover. Usually taking station
above the bombers, the fighters were relatively free to maneuver, and if enemy
interceptors were encountered, even at a distance, the fighters were free to pursue
them. Early in the Guadalcanal air campaign the navy's land-based fighter groups
employed this method. But a recurring problem, the same one that had occurred in
the China air war, was that this too often left the bombers uncovered. As the number of Allied fighters increased and the losses of Japanese bombers mounted, the
navy's fighter groups were obliged to switch to close-in, direct cover tactics
(*chokuen sentō*). But this tactic put a heavy psychological burden on the fighter
escorts, since it was mostly passive and allowed few pilot victories. Moreover, the
pilots involved in such a mission did not always carry out their assignments to the
letter, through either muddled instructions of the escort leader, misunderstanding of
his orders by his subordinate pilots, or simply inadequate flying and combat skills
on the part of these pilots, any one of which causes could leave the bombing force
unescorted and without cover. Indeed, all of these elements seem to have played a
part in the destruction of Admiral Yamamoto's G4M in 1943.[37]

I come now to the two most important reasons for the collapse of the Japanese
navy's air campaign over the Solomon Islands: the growing qualitative disparity
between Japanese and American aircrews, and the appearance of Allied aircraft
superior in performance to the Zero. At its higher levels, the Japanese naval air service was slow to grasp these new realities. Certainly little was done to exploit

incoming intelligence concerning new U.S. air technology and tactics. On their pa
American forces did this very quickly. Information concerning Japanese fighter ai
craft and tactics was disseminated rapidly and widely. As we have seen, even as earl
as the Battle of the Coral Sea, American fighter pilots flying F4F Wildcats had begun
to take the measure of the Zero, and information about the aircraft was widely disseminated throughout the combat theater.[38]

Salient among the lessons learned by American fighter pilots was the imperative
of not letting the Zero fight in its preferred environment: the relatively low-altitude
low-speed dogfight. In Southeast Asia early in the conflict many an Allied airman
had learned to his cost that the Zero's maneuverability and the skill of Japanese
pilots in exploiting it in tactics like the *hineri-komi* maneuver gave the Japanese a
deadly advantage under these conditions. One American recalled the seeming chaos
of a Japanese fighter formation that came on like a swarm, using random maneuvers to entice their opponents into acrobatic duels, a potentially fatal course for any
American pilot who tried to follow them.[39] But the advent of second-generation
American fighters with their superior speed, climb, and high-altitude performance,
and the appearance of American pilots wise to the strengths and weaknesses of their
opponents, came to marginalize the maneuverability of the Zero and the predilec-
tions of the pilots who flew it.[40] Pilots in the United States Navy, Marine Corps, and
Army Air Forces began to use their combat skills in the cockpits of larger, faster,
stronger aircraft: the Lockheed P-38 Lightning, the Vought F4U Corsair, and the
Grumman F6F Hellcat. American emphasis on individual gunnery, deflection
shooting, the new "finger four" flight formations, and tactics like the Thach Weave
began to have a telling effect in air combat.[41] Against these aircraft, and the techniques and tactics of the American pilots who flew them, the famed nimbleness of
the Zero was often of little avail, although on those increasingly rare occasions
when it fought on its own terms, it still was a deadly opponent.

But the Zero was not the only navy aircraft whose design and construction
made it a growing liability. The Aichi D3A ("Val") dive bomber, which had caused
such havoc in the Indian Ocean in the spring of 1942, by late fall of that year was
but a slow-moving and weakly protected target for enemy fighters, and the
Nakajima B5N ("Kate"), the terror of Pearl Harbor, was not much better. The aircrews of the Mitsubishi G3M ("Nell") and G4M ("Betty") bombers that had
ranged so far over Chinese skies and Southeast Asian waters now found that their
planes too often became fiery deathtraps under the guns of American aircraft with
heavier armament, greater armor, and better climbing and diving speeds.

Undoubtedly, however, it was less the inferiority of aircraft than the severe
drop-off in the quality of aircrews that accounted for the mounting Japanese losses
in the Solomons campaign.[42] Certainly a leading cause of the navy's defeat in the
Solomons air campaign was its inability to replace aircrews effectively and in sufficient numbers. There was no regular system of rotation of individual personnel, as
in the American air services. Instead, veteran air groups were simply used up,
through death, wounds, disease, or physical exhaustion, to be replaced by new units

that over time were increasingly composed of aircrews of less training and skill. Moreover, even if there could have been individual rotation, as operations became extended there were never enough reserves to permit the rotation back to Japan of those who had been longest in combat. "They won't let you go home unless you die" *(shinanakute wa kaeshite moraenai)* became a common and bitter phrase among Japanese navy pilots in the southwestern Pacific. For this reason, combat fatigue was a contributing cause of the continuing high attrition rate among older pilots.[43]

Compounding the effect of the attrition rate on the combat-effectiveness of Japanese air units was the problem of insufficiently trained personnel. While there were plenty of younger pilots to replace those who were older and highly skilled but who had succumbed to combat or combat fatigue, they lacked the necessary skills and experience. Thrown into combat without these qualities, they were lost more rapidly, and the relationship between inadequate training and attrition became a downward-spiraling vicious circle.[44]

In the autumn of 1942 the American intelligence report quoted earlier provided a blunt summary of the extent to which the overall competence and combat proficiency of Japanese naval aircrews had deteriorated. The report asserted that the inexperienced crews

> made glaring tactical mistakes, unnecessarily exposed themselves to gunfire, got separated and lost mutual support, and at times seemed completely bewildered. Both bomber and fighter pilots ceased to display the aggressiveness that marked their earlier combat. Bombers ceased to penetrate to their target in the face of heavy fire, as they had formerly done; they jettisoned their bombs, attacked outlying destroyers, gave up attempts on massed transports in the center of a formation. Fighters broke off their attacks on Allied heavy and medium bombers before getting within effective range, and often showed a marked distaste for close-in combat with Allied fighters.[45]

One effect of the deterioration of air combat skills and experience was the disintegration of the cohesion of Japanese tactical formations, particularly the three-man *shotai*. I mentioned in the previous chapter the empathy that was said to exist in the immediate prewar years between pilots who constantly trained together, a "sixth sense" that supposedly allowed them to think and act together in combat when not actually in communication by sight or voice. But by the end of 1942 this extrasensory pilot-to-pilot communication was gone, if it had indeed existed, and the tactical formations it supposedly had held together began to fall apart.

Directly related to this decline in combat capability was the vulnerability of Japanese aircraft. Throughout the war, novice American pilots also made mistakes in combat, but on many occasions the sturdy construction of their aircraft (plus armor and self-sealing tanks) allowed them to survive and fight again, and more skillfully, another day. All too often, the first mistake of a Japanese novice was his last.[46]

Even when the navy was able to pull an air group out of operations for training in a rear area, the shrinking nucleus of capable, combat-tested pilots to conduct that training meant a sharp drop-off in its effectiveness. This situation affected both carrier- and land-based air groups. During the Solomons air campaign, carrier aircrews were land-based at Rabaul and the Solomons on several occasions to augment land-based air groups, most notably during operations "I" and "RO" (see below). The losses they suffered simply served to cause further deterioration in the quality of what should have been the navy's best aircrews—the carrier pilots of the fleet.

With Guadalcanal in their hands, the Allies stepped up air attacks on Japanese positions in the northern Solomons, in eastern New Guinea, and on the defense barrier that the Japanese were trying desperately to establish along the Bismarck Archipelago. The growth of Allied aerial might and the waning ability of Japan's air forces in the southwestern Pacific to respond to its attacks were dramatically evident in the slaughter, by American land-based bombers and fighters, of Japanese warships and transports attempting to transit the Bismarck Sea in March 1943. Determined to hold back further enemy blows by counter air offensives against American shipping and advance bases in the southwestern Pacific, Adm. Yamamoto Isoroku, commander of the Combined Fleet, took personal command at Rabaul of Operation "I." This counteroffensive, directed first against Guadalcanal and then against Allied positions in eastern New Guinea, assembled both land-based air groups and carrier-based aircraft of the Third Fleet brought in from Truk. Together they should have numbered about 700 aircraft, but such was the poor state of the operational maintenance of the navy's aircraft at this point in the war that only 350 could be mustered.[47] Still, the raids collectively comprised the biggest air operations since the attack on Pearl Harbor.

Yet once again, despite the ferocity of the attacks, the operation was worn down by Allied air superiority, and the results were far less than Yamamoto believed at the time, especially in comparison with the heavy losses in aircraft (over fifty), which the Japanese navy could no longer afford. Worst of all, the inroads of American intelligence into the navy's plans for air operations were shockingly demonstrated by the aerial ambush of Admiral Yamamoto, whose aircraft was shot down while making an inspection tour of the front lines upon the conclusion of Operation "I." Okumiya Masatake, who attended the study conference at Rabaul that evaluated the operation, later recalled the general sense of gloom that attended the conference and the belief that American aircraft were now regularly matching and exceeding Japanese aircraft in performance as well as in numbers.[48]

Up until mid-1943, Rabaul was the main base for Japanese aerial offensives in the southwestern Pacific. In the autumn of that year, Allied air forces, led by American heavy bombers—B-17s and B-24s—turned such relentless assaults against Rabaul that, far from remaining a springboard for the southward expansion of Japanese air power, it became a stronghold under siege. Determined to hold on to the base as the linchpin of the Bismarcks barrier, Admiral Yamamoto's successor, Adm. Koga Mineichi, attempted to keep Rabaul supplied with sufficient fighter aircraft, but these were successively destroyed in the futile defense of the redoubt. Thus, in the words of a recent study, the Japanese air defense of Rabaul and its three airfields became a "giant aerial meat grinder" that devoured both fighter aircraft and what was left of the navy's best fighter pilots.[49]

In early November, in a reprise of Yamamoto's ill-fated Operation "I," Koga concentrated at Rabaul all the available land-based aircraft of the Eleventh Air Fleet, along with the entire aircraft strength (approximately one hundred planes) of the three carriers *(Zuikaku, Shōkaku,* and *Zuihō)* of the Third Fleet at Truk for attacks on the U.S. carrier forces harassing Rabaul. At the start of this Operation "RO," Koga had on hand approximately 365 aircraft. By the time it had ended, he had lost over two hundred aircraft, both to the air defenses of the American task group and to the American aircraft over Rabaul, without having caused significant damage to the besiegers.[50] So severely did "RO" reduce the pool of competent carrier pilots in the Combined Fleet that Koga could not put up any air defense of Tarawa in the Gilberts when the United States Marines stormed ashore on 20 November.

Meanwhile, the Allied air assault on Rabaul, now based on Allied airfields in the Solomons and eastern New Guinea, continued apace. By the end of January 1944, after the loss of some 250 aircraft in an attempt to defend it, Rabaul was finished as an effective air base, and the *coup-de-grâce* to the navy's air power in the southwestern Pacific was delivered in February, when an American carrier task force destroyed the navy's remaining air reserves on Truk, far to the rear of Rabaul. After this disaster, Admiral Koga ordered Rabaul abandoned, the majority of the remaining naval air units flying out on 20 February, leaving only a few aircraft to conduct aerial guerrilla warfare against the Americans storming up from the Solomons. Yet the enemy chose not to expend the men and materiel to take this once most formidable Japanese base from its enfeebled garrison. Bypassed but frequently bombed, Rabaul was left to wither on the vine.[51]

THE END OF CONVENTIONAL JAPANESE CARRIER AVIATION, 1943–1944

By the beginning of 1944, then, the land-based element of Japanese naval air power in the southwestern Pacific had been shredded. Yet on paper it would seem that by the late spring of 1944 the Japanese navy, through desperate efforts, had been able to build its air power back up to nearly the levels at which it had opened the Pacific War. True, the majority of the carriers with which Japan had opened the war had been sunk, and the few remaining prewar aircrews had been thrown into the furnace of combat in the central Pacific and consumed by early 1944. But wartime construction added new carriers to the fleet, the navy rushed new aircrews through its training programs, and the General Staff established a new carrier command, which attempted to match the new tempo and scale of carrier warfare being waged by the enemy. The navy's First Mobile Fleet was organized on 1 March 1944, supposedly similar in concept to the United States Navy's task forces now operating in the Pacific. Now acting as the central battle force of the Japanese navy, it was built around its nine carriers, including the new heavily armored *Taiho*. On their decks were crowded new, more powerful and more sophisticated aircraft types, including the Nakajima B6N torpedo bomber and the Yokosuka D4Y1, the fastest dive bomber of World War II.

In theory, therefore, the First Mobile Fleet was the second most powerful carrier force in the world. But in fact, shortages in every required element of this Japanese task force made it a feeble reflection of the original concept (see below). Of these deficiencies, none was worse than that of its air groups, which were filled with young pilots shockingly ill prepared for battle. Before the war, the average length of the navy's pilot training had been three and a quarter years, and the rigor of that training was discussed in chapter 2. By late 1944, every U.S. Navy pilot had undergone over two years of training. By June of the same year, the Japanese pilots who manned the air groups of the First Mobile Fleet had an average of only six months of training, and some had only two or three months. In the urgency of the time, as their instructors struggled to teach the tyros just to fly and shoot, the fine points of fighter combat were cast aside. Navigational training ceased altogether, and pilots were simply instructed to follow their leaders into action. But those leaders themselves were now correspondingly less experienced and prone to make mistakes unthinkable for their predecessors in 1941–42.[52]

This deplorable condition of air training was aggravated by a number of other elements. One was the fact that the new aircraft types—such as the Mitsubishi J2M Raiden fighter, the Yokosuka D4Y Suisei carrier bomber, and the Nakajima B6N torpedo bomber—were far more demanding of pilot skills than their predecessors. In the hands of inexperienced pilots they became deathtraps, as demonstrated by the increasing number of fatal accidents in the navy's air units. Because of unanticipated technical delays in equipping the navy's air groups with these latest aircraft, there was little time to train inexperienced aircrews in either their great combat potential or their dangerous quirks.[53] By 1944, moreover, the fuel problem, always tight for the Japanese navy and only temporarily relieved by the conquest of Southeast Asian oil fields, had really begun to bite. Aviation gas being in short supply meant that training and practice had to be sharply curtailed. There was even a shortage of airfields for training. Tawi-tawi, at the extreme end of the Sulu Archipelago, chosen by the First Mobile Fleet as its advance base, did not have an airfield, and the fleet's carrier pilots, apparently unable to use the carrier decks for training and practice, were inactive before the last great battle in which they were to take part.[54]

Despite these deficiencies, the Japanese navy remained confident of its ability to launch a smashing aerial offensive against the United States Navy's Task Force 58 when it approached the Marianas as part of the American offensive to break through Japan's defensive barrier in the central Pacific. In the plan for the navy's "A" operation, the main force to be used would be its shore-based air units rushed to the Marianas—Guam, Saipan, Tinian, and Rota—from which they were to launch mass attacks to cripple the American carriers. The land-based air assault units would be followed by attacks by the carrier aircraft of the First Mobile Fleet. Supposedly, with a 200-mile advantage in range over their American counterparts, the Japanese carriers would remain at a secure distance from enemy retaliation. The Japanese carrier aircraft could thus strike the enemy carriers, land on island bases in the Marianas, refuel, and launch a second attack on the enemy before returning to their own carriers.[55]

So it was planned. But the resulting Battle of the Philippine Sea, 19 June 1944, the last great carrier encounter of the Pacific War, turned into an air disaster that demonstrated the dramatic decline in Japanese naval air power since the glory days early in the war. The specific moves of the campaign lie beyond our concerns. Suffice it to say that American carrier fighters obliterated the Japanese land bases before their air groups could get into the fight, and Admiral Ozawa and the First Mobile Fleet plunged into his assault on the American carriers without the promised land support. In the ensuing Japanese attacks, the slaughter of Ozawa's carrier air groups was so great—and, by American standards, so easy—that it became known by the victors as the "Great Marianas Turkey Shoot."

The reasons for the debacle were twofold. On the American side, beyond the question of numerical superiority, which was significant, there were a number of spectacular advances: first, radar and its contribution to long-range interception of enemy air attacks; second, faster, more powerful, more rugged aircraft than ever before; third, the improvement in tactical formations for carrier battle; fourth, the superb performance of the combat information centers on all the major fleet units; and fifth and above all, the aggressiveness and cool professionalism of the superbly trained American aviators.

The Japanese side presented an exact opposite, particularly in the performance of its aircrew. The Japanese pilots orbited ineffectively around the American carriers at a distance of 100 miles at the start, losing the one chance they had for victory: a quick, violent strike regardless of loss. Many of the fighter pilots seemed content to stay out of the action entirely. In contrast to the outstanding discipline of the Kanoya Air Group bombing crews when they destroyed the *Repulse* and *Prince of Wales* off Malaya in December 1941, the Japanese dive and torpedo bombers at the Philippine Sea failed to keep their formations and, separating, lost all chance of coordinated attack. The aim of the Japanese carrier pilots was so off the mark that one American aviator declared contemptuously after the slaughter that they "couldn't hit an elephant if it was tied down."[56]

In his masterful history, Samuel Eliot Morison provided a more magnanimous verdict, though one no less devastating in its appraisal of the fundamental cause of the Japanese defeat:

Ozawa may be said to have conducted his fleet well. The Japanese plane searches kept him fairly in touch with the movements of Task Force 58 for twenty-four hours or more before Spruance knew where he was. [He] avoided the usual (and always disastrous) Japanese strategy of feint and parry; he kept his inferior force together and gave battle at a distance that prevented his enemy from striking back immediately. His handling of the fueling problem, in view of the shortage of oil and scarcity of tankers, was masterly. But all this availed him naught because his air groups were so ill-trained. Ozawa had fine ships and good planes, but his aviators were weak-winged through inexperience, and land-based air failed him completely.[57]

When the battle was over, in addition to the destruction of a large number of its land-based air groups, the Japanese navy had lost its last carrier air groups and had failed either to damage Task Force 58 or to halt the American drive through the Marianas.

The utter Japanese defeat at the Battle of the Philippine Sea marks the chronological terminus of my discussion of Japanese naval air power in World War II. After it was over, the Japanese navy never again launched a significant effort to contest the American hegemony of the skies over the Pacific. By war's end, save for the old *Hōshō,* all of her once proud carrier forces either lay at the bottom of the grand abysses of the Pacific or were careened, abandoned, and useless in the shallower waters of Japanese home ports.[58] (Photo. 7-3.) The last desperate effort by Japanese naval air units to stem the Allied tide in the western Pacific, the organization of the "special attack" *(tokkō)* corps—the kamikaze units, as they are best known in the West—was largely directed toward American surface units. In any event, the suicide tactic was simply not contemplated as a significant element in prewar air combat doctrine in the Japanese navy and therefore has little relevance to the scope of this work. At war's end, there were approximately fifty-nine hundred aircraft left on the navy's homeland airfields, but with little fuel to fly them and a dwindling number of pilots who could fly them more than one way. Within months, as the occupation forces began dismantling what was left of Japan's military machine, even these machines had been turned by American bulldozers into hundreds of acres of crumpled wings, propellerless engines, and overturned fuselages.[59] (Photo. 7-4.)

REFLECTIONS ON THE DESTRUCTION OF JAPANESE NAVAL AIR POWER

The grand causes of Japan's catastrophic collapse have been illuminated by a number of magisterial works on World War II. In addition, the late David Evans and I dealt more specifically with the nation's defeat at sea in the last chapter of our volume on the prewar Japanese navy. I now sharpen my focus on the causes of the destruction of Japanese naval air power, 1942–44. While the reasons are multiple, a few general categories stand out: first, the failure of the navy to anticipate the kind of air combat it would be obliged to wage; second, once in the new kind of air war, the failure to make the right decisions to deal with its realities; and third, the inability of Japanese industry and technology to support Japanese naval aviation against the emerging numerical and qualitative superiority of American air power.

Photo. 7-3. The carrier *Amagi* capsized in Kure Harbor, 8 October 1945
Source: Fukui, *Shashin Nihon kaigun zen kantei shi,* 1:336.

In prewar Japanese strategic-planning documents there were numerous references to the necessity to prepare for a war of attrition against the United States. But
in addition to underestimating the ability of the United States to force the pace of
attrition, the Japanese navy's strategy to wage such a war was based on a disregard
of the fundamental reality of the Pacific. The navy's plans called for the creation of
a great chain of island air bases that would form a defensive barrier around the
nation's empire of conquest in the central and southwestern Pacific against any
American counteroffensives to retake it. Shifting the navy's long-range bombers
from one to another of these "unsinkable carriers," as Yamamoto had viewed them,
the navy had believed that it could launch preemptive attacks against any enemy
advance.[60] Here, the navy clearly misjudged the vast distances over which it would
have to fight. The distances between Japanese bases throughout the western and
southwestern Pacific proved too great even for the longest reach of its land-based air-

Photo. 7-4. Wrecked Mitsubishi G4M (Type 1) bombers and other aircraft at Atsugi airfield, autumn 1945
Source: Mikesh, *Broken Wings of the Samurai.*

craft, and thus it proved impossible to provide the flexible defense that Yamamoto had envisioned. And thus, one by one, without substantial help from the nearest air garrisons, the navy's air bases fell before the American amphibious tidal wave.

The unrealistic quality of the navy's plans for winning an extended war is also apparent in its personnel policies and aircraft design priorities. The creation of a small but elite pool of naval aviators with no substantial reserve to back it up, nor any training program in place with which to do so, speaks of the mistaken assumption of a short, victorious conflict. That assumption is confirmed by the design and production of aircraft that provided scant means to protect the personnel who flew and fought in them and thus did nothing to preserve that precious elite once the air war of attrition began.

I have touched upon the navy's failure to create adequate reserves of trained aircrews at several points in these pages. With half of the naval air arm insufficiently trained at the opening of the Pacific War, it was difficult to fill the needs of frontline air groups with fully qualified personnel as its elite formations were steadily ground down. By stripping the carrier air groups of both capable leadership and the best pilots, the land-based groups were kept reasonably combat-ready into the spring of 1943. But by that time land-based aircrews had themselves been decimated, with no effective on-site training reserve to replace combat losses. The consequences of these training policies were ultimately fatal. Once the navy recognized that it was far better to have lots of competent pilots than a handful of outstanding ones, it was too late. The terrible shredding in combat of the navy's top air units, the ever-increasing need for their replacement, and the decreasing time and fuel available for adequate training to provide such replacement had by late 1943 left the navy with little but the greenest trainees, who were quickly sacrificed in the fire of combat.[61]

American air personnel policies before and during the Pacific War stood in sharp contrast. The American emphasis on training far greater numbers of aviators, albeit at a somewhat lower standard of performance, the assignment of training units aboard aircraft carriers, and the provision of aircraft that offered aircrews greater lifesaving protection gave American aviators an overwhelming advantage in air combat by the end of 1942. In sum, as Fuchida Mitsuo and Okumiya Masatake concluded in their account of the Battle of Midway, the Japanese naval air service "failed to realize that aerial warfare is a battle of attrition and that a strictly limited number of even the most skillful pilots could not possibly win out over an unlimited number of able pilots."[62]

It has been commonplace in Western accounts to view the Japanese tradition as indifferent to the expenditure of human life in battle. Specifically, it has been argued that the Japanese navy undervalued the lives of its few precious aviators. Yet there were elements complicating this picture. One must understand that the pilots themselves, embracing a Bushido ethos, did not want armor and self-sealing fuel tanks on their aircraft, since such additions seemed to imply a selfish concern for their own survival. There was also an intangible, that of the stoicism and *gaman* (perseverance) that pervaded Japanese society. Japanese were simply ready to put up with combat conditions that in the West would have been considered intolerable.[63]

As we have seen, the navy pursued aircraft designs in which safety factors—armor, self-sealing gas tanks, structural integrity—that might have saved the lives of pilots were sacrificed for greater performance, speed, and maneuverability. Once the harsh lessons of the China and Pacific wars had been absorbed, the inability of the navy to provide armor and self-sealing tanks was due to a combination of bureaucratic inflexibility and a weak industrial infrastructure rather than to any opposition to these features in themselves.

Of course, as Eric Bergerud reminds us, the devastating attrition rate for the navy's aircrews was also due to "operational"—that is, noncombat—losses that affected Japanese and Allied aircrews alike. Erratic and often violent weather, unfamiliar and often mountainous terrain, navigational mistakes over the ocean, primitive and often bomb-damaged runways, aircraft fatigue, pilot error, and mechanical failures—omnipresent dangers that confronted the Allies as well—took a horrendous toll of Japanese aircraft and aircrews. But for Japanese aircrews the 1,000-mile round trip from Rabaul to Guadalcanal and back posed far greater risks of dangerous weather and navigational error than their enemy counterparts based at Henderson Field and other American bases in the Solomons.[64] Moreover, the Japanese navy, while it made every effort to rescue downed pilots, never developed anything like the Allied system of sea rescue.[65] Although the naval air service actively rotated pilots early in the war, after the major pilot losses at Guadalcanal the rotation system began to break down.

Moreover, it was not just the decline in the quality of aircrews that accelerated the erosion of Japanese naval air power in the Pacific. Heavy losses in trained ground crews also weakened the navy's air groups. I have said that the most significant personnel losses at Midway occurred not in fighter cockpits but among trained maintenance personnel who went down with the four carriers. Similarly, the loss of skilled ground crews, often abandoned to their fates when the navy evacuated remaining aircrews from islands under siege, substantially weakened the land-based air groups.[66]

In the southwestern Pacific, the problem of distance was more strictly logistical. Wastage—not just through combat but through accident, the wearing out of equipment, corrosion due to humidity and salt air, and obsolescence of equipment—is an inherent problem of naval air war. To keep aircraft combat-ready requires reasonably effective logistical services. But in the grinding Solomons air campaign the Japanese naval air arm simply lost the battle of maintenance and supply. Failure to supply land-based air groups with sufficient aircraft early in this stage of the Pacific War meant that they went into battle with forces that were too slender, and for that reason accomplished little and missed favorable opportunities at the outset of the campaign. Later, the extreme distances between the homeland and the fighting front made it difficult to make up for these missed opportunities. Rabaul, the main base from which the naval air service waged the campaign, was some 2,400 miles from the Japanese homeland. This distance proved a hindrance to a steady and continuing supply and maintenance of front-line land-based air units because of weaknesses in the navy's logistical system. Central to the problem was the fact that the navy's air arm seems to have had no smoothly functioning system of ferrying heavier replacement aircraft—twin-engined bombers and flying boats—to Pacific combat theaters. It was obliged to detail combat aircrews back to Japan to pick up replacement aircraft and stage them through island bases to front-line units. Fighters and smaller aircraft were initially crated and sent to combat zones by cargo vessels or carriers, though later they too were flown out, usually from Truk.[67] As the number of skilled pilots decreased, green pilots often crashed the aircraft they were ferrying, further reducing the number of planes available.

But supply means more than just the availability of additional aircraft. Air war requires constant maintenance and repair, and the number of serviceable aircraft available to an air unit at any given time will greatly depend on the level of maintenance available to keep the aircraft flying. Here the Japanese naval air service fell down badly. While each air group was staffed with its own maintenance personnel, they were capable of undertaking only routine maintenance and simple repairs. Major or more complicated repairs proved difficult, in large part because of the trouble of dispatching skilled technicians from rear-area repair facilities and of sending damaged aircraft and equipment back to those same facilities. Moreover, just as with flight personnel, the average quality of ground crew deteriorated over time, thus lowering the serviceability rate and further compounding the problem of maintaining adequate numbers of aircraft and crews.[68]

Constant maintenance also requires a steady flow of supplies, particularly spare parts. For the first year of the Pacific War the production of parts, engines, weapons, and radios for the navy's air groups was more than adequate.[69] The problem of aviation ordnance was serious, however. Production of aircraft armament at the outset of hostilities was generally 80–90 percent of orders and use, depending on the type of weapon. Though the navy had more than adequate stocks of bombs, on the eve of the war it had on hand only 10–30 percent of anticipated needs in 20-millimeter aircraft cannon shells and Type 91 aerial torpedoes. Through crash conversion of industrial facilities from production of surface naval ordnance to the needs of naval air units, interruption of the flow of aviation ordnance to those units was prevented after the opening of hostilities.[70]

But as the naval air arm's area of operations expanded in the first six months of the war and distances between the Japanese islands and the Pacific combat theaters greatly increased, the transportation of ordnance and supplies became a major problem, particularly in situations of urgent need. Then the naval air service began to pay the price for its extremely limited air transport capacity. Not only were there too few transport aircraft available, but there was also a limited number of air transport personnel with sufficient skill to undertake efficient transport loading and to prevent breakage and wastage en route to the combat theater. For that reason, most bombs, torpedoes, ammunition, and fuel were supplied to each land-based air group by maritime transport, but since this means was quite limited even before the destruction of the Japanese transport fleet by the American submarine campaign, the allocation of supplies to advance air bases increasingly became a matter of severe prioritization.[71]

It was only in the area of aviation fuels that the Japanese naval air service felt no problem in supply until 1944. During 1942 the amount of oil from the Netherlands East Indies was greater than anticipated, as the facilities damaged or destroyed in the conquest of the Dutch oil fields were quickly repaired. Moreover, the American submarine campaign against the tanker routes from the Indies to the Japanese homeland had not yet begun to make serious inroads in supply. But if the supply of aviation fuels was greater than anticipated, so was consumption. At the outbreak of the war, the navy had believed that it had stocks adequate for two years of combat. But the great carrier battles of 1942 and the grinding air campaign in the southwestern Pacific had devoured an enormous amount of aviation fuel, and the reduction in stocks that had occurred by the end of 1943 was compounded by the death grip that the Allies began to apply to Japanese tank transportation by 1944. By the latter part of that year the navy's aviation fuel si uation had become so desperate that it began investigating the possibility o extracting aviation fuel from pine roots.[72]

Linked to the question of transport and supply was the paucity of advance air bases, which in turn was created by the navy's inadequate civil-engineering capacity, a matter touched upon earlier. In the spring of 1942 the advances of the Japanese army and navy simply outran the ability of the primitively equipped construction units to build an adequate network of new bases quickly. For the most part, the navy's land-based air groups were obliged to use Allied airfields captured in the first several months of the war. But these were few in relation to the numbers of aircraft needed to conduct the offensive operations that might have continued to keep Allied forces off balance. In contrast, the ability of the United States Navy's "Sea-Bees" to create airstrips almost overnight gave Allied air forces a devastatingly longer reach.

The origin of nearly all of these dilemmas for the Japanese naval air arm can be traced back to the navy's assumption that it would fight a short, decisive war. In such a conflict, few of these problems would have been critical. As it was, the extended conflict that Japanese naval aviation found itself obliged it to fight exhausted its airmen, destroyed its best aircraft, and overtaxed its facilities and resources.

If the catalogue of failures to anticipate the nature of an air war in the Pacific was fundamental to the navy's defeat in that conflict, so too were the collective demonstrations of the navy's inability or unwillingness to make the necessary changes once the war had begun. The first of these changes should have been recognition, at the very top of the naval high command, that the first six months— indeed, the first month—of the Pacific War had proven beyond doubt the dominance of air power over the big-gun capital ship. Such a clear-headed recognition should have resulted in an early decision to abandon the concept of the great and supposedly decisive gun duel at sea and, flowing from that decision, a decisive step to reorder the basic force structure of the Japanese navy.

In a thunderclap, the Japanese navy itself had brought such a realization and such a decision to the United States Navy in the opening hours of the war. At Pearl Harbor the obsolescent American battle line had been critically disabled, thus free- ing the United States Navy from its reliance on the capital ship and from whatever lingering faith it might have had in its preeminence. Air power, both land- and carrier-based, became the focus of innovative American tactical thinking and the recipient of a major portion of American industrial output.

In contrast, the Japanese navy was slow to give up its prewar big-gun/big-ship convictions. On the eve of the Pacific War, with the great increase in the performance of aircraft, air power advocates in the Japanese navy like Inoue Shigeyoshi had argued that aviation was now the dominant arm in naval warfare, and in the first few months of the conflict it was air power that scored the most dramatic and crushing victories. These should have been enough to guarantee that the locus of naval decision had indeed changed. Yet the Japanese navy's high command had been reluctant to discard its conviction that the battleship was the supreme arbiter at sea and that aviation's subsidiary role was to support the battle line. The Battle of Midway demonstrates this reluctance. On the one hand, after the loss of its four carriers, Yamamoto recalled the strike force, despite the fact that it included some of the world's most formidable battleships. This reluctance to wager his capital ships against the two remaining American carriers in daylight seems to have been Yamamoto's homage to air power. On the other hand, in the navy's major reorganization of its fleets after Midway, only the Third Fleet was to be a carrier force, and the purpose of that fleet was to provide protective cover over the battle line.[73]

In other words, while the Japanese navy's recognition of the tremendous power of aviation may have been deepened after Midway, it did not go much beyond the decision to create superior air power. To be fair, this failure to act upon the realities of the air power revolution stemmed from the fact that it was beyond the nation's industrial capacity to produce adequate numbers of both warships and aircraft. One can argue with twenty-twenty hindsight that a bold decision should have been made to limit warship construction severely and go flat out for air power, particularly the production of heavy land-based bombers. But because ships were also badly needed, this proved impossible.[74]

The durability of the grip of the big-gun/big-ship orthodoxy on Japanese naval thinking far into the Pacific conflict had another unfortunate consequence: the failure to give airmen substantial authority over the strategy and conduct of the navy's air war.[75] One must remember that in no other navy, not even the United States Navy, were land-based air elements so much an element of naval power. A look at the administrative organization of the Combined Fleet (Fig. 6-6) shows how clearly its land-based air groups were integrated into it. Yet, as was mentioned earlier in these pages, few qualified aviators had high-ranking positions within either the Combined Fleet or the navy's high command in Tokyo (the General Staff, the Navy Ministry, or any of the navy's semiautonomous bureaus and departments). Yamamoto Isoroku was the single most important exception, but his orientation toward air power was far less radical than that of Inoue Shigeyoshi, who was not a qualified aviator and whose influence was far smaller. Thus, throughout the war most of the navy's decisions concerning air operations were made by men whose experience and viewpoint had to do with capital ships, not with air power.[76]

One can think of a number of instances in which having airmen in command might have made a difference in decision making. One was the failure of Admiral Nagumo to authorize a third strike against Pearl Harbor that would have had the fuel storage tanks as a prime objective. Had the senior aviators in Nagumo's command been able to persuade their nonaviator commander to launch a final attack on this objective, the results might well have caused a military setback to the United States far beyond the crippling of the aging capital ships of the Pacific Fleet.[77]

It seems hardly possible that airmen in command positions in Tokyo would have been as neglectful of the health and morale of the navy's front-line land-based air units in the southwestern Pacific and the necessity to work out a rotation system for individual airmen that would have permitted new and inexperienced personnel to be gradually integrated with veteran aircrews. Japanese naval aviators may have brought their own prejudices and misperceptions to the air war, but they were infinitely more aware of the realities of aerial combat than the naval brass in Tokyo—mostly trained in surface warfare—who directed the air strategy from afar.[78]

A third and final example of the inadequate influence of the air element in the Japanese navy was the failure to push through to production a heavy bomber of the range, durability, and payload capacity of the American B-17 and B-24. As Okumiya Masatake and Horikoshi Jiro pointed out in their retrospective study of the air campaigns of the Pacific War, the B-17—and to a lesser extent its companion, the B-24 Liberator—gave Allied strategic air operations two great advantages: tremendous reach and invulnerability to all but the most concentrated fighter attacks. The great range of the American heavy bombers permitted them to operate from bases beyond the range of the Japanese navy's medium bombers. They thus facilitated long-range reconnaissance and intelligence collection, which undid the traditional Japanese strategy of keeping one's own movements hidden while discovering those of the enemy. The ruggedness of construction and the lethal firepower of these bombing aircraft meant that it took a good number of Japanese fighters to destroy a single B-17 or B-24 and usually cost a number of attackers in the process. The Japanese navy could ill afford to devote its dwindling numbers of fighter planes to the mass attacks needed to bring these airborne fortresses down, and it was not able to put into production a bomber of similar range, armor, armament, payload, and durability. Lt. Comdr. Kofukuda Mitsugu, flight commander of the Sixth Air Group based at Buin during the Solomons Islands air campaign, concluded that this inability to produce a truly strategic bomber was one of the most decisive Japanese failures of the Pacific War.[79]

In all this, one cannot help but wonder what might have been accomplished for Japanese naval air power if Inoue Shigeyoshi had early on been given the same scope and authority as Gen. "Hap" Arnold in the United States Army. For Inoue's vision of an essentially air power navy had been as radical as Arnold's view of the role of his own service, if not more so.

Among the decisions most fundamentally needed upon the outbreak of the war, but the one that was perhaps the nearest to impossibility, was an effective integration of the efforts of the Imperial Japanese Navy and the Imperial Japanese Army. In chapter 4 I mentioned the ways in which the duplication of separate research and development efforts between the two services hampered Japanese aircraft design and production before the war. At the outset of the war interservice cooperation in the initial strategic offensives went off smoothly enough. Later, when the conflict turned against Japan, the two services turned to bickering as men and resources became increasingly scarce.

Even before then, differences in training, missions, and equipment severely mpered cooperation. At the front lines in the southwestern Pacific during the war, inability to integrate the Japanese army's air strength with that of the navy was itical. Because the majority of the navy's operations there were conducted over long overocean distances, operations in which army pilots were poorly trained, the army was unable to contribute its aircraft and personnel to the struggle in sufficient numbers. In consequence, the navy's Zeros were forced to fight alone against an increasingly superior number of enemy fighters and bombers of various types and of various services.[80]

Finally, the fiery descent of Japanese naval air power in the Pacific War can be attributed to the discrepancies in strength and versatility between American and Japanese industry. I have written of the tremendous surge in the navy's air arm in the years immediately prior to the Pacific War. In that period, the technical skills of its aircrews and the quality of its aircraft and weapons rapidly became among the best in the world. But the navy's leadership decided on war without adequate fore-thought as to the prospects of fighting a long war with an enemy so superior in industrial, scientific, and technological resources.[81] The late David Evans and I have explored the consequences of this disparity at some length in our study on the Japanese navy.[82] Here I shall give only four examples of how this gap adversely affected Japanese naval air power. The first two examples, radar and the VT fuze, exemplify the tremendous advance of Allied technology during the war.

Radar was the single most important technological advantage held by the United States Navy in the Pacific War.[83] Its applications were numerous, of course, but in the naval air war, in combination with the installation of the combat infor-mation center aboard U.S. warships, it enormously strengthened the air defenses of Allied fleet units, particularly in vectoring combat air patrols toward inbound Japanese air strikes. Conversely, by the end of the war, radar sets installed in U.S. naval aircraft helped their pilots to identify and attack Japanese air and surface tar-gets. In contrast, shipborne and airborne radar lagged in the Japanese navy for rea-sons that Evans and I spelled out in our earlier study.[84] By the second year of the Pacific War, land-based air groups at the navy's larger bases had radar sets, but they were unreliable, and their range was limited to 100 kilometers (60 miles). But the central problem in the navy's use of radar, aboard carriers or ashore, was the fact that there was no control system to coordinate information so obtained, such as the American combat information center. And behind that difficulty was the abysmal nature of the navy's aerial communications. In the case of carriers, these multiple difficulties obliged any carrier force to maintain constant air patrols over the carri-ers during combat operations.

The VT, or proximity, fuze was another Allied technological advance that helped to break the back of Japanese naval air power. Antiaircraft fire was a great killer of aircraft on both sides during the Pacific War, but American antiaircraft fire was particularly dangerous to Japanese fighters and bombers because of their frag-ile construction. Then in 1943 the appearance of the American proximity fuze changed antiaircraft defenses from dangerous to deadly. Installed in antiaircraft shells and activated by electrical waves reflected off the surface of the target, the fuze vastly simplified the process of destroying enemy aircraft. Prior to its introduction, to knock a plane out of the skies by antiaircraft fire required the convergence of two separate processes: the delivery of a shell near the target and the detonation of that shell by a time fuze preset for the correct distance downrange. With the introduction of the VT fuze, the second process was eliminated, since the fuze itself determined the detonation of the shell at the point where it would be most likely to destroy the target.[85] Thus, the mechanism enormously enhanced the antiaircraft fire of American warships. Between January 1943, when it was introduced, and the end of the war, the fuze is judged to have been the key element in the destruction of 305 Japanese aircraft lost to shipboard antiaircraft fire. Together with radar and the inexperience of Japanese naval aircrews during the same period, this lethal weapon shredded the air attack systems described in chapter 6.[86]

Still another example centers on the design of American aircraft engines, whose performance stands in sharp contrast to Japanese wartime power plants.[87] From the beginning of the Pacific War, the design staffs of the huge American aircraft industry, in close cooperation with the American military services, were continually engaged in designing and constructing the best lines of aircraft and aircraft engines to meet the wide diversity of combat needs and changing wartime requirements of the services. At the same time, American industry still made the standardization of production an overarching priority, since it not only speeded production but also simplified the problem of replacement parts and maintenance skills available on the distant front lines.[88]

In particular, the progress of American manufacturers in the continual improvement of aircraft engines put them well ahead of their counterparts anywhere else on the globe. In this effort, they were able to call upon the expertise and services of America's wide network of laboratories and research centers, and also upon the abundant natural resources of the country, including the broad range of raw materials for engine parts. Favored by these advantages, the United States was able to produce the world's lightest and most powerful engines, eventually improved even further by turbo-superchargers. This availability of greater engine power in a lighter "package" meant that aircraft designers had a greater range of options and opportunities. In turn, this meant that aircraft of ever-increasing engine power, range, and performance—the Hellcat, the Lightning, the Corsair—became available in awesome numbers on the decks of American carriers and on the runways of advance bases in the Pacific.

In contrast, as shown in chapter 4, the Mitsubishi Zero reflected the limitations of the Japanese aircraft industry. Horikoshi Jirō, the designer of the Zero, produced a fighter plane of outstanding performance, even though the Navy General Staff had presented him with an almost impossibly conflicting set of requirements and specifications. Yet the aircraft suffered a series of ultimately fatal weaknesses, at least half of which were due to its small engine. In the later stages of the Pacific War this discrepancy in power plants was to prove a fatal weakness in encounters between Japanese and American fighter aircraft. In the fall of 1942 the P-38 Lightning, with twin 1,000-horsepower engines, appeared in the skies over Guadalcanal. The spring of 1943 saw the entry of the F4U Corsair, with a 2,000-horsepower engine, in the Solomons campaign. At about the same time, the F6F Hellcat, with its 2,000-horsepower engine, became part of the American air arsenal in the southwestern Pacific. By the summer of 1943, therefore, the Allies' combination of new tactics and new and more powerful aircraft had begun to drive the once-dreaded Zero from the skies. The Japanese navy (as well as the army) developed better fighter aircraft, of course, but these were produced in far smaller numbers, and the navy continued to rely mainly on the Zero up to the end of the war. That it was obliged to do so speaks volumes for the limited manpower base of Japanese engineering, which took twice as long to develop a new airplane as its American counterpart.[89]

I have one final comparison to make that demonstrates how, by midwar, all of these elements of American material superiority—industrial, technological, and logistical—combined with American innovative and organizational skills, ultimately sent Japanese naval air power to fiery destruction. I have written in chapter 6 that the Japanese navy's single most impressive tactical innovation in the prewar years was the concentration of carrier air power manifest in the First Air Fleet. While it existed, the First Air Fleet, which gave new directions to war at sea, was the most powerful formation afloat, and one can argue that its disbandment soon after the Midway battle was a major tactical mistake. But in any event, it represented a concept in naval air power—the hit-and-run strike force—that by the end of 1943 had been superseded and overwhelmed by the task force concept. As developed by the United States Navy, the task force was a multicomponent fleet supplied by a mobile fleet train. At its core were several carriers, and the aircraft it was able to assemble represented an aerial armada capable of providing continuous, round-the-clock offensive air operations against a target. With such a fleet organization the United States Navy was now able to pound Japanese bases relentlessly for days at a time and to prevent any Japanese planes from even getting into the air. The Japanese First Mobile Fleet, despite its concentration of air power and because of the absence of any effective logistical system to support it, could never have undertaken such an operation.

Thus, in the end the Japanese naval air service was outproduced, outorganized, outmanned, and outfought. But for a brief time its combat performance in an age of industrial war had been dazzling. In that conflict its Zero Fighter, dainty as a dragonfly and dangerous as a rapier, was to prove the transcendent symbol of the amazing qualities and fatal weaknesses of Japanese naval air power. Dazzling in its quickness, extraordinary in its reach, and possessed of great of firepower, its vulnerabilities in design and frailties in construction were ultimately discovered and exploited by its foes. Collectively, moreover, its assets embodied the central assumption with which the Imperial Japanese Navy went to war: that speed, maneuverability, and firepower would deliver a slashing stroke at the outset and would bring

Photo. 7-5. A Mitsubishi A6M5a (Type 0) carrier fighter, recovered from Yap, restored by Mitsubishi Heavy Industries and exhibited at the company's Nagoya plant
Source: Mikesh, *Broken Wings of the Samurai.*

the giant to his knees before he could assert his massive strength. Ultimately the most critical failure of Japanese naval air power was the failure of the navy's leaders, before the war ever began, to conceive the possibility that the initial stroke would not be mortal to the enemy, and that given time and superior strength, he would be able to apply his death grip.

There are not many Zero fighters left today. A few still rust away amid the jungles and weeds on islands in the tropical Pacific. Fewer still, beautifully restored and maintained, grace the floors of air museums in Japan and the United States, even today an object of admiration and awe to those who view them. (Photo. 7-5.) For if they never could have provided the margin of victory for the nation and the navy in the Pacific War, the precision, the skill, and the technical mastery with which they were crafted lived on and gave wings to the phoenix of postwar Japanese technology.

Appendix 1

Biographical Sketches

This appendix provides biographical sketches of the principal naval figures mentioned in the text. Each individual listed here is identified with the symbol † where first discussed in the text. The information was drawn from the following sources: Hata, *Nihon riku-kaigun sōgō jiten;* Kaigun Rekishi Hōzonkai, *Nihon kaigun shi,* vols. 10 and 11; Toyama, *Riku-kaigun shōkan jinji sōran,* vol. 2; Hata and Izawa, *Japanese Naval Aces;* and communications with Todaka Kazushige.

AIKŌ FUMIO (1901 – 1991). Born in Kagoshima, he graduated from the Naval Academy (51st class) in 1924. After holding several small ship commands, he was appointed a special student at the Yokosuka Naval Air Base, September 1938, and, concurrently, a member of the Weapons Division of the Naval Air Arsenal. In 1939 he served as an aerial torpedo specialist with the Combined Fleet, studying shallow-water launching techniques. Attached to the Second Carrier Division in March 1940, he became a member of the Technical Bureau of the Navy Aviation Department in May of that year. He was promoted to the rank of commander in October 1941. In April 1944 he became chief of the Torpedo Section, Second Division, Air Weapons Bureau, Munitions Ministry. He attained the rank of captain in October 1944 and was posted to the Naval Aviation Department in March 1945.

ANDŌ MASATAKA (1880–1956). Born in Gifu Prefecture, he was the nephew of an admiral. He graduated from the Naval Academy (28th class) in 1900 and studied at the Naval Staff College, 1909–11. After study in Britain, 1911–14, he was assigned to the Navy General Staff, 1914–19. Promoted to captain in 1919, he became an instructor at the Naval Staff College in January 1920. He held a battle-ship command in 1922 and was promoted to rear admiral in 1924. He was named commander of the Kasumigaura Naval Air Group (where he took pilot training) in 1925. Following a tour of Europe and the United States, 1927–28, he was pro-moted to vice admiral and named chief of the Naval Aviation Department in 1928. He retired in 1931.

EGUSA TAKASHIGE (1910–1944). Born in Hiroshima Prefecture, he married the sis-ter of skilled fighter pilot Okamura Motoharu (q.v.). After graduating from the Naval Academy (58th class) in 1929, he was assigned to the Kasumigaura Naval Air Base for flight training in 1932, and there specialized in dive bombing. He was assigned to several land-based air groups, 1934–36, and as a member of the carrier *Hōshō*'s air group participated in air operations on the China coast in 1937. He was appointed division leader and instructor at the Yokosuka Naval Air Base in 1939, by which time he was established as a leading expert in dive bombing. He practiced extensively for the destruction of U.S. carriers based at Pearl Harbor, but since no carriers were in the harbor at the time of attack, he led his dive-bomber group against other targets of opportunity, including the battleship *Nevada*. He also participated in strikes against Wake Island and Port Darwin in the spring of 1942, as well as in dive-bombing attacks against British naval units in the Indian Ocean. He led the air group of the carrier *Sōryū* at Midway in June 1942 and was badly burned when that ship was attacked and sunk by U.S. air units. Posted as group leader with the Yokosuka Naval Air Group in September 1942, he was killed in the defense of Saipan on 15 June 1944.

FUCHIDA MITSUO (1902–1976). Carrier bomber pilot and famed veteran of the Pacific War. He was born in Nara Prefecture. Following his graduation from the Naval Academy (52d class) in 1924, he was sent to the Kasumigaura Naval Air Reconnaissance School in 1928. Assigned to the carrier *Kaga* in 1929 and then to the Sasebo Air Group the following year, he took flight training in 1932, following which he was assigned as air officer on several cruisers during 1933. He took spe-cialized training in horizontal bombardment at the Yokosuka Naval Air Base in 1936. Promoted to lieutenant commander in 1936, he was given command of the Thirteenth Special Air Group based at Nanking in 1938. He was posted to the staff of the Second Combined Air Group in 1938, following which he commanded, con-secutively, the air groups of the carriers *Ryūjō* and *Akagi*, 1938–39. He was pro-moted to commander in October 1941 and given command of the *Akagi* air group while concurrently serving as senior air officer of the First Air Fleet. In this capac-ity he led the first wave in the attack on Pearl Harbor on 7 December 1941 and helped plan the Midway campaign, during which he was injured in the destruction of the carrier *Akagi*. He was appointed instructor at the Naval Staff College in late 1942 and served on the staff of the First Air Fleet in 1943 and of the Combined Fleet in 1944. He attained the rank of captain in 1944. After the war he became a rice farmer and converted to Christianity. During the 1950s he frequently traveled to the United States to minister to Japanese immigrants there, and in 1966 he became an American citizen.

GENDA MINORU (1904–1989). Renowned fighter pilot, air tactician, and doctrinal innovator. A native of Hiroshima Prefecture, he graduated from the Naval Academy (52d class) in 1924 and studied at the Naval Staff College, 1935–37. After flight training, 1928–29, he was assigned to the carrier *Akagi* as a carrier fighter pilot in 1931. He was posted to the Yokosuka Naval Air Base in 1932 as a flight instructor and while there organized and led an acrobatic team known as the "Genda Circus." He was a division officer in the air group of the carrier *Ryūjō* in 1933, following which he served on the staff of the Second Combined Air Group and as such saw duty in China in the autumn of 1937. He was named senior flight instructor for the Yokosuka Air Group in 1938 and served as assistant naval attaché in London, 1938–40. He was promoted to commander and posted as senior air officer in the First Carrier Division in November 1940. Posted as senior air officer of the First Air Fleet in April 1941, he helped draw up tactical plans for the Pearl Harbor strike and participated in fleet operations in the Indian Ocean and at Midway in the spring of 1942. As air officer on the carrier *Shōkaku* he saw action in the Solomon Islands campaign in the summer and autumn of 1942. Appointed senior air officer in the Operations Division of the Navy General Staff in December 1942, he attained the rank of captain in 1944. He was given command of the 343d Naval Air Group in January 1945 and was charged with regaining control of the air over Japan through the use of the most advanced fighter aircraft. He ended the war at the Sasebo Naval Base. Recalled to duty after the war, he was appointed a major general and made deputy chief of staff in the Japan Air Self-Defense Force. He was named head of the Air Defense Command in 1957 and was promoted to general and appointed Chief of Staff of the Air Self-Defense Force in 1959. He retired in 1962 and was elected to the House of Councilors that same year.

IKEGAMI TSUGUO (1902–1986). A native of Kumamoto Prefecture, he graduated from the Naval Academy (51st class) in 1923. He was a division officer of the Ōmura Air Group and as such participated in air maneuvers in 1937 that pitted fighters (led by Ikegami) against attacking G3M medium bombers from Kanoya. He was group leader in the Thirteenth Air Group, 1937–38, and was thus heavily engaged in the early air combat of the China War. He was on the staff of the Twenty-third Air Flotilla, 1942–43, and was posted to the Naval Aviation Department, August 1943, concurrently serving on the Navy General Staff, August 1944. He held an additional assignment as a member of the Planning Group, War Materiel Bureau, Imperial

General Headquarters, 1944. Promoted to captain in 1944, he ended the war as chief of the First Section, General Affairs Bureau, Naval Aviation Department.

INOUE SHIGEYOSHI (SEIMI) (1889–1975). First-rate naval theorist and advocate of air supremacy. Born in Miyagi Prefecture, he graduated from the Naval Academy (37th class) in 1909 and from the Naval Staff College in 1924. His early naval career, which included two years on detached duty in Switzerland, 1918–20, and an assignment as naval attaché in Rome, 1927–28, mixed sea billets with some impressive staff assignments ashore. By 1935 he had attained flag rank and in 1937 was appointed chief of the Naval Affairs Department in the Navy Ministry. Two years later he became chief of staff of the China Area Fleet and attained the rank of vice admiral. In his capacity as chief of the Naval Aviation Department, to which he had been appointed in 1940, he voiced a scathing criticism of the navy's shipbuilding plans and its general strategic posture. In doing so he clearly foresaw the nature of the coming war with the United States but so irritated the navy brass with his criticisms that he was eased out of his position and transferred in August 1941 to command of the Fourth Fleet, with headquarters at Truk. As such he was in overall command of the forces that took Guam and Wake islands at the outset of the Pacific War. Subsequently, with his headquarters at Rabaul, he was overall commander for Operation "MO," which was designed to take Port Moresby and which led to the Japanese reverse at the Coral Sea in May 1942. Relieved of command of the Fourth Fleet in October of that year, he became superintendent of the Naval Academy. Toward the end of the war he came back into favor and assumed the position of navy vice minister, chief of the Navy Technical Department, and chief (once again) of the Naval Aviation Department. He attained the rank of admiral by war's end.

KAMEI YOSHIO (1896–1944). Veteran fighter pilot. Born in Tokyo, he graduated from the Naval Academy in 1918. He took his flight training in 1920–21 and became an instructor at the Kasumigaura Air Group in 1922. After a tour aboard the carrier *Hōshō*, 1923–24, he was a division leader with the Yokosuka Air Group, 1925–26. An observation tour of Europe and the United States followed, 1927–28, after which he was division officer in the Ōmura and Yokosuka air groups, 1928–29. He was air group leader in the Yokosuka Air Group, 1930–33, and air officer on the carriers *Ryūjō* and *Kaga*, 1933–34. During these years he was one of the first in the naval air service dedicated to improving the capabilities of fighter aircraft as opposed to bombers. He was executive officer and instructor at the Kasumigaura Naval Air Base, 1936–37. Again air officer on the *Kaga* in 1937, he was appointed to the staff of the First Carrier Division in December of that year. Following a posting as executive officer of the Ōita Air Group in December 1938, he was assigned to the staff of the Twelfth Combined Air Group, 1939–40. Promoted to captain in November 1940, in April 1941 he was given command of the newly formed Third Air Group, a fighter unit that spearheaded the Japanese naval air assault on the Philippines the following December. In preparation for this long-range operation, he was instrumental in developing techniques to reduce fuel consumption by the unit's aircraft. He commanded the carrier *Ryūhō* in November 1942 and was second in command of the First Air Fleet in March 1944. He was given command of the naval air defense of the Marianas in July 1944 and was killed in action in August. He was posthumously promoted to rear admiral.

KANEKO YŌZŌ (1882–1941). Born in Hiroshima, he was one of the pioneers of Japanese naval aviation. His brother was a rear admiral. He graduated from the Naval Academy (30th class) in 1902 and was a member of a joint army-navy commission to study the military uses of balloons in 1910. He was sent to France, 1911–12, to study aeronautics and undergo pilot training. He was attached to the Yokosuka Naval Base in 1912 and undertook the navy's first successful flight at Oppama in November of that year. Assigned to the seaplane tender *Wakamiya Maru* in March 1914, he participated in the navy's expedition against Tsingtao in September 1914. In 1916 he was appointed group leader of the newly formed Yokosuka Air Group. He made an observation trip to Europe, 1916–17, and was promoted to commander, 1917. After several postings in a training capacity, 1918–19, he became commander of the Sasebo Air Group in 1920. Promoted to captain in 1921, he successively held a cruiser command, a posting to the Navy General Staff, and an instructorship at the Naval Staff College, 1922–24. Promoted to admiral in 1926, he retired the next year.

KASHIMURA KAN'ICHI (1913–1943). One of the navy's top dogfighting experts. Born in Kagawa Prefecture, he entered the navy as a seaman. He undertook pilot training in 1934 and was assigned, successively, to the Ōmura, Yokosuka, and Kanoya air groups, 1934–36. Posted to the Thirteenth Air Group in 1937, he participated in the navy's fighter combat over central China, losing no time in downing several enemy aircraft. During a raid on Nan-ch'ang in December 1937, his unit battled with a large group of Chinese Curtiss Hawk fighters and in the encounter lost a substantial part of his port wing, though he managed to bring his aircraft safely back to base in a much heralded demonstration of pilot skill. With a score of eighteen enemy aircraft to his credit, he was posted to the Yokosuka Air Group in 1938 but returned to central China with the Twelfth Air Group in 1939 and was heavily engaged in strikes against Chinese bases there. Promoted to warrant officer in 1941 and flight warrant officer the next year, he was assigned to the 582d Air Group and participated in the losing air campaign over the Solomons in the autumn of 1942. He failed to return from an air battle over the Russell Islands in March 1943.

KIKUCHI TOMOZŌ (1896–1988). A native of Fukushima Prefecture, he graduated from the Naval Academy (45th class) in 1917 and was a student pilot in 1922. Assigned to the Kasumigaura and Yokosuka naval air groups, 1923–26, along with Kuwabara Torao (q.v.) and others, he was involved in the early development of torpedo bombing in the navy. Assigned, successively, to the carriers *Hōshō, Kaga,* and *Akagi,* 1927–29, he was air officer of the *Akagi* in 1934 and staff officer of the Second Carrier Division in 1935. Promoted to commander in 1935, he held staff positions at several land-based air groups, 1937–38. Commander of the Takao Air Group in 1939, he was promoted to the rank of captain that year and was appointed captain of the carrier *Hōshō* in 1940. Attached to the Naval Aviation Department in 1942, he was made captain of the carrier *Zuikaku* in 1943 and the carrier *Taihō* in 1944. Promoted to rear admiral in October 1944, he successively served as chief of staff of the Second and First air fleets, 1944–45.

KIRA SHUN'ICHI (1889–1947). One of the pioneers of Japanese naval aviation. Born in Ōita Prefecture, he graduated from the Naval Academy (40th class) in 1912 and passed through the Naval Staff College in 1936. He underwent flight training, 1916–17, and was assigned first to the newly formed Yokosuka Air Group and then to the seaplane tender *Wakamiya,* 1917–18. He served as division leader and instructor at the Yokosuka Air Group, 1919–20, and as a member of the navy's Provisional Aviation Training Department in 1921. He was instructor at the Kasumigaura Air Group in 1922. He was appointed air officer of the navy's first carrier, the *Hōshō,* in 1923 and in March of that year became the first Japanese aviator to land on that ship. He made an observation trip to Europe and the United States, 1925–26, following which he was appointed air officer on the carrier *Akagi* in 1927, assigned to the Yokosuka Air Group in 1928, and posted to the Naval Air Arsenal in 1929. He was promoted to the rank of captain in 1934 and given command of the carrier *Ryūjō* in 1935. Named chief of the Testing Division, Naval Air Arsenal, in 1937 and 1939, he assumed command of the Twelfth Combined Air Group in 1940. Attaining the rank of rear admiral in 1940, in May 1942 he was given command of the Twenty-second Air Flotilla, which had participated in the aerial conquest of the Netherlands East Indies. He was promoted to vice admiral in 1943 and attached to the Navy General Staff in 1944.

KOBAYASHI YOSHITO (1899–1950). Born in Tottori Prefecture, he graduated from the Naval Academy (49th class) in 1921. After flight training, 1924–25, he was assigned, successively, to the Ōmura, Kasumigaura, and Yokosuka air groups, 1925–27. Following assignment to the carrier *Akagi* in 1927, he was sent to Britain for advanced flight training, 1929–30. He served as division leader in the Yokosuka Air Group in 1930 and aboard the carrier *Kaga* in 1932. He commanded the air group of the carrier *Ryūjō* in 1936 and was on the staff of the Second Carrier Division in 1937. Promoted to commander in 1938, he served in the Naval Aviation Department, 1938–40, and was sent to Germany as a resident observer in 1941. He commanded the 253d Air Group based at Kavieng, 1942–43. Promoted to captain in May 1943, he was assigned to the Naval Air Arsenal in July of that year. In 1944 he was assigned to the Training Division of the Naval Aviation Department and ended the war as executive officer of the Yokosuka Air Group.

KOGA MINEICHI (1885–1944). A native of Saga Prefecture, he graduated from the Naval Academy (34th class) in 1906 and finished courses at the Naval Staff College in 1912 and 1915. After his promotion to captain in 1926, he was assigned to several important ship commands and several influential administrative positions ashore. Promoted to rear admiral in 1932 and made chief of the Intelligence Division of the Navy General Staff in 1933, he served as vice chief of the General Staff in 1937. He was commander of the China Area Fleet in 1941 and as such participated in the attack on Hong Kong that December. Upon the death of Adm. Yamamoto Isoroku (q.v.), he succeeded him as commander-in-chief of the Combined Fleet in May 1943 but died when his plane crashed in a storm off the Philippines in 1944.

KUSAKA RYŪNOSUKE (1892–1971). A native of Ishikawa Prefecture. His cousin was also a vice admiral. He passed through the Naval Academy (41st class) in 1913, the Naval Gunnery School in 1920, and the Naval Staff College in 1926. After several shipboard assignments he was appointed instructor at both the Kasumigaura Air Group and the Naval Staff College. Promoted to commander in 1930, he was assigned to the staff of the First Carrier Division and four years later, with the rank of captain, was posted to the Naval Aviation Department. There followed various staff assignments at sea and in Tokyo, interspersed with carrier commands. He attained the rank of rear admiral in 1940, and when the First Air Fleet was reorganized into the Pearl Harbor Strike Force, he was made its chief of staff. He played a major role in formulating the plans for the Pearl Harbor and Midway operations. After serving as chief of staff, Southeast Area Fleet, 1943–44, he became chief of staff of the Combined Fleet. He ended the war as a vice admiral in command of the Fifth Air Fleet based on Kyūshū.

KUWABARA TORAO (1894–1987). Active in the early development of aerial torpedo techniques and aircraft, he was born in Shizuoka Prefecture and passed through the Naval Academy (39th class) in 1909. He was given aviation training in 1915 and traveled through Europe and the United States in 1917. He was a member of the Japanese delegation to the Washington Naval Conference, 1921–22, and commanded the Kasumigaura Air Group in 1923. He held a number of command positions with various land-based air groups, 1923–30, and attained the rank of captain in 1928. He was given command of the carrier *Ryūjō* in 1933. Promoted to rear admiral in 1938, he commanded, successively, the Second and First combined air groups, which took the lead in aerial operations in central China, 1938–39. He commanded the Eleventh Combined Air Group in 1940 and, successively, the Fourth and Third air flotillas in 1941. Promoted to vice admiral in 1942, he ended the war as an administrator in the Naval Air Arsenal.

MAEDA KŌSEI (1897–1963). Born in Tokyo, he graduated from the Naval Academy (47th class) in 1919. Along with Kuwabara Torao (q.v.), Kikuchi Tomozō (q.v.), Saitō Masahisa (q.v.), and others, as a young lieutenant he developed the navy's aerial torpedo doctrine. He was air officer of the Genzan Air Group in 1940 and commanded the Saeki Air Group in 1941. On the staff of the Eleventh Air Fleet, he was consulted in the plans being developed for shallow-water aerial torpedo attack. Promoted to captain in 1941, he took over the Genzan Naval Air Group in October of that year. He thus participated in the sinking of the British capital ships *Repulse* and *Prince of Wales* in December 1941. He was posted as executive officer and senior instructor of the Kasumigaura Air Group in 1942 and commanded the 761st Air Group of medium bombers in the battle for the Marianas in July 1944.

MATSUNAGA TOSHIO (1888–1955). Born in Kōchi Prefecture, he graduated from the Naval Academy (37th class) in 1909 and passed through the Naval Staff College in 1921. Although he had no flight training, from his early career he was involved in naval aviation, being attached to the Yokosuka and Kasumigaura air groups in the early 1920s. He held a number of staff positions on the Navy General Staff, in the Navy Ministry, and in the Naval Aviation Department in the latter part of that decade. Executive officer of the carrier *Akagi* in 1928, he was promoted to captain in 1930 and commanded the carrier *Ryūjō* in 1933. He retired as rear admiral in 1936.

MOCHIZUKI ISAMU (1906–1944). Famed fighter pilot and supposedly the inventor of the half-loop and roll technique known as the *hineri-komi* maneuver. A native of Saga Prefecture, he entered the navy as a seaman in 1925 and completed the 9th Pilot Training Class in 1926. After serving aboard the carriers *Hōshō* and *Kaga,* he was posted to the Yokosuka Air Group, 1932–36, where he established a reputation as one of the best fighter pilots in Japan. Promoted to warrant officer, he was transferred to the Ōmura Air Group in 1937. Upon the outbreak of the China War he was posted to the Thirteenth Air Group and sent to the navy's Kunda Air Base outside of Shanghai, July 1937–January 1938, during which time he shot down seven enemy aircraft. He was instructor for several land-based air groups in Japan, 1938–41. Appointed division officer of the newly organized 281st Air Group, he was sent to the northern Kuriles in March 1943. While stationed on the navy's Roi-Namur Air Base on Kwajalein in the Marshalls in late 1943, he was killed in combat on the ground after all the navy's aircraft had been destroyed in the American assault on the island in February 1944.

MURATA SHIGEHARU (1909–1942). Famed torpedo pilot who perfected the shallow-water torpedo-launching techniques used with devastating effect at Pearl Harbor. A native of Nagasaki Prefecture, he passed through the Naval Academy (58th class) in 1930. After several shipboard assignments in the early 1930s, he undertook flight training at Kasumigaura, 1933–34. A member of several land-based air groups in China, 1937–38, he took part in the navy's aerial assault on the U.S. gunboat *Panay* in December 1937. After a stint aboard the carrier *Akagi* in 1938, he was one of two officers who completed a special course in special aerial torpedo attack, 1939–40. After service with the Ōmura and Yokosuka air groups in 1940, he saw duty in 1941 on three different carriers, the *Shōkaku, Ryūjō,* and *Akagi.* He led the torpedo squadron from the *Akagi* during the Pearl Harbor operation, following which he participated in operations in the Bismarck Archipelago and against Port Darwin, Java, and Ceylon, January–March 1942. Commanding the *Shōkaku*'s attack squadron at the Battle of the Santa Cruz Islands, he was killed in action leading an attack against the U.S. carrier *Hornet* in October 1942.

NAGUMO CHŪICHI (1886–1944). Victorious commander of Japanese carrier forces in the spring of 1942. Born in Yamagata Prefecture, he graduated from the Naval Academy (36th class) in 1908 and passed through the Naval Staff College in 1920. During his career he held numerous sea commands ranging from gunboats to carrier groups. As a torpedo expert, he was a strong advocate of combining sea and air power, though he was never comfortable in command of carriers because he lacked expertise in aviation. Nevertheless, he was given command of the First Air Fleet in 1941. In that position, despite his opposition to Yamamoto's plans for the Pearl Harbor operation and the subsequent criticism from some quarters that his refusal to sanction a third strike was overly cautious, he directed Japan's carrier forces during their greatest victories of the Pacific War: the Hawai'i operation, the attacks on Rabaul and Port Darwin, and the sweeping away of Allied naval forces from the eastern Indian Ocean in the winter and spring of 1942. With the sinking of his four carriers at Midway, however, he evidently lost whatever aggressiveness he had had and was relegated to shore commands, 1942–43. Called back to the front lines in 1944, he was given command of an essentially paper fleet at Saipan and died by his own hand in the futile defense of that island against American forces that June.

NAKAJIMA CHIKUHEI (1884–1949). Naval officer, aviation advocate, aircraft engineer, industrialist, and politician. Born in Gumma Prefecture, he graduated from the Naval Engineering School in 1908. He was also a student in the elective course of the Naval Staff College, 1911–12. A member of the Committee for the Study of the Military Uses of the Balloon in 1911, he was promoted to lieutenant senior grade and was sent to learn aircraft maintenance at the Glenn Curtiss School of Aviation at Hammondsport, N.Y., but on his own initiative took up flight training there, June–December 1912. He was attached to the Yokosuka Naval Base in 1912 and to the Yokosuka Naval Arsenal in 1913. As a member of the Office of Ship Construction at the arsenal, he was sent to France to observe naval construction. He resigned from naval service in 1917 to found his own aircraft company and eventually became a leading aircraft manufacturer in Japan. Elected to the Japanese Diet, he became a powerful political figure and held several ministerial posts in the 1930s.

NAKANO CHŪJIRŌ (1903–1977). Graduated from the Naval Academy (51st class) in 1923. After attending the 14th Aviation Student Class, from which he graduated with honors in 1926, he went on to take training in fighter tactics in the short course at the Japanese army Air Gunnery School at Akino. He was transferred to the Ōmura Air Group, where, with Kamei Yoshio (q.v.), he laid the foundation of the navy's fighter tactics in late 1929. He commanded the fighter squadron aboard the carrier *Kaga*, 1937–38, and did the same in the Thirteenth Air Group in 1939. In 1943–44 he commanded the fighter squadron of the 201st Air Group, seeing combat in the Solomon Islands–Bismarcks theater.

NANGŌ MOCHIFUMI (1906–1938). A navy fighter ace, he was a descendant of a distinguished naval family, his grandfather being a high official in the early Navy Ministry and his father being a rear admiral. He was born in Tokyo. After attending the prestigious Peers School, he passed through the Naval Academy (55th class) in 1927. He had a number of shipboard assignments, 1927–30, before graduating from the 22d Aviation Student Class in 1932. As a fighter pilot, he served first with the Tateyama Naval Air Group in 1932 and then aboard the carrier *Akagi* in 1933. He served as assistant naval attaché in London, 1935–37. He was a member, successively, of the Yokosuka, Ōmura, Kisarazu, and Thirteenth air groups in 1937, and as leader of six Mitsubishi A5M fighters he participated in the massacre of a much larger formation of Chinese fighters over Nan-ch'ang on 2 December 1937. He was air group leader aboard the carrier *Sōryū* in March 1938 and was shot down and killed in combat over Nan-ch'ang in July of that year and posthumously promoted to lieutenant commander. At the time of his death he was credited with having shot down eight enemy aircraft.

NARUSE SEIJI (1893–1960). Specialist in the development of aerial torpedoes. Born in Kagawa Prefecture, he graduated from the Tokyo University School of Engineering and entered the navy as an ordnance lieutenant in 1920. After a tour at the Yokosuka Naval Arsenal, 1920–21, he was assigned to the Torpedo Testing Department of the Kure Naval Arsenal in 1921. He was sent to Britain, 1925–26, to observe torpedo developments in that country. Through the good offices of the Whitehead Torpedo Company, he was given an explanation of a six-cylinder steel aerial torpedo that became the model for his development, in 1929, of a 45-centimeter (18-inch) aerial torpedo. This was the prototype for the Type 91 aerial torpedo that was adopted by the navy in 1931. Named ordnance inspector in the Navy Technical Department in 1931, he was promoted to captain and made a member of the Torpedo Testing Department at the Kure Naval Arsenal in 1938. He served in the Weapons Department of the Naval Air Arsenal in 1941, was appointed head of the Torpedo Attack Section of the Naval Aviation Department in 1943, and ended his career as an ordnance rear admiral.

NITTA SHIN'ICHI (1902–37). An expert bomber pilot and strong advocate of the superiority of bombing aircraft, he was born in Yamaguchi Prefecture and graduated from the Naval Academy (51st class) in 1923. After several tours aboard carriers in the early 1930s, he was appointed instructor at the Yokosuka Air Base in 1935. Promoted to lieutenant commander in 1936, he was appointed group leader of the Eleventh Air Group, whose bombing aircraft were judged to have inflicted major damage on the capital ships of the Combined Fleet in the annual fleet exercises of that year. Shortly after the outbreak of the China War he led a flight of G3M bombers from Kanoya to Taihoku (Taipei), 8 August 1937, and from there in a series of bombing raids against the Hang-chou area, 14–16 August. Shot down over Yang-chou on 16 August, he was posthumously promoted to commander.

ODAWARA TOSHIHIKO (1899–1945). Combat-tested fighter pilot. Born in Kagoshima Prefecture, he passed through the Naval Academy (48th class) in 1920. He graduated from the 10th Aviation Student Technical Class in 1923 and served, successively, in the Kasumigaura, Ōmura, and Yokosuka air groups, 1924–28. His assignments over the next four years interspersed service aboard the carrier *Hōshō* with duty at the Yokosuka Naval Air Arsenal's Testing Department. Promoted to lieutenant commander in 1932, he was fighter squadron commander and instructor at the Yokosuka Naval Air Base, 1933–35. It was at about this time that he became involved in a heated controversy with Comdr. Okamura Motoharu (q.v.) over the proper emphasis—speed versus maneuverability—in fighter design, Odawara insisting on speed. He was posted to the First Carrier Division in 1935 and was appointed air officer of the Ōmura Air Group in 1936, following which he was placed on the staffs, successively, of the Second and Third fleets, July–December 1937. Promoted to commander in December 1937, he was made air officer of the carrier *Sōryū*. He was a member of the Training Bureau of the Naval Aviation Department, 1938–40, and was on the staff of the Eleventh Combined Air Group, 1940–41. Promoted to captain in October 1941, he commanded the Kanoya (later renamed the 751st) Air Group, 1942–43, with service in the southwestern Pacific. Following a number of high-level administrative assignments in Tokyo, he was made chief of staff of the First Air Fleet in 1944. He was killed in action on Okinawa in January 1945 and posthumously promoted to rear admiral.

OKAMURA MOTOHARU (1900–1948). Fighter and test pilot. A native of Kōchi Prefecture, he was the brother-in-law of the navy's dive-bombing ace, Egusa Takashige (q.v.) He graduated from the Naval Academy (50th class) in 1922 and took flight training in 1925–26. His next six years were divided between assignments to land-based air groups (Ōmura and Yokosuka) and aboard carriers (the *Hōshō* and *Kaga*). Appointed division leader at the Yokosuka Air Group, 1932–34, he was one of the original members of the "Flying Circus" of Lt. Genda Minoru (q.v.). Also serving as a test pilot at Yokosuka at this time, he severely injured his hand while testing an experimental aircraft, an accident that ended his career as a fighter pilot. He was one of the navy airmen of these years who insisted that maneuverability should be the priority in aircraft design, rather than speed or rate of climb, a view heatedly opposed by contemporary fighter pilots like Odawara

Toshihiko (q.v.). Twice posted to carriers (the *Akagi* and *Kaga*), 1934–35, he was air group leader at several land-based air groups (Ōmura and Saiki) in 1936 and was commander of three others (Saiki, Ōita, and the Twelfth), 1937–40. He commanded but did not fly with the 202d (the former Third) Air Group, based at Kendari in the Celebes, during its 1942–43 combat tour. Promoted to captain, he commanded the 341st Air Group in 1944. In September 1944 he was given command of, but did not fly with, the 721st Air Group, a suicide unit, and ended the war as commander of the Kōchi Air Group. Posted as chief of personnel in the navy's demobilization office, 1945–46, he committed suicide in 1948.

OKUMIYA MASATAKE (1909–). Born in Kōchi Prefecture, he passed through the Naval Academy (58th class) in 1930. He completed his flight training in 1933, and with the exception of a posting aboard the carrier *Ryūjō*, 1934–36, all his assignments, 1933–41, were in land-based air groups (Ōmura, Kanoya, the Thirteenth, Yokosuka, Yatabe) and the Eleventh Combined Air Group. He was staff officer, successively, of the Fourth and Second carrier divisions, 1942–44, during which time he witnessed fierce air combat in the southwestern Pacific. Promoted to commander in 1944, he ended the war in an administrative billet on the Navy General Staff. In 1954 he entered the Japanese Air Self-Defense Force, where he served for ten years in both staff and line positions, ending his career at the rank of lieutenant general. He is the author of a number of books on Japanese naval aviation in the Pacific War.

ŌNISHI TAKIJIRŌ (1891–1945). High-ranking naval officer closely identified with the navy's kamikaze effort at the end of the Pacific War. A native of Hyōgo Prefecture, he passed through the Naval Academy (40th class) in 1912. After studying air combat and reconnaissance in Britain, 1918–21, he was assigned to the Yokosuka Air Group. In the mid-1920s he was an instructor at the Kasumigaura Naval Air Base. As the 1930s progressed, he held staff and line positions of increasing responsibility in naval aviation, including flight commands ashore and on carriers (the *Hōshō* and *Kaga*) and staff assignments with the Naval Aviation Department. Promoted to rear admiral in 1939, he was made chief of staff of the Eleventh Air Fleet in 1941. As such, he had a part in Yamamoto Isoroku's Pearl Harbor attack plan and in the coordination of the devastating air attacks on the Philippines from bases on Taiwan. Attaining the rank of vice admiral in 1943, he held several important administrative positions in Tokyo before being sent to the Philippines in October 1944 to take command of the First Air Fleet, by then an entirely land-based air command. In that capacity he developed the concept of aerial suicide attacks on American warships and directed the first such attacks. He took up the position of vice chief of the Navy General Staff in May 1945, and on 15 August 1945, after hearing the emperor's surrender broadcast, committed ritual suicide.

OZAWA JISABURŌ (1886–1966). One of the ablest flag officers in the Japanese navy during the Pacific War. Born in Miyazaki Prefecture, he graduated from the Naval Academy (37th class) in 1909 and from the navy's Torpedo School in 1917. He served mostly at sea as commander, successively, of a destroyer squadron, a cruiser, and a battleship. As rear admiral he served as chief of staff of the Combined Fleet, 1937, and as commander of the First Carrier Division. Later, as a vice admiral, he commanded the Southern Expeditionary Fleet, which supported the Japanese conquest of Malaya and the Netherlands East Indies in the winter of 1941–42, and which supported operations in the Indian Ocean in the spring of 1942. In 1944, as commander of the First Mobile Fleet and the Third Fleet (the navy's principal carrier forces at that time), he was outmatched and outfought by Admiral Spruance's Task Force 58 in the Battle of the Philippine Sea. In command of the decoy force in the Leyte Gulf campaign, he saw his carriers smashed at the Battle of Cape Engano in October 1944. He ended the war as commander of the Combined Fleet, which by then existed largely as a paper force.

SAITŌ MASAHISA (1897–1996). Born in Miyagi Prefecture, he was married to the younger sister of the wife of Yamamoto Isoroku. He graduated from the Naval Academy (47th class) in 1919 and underwent flight training in 1922–23. Most of his early years in naval aviation, 1925–31, he spent either with the Kasumigaura Air Group or as one of the flight crew aboard the carrier *Hōshō*. It was during these years that, along with Kuwabara Torao (q.v.), Kikuchi Tomozō (q.v.), and others, he helped develop the navy's aerial torpedo doctrine. Following an observation tour of the United States in 1934, he was air group leader, successively, aboard the carriers *Ryūjō* and *Akagi*, 1934–35. Promoted to commander in 1936, he had a tour in the Technical Bureau of the Naval Aviation Department in 1937. He spent the years 1937–40 in senior positions with various land-based air groups (Yokosuka, the Fifteenth, Kasumigaura, Ōmura, and Kisarazu). Promoted to captain in 1941, he was named commander of the famed Tainan Air Group and took it into combat in the Solomon Islands air campaign in 1942. He served in top positions with the Naval Aviation Department, 1942–44. His last two years were with land-based air groups in the Japanese home islands (the 221st, the 252d, and Yokosuka).

SAKAI SABURŌ (1916–2000). Of all the navy's fighter pilots, the one best known in the West. Born in Saga Prefecture, he enlisted in the navy as a seaman in 1933. He underwent flight training at Tsuchiura, 1937–38, and was posted to the Twelfth Air Group—then engaged in air combat over central China—in 1938. He was posted to the Twelfth again in 1941 and participated in attacks on Cheng-tu and Lan-chou, during which time he was credited with numerous kills. Promoted to pilot officer first class in June 1941, he was transferred to the Tainan Air Group. Upon the outbreak of the Pacific War he participated as a division officer in air battles over the Philippines and the Netherlands East Indies. In those months he boosted his record of enemy aircraft destroyed, including, supposedly, the B-17 piloted by Colin Kelly. In April 1942 the Tainan Air Group was advanced to Rabaul, and it was there at the time of the American landings on Guadalcanal. On 7 August, the first day of air battle over that island, Sakai was severely wounded in aerial combat and made a heroic and agonizing flight back to base. He was subsequently transferred back to the Ōmura Air Group in the home islands and then to the Yokosuka Air Group as instructor. He participated in one more air combat, off Iwo Jima in June 1944, but was forced to give up air combat because of failing eyesight. His autobiography was published in English under the title *Samurai!*

SHIBATA TAKEO (1904–1994). Fighter pilot and fighter plane advocate. Born in Fukushima Prefecture, he passed through the Naval Academy (52d class) in 1924. He underwent aviation training, 1928–30, and served aboard the carriers *Kaga* and *Hōshō,* 1930–32. After additional flight training in 1933, he was assigned to the Ōmura Air Group, 1935–36, during which time he was one of a number of pilots who effectively articulated the importance of fighter aircraft as opposed to a force structure that emphasized bombers. He commanded the fighter squadron aboard the carrier *Kaga,* 1936–37, and was a test pilot for the Naval Air Arsenal in 1938. He was air group leader of the Twelfth Air Group, 1938–39, then involved in combat over central China. Following a staff position at the Kure Naval Base, 1939–40, he was posted as air officer of the First Air Group's fighter squadron in 1941. Promoted to commander, he was executive officer of the famed Third Air Group, 1941–42. He was posted to a number of other land-based air groups, 1942–44, including a tour as commander of the 204th Air Group at Rabaul during the furious air combat over that base, March–September 1944. Promoted to captain in 1944, he ended the war as commander of the 312th Air Group.

SHINDŌ SABURŌ (1911–2000). A renowned fighter pilot, he was born in Hiroshima, graduated from the Naval Academy (60th class) in 1932, and passed through the 26th Aviation Student Class in 1935. He was assigned to the Twelfth Air Group early in the China War and in August 1940 participated in the first attack on Chungking that employed the new Zero fighter aircraft. The next month he commanded a flight of thirteen Zeros that engaged Chinese interceptors in a fierce battle over the same city. He was division officer aboard the carrier *Akagi,* April–December 1941, and as such led thirty-six Zeros in the second wave in the attack on Pearl Harbor. Serving with several land-based air groups and aboard the carrier *Ryūhō,* he participated in the air campaign in the Solomon Islands, 1943–44.

SHIRANE AYAO (1916–1944). One of the navy's noted air aces. Born in Tokyo, he passed through the Naval Academy (64th class) in 1937. He completed flight training in March 1939 and was posted to the Twelfth Air Group, then based at Hankow. As a fighter pilot with that unit he was involved in the first several operations over Chungking that involved Zero fighters in the late summer of 1940.

After the outbreak of the Pacific War, as division officer of the fighter squadron aboard the carrier *Akagi,* he participated in the attack on Port Darwin and fought at Midway. Transferred to the carrier *Zuikaku* as a division officer in July 1942, he fought in the Battle of the Eastern Solomons. He served with the Yokosuka Air Group, 1942–44, and in October 1944 took command of the fighter squadron of the 341st Air Group, based at Mabalacat, Luzon. He participated in air battles over Leyte and was killed in action against American fighters in November 1944. At the time of his death he had nine confirmed enemy aircraft kills to his credit.

TAKAHASHI SADAMU (1912–). Prominent in the perfection of Japanese dive-bombing techniques, he was born in Ehime Prefecture, graduated from the Naval Academy (61st class) in 1933, and completed his flight training in 1935. After assignments with several land-based air groups he was appointed a division leader of dive bombers aboard the carrier *Ryūjō* in 1938 and with the Fourteenth Air Group in 1939. It was during his tours as instructor at several air bases, 1940–41, that he perfected the techniques that were disseminated throughout the navy's dive-bombing units and used with such effect in the first six months of the Pacific War. He was commander of the carrier *Zuikaku*'s squadron Type 99 dive bombers and as such participated in the battle of the Eastern Solomons, August 1942 (where he missed a major opportunity to locate and destroy the crippled American carrier *Enterprise*). In October, at the Battle of Santa Cruz, he led another flight of dive bombers, but his aircraft was so badly shot up that after fighting the controls for six hours, he was obliged to ditch at sea and was fortunate to be rescued by nearby Japanese ships. Takahashi also participated in Operation I-GO, April 1943, after which he was posted back to Japan, where he served out the rest of the war. In the postwar years he served with the Maritime Self-Defense Force and was later hired by Japan Air Lines.

TORISU TAMAKI (1877–1949). Born in Saga Prefecture. He graduated from the Naval Academy (25th class) in 1897 and from the Naval Staff College in 1909. He held a number of staff appointments at sea and ashore, 1905–12, and was dispatched to Britain as an observer in 1912. He attained the rank of captain in that year, was resident officer in Britain, 1916–17, and following his return wrote a report on British naval operations during World War I. He was naval attaché in London, 1922–23. The remainder of his career was largely spent in higher staff positions and major base commands. Retiring in 1931, he was equerry to Prince Fushimi, 1938–45.

TSUNODA HITOSHI (1906–N.A.). A native of Aomori Prefecture, he graduated from the Naval Academy (55th class) in 1927 and completed courses at the Naval Staff College in 1940. He underwent flight training in 1930–31 and again in 1934. His service during the years 1931–39 was largely spent either with land-based naval air groups (Sasebo and Yokosuka) or as air officer aboard cruisers. He was made instructor in air combat tactics at the Yokosuka Air Group in 1940 and was attached to the Combined Fleet in November 1941. He joined the Naval Aviation Department in 1942 and was appointed commander in 1943. He was posted to the staff of the Third Air Fleet in February 1945 and ended the war as commander of the Thirteenth Air Flotilla. After the war he joined the war history editorial staff in the Self-Defense Agency and thus may be regarded as an authoritative source on Japanese naval air history.

WADA HIDEHO (1886–1972). Pioneer in Japanese naval aviation, pilot, and carrier commander. Born in Tokyo, he graduated from the Naval Academy (34th class) in 1906 and completed study at the Naval Staff College in 1912. He was appointed a member of the Aviation Research Committee at Yokosuka in 1914 and served aboard the seaplane carrier *Wakamiya Maru*, 1914–15, during which time he participated in operations against German ships and aircraft at Tsingtao. After a tour of Allied countries, 1916–17, he became aviation instructor aboard the *Wakamiya* (the former *Wakamiya Maru*) in 1917 and was executive officer of the Yokosuka Air Group in 1918. During the next five years he held various posts in the Navy Ministry, in the Naval Staff College, and on the Navy General Staff. Promoted to the rank of commander in 1922 and captain in 1926, he became executive officer and chief instructor at the Kasumigaura Air Group in 1923 and commanded the Sasebo Air Group in 1924 and the Yokosuka Air Group in 1927. He was captain of the carrier *Hōshō* in 1929 and the carrier *Akagi* in 1930, and as such was one of the few Japanese naval aviators who ever held carrier commands. Hospitalized during 1931–32 after being struck by an aircraft landing on the deck of the *Akagi*, he was posted to the Naval Aviation Department in 1932 and, concurrently, was chief of the Aircraft Division of the Naval Air Arsenal. Promoted to rear admiral that same year, he commanded the Kasumigaura Air Group in 1933 and the First Carrier Division in 1934. He ended his career as a vice admiral, attached to the Navy General Staff. His published reminiscences are a valuable source for the early history of Japanese naval aviation.

YAMADA CHŪJI (1883–1971). One of the pioneers of Japanese naval aviation. Born in Aichi Prefecture, he graduated from the Naval Academy (33d class) in 1905 and passed through the Naval Staff College in 1911. He took flight training at the Glenn Curtiss School of Aviation at Hammondsport, N.Y., June–December 1912, served aboard the seaplane carrier *Wakamiya Maru* in 1914, and participated in the campaign against German naval and air units at Tsingtao. Following a posting as executive officer of the navy's first land-based air unit, the Yokosuka Air Group, in 1916, his assignments over the next three years were divided between that unit and service on the *Wakamiya* (formerly the *Wakamiya Maru*). Appointed to the Navy Technical Department in 1920, he served with various land-based air groups (Yokosuka, Sasebo, Ōmura) in executive or command positions, 1923–24. Promoted to commander in 1923 and captain in 1928, he held executive or command positions with the Kasumigaura and Yokosuka air groups, 1928–32. He served as chief of the Testing Division, and then as chief of the Aircraft Division, of the Naval Air Arsenal, 1933–34. He was promoted to rear admiral in 1934 and retired while on the Navy General Staff in 1936. He was briefly recalled to active service in March 1945 as a member of a special commission on naval air weapons.

YAMAGUCHI TAMON (1892–1942). Born in Shimane Prefecture, he graduated from the Naval Academy (40th class) in 1912 and passed through the Naval Staff College in 1924. His early career, 1913–21, was devoted to destroyers, submarines, and torpedo warfare. He studied at Princeton University, 1921–23, and was a member of the Japanese delegation to the London Naval Conference in 1929. Promoted to captain in 1934, he served as naval attaché, Washington, 1934–36. Promoted to rear admiral in 1938, he was given command of the First Combined Air Group and as such directed its saturation-bombing campaign in central China in 1940. He commanded the Second Carrier Division (carriers *Hiryū* and *Sōryū*) and thus participated in the Pearl Harbor strike and the Battle of Midway. He went down with his ship when the *Hiryū* was sunk at Midway.

YAMAJI KAZUYOSHI (1869–1963). Born in Aichi Prefecture. His wife was the daughter of Adm. Yamamoto Gombei. He graduated from the Naval Academy (17th class) in 1890 and passed through the Naval Staff College in 1906. After study in Britain, 1900–1903, he held a number of ship commands before being assigned to the Navy General Staff in 1911. Promoted to captain in 1908, in 1913, together with Lt. Kōno Sankichi, he made a tour of Europe and the United States gathering information on the progress of naval aviation abroad. Promoted to rear admiral in 1914 and vice admiral in 1918, he spent the remainder of his career, 1916–22, in base and battleship division commands.

YAMAMOTO EISUKE (1876–1962). Conceptual father of Japanese naval aviation. A native of Kagoshima Prefecture, he was the nephew of Adm. Yamamoto Gombei, the most influential figure in the navy of the late Meiji era. Born in Kagoshima Prefecture, he graduated from the Naval Academy (24th class) in 1897 and from the Naval Staff College in 1907. Promoted to lieutenant commander in 1907, he became interested in aviation and was influential, quite possibly through his family connections, in provoking the navy's interest in this emerging dimension of warfare. He held increasingly important positions on the Navy General Staff, in the Navy Technical Department, and in the Naval Staff College, 1915–27, and was promoted to vice admiral in 1924. He was named the first chief of the Naval Aviation Department in 1927, following which he held important fleet commands, ending his career with his service on the Supreme War Council in 1932.

YAMAMOTO ISOROKU (1884–1943). Along with Tōgō Heihachirō, Yamamoto is one of the two Japanese naval figures best known in the West, his fame resting largely on his role in planning the Hawai'i operation in 1941 and the Midway campaign of 1942. He was born Takano Isoroku but was adopted in his youth by the Yamamoto family. After graduation from the Naval Academy in 1904, he was just in time to participate in the Battle of Tsushima, losing two fingers in that action. After a number of shipboard assignments he passed through the "B" course at the Naval Staff College in 1911 and the "A" course in 1916. Promoted to lieutenant commander in 1915, he was sent for study in the United States, where he attended Harvard University, 1919–21. He attained the rank of commander in 1919 and after a tour as executive officer aboard a cruiser and a tour of Europe and America, 1923–24, was promoted to captain. After a posting as executive officer with the Kasumigaura Air Group in 1924 and serving as naval attaché in Washington, 1925–28, his next several assignments all dealt with naval aviation: captain of the aircraft carrier *Akagi,* 1928, chief of the Technical Bureau of the Naval Aviation Department, 1930–33, and commander of the First Carrier Division, 1933. He had been promoted to rear admiral in 1929 and attained the rank of vice admiral in 1934. Following his responsibilities at the London Naval Conference, he was made chief of the Naval Aviation Department in 1935. Appointed navy vice minister in 1936, he served concurrently as chief of the Naval Aviation Department, 1938–39. Following his appointment as commander in chief of the Combined Fleet, he was promoted to admiral. In April 1943, while making an inspection tour of the southwestern Pacific theater, the naval aircraft in which he was riding was shot down over Bougainville by American fighter planes. He was posthumously promoted to admiral of the fleet.

YOKOYAMA TAMOTSU (1909–1981). He graduated from the Naval Academy (59th class) in 1931 and completed his flight training at Kasumigaura in 1935. He served with the Tateyama, Saiki, Ōmura, Thirteenth, and Kisarazu air groups, 1935–37. As a member of the fighter squadron of the carrier *Sōryū,* 1938–39, he saw considerable combat over central China, and as a division leader in the Twelfth Air Group was one of the first to command a unit of Zero fighters in combat—an attack on Chungking, 19 August 1940. Air group leader of the famed Third Air Group, he led Zero fighters in attacks on Iba and Clark airfields in the Philippines, 8 December 1941. After serving as staff officer of the Twenty-sixth Air Flotilla, Rabaul, in 1943, he took command of the Tsukuba Air Group in the home islands in June 1944 and of the 203d Air Group in the defense of southern Kyūshū in May 1945. After the war he held several senior positions in the Japan Air Self-Defense Force, retiring in 1964. His memoirs are a valuable source of information on Japanese naval aviation in the China and Pacific wars.

Appendix 2

Glossary of Naval Aviation Terms

Information for this appendix was drawn from the following sources: Hata and Izawa, *Japanese Naval Aces,* xiii–xiv; Lundstrom, *First Team: Pacific Naval Air Combat,* 183–86; and consultation with Osamu Tagaya.

Aircraft

Kansen (Kanjō sentōki):	Carrier fighter. Japanese romanized symbol: f^c.
Kanbaku (Kanjō bakugekki):	Carrier bomber (usually meaning a dive bomber). Japanese romanized symbol: f^b.
Kankō (Kanjō kōgekki):	Carrier attack bomber (sometimes employed as a torpedo bomber, sometimes as a horizontal attack aircraft). Japanese romanized symbol: f^o.
Hikōtei:	Flying boat
Suitei (suijō teisatsuki):	Reconnaissance seaplane. Japanese romanized symbol: f^{sr}.
Rikkō (rikujō kōgekki):	Medium land-based bomber. Japanese romanized symbol: $f1^o$.

Administrative Organizations
(See also app. 3 and app. 5.)

Kōkū kantai:	Air fleet (sea- or land-based)
Kōkū sentai:	Carrier division or land-based air flotilla
Kōkūtai:	In the broadest terms, this could comprise both a flight element and a base element of a land-based air group. In terms of the flight element, it was generally composed of eighteen to twenty-seven aircraft (sometimes more) and took the name of the air base where it was originally formed. It could be either homogenous or composed of different types of aircraft.
Hikōtai:	A carrier flight echelon or the flight echelon of a land-based *kōkūtai*
Hikō buntai:	The smallest administrative unit of aviation personnel (as opposed to operational/tactical formations of aircraft)

Operational/Tactical Formations

Hikōkitai:	A carrier aircraft echelon that took the name of the carrier on which it was embarked (and that was as much a part of the carrier's complement as any of the crew) or the flight echelon of a land-based *kōkūtai* that took the name of the air base on which it was located
Daitai:	Eighteen to twenty-seven aircraft
Chūtai:	Nine aircraft
Shōtai:	Three aircraft

Aviation Personnel

Fukuchō:	Executive officer; second in command of a ship or an air group
Hikōchō:	Air officer in charge of flight operations on a carrier or with a land-based *kōkūtai*. His was essentially a desk position, and he did not normally fly with his unit in combat.
Hikō buntaichō:	Sometimes called a *buntaichō*. Leader of a *chūtai* of around nine aircraft. Though *buntai* really has no appropriate English translation, for lack of any other accurate English term *buntaichō* has sometimes been translated as "division leader."
Hikōtaichō:	Air group leader; the senior officer of an air group in combat
Seibichō:	Maintenance officer of either a land-based *kōkūtai* or a carrier-based *hikōkitai*
Shirei:	Commander of a *kōkūtai*; the equivalent of the *kanchō* (captain) of a ship. Usually an aviator of some experience. As a rule he did not fly with the air group in combat.

Appendix 3

Generic Organization of Japanese Naval Aviation

Information for this appendix was drawn from the following sources: Lundstrom, *First Team: Pacific Naval Air Combat*, 184; Hata and Izawa, *Japanese Naval Aces*, xiv; and consultation with Osamu Tagaya.

The generic administrative and operational organization of Japanese naval aviation on the eve of the Pacific War can be confusing for many reasons: organizational equivalents do not always exist in Western terminology (e.g., *hikō buntai*, a unit of personnel, has no equivalent in Western air services); the same Japanese term will have a different English translation depending upon whether the organization in question is sea-based or land-based (e.g., *kōkū sentai*); there are not always equivalents between sea-based and land-based units; and at the lowest levels, distinction has to be made between personnel units (e.g., *hikō buntai*) and aircraft units (e.g., *daitai*, *chūtai*, and *shōtai*).

Administrative		Operational		
Sea-Based	Land-Based	Sea-Based	Land-Based	C.O. Rank
Kōkū kantai (air fleet)		*Kidō butai* (striking force)	*Kichi kōkūtai* (base air force)	Vice Adm.
Kōkū sentai (carrier division)	(air flotilla)	*Kūshū butai* (air attack force)	—	Rear Adm.
Kōkū bōkan (aircraft carrier)	*Kōkūtai* (air group)	—	—	Capt.
Hikōtai (flight echelon)		*Hikōkitai* (aircraft echelon)	same	Comdr. or Lt. Comdr.
—		*Daitai* (27 aircraft)	same	Lt. Comdr. or Lt. s.g.
Hikō buntai		*Chūtai* (9 aircraft)	same	Lt. s.g. or Lt. j.g.
—		*Shotai* (3 aircraft)	same	Lt. j.g., WO, or CPO

Appendix 4

Naval Aviation Vessels

This appendix details the specifications and histories of the naval aviation vessels in the Japanese inventory at the outbreak of the Pacific War. In all cases, the vessels are depicted as they would have appeared in December 1941.

The hangar-deck dimensions of many of these vessels are known only approximately. Even "exact" dimensions can be misleading, as the spaces themselves were invariably irregular in shape. Thus, the square-footage figure provided should be used as a rough measure of the aircraft-carrying capacity of the vessel rather than as a hard-and-fast figure.

The following abbreviations are used in this appendix:

OA	overall length;
PP	length between perpendiculars (length between the stem and the rudder post centerline);
WL	waterline;
DP	dual purpose (ordnance intended for use against both ships and aircraft);
AA	antiaircraft;
HA	high altitude;
LA	low altitude;
MG	machine gun.

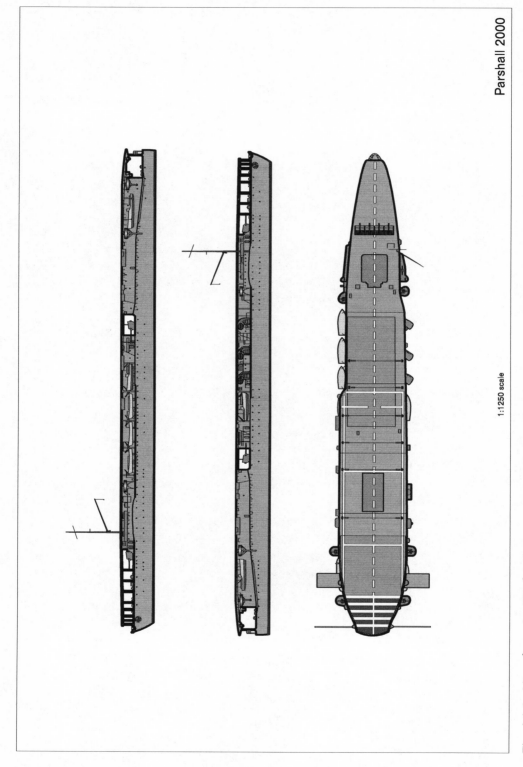

1:1250 scale

Fig. A4-1. Aircraft carrier *Hōshō*

The following plans and photographic sources were used in compiling this appendix: *SZ*, 1; Jentschura et al., *Warships of the Imperial Japanese Navy*; Chesneau, *Aircraft Carriers of the World*; Hasegawa, *Nihon no kōkūbōkan*; Katō Sadatoshi, *Nihon kaigun kantei zumen*, no. 3; D. Brown, *Aircraft Carriers*; Nakamura, *Taiheiyō sensō shi shirizu*, nos. 13 and 14; *Maru* Magazine, *Nihon kaigun kantei shashinshū*, nos. 5 and 6; Watts and Gordon, *Imperial Japanese Navy*; and additional miscellaneous plans in the possession of the illustrator.

Hōshō

Builder:	Asano Shipbuilding Co., Tsurumi
Laid down:	16 Dec 1919
Launched:	13 Nov 1921
Commissioned:	27 Dec 1922
Displacement:	7,470 tons (standard), 9,630 tons (normal)
Length:	551ft 6in (OA), 541ft 4in (WL), 510ft 0in (PP)
Beam:	59ft 1in
Draught:	20ft 3in
Machinery:	2 sets Parsons geared turbines, 12 Kampon boilers, 2 shafts
Performance:	30,000shp; 25 knots
Bunkerage:	2,695 tons fuel, 940 tons coal
Range:	8,000nm at 14 knots
Flight-deck dimensions:	519ft 0in × 74ft 6in
Elevators:	2 (42ft 4in × 27ft 10in, 44ft 11in × 36ft 1in)
Arrester wires:	6
Hangar decks:	1
Hangar dimensions:	423ft 6in × 55ft 0in (max); 23,292sq ft (approx)
Aircraft:	11
Armament:	16 × 25mm AA
Armor:	None
Complement:	550

NOTES: Originally laid down as an oiler. Work was suspended on the *Hōshō*'s hull when Japan decided to complete her instead as the navy's first aircraft carrier. As such, her hull form was little changed from the original design, a single hangar being added on top of the old weather deck. Originally a simple island was fitted on the starboard side, but this was removed shortly after her trials owing to the hazards it created for landing aircraft on the small flight deck.

The *Hōshō*'s flight deck provided much of the early experimentation in Japanese

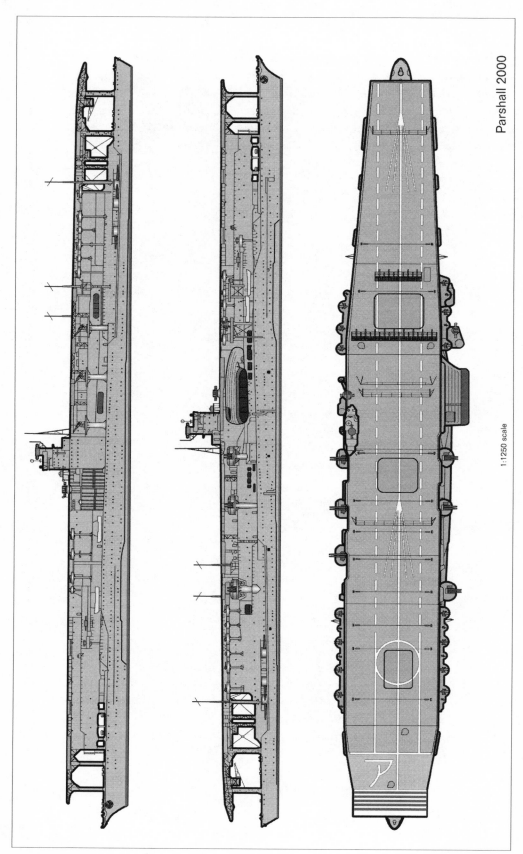

Parshall 2000

1:1250 scale

Fig. A4-2. Aircraft carrier *Akagi*

naval aviation in the 1920s. Among other things, she was a test bed for both arresting-gear systems and optical landing aids (lights). By the outbreak of the Pacific War, the *Hōshō* was clearly a second-rate unit and consequently spent most of her time as a training ship. She did, however, participate in the Midway campaign by providing fighter cover for the Main Body. Although attacked by U.S. carrier aircraft at Kure in 1945, the *Hōshō* survived the war and was used as a repatriation ship. She was scrapped in 1947.

Akagi

Builder:	Kure Naval Dockyard
Laid down:	6 Dec 1920
Launched:	22 Apr 1925
Commissioned:	25 Mar 1927

As Built

Displacement:	26,900 tons (standard), 34,364 tons (normal)
Length:	857ft 0in (OA), 816ft 7in (WL), 764ft 5in (PP)
Beam:	95ft 0in
Draught:	26ft 6in
Machinery:	Gijitsu Honbu geared turbines, 19 Kampon boilers, 4 shafts
Performance:	131,000shp; 31 knots
Bunkerage:	3,900 tons fuel oil, 2,100 tons coal
Range:	8,000nm at 14 knots
Flight-deck dimensions:	562ft 0in × 100ft 0in, plus 60ft (approx) and 160ft (approx) flying-off platforms at hangar-deck levels
Elevators:	2 (38ft 6in × 42ft 8in, 42ft 0in × 27ft 6in)
Arrester wires:	Longitudinal system initially, then 6 wires (electrically controlled)
Hangar decks:	3 (upper, middle, and lower; lower used for disassembled aircraft stowage only)
Hangar dimensions:	upper 516ft × 75ft (approx), middle 557ft × 75ft (approx), lower 170ft × 50ft (approx); upper and middle hangar area 80,475sq ft total (approx), lower hangar 8,515sq ft (approx)
Aircraft:	60
Armament:	10 × 8in/50-cal LA, 12 × 4.7in/45-cal HA, 22 MGs
Armor:	6in belt, 3.1in deck
Complement:	1,600

As Reconstructed (1935–38)

Displacement:	36,500 tons (standard), 41,300 tons (normal)
Length:	855ft 3in (OA), 821ft 5in (WL), 770ft 0in (PP)
Beam:	102ft 9in
Draught:	28ft 7in
Machinery:	Gijitsu Honbu geared turbines, 19 Kampon boilers, 4 shafts
Performance:	133,000shp; 31.25 knots
Bunkerage:	5,775 tons fuel oil
Range:	8,200nm at 16 knots
Flight-deck dimensions:	817ft 6in × 100ft 0in
Elevators:	3 (38ft 6in × 42ft 6in, 42ft 0in × 27ft 6in, 37ft 6in × 41ft 3in)
Arrester wires:	9 (hydraulic)
Hangar decks:	3 (upper, middle, and lower; lower used for disassembled aircraft stowage only)
Hangar dimensions:	upper and middle 620ft × 75ft (approx), lower 170ft × 50ft (approx); upper and middle hangar area 93,000sq ft (approx), lower hangar 8,515sq ft (approx)
Aircraft:	91
Armament:	6 × 8in/50-cal LA, 12 × 4.7in/45-cal HA, 28 × 25mm AA
Armor:	6in belt, 3.1in deck
Complement:	2,000

NOTES: The *Akagi* was originally laid down as a battle cruiser in 1920. Subsequent to the Washington Naval Treaty of 1922, she was taken in hand in late 1923 for completion as an aircraft carrier. After significant alterations—including major revisions to the armor belt to conserve top weight for usage in the aircraft hangars—the *Akagi* was launched in 1925 and commissioned two years later.

As constructed, the *Akagi* had three aircraft flight decks and no superstructure. The validity of this arrangement was called into question as aircraft and flight-deck operational techniques evolved in the 1930s. After a major refit beginning in October 1935, she emerged in August 1938 with a single full-length flight deck, enlarged hangar space, a third lift, and a true carrier "island" carried on the port side of the flight deck. Antiaircraft armament was also increased.

As Japan's first true fleet carrier, the *Akagi* (along with the *Kaga*,) acted as a test bed for the development of Japanese naval air doctrine throughout the 1930s. She served as flagship of Carrier Division 1 and as flagship of the First Air Fleet from April 1940 onward. She participated in actions against China and in every major carrier campaign during the opening stages of the Pacific War. She was scuttled on 5 June 1942 during the Battle of Midway, after receiving two bomb hits that resulted in uncontrollable fires and induced explosions.

Kaga

Builder:	Kawasaki Dockyard Co. and Yokosuka Naval Dockyard
Laid down:	19 Jul 1920
Launched:	17 Nov 1921
Commissioned:	31 Mar 1928

As Built

Displacement:	26,000 tons (standard), 33,693 tons (normal)
Length:	782ft 6in (OA), 771ft 0in (WL), 715ft 1in (PP)
Beam:	97ft 0in
Draught:	26ft 0in
Machinery:	Brown-Curtiss geared turbines, 12 Kampon boilers, 4 shafts
Performance:	91,000shp; 28.5 knots
Bunkerage:	3,600 tons fuel oil, 1,700 tons coal
Range:	8,000nm at 14 knots
Flight-deck dimensions:	560ft 0in × 100ft 0in, plus 60ft (approx) and 160ft (approx) flying-off platforms at hangar-deck levels
Elevators:	2 (37ft 8in × 39ft 5in, 35ft 0in × 52ft 0in)
Arrester wires:	6 (electrically controlled)
Hangar decks:	3 (upper, middle, and lower; lower used for disassembled aircraft stowage only)
Hangar dimensions:	upper 415ft × 65ft (approx), middle 470ft × 75ft (approx), lower 116ft × 48ft (approx); upper and middle hangar area 62,225sq ft (approx), lower hangar 5,568sq ft (approx)
Aircraft:	60
Armament:	10 × 8in/50-cal LA, 12 × 4.7in/45-cal HA, 2 MGs
Armor:	6in belt, 1.5in deck
Complement:	1,340

As Reconstructed (1934–35)

Displacement:	38,200 tons (standard), 42,541 tons (normal)
Length:	812ft 6in (OA), 788ft 5in (WL), 738ft 2in (PP)

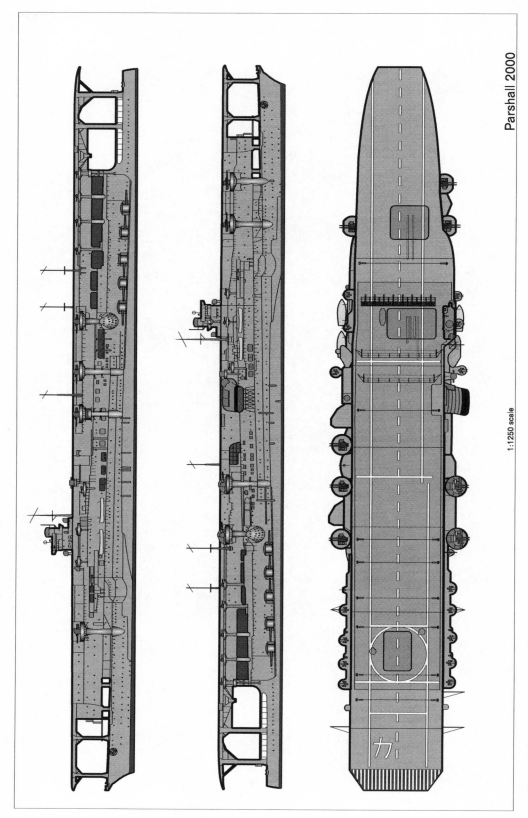

Parshall 2000

1:1250 scale

Fig. A4-3. Aircraft carrier *Kaga*

Beam:	106ft 8in
Draught:	31ft 1in
Machinery:	Kampon geared turbines, 8 Kampon boilers, 4 shafts
Performance:	127,400shp; 28 knots
Bunkerage:	8,208 tons fuel oil, 600 tons avgas
Range:	10,000nm at 16 knots
Flight-deck dimensions:	815ft 6in × 100ft 0in
Elevators:	3 (37ft 8in × 39ft 5in, 35ft 0in × 52ft 0in, 42ft 0in × 31ft 5in)
Arrester wires:	9 (hydraulically controlled)
Hangar decks:	3 (upper, middle, and lower; lower used for disassembled aircraft stowage only)
Hangar dimensions:	upper and middle 615ft × 88ft (approx), lower 116ft × 48ft (approx); upper and middle hangar area 108,240sq ft (approx), lower hangar 5,568sq ft (approx)
Aircraft:	91
Armament:	10 × 8in/50-cal LA, 16 × 5in/40-cal DP, 22 × 25mm AA
Armor:	6in belt, 1.5in deck
Complement:	2,016

NOTES: Because of the limitations on capital ship construction imposed by the Washington Naval Treaty, work on the battleship *Kaga* was halted in 1922. Following the destruction of the then-building *Amagi* in the Tokyo earthquake of 1923, the *Kaga* was selected to replace her for completion as an aircraft carrier. Alterations included revisions to armor layout to conserve top weight. She was launched in 1925 and commissioned three years later after an extensive fitting-out period. Like the *Akagi,* the *Kaga* had three aircraft flight decks and no superstructure as built. After only six years in service she underwent a major refit beginning in June 1934. Her hull was lengthened, a single full-length flight deck erected, hangar spaces enlarged, a third lift added, and an island built on the starboard side of the flight deck. Her heavy antiaircraft armament was upgraded, and light AA was also increased.

The *Kaga* participated in actions against China and in every major carrier campaign during the opening stages of the Pacific War. She was sunk on 4 June 1942 during the Battle of Midway, as the result of four bomb hits producing fires and induced explosions.

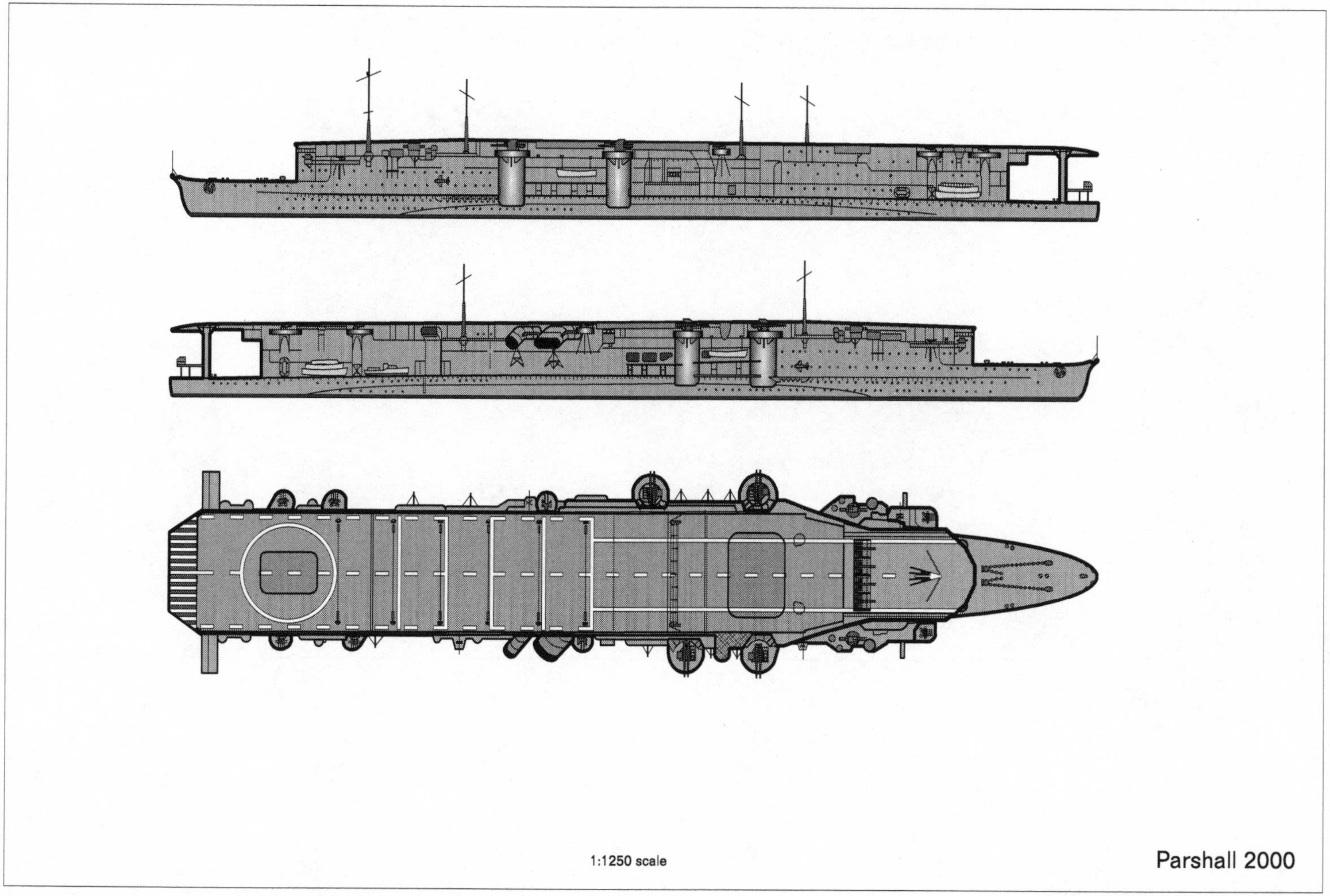

Parshall 2000

1:1250 scale

Fig. A4-4. Aircraft carrier *Ryūjō*

Ryūjō

Builder:	Yokohama Dockyard Co.
Laid down:	26 Nov 1929
Launched:	2 Apr 1931
Commissioned:	9 May 1933

As Built

Displacement:	12,500 tons (standard)
Length:	590ft 3in (OA), 575ft 5in (WL), 548ft 7in (PP)
Beam:	66ft 8in
Draught:	18ft 3in
Machinery:	2 sets geared turbines, 6 Kampon boilers, 2 shafts
Performance:	65,000shp; 29 knots
Bunkerage:	2,490 tons fuel oil
Range:	10,000nm at 14 knots
Flight-deck dimensions:	513ft 6in × 75ft 6in
Elevators:	2 (51ft 6in × 36ft 5in, 35ft 5in × 26ft 3in)
Arrester wires:	6
Hangar decks:	2
Hangar dimensions:	both 336ft 0in × 62ft 2in (approx); 41,664sq ft (approx)
Aircraft:	48
Armament:	12 × 5in/40-cal DP, 24 MGs
Armor:	None
Complement:	600

As Reconstructed (1934–36)

Displacement:	10,600 tons (standard), 12,732 tons (normal)
Length:	590ft 3in (OA), 576ft 6in (WL), 550ft 4in (PP)
Beam:	68ft 2in
Draught:	23ft 3in
Machinery:	2 sets geared turbines, 6 Kampon boilers, 2 shafts
Performance:	66,269shp; 29 knots
Bunkerage:	2,490 tons fuel oil
Range:	10,000nm at 14 knots
Flight-deck dimensions:	513ft 6in × 75ft 6in
Elevators:	2 (51ft 6in × 36ft 5in, 35ft 5in × 26ft 3in)
Arrester wires:	6

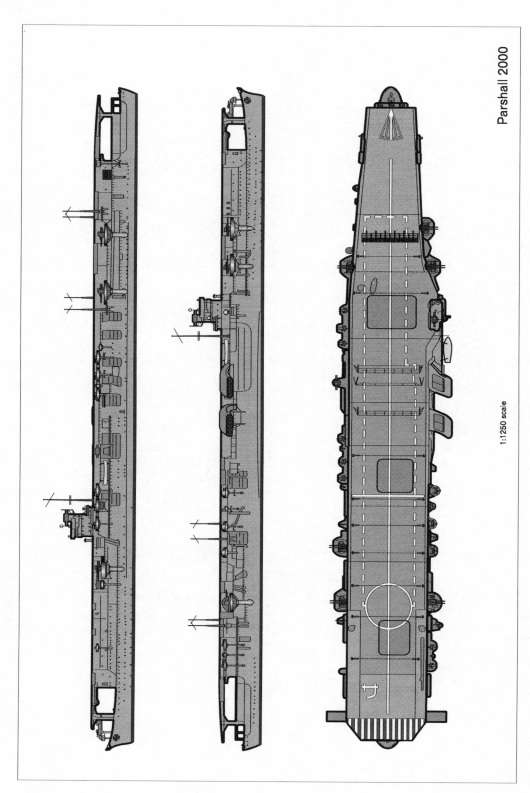

Parshall 2000

1:1250 scale

Fig. A4-5. Aircraft carrier *Sōryū*

Hangar decks:	2
Hangar dimensions:	both 336ft 0in × 62ft 2in (approx); 41,664sq ft (approx)
Aircraft:	48
Armament:	8 × 5in/40-cal DP, 4 × 25mm AA, 24 × 13.2mm AA
Armor:	None
Complement:	924

NOTES: Owing to the aggregate tonnage dedicated to the *Akagi* and *Kaga* (nearly 53,000 tons), under the limitations of the Washington Naval Treaty Japan was left with only 30,000 tons of allowable carrier construction. The Japanese were determined to spread this remaining tonnage across as many hulls as possible while still ensuring that each carrier was capable of operating a useful air wing. The result of these irreconcilable design pressures was the *Ryūjō*, a carrier that was supposed to embark forty-eight aircraft, displace only 8,000 tons, and maintain battle speed with the fleet. Not surprisingly, the *Ryūjō* was a failed compromise in a number of respects. Her original aircraft complement having been deemed insufficient after her ordering, a second aircraft hangar was almost arbitrarily placed on top of her original single-hangar design. As built, she was lightly constructed, lacking in longitudinal girder strength and freeboard, and dangerously top-heavy. The *Ryūjō* was badly damaged while on maneuvers in the monster typhoon of 1934, where her structural liabilities were brought into glaring focus. She went back to the yards after a little more than a year in service.

When the *Ryūjō* reemerged, her hull had been strengthened, ballasted, and widened. This modification, in combination with the removal of a pair of her 5-inch DP mounts, greatly improved the *Ryūjō*'s stability, but her marginal freeboard had been lowered still further. Subsequent work to heighten her forecastle improved this condition somewhat. However, by 1940 the improvement (and enlargement) of combat aircraft had made it impossible for her smaller aft elevator to stow any combat aircraft (except possibly the B5N, which had folding wings), meaning that she was essentially a single-lift carrier. Furthermore, the diminutive size of her flight deck made it impossible for her to operate more than a half-dozen nonfighter aircraft in a single strike package. In all, the *Ryūjō* was of distinctly marginal utility as a light fleet carrier.

The *Ryūjō* saw extensive service in the opening phases of the Pacific War, mostly in support of Japanese amphibious operations. She was sunk on 24 August 1942 during the Battle of the Eastern Solomons, the victim of four bombs and a torpedo hit that left her a blazing wreck.

Sōryū

Builder:	Kure Naval Dockyard
Laid down:	20 Nov 1934
Launched:	21 Dec 1935

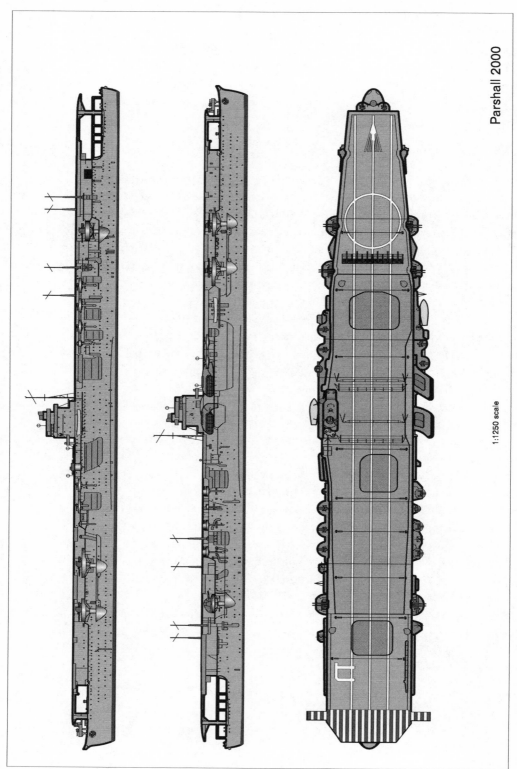

Parshall 2000

1:1250 scale

Fig. A4-6. Aircraft carrier *Hiryū*

Commissioned:	29 Jan 1937
Displacement:	15,900 tons (standard), 18,800 tons (normal)
Length:	746ft 5in (OA), 729ft 9in (WL), 677ft 7in (PP)
Beam:	69ft 11in
Draught:	25ft 0in
Machinery:	4 sets geared turbines, 8 Kampon boilers, 4 shafts
Performance:	152,000shp; 34.5 knots
Bunkerage:	3,670 tons fuel oil, 150,000 gallons avgas
Range:	7,750nm at 18 knots
Flight-deck dimensions:	711ft 6in × 85ft 4in
Elevators:	3 (37ft 9in × 52ft 6in, 37ft 9in × 39ft 4in, 38ft 8in × 32ft 10in)
Arrester wires:	9 (hydraulically controlled)
Hangar decks:	2
Hangar dimensions:	upper 562ft × 60ft × 15ft (approx), lower 467ft × 60ft × 14ft (approx); 61,740sq ft (approx)
Aircraft:	68
Armament:	12 × 5in/40-cal DP, 28 × 25mm AA
Armor:	1.8in belt, 1in deck (2.2in over the magazines)
Complement:	1,100

NOTES: The *Sōryū*, the first of Japan's third-generation carriers, established the basic format for all future Japanese carrier classes: a high-aspect cruiserlike hull mounting powerful machinery for high speed, twin downswept stacks to vent exhaust gases away from the flight deck, dual hangar decks served by three lifts, light construction, and little or no armor protection. As such, she approached the ideal carrier (at least according to Japanese naval doctrine): long on speed, range, and offensive capabilities, but lacking in defensive staying power.

The *Sōryū* served alongside her larger sister *Hiryū* in Carrier Division 2 for most of her career. The *Sōryū* was involved in actions in China and in every major carrier campaign during the opening stages of the Pacific War. She was the first of the four Japanese carriers sunk during the Battle of Midway on 4 June 1942. Smashed by three bomb hits among her parked aircraft and in her hangars, she was soon ablaze from stem to stern, sinking some nine hours later.

Hiryū

Builder:	Yokosuka Naval Dockyard
Laid down:	8 Jul 1936
Launched:	16 Nov 1937
Commissioned:	5 Jul 1939

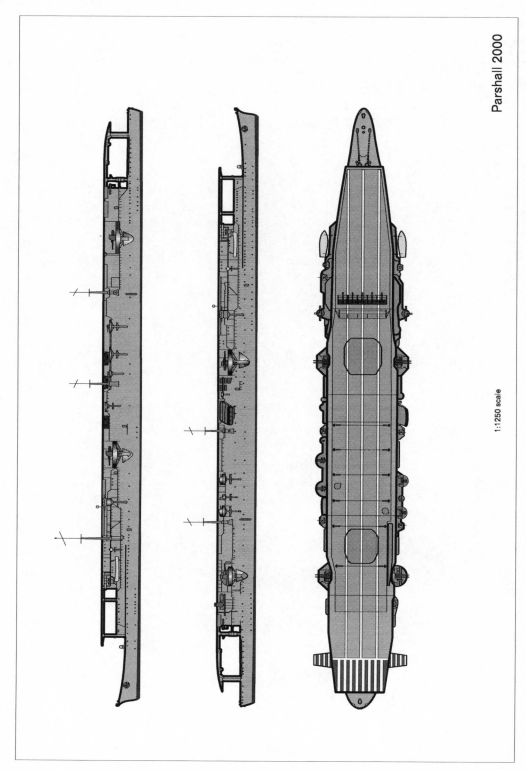

Parshall 2000

1:1250 scale

Fig. A4-7. Aircraft carrier *Zuihō*

Displacement:	17,300 tons (standard), 20,250 (normal)
Length:	745ft 11in (OA), 721ft 9in (WL), 687ft 5in (PP)
Beam:	73ft 3in
Draught:	25ft 9in
Machinery:	4 sets geared turbines, 8 Kampon boilers, 4 shafts
Performance:	153,000shp; 34.5 knots
Bunkerage:	4,400 tons fuel oil (approx)
Range:	10,330nm at 18 knots
Flight-deck dimensions:	711ft 6in × 88ft 6in
Elevators:	3 (42ft 8in × 52ft 6in, 42ft 8in × 39ft 4in, 38ft 8in × 42ft 8in)
Arrester wires:	6 aft, 3 forward, all hydraulic
Hangar decks:	2
Hangar dimensions:	upper 562ft × 60ft × 15ft (approx), lower 467ft × 60ft × 14ft (approx); 61,740sq ft (approx)
Aircraft:	73
Armament:	12 × 5in/40-cal DP, 31 × 25mm AA
Armor:	3.5in belt (magazines 5.9in), 1in deck (2.2in over the magazines)
Complement:	1,100

NOTES: The *Hiryū*, a slightly enlarged version of the *Sōryū*, improved on her smaller sister in a number of respects, notably combat range—owing to a 20 percent increase in her fuel capacity—and protection, although by contemporary foreign standards her defensive arrangements were still woefully inadequate. Nevertheless, with her long range, high speed, and relatively large airwing, she was judged by the Japanese to be a highly useful design that was to be reincarnated in the late-war *Unryū*-class ships.

The *Hiryū* was involved in operations against China and was heavily used during the opening phases of the Pacific War. She was the last of four Japanese carriers sunk at the Battle of Midway, receiving four bomb hits on her forward flight deck that started insurmountable fires.

Shōhō AND *Zuihō*

Shōhō

Builder:	Yokosuka Naval Dockyard
Laid down:	3 Dec 1934
Launched:	1 Jun 1935
Commissioned:	26 Jan 1942

Zuihō

Builder:	Yokosuka Naval Dockyard
Laid down:	20 Jun 1935
Launched:	19 Jun 1936
Commissioned:	27 Dec 1940
Displacement:	11,262 tons (standard), 13,950 tons (normal)
Length:	674ft 2in (OA), 660ft 11in (WL), 606ft 11in (PP)
Beam:	59ft 8in
Draught:	21ft 7in
Machinery:	2 sets geared turbines, 4 boilers, 2 shafts
Performance:	52,000shp; 28 knots
Bunkerage:	2,600 tons fuel oil (approx)
Range:	7,800nm at 18 knots
Flight-deck dimensions:	590ft 6in × 75ft 6in
Elevators:	2 (42ft 8in × 39ft 4in, 39ft 4in × 35ft 5in)
Arrester wires:	6
Hangar decks:	1
Hangar dimensions:	406ft 10in × 59ft 0in; 24,013sq ft (approx)
Aircraft:	30
Armament:	8 × 5in/40-cal DP, 8 × 25mm AA
Armor:	None
Complement:	785

NOTES: These ships were originally laid down as submarine tenders (the *Tsurugisaki* and *Takasaki* respectively) but were ostensibly intended for conversion to either fleet oilers or light carriers as needed. Yet as it happened, the *Zuihō*'s conversion to a carrier took some four years. Both the *Zuihō* and *Shōhō* were useful light carriers as they finally emerged, but their insufficient aircraft complement prevented them from operating independently. Strictly speaking, the *Shōhō* was not in commission at the beginning of the Pacific War. However, she had previously been in commission as a submarine tender and was only a little more than a month away from being recommissioned as an aircraft carrier when the war began.

The *Shōhō* was lost during her first combat deployment, during the Battle of the Coral Sea on 7 May 1942. She was struck by no fewer than eleven aerial bomb and seven torpedo hits, and sank within minutes. The *Zuihō* participated in several campaigns, finally being lost during the Battle of Cape Engano on 25 October 1944, a victim of multiple bomb and torpedo hits.

Shōkaku AND *Zuikaku*

Shōkaku

Builder:	Yokosuka Naval Dockyard
Laid down:	12 Dec 1937
Launched:	1 Jun 1939
Commissioned:	8 Aug 1941

Zuikaku

Builder:	Kawasaki Dockyard, Kobe
Laid down:	25 May 1938
Launched:	27 Nov 1939
Commissioned:	25 Sep 1941
Displacement:	25,675 tons (standard), 29,800 tons (normal)
Length:	844ft 10in (OA), 820ft 2in (WL), 774ft 6in (PP)
Beam:	85ft 4in
Draught:	29ft 1in
Machinery:	4 sets geared turbines, 8 Kampon boilers, 4 shafts
Performance:	160,000shp; 34.25 knots
Bunkerage:	3,500 tons fuel oii, 150 tons avgas
Range:	9,700nm at 18 knots
Flight-deck dimensions:	794ft 7in × 95ft 2in
Elevators:	3 (52ft 6in × 42ft 6in, 42ft 6in × 39ft 4in, 42ft 6in × 38ft 6in)
Arrester wires:	6 aft, 3 forward
Hangar decks:	2
Hangar dimensions:	upper 623ft × 78ft (approx), lower 525ft × 78ft (approx); 87,675sq ft (approx)
Aircraft:	84
Armament:	16 × 5in/40-cal DP, 42 × 25mm AA
Armor:	5.9–8.5in belt, 6.7in deck
Complement:	1,660

NOTES: With the possible exception of the later *Taihō*, the magnificent *Shōkaku*-class carriers were the finest expression of Japanese carrier design and were arguably the best aircraft carriers in the world until the emergence of the American *Essex* class in 1943. Combining all the virtues of the *Sōryū* with greatly increased protection and expanded

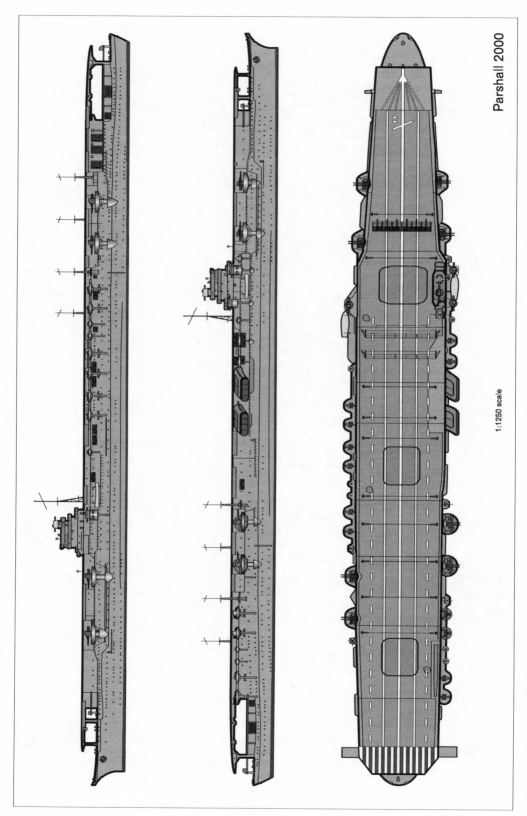

Parshall 2000

1:1250 scale

Fig. A4-8. Aircraft carrier *Shōkaku*

aircraft-handling capacity, the *Shōkakus* had few drawbacks besides an unarmored flight deck. Their impending entry into the imperial fleet factored heavily into the Combined Fleet's calculations for the feasibility of the Pearl Harbor attack.

The *Shōkakus* were the most active Japanese carriers during the Pacific War, participating in almost every major campaign except the Battle of Midway. The *Shōkaku* succumbed to damage from three or four submarine torpedo hits during the Battle of the Philippine Sea on 19 June 1944. The *Zuikaku* was sunk during the Battle of Cape Engano on 25 October 1944, having been hit by numerous aerial bombs and torpedoes.

Taiyō (formerly *Kasuga Maru*)

Builder:	Mitsubishi, Nagasaki
Laid down:	6 Jan 1940
Launched:	19 Sep 1940
Commissioned:	15 Sep 1941
Displacement:	17,830 tons (standard), 20,000 tons (normal)
Length:	591ft 4in (OA), 569ft 11in (WL), 551ft 2in (PP)
Beam:	73ft 10in
Draught:	26ft 3in
Machinery:	2 sets geared turbines, 4 boilers, 2 shafts
Performance:	25,200shp; 21.1 knots
Bunkerage:	?
Range:	6,500nm at 18 knots
Flight-deck dimensions:	564ft 3in × 77ft 0in
Elevators:	2 (39ft 5in × 42ft 8in, 42ft 8in × 39ft 5in)
Arrester wires:	8
Hangar decks:	1
Hangar dimensions:	300ft long (approx)
Aircraft:	27
Armament:	6 × 4.7in HA, 8 × 25mm AA
Armor:	None
Complement:	747

NOTES: The *Taiyō* was formerly a 17,100grt passenger liner taken in hand for quick conversion to an escort carrier at Sasebo Naval Yard in 1940. During her conversion a single hangar deck was added, her boilers were rerouted to vent over the side, and minimal antiaircraft armament and fire-control equipment were fitted. Interestingly, no arrester gear was installed, which undoubtedly complicated the handling of modern high-performance carrier aircraft.

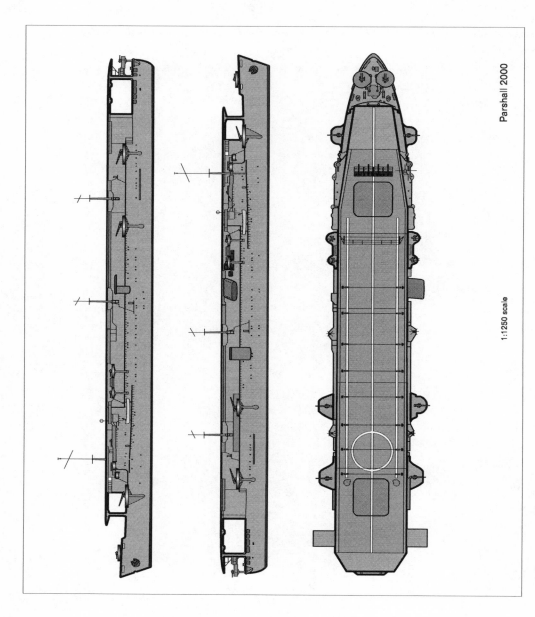

Parshall 2000

1:1250 scale

Fig. A4-9. Aircraft carrier *Taiyō*

The *Taiyō* was used mainly for aircraft transport and training duties during the Pacific War. She was sunk by the U.S. submarine *Rasher* on 18 August 1944 off Luzon, the Philippines.

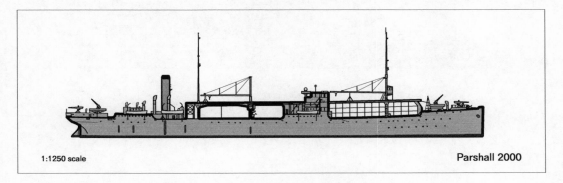

Fig. A4-10. Seaplane carrier *Notoro*

Notoro

Builder:	Kawasaki, Kobe
Laid down:	24 Nov 1919
Launched:	3 May 1920
Commissioned:	10 Aug 1920
Displacement:	14,050 tons (standard)
Length:	470ft 9in (OA), 455ft 0in (PP)
Beam:	58ft 0in
Draught:	26ft 6in
Machinery:	2 sets vertical triple-expansion reciprocating engines, 4 Miyabara boilers, 2 shafts
Performance:	5,850shp; 12 knots
Bunkerage:	1,000 tons fuel oil
Range:	?
Aircraft:	10–16 seaplanes
Armament:	2 × 4.7in LA, 2 × 80mm AA
Armor:	None
Complement:	155

NOTES: Originally built as an oiler, the *Notoro* was converted to a seaplane carrier in 1924. However, she retained capabilities as an oiler and was reconverted to this purpose in 1942.

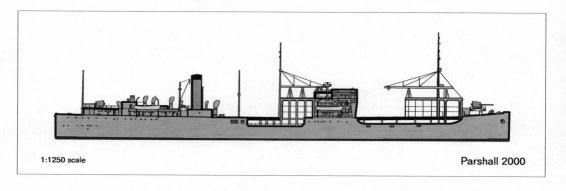

1:1250 scale   Parshall 2000

Fig. A4-11. Seaplane carrier *Kamoi*

Kamoi

Builder:	New York Shipbuilding Co., Camden, N.J.
Laid down:	14 Sep 1921
Launched:	8 Jun 1922
Commissioned:	12 Sep 1922
Displacement:	19,550 tons (normal), 17,000 (standard)
Length:	496ft 3in (OA), 496ft 0in (WL), 488ft 6in (PP)
Beam:	67ft 0in
Draught:	27ft 8in
Machinery:	2 sets Curtiss turbo-electric drive, 2 Yarrow boilers, 2 shafts
Performance:	9,000shp; 15 knots
Bunkerage:	2,500 tons coal
Range:	10,000nm at 10 knots
Aircraft:	12–16 seaplanes
Armament:	2 × 5.5in LA, 2 × 80mm AA
Armor:	None
Complement:	?

NOTES: Completed as a fleet oiler, the *Kamoi* was converted to a seaplane carrier by Uraga Dock Co., Tokyo, in 1933. She was reclassified as a fleet oiler in 1943.

Chitose AND *Chiyoda*

Chitose

Builder:	Kure Naval Dockyard
Laid down:	26 Nov 1934
Launched:	29 Nov 1936
Commissioned:	25 Jul 1938

Chiyoda

Builder:	Kure Naval Dockyard
Laid down:	14 Dec 1936
Launched:	19 Nov 1937
Commissioned:	15 Dec 1938
Displacement:	12,550 tons (normal), 11,023 (standard)
Length:	631ft 7in (OA), 603ft 4in (WL), 570ft 10in (PP)
Beam:	61ft 8in
Draught:	23ft 8in
Machinery:	2 sets geared turbines, 4 Kampon boilers, 2 diesel engines, 2 shafts
Performance:	44,000shp (+ diesels = 12,800bhp); 29 knots
Bunkerage:	3,600 tons fuel oil
Range:	8,000nm at 18 knots
Catapults:	4
Hangar decks:	1
Hangar dimensions:	300ft long (approx)
Aircraft:	24 seaplanes
Armament:	2 × 5in/40-cal DP, 12 × 25mm AA
Armor:	None
Complement:	?

NOTES: These ingenious multipurpose vessels were designed as seaplane carriers that could be converted to fast oilers, submarine tenders, or light aircraft carriers at need. They could also operate midget submarines from the hangar deck via a ramp and gate mechanism in the stern. Both were converted to light carriers in 1942–43.

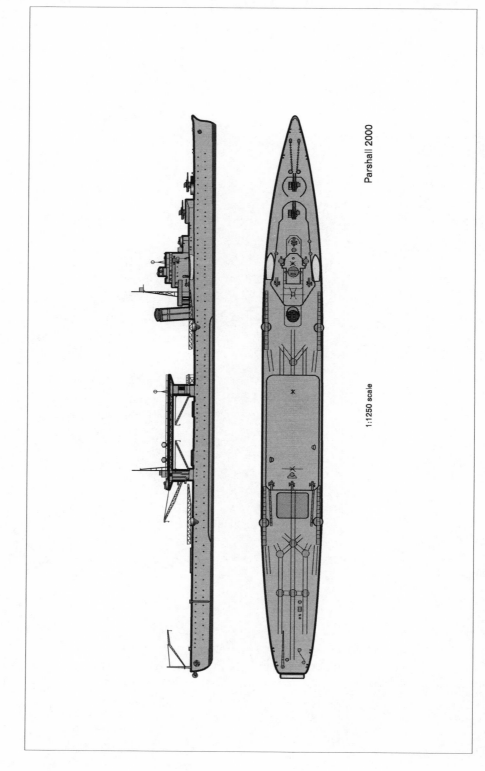

Parshall 2000

1:1250 scale

Fig. A4-12. Seaplane carrier *Chitose*

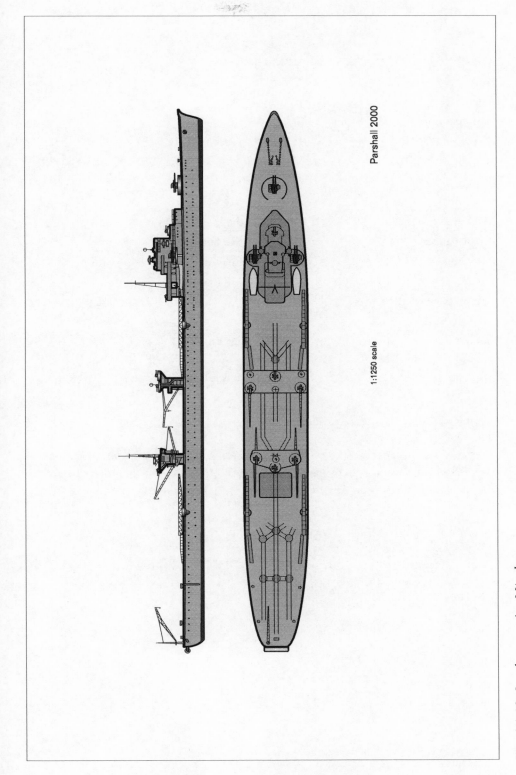

Parshall 2000

1:1250 scale

Fig. A4-13. Seaplane carrier *Mizuho*

Mizuho

Builder:	Kawasaki, Kobe
Laid down:	1 May 1937
Launched:	16 May 1938
Commissioned:	25 Feb 1939
Displacement:	12,150 tons (normal), 10,929 (standard)
Length:	631ft 6in (OA), 602ft 6in (WL), 570ft 10in (PP)
Beam:	61ft 8in
Draught:	23ft 3in
Machinery:	2 × 4-cycle diesels, 2 shafts
Performance:	15,200bhp; 22 knots
Bunkerage:	3,600 tons fuel oil
Range:	8,000nm at 16 knots
Catapults:	4
Hangar decks:	1
Hangar dimensions:	300ft long (approx)
Aircraft:	24 seaplanes
Armament:	6 × 5in/40-cal DP, 12 × 25mm AA
Armor:	None
Complement:	?

NOTES: A less successful variant of the earlier *Chitose* class, the *Mizuho* was hampered by a diesel propulsion system that delivered 5 knots less speed than her planned 27 knots. She was sunk by an American submarine near Japan in May 1942.

Appendix 5

Naval Air Bases and Land-Based Air Groups

Information for this appendix was drawn from the following sources: *KKG*; Nagaishi, *Kaigun kōkūtai nenshi*; Hata and Izawa, *Japanese Naval Aces*; and letter from Osamu Tagaya to author, 14 September 2000.

GENERAL REMARKS

The navy's land-based air service—the *kōkūtai* system—was established in 1916 and provided that naval air bases and air groups be organized, as needed, at naval ports *(gunkō)* and strategic ports *(yōkō)*, taking their designations from the names of those places and functioning under the authority of those stations. Air groups and air bases outside those ports were placed under the command of the nearest naval base *(chinjufu)*.

From the establishment of the navy's first land-based air unit at Yokosuka in 1916 until near the end of the Pacific War, the term *kōkūtai* was taken to mean both a naval air base and the flying unit stationed at that base. The flying unit *(hikōkitai* or *hikō-tai)* operated the aircraft, and the rest of the personnel of any *kōkūtai* operated and maintained the ground facilities of the base at which the air unit was stationed. This is important to understand, since much writing in the West on the *kōkūtai* has focused only on the flying element (the air group), giving the mistaken impression that a *kōkūtai* was akin to a U.S. Navy or Army Air Corps "group" (a formation of aircraft, together with their attendant flight and maintenance crews, which functioned independently of the air base). In fact, because the Japanese navy was very conservative in its organization, for most of its existence the *kōkūtai* system combined both functions. Just as aircraft and flight crew *(hikōtai)* on board a Japanese carrier or seaplane tender were made an integral part of their ship's complement, when land-based or shore-based (seaplane) air units were formed, the air bases at which they were stationed were seen as the equivalent of the ships of which the carrier-based *hikōtai* formed a part. Because this structure inherently lacked flexibility and hampered front-line operations as the Pacific War progressed, in March 1944 the navy's land-based forces were restructured, and certain *hikōtai* were given independent numerical designations and an identity of their own outside the parent *kōkūtai* structure. With the above explanation as a background, the reader should understand that throughout this work, and specifically in this appendix, the use of the term *kōkūtai*—air group—does indeed usually refer to its flying echelon, since it is that element that has been the greater focus of this study.

In 1919 the navy set out new regulations that provided for the organization, in time of war, emergencies, or maneuvers, of "special air groups" *(tokusetsu kōkūtai)*, which could be designated either by a place or by a numerical designation. They could be either land- or carrier-based, but in general they were land-based and would be given numerical designations. In most cases the nuclei of these air groups were to be created from elements drawn from existing air groups. The first such unit was the Eleventh Air Group, established briefly in 1936.

While the regulations establishing land-based air groups were set forth in 1916 and 1919, it was not until the early 1930s that the navy, in a series of regulations and instructions, set forth the specific internal organization of air groups, their locations, their functions, and their training, though these changed from time to time right up to the end of the Pacific War.

In November 1936, during a period of political tension with China, the navy arranged for the organization of special combined air groups *(tokusetsu rengō kōkūtai)*, which were composed of two or more air groups in order to provide greater air strength under a single command. The First and Second combined air groups were formed in July 1937, at the beginning of the China War, and were the backbone of the navy's air operations in the first several years of that conflict.

Standing combined air groups *(jōsetsu rengō kōkūtai)*, intended to be more permanent, were established by navy regulations in December 1938. Two of these were established before the Pacific War: the Eleventh, organized in December 1938, and the Twelfth, formed in 1939. By 1941 the navy's land-based air groups were almost always composed of one type of aircraft. (The exception was the Chitose Air Group, based in Micronesia and composed of both medium bombers and fighters.) On 1 November 1942 all land-based air groups identified with base names were given numerical designations.

AIR GROUPS, 1916–1941

In the following list of air groups organized prior to 8 December 1941, only those that were significantly engaged in either the China War or the Pacific War are provided with combat summaries.

YOKOSUKA AIR GROUP. Organized 1 April 1916 at Yokosuka, Shinagawa Prefecture. The oldest air group in the Japanese navy, it remained in existence until the end of the Pacific War. From its earliest years its primary missions were training and research. It soon became the navy's main center for research into air combat tactics and the testing of new aircraft. In the early 1930s Yokosuka became the mecca of navy fighter pilots as a center for training in dogfighting, and it was the home base for a number of "flying circuses" that put on acrobatic performances for the Japanese public. By the 1930s, too, the air group's fighter squadron was flight-testing aircraft under research by the Naval Air Arsenal. It was not assigned a combat role until 1944 in the Marianas.

SASEBO AIR GROUP. Organized 12 September 1920 at Sasebo, Nagasaki Prefecture. Equipped mostly with reconnaissance seaplanes and flying boats.

KASUMIGAURA AIR GROUP. Organized 1 November 1922 at Kasumigaura, Ibaraki Prefecture, as a flight-training unit and thus equipped mostly with training aircraft—both floatplanes and wheeled aircraft. In later years specialized and advanced flight training at Kasumigaura was transferred to Yokosuka. It was incorporated into the Eleventh Combined Air Group in 1938.

ŌMURA AIR GROUP. Organized 1 December 1922 at Ōmura, Nagasaki Prefecture. In November 1940 it was made a training group for pilots of carrier attack and reconnaissance aircraft and assimilated into the Twelfth Combined Air Group.

TATEYAMA AIR GROUP. Organized 1 June 1930 at Tateyama, Chiba Prefecture, comprising fighters, dive bombers, attack bombers, medium bombers, and seaplane reconnaissance aircraft. The group was used to test aircraft prototypes and initial production models in the mid-1930s. It later became a training unit and was attached to the Yokosuka Naval Base by the outbreak of the Pacific War.

KURE AIR GROUP. Organized 1 June 1931 at Kure, Hiroshima Prefecture, and composed of various types of aircraft but principally known as a cold-weather testing unit for the naval air service. It was attached to the Kure Naval Base by the outbreak of the Pacific War.

ŌMINATO AIR GROUP. Organized 1 November 1933 at Ōminato, Aomori Prefecture, and composed of seaplanes and wheeled aircraft, including medium bombers. It was attached to the Ōminato Defense Base by the opening of the Pacific War.

SAEKI AIR GROUP. Organized 15 February 1934 at Saeki, Ōita Prefecture, and composed of seaplanes and wheeled aircraft. It was attached to the Kure Naval Base by the opening of the Pacific War.

MAIZURU AIR GROUP. Organized 1 October 1935 at Maizuru, Kyōto Prefecture, and composed of seaplanes. It was attached to the Maizuru Naval Base by the opening of the Pacific War.

KANOYA AIR GROUP. Organized 1 April 1936 at Kanoya, Kagoshima Prefecture, as both a medium-bomber and fighter group. It was made part of the First Combined Air Group in early July 1937 and became one of the most active air groups in the China War, 1937–38. It became an exclusively medium-bomber unit in March 1938 and was incorporated into the Twenty-first Air Flotilla of the Eleventh Air Fleet on 15 January 1941. Half of the unit was sent to Saigon in early December 1941 and led the attack on the *Prince of Wales* and *Repulse;* the other half fought in the Philippines air campaign. Transferred to the Bismarcks in September 1942, it was heavily involved in air combat in the southwestern Pacific. On 1 October 1942 it was split into the 751st Air Group (medium bombers) and the 253d Air Group (carrier fighters).

KISARAZU AIR GROUP. Organized 1 April 1936 at Kisarazu, Chiba Prefecture. It was the navy's first land-based bomber unit. In July 1937 it was made part of the First Combined Air Group and dispatched to central China. It was heavily engaged in bombing operations in northern and central China from August 1937 to December 1938. It returned to Japan in January 1940 to become a medium bomber training unit. In April 1942 it was made part of the Twenty-sixth Air Flotilla and became an operational unit once more. Sent to Rabaul in August 1942, it was redesignated the 707th Air Group in November of that year.

CHINKAI AIR GROUP. Organized 1 October 1936 at Chinkai (Chinhae), Korea, and composed of seaplanes. It remained attached to the Chinkai Defense Base for its entire existence.

YOKOHAMA AIR GROUP. Organized 1 October 1936 at Yokohama, Kanagawa Prefecture, and composed entirely of flying boats. Incorporated into the Fourth Fleet, it was sent to Micronesia, February–October 1940. It was incorporated into the Fourth Combined Air Group in November 1940 and into the Twenty-fourth Air Flotilla on 15 January 1941. The group took part in raids against Allied bases in the central Pacific on 8 December 1941, following which it was sent to Rabaul on 14 February 1942. It was made part of the Twenty-fifth Air Flotilla of the Eleventh Air Fleet on 1 April 1942, and the forward detachment of the air group was destroyed by enemy air attack at Tulagi on 7 August 1942.

TAKAO AIR GROUP. Organized 1 April 1938 as a land-based bomber group. It was originally based at Takao (Kaohsiung), Taiwan. Briefly based at Shanghai in August 1938, it undertook attacks in central China and in September was sent to Santsao, near Canton, for operations in southern China, returning to Takao in December of that year. It became part of the First Combined Air Group in January 1940 and was sent to Hankow in May for operations against central China, after which it was sent back to Japan. Following incorporation into the Twenty-third Air Flotilla on 10 April 1941 and training in Micronesia in May and June, it was again sent to Hankow for operations in central China in July. A detachment of the group returned to Takao in September 1941 and on 8 December participated in raids against the Philippines, but the main unit advanced to the East Indies, from which it launched raids on Port Darwin, Australia, in 1942 and 1943. In September 1942, elements of the group were sent to Rabaul, from which they became heavily engaged in air combat in the Solomons. The unit was redesignated the 753d Air Group on 1 October 1942.

SUZUKA AIR GROUP. Organized 1 October 1938 at Suzuka, Mie Prefecture, as a training group. It was placed within the Eleventh Combined Air Group in December.

KAGOSHIMA AIR GROUP. Organized 15 December 1938 at Kagoshima, Ibaraki Prefecture, as a training group. It was equipped with training and reconnaissance seaplanes and placed within the Eleventh Combined Air Group.

ŌITA AIR GROUP. Organized 15 December 1938 at Ōita, Ōita Prefecture, as a mixed group of fighters and attack aircraft. The unit was placed within the Twelfth Combined Air Group in December 1939 and made a training group in November 1940.

TSUKUBA AIR GROUP. Organized 15 December 1938 at Tsukuba, Ibaraki Prefecture, as a training group for land-based fighters and placed within the Eleventh Combined Air Group.

CHICHIJIMA AIR GROUP. Organized 1 April 1939, on Chichijima, Bonin Islands. Placed under the Seventh Base Force of the Fifth Fleet, it was composed of reconnaissance seaplanes.

CHITOSE AIR GROUP. Organized 1 October 1939 as a medium-bomber unit, a fighter unit being added later. On 15 November 1940 it was placed within the Fourth Combined Air Group and on 15 January of the next year was incorporated into the Twenty-fourth Air Flotilla of the Fourth Fleet. Sent to Saipan for training in late spring of 1941 and then deployed in Micronesia: Truk and the Marshalls (Roi on Kwajalein and Taroa on Maloelap). Elements based on Roi attacked Wake Island on 8 December 1941. In September 1942 the bomber unit was sent to Rabaul, where it was later destroyed in combat. The fighter unit was redesignated the 201st Air Group and fought extensively over the Solomons, New Guinea, and the Philippines, where it provided cadre for early kamikaze missions.

USA AIR GROUP. Organized 1 October 1939 at Ōita, Ōita Prefecture, and composed of dive bombers and carrier attack aircraft. Placed within the Twelfth Combined Air Group in December 1939, it was made a training unit in December 1940.

HYAKURIGAHARA AIR GROUP. Organized 1 December 1939 at Hyakurigahara, Ibaraki Prefecture, as a training group for land-based aircraft and placed within the Eleventh Combined Air Group.

IWAKUNI AIR GROUP. Organized 1 December 1939 at Iwakuni, Yamaguchi Prefecture, as a training group for land-based aircraft. It was placed under the command of the Kure Naval Base, and training in reconnaissance and responsibilities for the Flight Reserve Enlisted Trainee Program were added in 1941.

YATABE AIR GROUP. Organized 1 December 1939 at Yatabe, Ibaraki Prefecture, as a training group for land-based aircraft and placed within the Eleventh Combined Air Group.

MIHORO (BIHORO) AIR GROUP. Organized 1 October 1940 at Mihoro (Bihoro), Hokkaidō, as a medium-bomber group. It was made part of the Second Combined Air Group on 15 November 1940 and then of the Twenty-second Air Flotilla in January of the next year. The group took part in operations in central China in March 1941, and in October it was moved to southern Taiwan and then, in December, to Saigon. Flying from that base, aircraft of the group participated in the destruction of the *Repulse* and *Prince of Wales* on 10 December 1941. Returning to Japan in April 1942, the group was dispatched to Tinian in the Marianas in October of that year and was renamed the 701st Air Group in November.

GENZAN AIR GROUP. Organized 15 November 1940 at Genzan (Wonsan), Korea, as a mixed group of carrier fighters and medium bombers, and attached to the Second Combined Air Group. It was transferred to the Twenty-second Air Flotilla in January 1941 and moved to mainland China bases in April of that year. The group's medium-bomber squadron undertook bombing missions in Szechwan Province, and the fighter squadron was assigned routine patrol function over the group's Hankow base. In September the group returned to Genzan for training and was made part of the Twenty-second Air Flotilla. The bombing squadron was sent to airfields near Saigon in December 1941 and participated in the destruction of the *Repulse* and *Prince of Wales*. It subsequently undertook attacks on Singapore and bombing missions in the Netherlands East Indies. In March and April 1942 the bombing squadron undertook operations over the Indian Ocean and in Burma. It was sent to Rabaul in April and took part in the Battle of the Coral Sea. The group's fighter squadron became independent as the 252d Air Group in September 1942.

HAKATA AIR GROUP. Organized 15 November 1940 at Kasuya, Fukuoka Prefecture, as a training group, composed of reconnaissance seaplanes, and placed under the Twelfth Combined Air Group.

TŌKŌ AIR GROUP. Organized 15 November 1940 at Tōkō (Tung-ch'ang), Takao Province, Taiwan. It was composed entirely of flying boats and placed within the First Combined Air Group. In January 1941 it was made part of the Twenty-first Air Flotilla, which was based on Taiwan. As such, it took part in operations against Allied forces in the conquest of the Netherlands East Indies. In the summer of 1942 it was moved to Rabaul and the Shortlands, and it took part in the fighting in the southwestern Pacific that autumn. It was redesignated the 851st Air Group that November.

TSUCHIURA AIR GROUP. Organized 15 November 1940 at Tsuchiura, Ibaraki Prefecture. It was placed under the Eleventh Combined Air Group and given responsibilities for the Flight Reserve Enlisted Trainee Program.

FIRST AIR GROUP. Organized 10 April 1941 at Kanoya, Kagoshima Prefecture, as a mixed group of fighters and medium bombers, placed under the Twenty-fourth Air Flotilla, Fourth Fleet, and sent to the Marshall Islands. It served briefly in central China in the summer of that year. In September of that year the fighter squadron was abolished, and its pilots and aircraft were transferred to the Third and Tainan air groups. The medium-bomber squadron was absorbed into the Twenty-first Air Flotilla based on Taiwan and participated in the attacks on the Philippines and the Netherlands East Indies early in the Pacific War. In February 1942 it was transferred to Rabaul and made part of the Twenty-fourth Air Flotilla. Eventually most of the group was transferred to Micronesia. It was redesignated the 752d Air Group in November 1942.

KOMATSUSHIMA AIR GROUP. Organized 1 October 1941 at Naka County, Tokushima Prefecture, as a reconnaissance seaplane group and incorporated into the Twelfth Combined Air Group. It was transformed into a training group early in the Pacific War.

SEVENTEENTH AIR GROUP. Organized 1 October 1941 at Truk, central Caroline Islands, as a reconnaissance seaplane group and made part of the Fourth Base Force under the command of the Fourth Fleet.

TAINAN AIR GROUP. Organized 1 October 1941 at Tainan, Taiwan, as a purely fighter air group and enrolled in the Twenty-third Air Flotilla. It was one of the two most redoubtable fighter groups in the Japanese navy (the other being the Third Air Group), compiling a ferocious combat record in Southeast Asia and the southwestern Pacific in the first year of the Pacific War. It opened the war with fierce attacks on American air bases in the Philippines and moved in January 1942 to Tarakan in Borneo, from which it carried out attacks on other Dutch bases on the island. At the end of January the group transferred to Balikpapan for air combat over eastern Java. On 1 April 1942 it was integrated into the Twenty-fifth Air Flotilla and sent to Rabaul. From that base the group participated in air battles over eastern New Guinea. After the American invasion of the Solomons in the summer of 1942, the group was involved in a grinding war of attrition in that theater in which its veteran pilots were successively lost. Redesignated the 251st Air Group, the unit was sent back to Japan with only twenty-two survivors of the original organization. The 251st went on to have its own distinguished combat record in the southwestern Pacific before it too was shredded in 1944.

Special Air Groups, 1936–1941

Eleventh Air Group. Organized 24 September 1936 on Taiwan at a time of crisis on the continent (the Pakhoi Incident) and rising Sino-Japanese tensions. It was abolished that November, after the crisis blew over.

Twelfth Air Group. Organized 11 July 1937 at Saeki, Ōita Prefecture, from elements of the Saeki Air Group and composed of fighters, dive bombers, and attack aircraft. It became part of the Second Combined Air Group and was sent to the continent, where it participated in the early air operations in central China, including attacks on Hankow. In March 1938 it became largely a fighter unit. With the fall of Hankow in 1938, the group moved to an air base outside that city, where it saw little combat for the next two years. In the summer of 1940 its new Zero fighters were heavily engaged in escort operations for large-scale bombing raids against Chungking. One of the last air groups to serve in China, it was disbanded on 15 September 1941.

Thirteenth Air Group. Organized 11 July 1937 at Ōmura, Nagasaki Prefecture, as part of the Second Combined Air Group and equipped with the latest fighters, dive bombers, and attack bombers. It was deployed to Shanghai in early 1937 after the Japanese capture of the airfields there. Heavily engaged in the early aerial battles in the China War, with the fall of Nanking it was moved to airfields outside that city. Reorganized in March 1938 as a predominantly medium-bomber force and equipped entirely with medium bombers in November 1938, it became the only G3M bomber unit in China, September 1940–April 1941.

Twenty-first Air Group. Organized 11 July 1937 at Kure, Hiroshima Prefecture, and composed of seaplane reconnaissance aircraft. It was sent to patrol sea routes off the north China coast in August 1937 and disbanded that October.

Twenty-second Air Group. Organized 11 July 1937 at Sasebo, Nagasaki Prefecture, and composed of reconnaissance seaplanes. It was sent to patrol sea routes off the north China coast in August 1937 and disbanded that October.

TWENTY-THIRD AIR GROUP. Organized 11 July 1937 at Sasebo, Nagasaki Prefecture, and composed of reconnaissance seaplanes. It was sent to patrol sea routes off the north China coast in August 1937 and disbanded that October.

FOURTEENTH AIR GROUP. Organized 6 April 1938 as a mixed unit of fighters, dive bombers, and attack aircraft and placed under the Fifth Fleet. It was sent to Santsao, near Canton, to support ground operations in Kwangtung Province and was later assigned escort duty on bombing missions in the interior of southern China. Made an all-fighter unit in November 1939, it moved to the newly captured airfield at Nan-ning and cooperated, in January 1940, with aircraft from the carrier *Akagi* and the Twelfth Air Group in attacks in the Kwei-lin/Liu-chou area. In the summer of 1940 it was sent to Hanoi to help interdict Chinese supply lines from French Indochina. It also participated in attacks on key points in Yunnan Province. In late spring of 1940 it was, along with the Twelfth Air Group, one of the last navy air groups in China. It was disbanded in July 1941.

FIFTEENTH AIR GROUP. Organized 25 June 1938 at Ōmura, Nagasaki Prefecture, from fighter and bomber units from the carrier *Soryū*. At the outset of the China War it was dispatched to An-ch'ing, Anhwei Province, and was soon heavily engaged in operations in China. Later in the year it was sent to Chiu-chiang for attacks on Hankow. It was disbanded on 1 December 1938 but reconstituted on 15 November 1939, sent to southern China, and incorporated into the Second Expeditionary Fleet's Third Combined Air Group. Its aircraft were incorporated into the Genzan Air Group on 15 November 1940.

SIXTEENTH [SEVENTH] AIR GROUP. Organized 15 November 1940 as the Seventh Air Group, attached to the Fourth Fleet's Third Base Force, and composed of reconnaissance seaplanes. In April 1940 it was dispatched to Palau, and it was redesignated the Sixteenth Air Group in April 1941.

SEVENTEENTH AIR GROUP. Organized 1 October 1941 and attached to the Fourth Fleet's Fourth Base Force. Composed of reconnaissance seaplanes, it was immediately dispatched to Truk.

EIGHTEENTH [EIGHTH] AIR GROUP. Organized 15 January 1940 as the Eighth Air Group, a reconnaissance seaplane group, on Saipan in the Mariana Islands and made part of the Fifth Base Force under the command of the Fourth Fleet. It was redesignated the Eighteenth Air Group on 1 April 1941.

NINETEENTH AIR GROUP. Organized 15 January 1941 at Kwajalein in the Marshall Islands as a reconnaissance seaplane air group and placed under the Sixth Base Force, Fourth Fleet. It was redesignated the 952d Air Group in November 1942 and was annihilated on 6 February 1944 in the defense of Kwajalein.

THIRD AIR GROUP. Organized 10 April 1941 as a mixed group of fighters and medium bombers and made part of the Twenty-third Air Flotilla. In July 1941 the group was sent to Hanoi, and in September it was reorganized into a purely fighter group and based on Taiwan. Conceived as one of the spearheads of the projected Japanese conquest of Southeast Asia, the group was composed of veteran pilots, some of whom like Kamei Yoshio, its commanding officer, and Shibata Takeo, its executive officer, had already gained fame in Japanese naval aviation circles. It took part in the initial attacks on American air bases on Luzon on 8 December 1941 and next flew to Davao, from whence it attacked Allied positions in Borneo and the Celebes. It was then moved forward to Kendari on the Celebes for attacks on Timor and from there to Balikpapan to participate in air battles for the conquest of Java. After being dispersed to various bases in the Netherlands East Indies, the group was reunited at Kupang, Timor. From bases at Kendari and Kupang the group launched attacks on key towns in northwestern Australia in March 1942. In September of that year the group became heavily engaged in attacks on Guadalcanal, in providing air cover for convoys, and in air defense in the southwestern Pacific. It was redesignated the 202d Air Group in November. Along with the Tainan Air Group, the Third Air Group was one of the most heralded of the navy's land-based air groups in the air combat of the Pacific War.

COMBINED AIR GROUPS, 1938–1939

ELEVENTH COMBINED AIR GROUP. Formed 15 December 1938 at Yokosuka and composed of the Kasumigaura, Tsukuba, Kagoshima, and Suzuka air groups. The Hyakurigahara and Yatabe air groups were added on 1 December 1939, when the Eleventh CAG took on a training function. The Tsuchiura Air Group was added on 15 November 1940.

TWELFTH COMBINED AIR GROUP. Formed 1 December 1939 at Kure and composed of the Ōita and Usa air groups. The Ōmura and Hakata air groups were added on 15 November 1940.

SPECIAL COMBINED AIR GROUPS, 1937–1940

FIRST COMBINED AIR GROUP. Formed 11 July 1937 as part of the Third Fleet and composed of the Kisarazu and Kanoya air groups, it was almost immediately sent to China, where it became one of the mainstays of the navy's aerial offensives there. On 1 December 1937 it was placed under the direct command of the Combined Fleet. After 1 April 1938 it was made a training unit within the Combined Fleet, but it returned as needed to China to take part in air operations there. On 15 January 1940 the Takao Air Group took the place of the Kisarazu Air Group, and on 15 November the Tōkō Air

Group was added. On 15 January 1941, as part of the major reorganization of Japanese naval aviation, the group was redesignated the Twenty-first Air Flotilla.

SECOND COMBINED AIR GROUP. Formed July 1937 as part of the Second Fleet, it was composed of the Twelfth and Thirteenth air groups. The unit was immediately dispatched to northern China, where it took part in the Japanese early aerial offensives in that region, but was transferred to central China in September and placed under the Third Fleet. The Fifteenth Air Group was added in June 1938 but was disbanded that September. In September 1940 the Twelfth and Thirteenth air groups were abolished, and in November their places were taken by the Genzan and Mihoro air groups. At the same time, the Second CAG was returned to Japan to become a training unit under the Combined Fleet, though it was returned temporarily to take part in operations in central China. It was redesignated the Twenty-second Air Flotilla on 1 January 1941.

THIRD COMBINED AIR GROUP. Formed 15 December 1938 as part of the Fifth Fleet and composed of the Fourteenth and Sixteenth air groups and the seaplane carrier *Kamikawa Maru*. It served in southern China in 1939–40 but was disbanded on 15 November 1940.

FOURTH COMBINED AIR GROUP. Formed 15 November 1940 as part of the Fourth Fleet and composed of the Yokohama and Chitose air groups. On 15 January 1941 it was redesignated the Twenty-fourth Air Flotilla.

Appendix 6

Principal Naval Aircraft

This appendix is divided into two sections: early aircraft and aircraft of the Pacific War. The first section lists the principal combat aircraft types found in the Imperial Japanese Navy from 1921 until the outbreak of the Pacific War. In most cases the aircraft illustrated is the last variant of a given model. The second section lists the principal combat aircraft types in the Imperial Japanese Navy designed and in production at the outbreak of the war on 8 December 1941. In those cases where an aircraft had multiple active variants (including noncombatant variants such as trainers and transports), only the latest combat variant fielded at the outbreak of the war is listed.

Each aircraft listed here is identified with the symbol • where first discussed in the text. Information for this appendix was drawn from the following sources: *NKS*; Mikesh and Abe, *Japanese Aircraft*; Francillon, *Japanese Aircraft*; and Hasegawa, *Nihon no kōkūbōkan*.

SECTION 1: EARLY AIRCRAFT

FIGHTERS

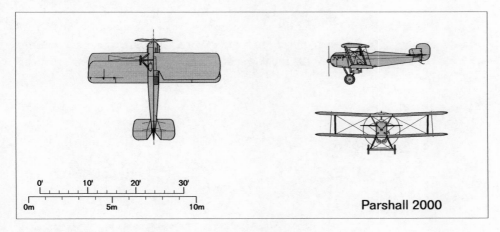

Fig. A6-1. Mitsubishi 1MF3 Type 10 carrier fighter

Mitsubishi 1MF3

Official designation:	Type 10 carrier fighter
Description:	Single-engined single-seat biplane carrier-borne fighter of wooden construction and fabric covering
Crew:	1
Power plant:	300hp Mitsubishi 8-cylinder water-cooled engine
Armament:	2 forward-firing fixed 7.7mm machine guns

Dimensions

Span:	27ft 10.5in
Length:	22ft 7.5in
Height:	10ft 2in

Weight

Empty:	2,073lb
Loaded:	2,821lb
Wing loading:	8.438lb/sq ft

Performance

Maximum speed:	132mph
Cruising speed:	?

Climb:	9,843ft in 10min
Service ceiling:	22,963ft
Endurance:	2.5hrs

NOTES: One of three types of aircraft whose designs were drawn up in the early 1920s with the assistance of British engineers and under Mitsubishi's first contract with the navy. The first aircraft to undertake flight operations from the deck of Japan's first carrier, the *Hōshō*.

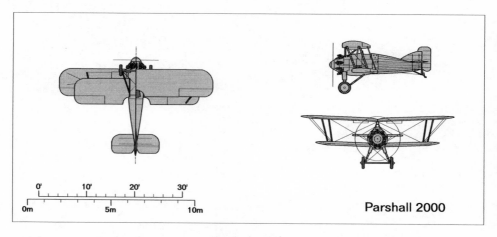

Fig. A6-2. Nakajima A1N1 Type 3 carrier fighter

Nakajima A1N1

Official designation:	Type 3 carrier fighter
Description:	Single-engined single-seat biplane fighter of wooden structure and fabric covering
Crew:	1
Power plant:	420hp Nakajima Jupiter VI 9-cylinder air-cooled radial engine
Armament:	2 forward-firing side-mounted 7.7mm machine guns
Bomb load:	2 × 30kg (66lb) bombs

Dimensions

Span:	31ft 9in
Length:	21ft 3.5in
Height:	10ft 8in

Weight

Empty:	2,094lb
Loaded:	3,196lb
Wing loading:	11.3lb/sq ft

Performance

Maximum speed:	148mph
Cruising speed:	92mph
Range:	200nm
Endurance:	2.5hrs

NOTES: This aircraft had its origin in a modified version of the Gloster Gamecock fighter. It was the first Nakajima naval fighter and the best fighter in Japan at the time of its appearance. An improved version, the A1N2, was adopted in 1930. Saw combat during the fighting in Shanghai in February 1932.

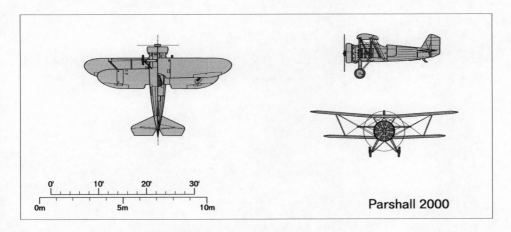

Fig. A6-3. Nakajima A2N1 Type 90 carrier fighter

Nakajima A2N1

Official designation:	Type 90 carrier fighter
Description:	Single-engined single-seat biplane fighter; all-metal fuselage with wood and metal fabric-covered wings
Crew:	1
Power plant:	460–580hp Nakajima Kotobuki 2 9-cylinder air-cooled radial engine
Armament:	2 forward-firing fixed 7.7mm machine guns

Dimensions

Span:	30ft 9in
Length:	20ft 3.25in
Height:	9ft 11in

Weight

Empty:	2,303lb
Loaded:	3,417lb
Wing loading:	11.3lb/sq ft

Performance

Maximum speed:	182mph
Cruising speed:	104mph
Climb:	9,843ft in 5min 45sec
Service ceiling:	29,527ft
Range:	270nm
Endurance:	3hrs

NOTES: The first Japanese fighter that was equal in performance to the world's best fighters of the time. Used by the navy's acrobatic teams of the early 1930s.

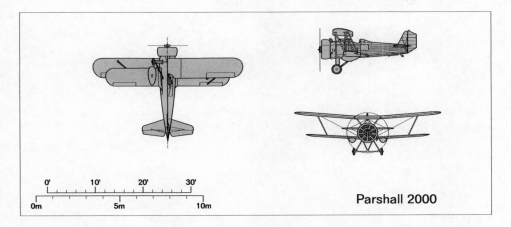

Parshall 2000

Fig. A6-4. Nakajima A4N1 Type 95 carrier fighter

Nakajima A4N1

Official designation:	Type 95 carrier fighter
Description:	Single-engined single-seat biplane fighter; metal structure with fabric covering
Crew:	1
Power plant:	670–730hp Nakjajima Hikari 1 9-cylinder air-cooled radial engine
Armament:	2 forward-firing fixed 7.7mm machine guns
Bomb load:	2 × 30kg or 60kg (66lb or 132lb) bombs

Dimensions

Span:	32ft 9.5in
Length:	21ft 9.25in
Height:	10ft 1in

Weight

Empty:	2,813lb
Loaded:	3,380lb
Wing loading:	15.74lb/sq ft

Performance

Maximum speed:	219mph
Cruising speed:	145mph
Climb:	9,843ft in 3min 30sec

Service ceiling:	25,393ft
Range:	457nm
Endurance:	3.5hrs

NOTES: Was the navy's first-line fighter at the opening of the war in China. As the last of the navy's biplane fighters, it was replaced by the Mitsubishi A5M Type 96 carrier fighter (q.v.).

ATTACK AIRCRAFT

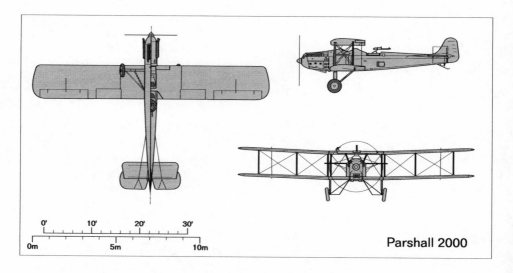

Parshall 2000

Fig. A6-5. Mitsubishi B1M1 Type 13 carrier attack aircraft

Mitsubishi B1M1

Official designation:	Type 13 carrier attack aircraft
Description:	Single-engined 3-seat biplane attack bomber; wooden structure with fabric covering; rearward-folding wings for carrier stowage
Crew:	2 or 3
Power plant:	450 Napier Lion 12-cylinder water-cooled engine
Armament:	Twin dorsal flexible 7.7mm machine gun and 2 forward-firing 7.7mm machine guns
Bomb load:	1 × 18in torpedo or 2 × 240kg (529lb) bombs

Dimensions

Span:	48ft 5.5in
Length:	32ft 1in
Height:	11ft 6in

Weight

Empty:	3,179lb
Loaded:	5,945lb
Wing loading:	9.339lb/sq ft

Performance

Maximum speed:	130mph
Service ceiling:	14,763ft
Climb:	9,843ft in 20min (Type 13-2)
Endurance:	2.6hrs

NOTES: Adopted by the navy in the late 1920s, this aircraft remained the navy's all-round combat aircraft until the beginning of Japan's war in China.

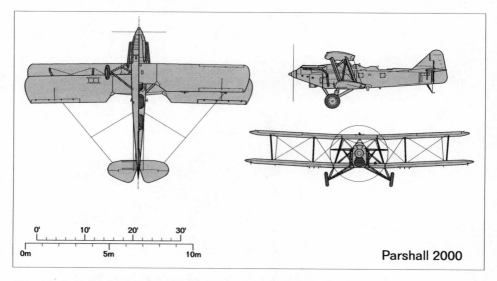

Parshall 2000

Fig. A6-6. Mitsubishi B2M1 Type 89 carrier attack aircraft

Mitsubishi B2M1

Official designation:	Type 89 carrier attack aircraft
Description:	Single-engined 2-bay biplane attack bomber; steel and aluminum construction with fabric covering; rearward-folding wings for carrier stowage
Crew:	3
Power plant:	650 Mitsubishi Type Hi 12-cylinder water-cooled engine
Armament:	1 forward-firing (from fuselage side) 7.7mm machine gun and 1 dorsal flexible 7.7mm machine gun
Bomb load:	1 Type 91 or Type 94 torpedo, or 1 × 800kg (1,763lb) bomb

Dimensions

Span:	49ft 11.25in
Length:	33ft 8.5in
Height:	12ft 2in

Weight

Empty:	4,982lb
Loaded:	9,936lb
Wing loading:	13.4lb/sq ft

Performance

Maximum speed: 132mph

Climb: 9,843ft in 18 min

Range: 960nm

Endurance: ?

NOTES: Adapted from a British Blackburn design, this aircraft was conceived by the navy as a replacement for the Mitsubishi B1M Type 13 carrier attack aircraft (q.v.). Although over two hundred were built between 1930 and 1935, this aircraft was not a success because of stability, engine, and other problems.

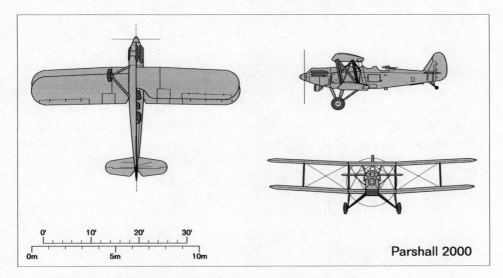

Parshall 2000

Fig. A6-7. Yokosuka B3Y1 Type 92 carrier attack aircraft

Yokosuka B3Y1

Official designation: Type 92 carrier attack aircraft

Description: Single-engined 3-seat biplane attack bomber; welded steel tube fuselage structure with fabric covering; rearward-folding wings for carrier stowage

Crew: 3

Power plant: 600–750hp Type 91 12-cylinder water-cooled engine

Armament: 1 fuselage-mounted forward-firing fixed 7.7mm machine gun and 1 dorsal flexible 7.7mm machine gun

Bomb load:	1 × 800kg (1,763lb) torpedo, or 2 × 250kg (551lb) bombs, or 6 × 30kg (66lb) bombs

Dimensions

Span:	44ft 3.25in
Length:	31ft 2in
Height:	12ft 2.75in

Weight

Empty:	4,078lb
Loaded:	7,054lb
Wing loading:	13.1lb/sq ft

Performance

Maximum speed:	136mph
Endurance:	4.5hrs

NOTES: Adopted by the navy in 1933 as a replacement for the Mitsubishi B2M Type 89 carrier attack aircraft (q.v.), this aircraft encountered numerous engine problems. It had a certain success at the beginning of the Japanese war in China, however, in horizontal bombardment against land targets.

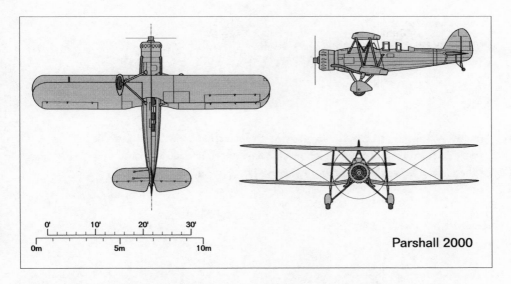

Parshall 2000

Fig. A6-8. Yokosuka B4Y1 Type 96 carrier attack aircraft

Yokosuka B4Y1

Official designation:	Type 96 carrier attack aircraft
Subsequent Allied code name:	"Jean"
Description:	Single-engined 3-seat biplane torpedo bomber; all-metal structure with light alloy and fabric covering
Crew:	3
Power plant:	600hp Hirō Type 91 air-cooled radial engine
Armament:	1 flexible rear-firing 7.7mm machine gun
Bomb load:	1 × 800kg (1,764lb) torpedo or 500kg (1,102lb) of bombs

Dimensions

Span:	49ft 2in
Length:	33ft 3in
Height:	14ft 3in

Weight

Empty:	4,409lb
Loaded:	7,937lb
Wing loading:	14.7lb/sq ft

Performance

Maximum speed:	173mph
Climb:	9,845ft in 14 min
Service ceiling:	19,685ft
Range:	850nm

NOTES: Acquired in 1936 by the navy as a replacement for the Yokosuka B3Y Type 92 carrier attack aircraft (q.v.), which had proved unreliable. Saw service in the early stages of the China War and operated on Japanese carriers until 1940.

RECONNAISSANCE AIRCRAFT

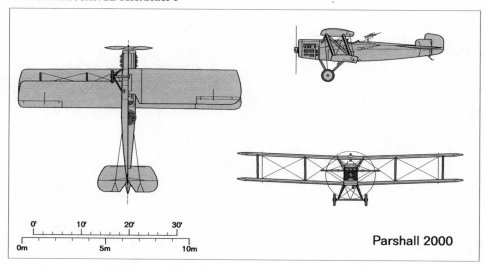

Parshall 2000

Fig. A6-9. Mitsubishi 2MR1 Type 10 carrier reconnaissance aircraft

Mitsubishi 2MR1

Official designation:	Type 10 carrier reconnaissance aircraft
Description:	Single-engined 2-seat reconnaissance biplane; wooden construction with fabric covering
Crew:	2
Power plant:	300hp Mitsubishi 8-cylinder water-cooled engine
Armament:	2 forward-firing fixed 7.7mm machine guns and twin dorsal flexible 7.7mm machine guns
Bomb load:	3 × 30kg (66lb) bombs

Dimensions

Span:	39ft 6in
Length:	26ft 0in
Height:	9ft 6in

Weight

Empty:	2,160lb
Loaded:	2,910lb
Wing loading:	7.168lb/sq ft

Performance

Maximum speed:	127mph
Climb:	9,843ft in 17min
Endurance:	3.5hrs

NOTES: This aircraft was acquired by the navy in 1922, and production continued until 1930. After it was withdrawn as an operational aircraft it was used for a number of years as a trainer.

DIVE BOMBERS

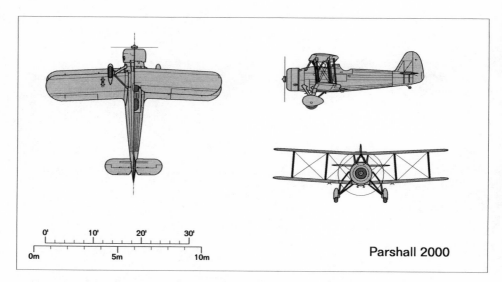

Parshall 2000

Fig. A6-10. Aichi D1A2 Type 96 carrier bomber

Aichi D1A2

Official designation:	Type 96 carrier bomber
Subsequent Allied code name:	"Susie"
Description:	Single-engined 2-seat carrier-borne biplane dive-bomber
Crew:	2 (pilot, radio operator/gunner)
Power plant:	1 Nakajima Hikari 9-cylinder air-cooled radial, 730hp at takeoff, driving a 2-bladed propeller
Armament:	2 fixed forward-firing 7.7mm Type 92 machine guns and 1 flexible rear-firing 7.7mm Type 92 machine gun
Bomb load:	1 × 250kg (551lb) bomb under the fuselage and 2 × 30kg (66lb) bombs under the wings

Dimensions

Span:	37ft 4in
Length:	30ft 6in
Height:	11ft 2in

Weight

Empty:	3,342lb
Loaded:	5,512lb

Performance

Maximum speed:	192mph at 10,500ft
Cruising speed:	138mph at 3,280ft
Climb:	9,845ft in 7min 51sec
Service ceiling:	22,900ft
Range:	500nm

NOTES: This aircraft was originally designated the Aichi D1A1 and was adopted by the navy in 1934 as the Type 94 carrier bomber. In 1935 Aichi designed the improved version of the aircraft shown here, the Aichi D1A2, which was accepted by the navy as the Type 96 carrier bomber. Although it was technically still an active combat aircraft at the outset of the Pacific War, it served in second-line units only.

SECTION 2: AIRCRAFT OF THE PACIFIC WAR

FIGHTERS

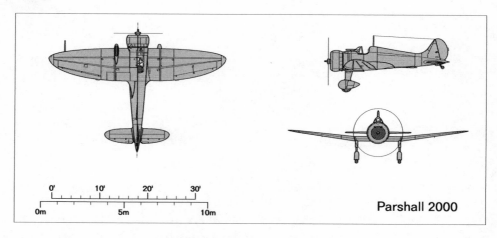

Fig. A6-11. Mitsubishi A5M4 Type 96 carrier fighter

Mitsubishi A5M4

Official designation:	Type 96 carrier fighter
Subsequent Allied code name:	"Claude"
Description:	Single-engined single-seat carrier-borne fighter; trainer version (A5M4-K) also produced
Crew:	1
Power plant:	1 Nakajima Kotobuki 41 or 41 KAI 9-cylinder air-cooled radial, 710hp at takeoff, driving a 3-bladed propeller
Armament:	2 × 7.7mm Type 89 machine guns
Bomb load:	2 × 30kg (66lb) bombs or 1 × 160-liter (35.2-imp-gal) drop tank

Dimensions

Span:	36ft 1in
Length:	24ft 10in
Height:	10ft 6in

Weight

Empty:	2,681lb
Loaded:	3,684lb

Performance

Maximum speed:	270mph at 9,845ft
Climb:	9,845ft in 3min 35sec
Service ceiling:	32,150ft
Range:	648nm

NOTES: Obsolescent but still in use in some front-line units (such as the carrier *Ryūjō*) during the early portions of the war.

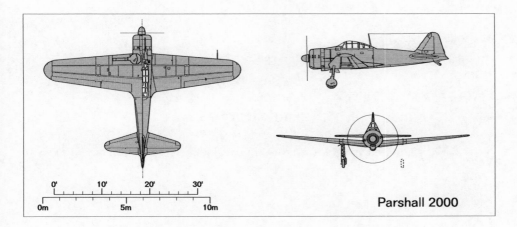

Fig. A6-12. Mitsubishi A6M2 Model 21 Type 0 carrier fighter

Mitsubishi A6M2 Model 21

Official designation:	Type 0 carrier fighter
Subsequent Allied code name:	"Zeke"
Description:	Single-engined single-seat carrier-borne and land-based fighter
Crew:	1
Power plant:	1 Nakajima NK1C Sakae 12 14-cylinder air-cooled radial, 940hp at takeoff, driving a 3-bladed propeller
Armament:	2 × 7.7mm Type 97 machine guns and 2 × 20mm Type 99 cannon
Bomb load:	2 × 60kg (132lb) bombs, 1 × 330-liter (72.6-imp-gal) drop tank

Dimensions

Span: 39ft 4in
Length: 29ft 8in
Height: 11ft 6in

Weight

Empty: 3,704lb
Loaded: 5,313lb

Performance

Maximum speed: 332mph at 14,930ft
Cruising speed: 207mph
Climb: 19,685ft in 7min 27sec
Service ceiling: 32,810ft
Range: 1,010nm (1,675nm max)

NOTES: The standard carrier and land-based naval fighter at the outbreak of the war.

ATTACK AIRCRAFT

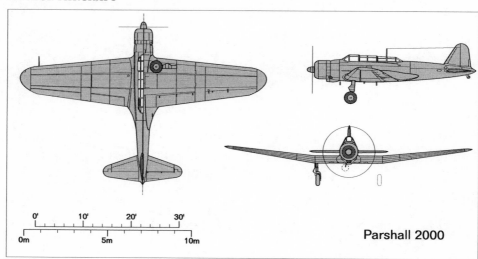

Fig. A6-13. Nakajima B5N2 Type 97 carrier attack aircraft

Nakajima B5N2

Official designation: Type 97 carrier attack aircraft

Subsequent Allied code name:	"Kate"
Description:	Single-engined 3-seat carrier-borne torpedo bomber
Crew:	3 (pilot, observer/navigator/bomb aimer, radio operator/gunner)
Power plant:	1 Nakajima NK1B Sakae 11 14-cylinder air-cooled radial, 1,000hp at takeoff, driving a 3-bladed propeller
Armament:	1 flexible rear-firing 7.7mm Type 92 machine gun
Bomb load:	1 × 800kg (1,764lb) torpedo or 800kg (1,764lb) of bombs

Dimensions
Span:	50ft 10in
Length:	33ft 9in
Height:	12ft 1in

Weight
Empty:	5,024lb
Loaded:	8,378lb

Performance
Maximum speed:	235mph at 11,810ft
Cruising speed:	161mph at 11,810ft
Climb:	9,845 in 7min 40sec
Service ceiling:	27,100ft
Range:	528nm (1,075nm max)

NOTES: At the outbreak of the Pacific War, B5N2s equipped all front-line carrier units. Older B5N1s were still in service in second-line units.

DIVE BOMBERS

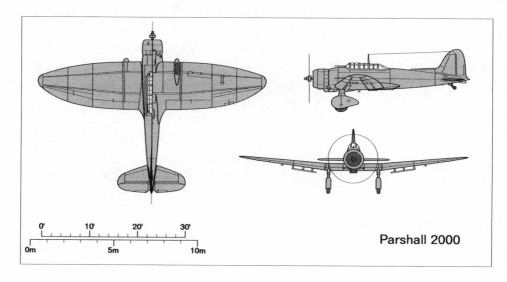

Parshall 2000

Fig. A6-14. Aichi D3A1 Type 99 carrier bomber

Aichi D3A1

Official designation:	Type 99 carrier bomber
Subsequent Allied code name:	"Val"
Description:	Single-engined 2-seat carrier-borne and land-based dive bomber
Crew:	2
Power plant:	1 Mitsubishi Kinsei 43 14-cylinder air-cooled radial, 1,000hp at takeoff, or Mitsubishi Kinsei 44 14-cylinder air-cooled radial, 1,070hp at takeoff, driving a 3-bladed propeller
Armament:	2 forward-firing 7.7mm Type 97 machine guns and 1 flexible rear-firing 7.7mm Type 92 machine gun
Bomb load:	1 × 250kg (551lb) bomb under the fuselage and 2 × 60kg (132lb) bombs under the wings

Dimensions

Span:	47ft 1in
Length:	33ft 5in
Height:	12ft 7in

Weight

Empty: 5,309lb
Loaded: 8,047lb

Performance

Maximum speed: 240mph at 9,845ft
Cruising speed: 184mph at 9,845ft
Climb: 9,845ft in 6min 0sec
Service ceiling: 30,050ft
Range: 795nm

NOTES: D3A1s equipped all front-line carrier dive-bomber formations at the beginning
of the Pacific War.

FLOATPLANES

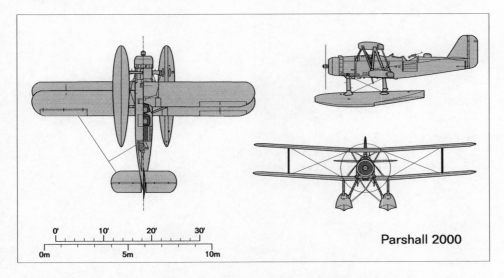

Fig. A6-15. Kawanishi E7K2 Type 94 reconnaissance seaplane

Kawanishi E7K2

Official designation: Type 94 reconnaissance seaplane
Subsequent Allied code name: "Alf"
Description: Single-engined 3-seat biplane twin-float reconnais-
                                sance seaplane
Crew: 3

Power plant:	1 Mitsubishi Zuisei 11 14-cylinder air-cooled radial, 870hp at takeoff, driving a 2-bladed propeller
Armament:	1 forward-firing 7.7mm Type 92 machine gun, 1 flexible rear-firing 7.7mm Type 92 machine gun, and 1 flexible downward-firing 7.7mm Type 92 machine gun
Bomb load:	4 × 30kg (66lb) bombs or 2 × 60kg (132lb) bombs

Dimensions

Span:	45ft 11in
Length:	34ft 5in
Height:	15ft 10in

Weight

Empty:	4,630lb
Loaded:	7,275lb

Performance

Maximum speed:	171mph at 6,560ft
Cruising speed:	115mph at 3,280ft
Climb:	9,845ft in 9min 6sec
Service ceiling:	23,165ft
Endurance:	11.32hrs

NOTES: Obsolescent but still used in front-line roles until 1943.

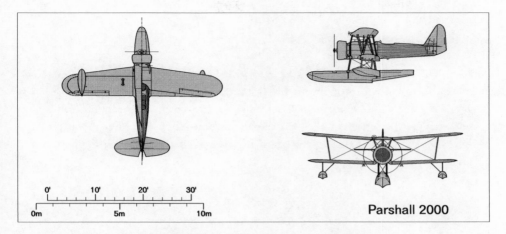

Parshall 2000

Fig. A6-16. Nakajima E8N2 Type 95 reconnaissance seaplane

Nakajima E8N2

Official designation:	Type 95 reconnaissance seaplane
Subsequent Allied code name:	"Dave"
Description:	Single-engined 2-seat biplane reconnaissance seaplane
Crew:	2
Power plant:	1 Nakajima Kotobuki 2 KAI 2 9-cylinder air-cooled radial, 630hp at takeoff, driving a 2-bladed propeller
Armament:	1 fixed forward-firing 7.7mm machine gun and 1 flexible rear-firing 7.7mm machine gun
Bomb load:	2 × 60kg (132lb) bombs

Dimensions

Span:	36ft 0in
Length:	28ft 10in
Height:	12ft 7in

Weight

Empty:	2,910lb
Loaded:	4,189lb

Performance

Maximum speed:	186mph at 9,845ft
Climb:	9,845ft in 6min 31sec

Service ceiling:	23,850ft
Range:	485nm

NOTES: This aircraft appeared in the mid-1930s as a catapult-launched light reconnaissance floatplane operating principally off battleships and cruisers. During the early stages of Japan's war in China it saw action largely as a reconnaissance aircraft and as a spotter for artillery fire but also occasionally as a dive bomber. After it was replaced early in the Pacific War by more modern floatplanes, it was retained for liaison and training purposes.

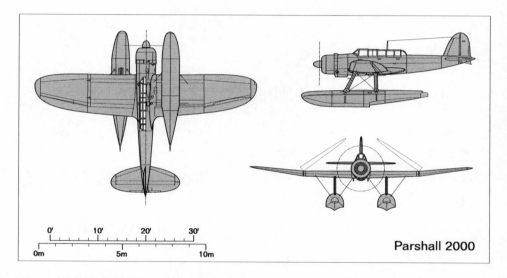

Parshall 2000

Fig. A6-17. Mitsubishi F1M2 Type 0 observation seaplane

Mitsubishi F1M2

Official designation:	Type 0 observation seaplane
Subsequent Allied code name:	"Pete"
Description:	Single-engined 2-seat biplane observation float seaplane; also produced in trainer version (F1M2-K)
Crew:	2 (pilot, radio operator/gunner)
Power plant:	1 Mitsubishi Zuisei 13 14-cylinder air-cooled radial, 875hp at takeoff, driving a 3-bladed propeller
Armament:	2 fixed forward-firing 7.7mm Type 97 machine guns and 1 flexible rear-firing 7.7mm Type 92 machine gun
Bomb load:	2 × 60kg (132lb) bombs

Dimensions

Span:	36ft 1in
Length:	31ft 2in
Height:	13ft 1in

Weight

Empty:	4,251lb
Loaded:	5,622lb

Performance

Maximum speed:	230mph at 11,285ft
Climb:	16,405ft in 9min 36sec
Service ceiling:	30,970ft
Range:	400nm

NOTES: Conceived as a replacement for the Nakajima E8N2 reconnaissance seaplane, this aircraft was produced in large quantities for the navy. It was originally designed as a short-range observation floatplane operating from cruisers, seaplane tenders, and shore bases. But its maneuverability and the exigencies the navy faced in the Pacific War led to its use across a range of functions: interceptor fighter, dive bomber, coastal patrol aircraft, and convoy escort.

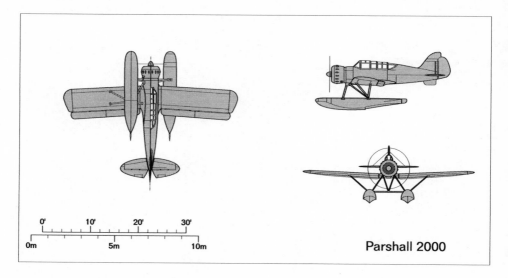

Fig. A6-18. Aichi E13A1 Type 0 reconnaissance seaplane

Aichi E13A1

Official designation:	Type 0 reconnaissance seaplane
Subsequent Allied code name:	"Jake"
Description:	Single-engined 3-seat twin-float reconnaissance seaplane
Crew:	3
Power plant:	1 Mitsubishi Kinsei 43 14-cylinder air-cooled radial, 1,000hp at takeoff, driving a 3-bladed propeller
Armament:	1 flexible rear-firing 7.7mm Type 92 machine gun
Bomb load:	1 × 250kg (551lb) bomb under the fuselage, or 4 × 60kg (132lb) bombs, or depth charges

Dimensions

Span:	47ft 6in
Length:	37ft 0in
Height:	24ft 3in

Weight

Empty:	5,825lb
Loaded:	8,025lb

Performance

Maximum speed:	234mph at 7,155ft
Cruising speed:	138mph at 6,560ft
Climb:	9,845ft in 6min 5sec
Service ceiling:	28,640ft
Range:	1,128nm

NOTES: Designed as a replacement for the Kawanishi E7K2 in the late 1930s, this aircraft went into production in early 1941 and was eventually produced in greater numbers than any other Japanese floatplane. Its outstanding feature was an endurance of almost fifteen hours. Operating from battleships, cruisers, and seaplane tenders, it participated in the navy's aerial assault on railways and antishipping patrols along the south China coast in late 1941 and flew reconnaissance missions during the navy's Hawai'ian operation.

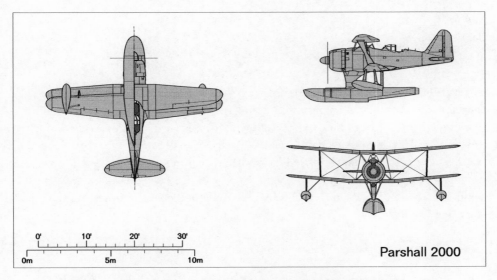

Fig. A6-19. Yokosuka E14Y1 Type 0 small reconnaissance seaplane

Yokosuka E14Y1

Official designation:	Type 0 small reconnaissance seaplane
Subsequent Allied code name:	"Glen"
Description:	Single-engined 2-seat submarine-borne twin-float reconnaissance seaplane
Crew:	2
Power plant:	1 Hitachi Tempu 12 9-cylinder air-cooled radial, 340hp at takeoff, driving a 2-bladed propeller

Armament:	1 flexible rear-firing 7.7mm Type 92 machine gun
Bomb load:	60kg (132lb) of bombs

Dimensions

Span:	36ft 1in
Length:	28ft 0in
Height:	12ft 5in

Weight

Empty:	2,469lb
Loaded:	3,197lb

Performance

Maximum speed:	153mph at sea level
Cruising speed:	104mph at 3,280ft
Climb:	9,845ft in 10min 11sec
Service ceiling:	17,780ft
Range:	476nm

NOTES: This small seaplane, designed to be carried aboard the navy's largest submarines for reconnaissance purposes, could be easily disassembled for storage in a watertight hangar aboard the submarine. It had two noteworthy appearances during the Pacific War. The first was its dawn reconnaissance over Pearl Harbor on 17 December 1941 to assess the damage inflicted by the navy's earlier attack on the warships and facilities there. The second was an attempt by an E14Y1, flying off a submarine, to fire-bomb the Oregon forests in August 1942, the only time Japanese forces ever struck at the American mainland.

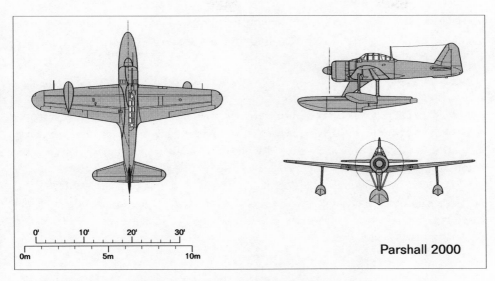

Fig. A6-20. Nakajima A6M2-N Type 2 seaplane fighter

Nakajima A6M2-N

Official designation:	Type 2 seaplane fighter
Subsequent Allied code name:	"Rufe"
Description:	Single-engined single-seat float seaplane fighter
Crew:	1
Power plant:	1 Nakajima NK1C Sakae 12 14-cylinder air-cooled radial, 940hp at takeoff, driving a 3-bladed propeller
Armament:	2 × 7.7mm Type 97 machine guns and 2 × 20mm Type 99 cannon
Bomb load:	2 × 60kg (132lb) bombs

Dimensions
Span:	39ft 4in
Length:	33ft 1in
Height:	14ft 1in

Weight
Empty:	4,235lb
Loaded:	5,423lb

Performance
Maximum speed:	270mph at 16,405ft

Cruising speed:	184mph at 16,405ft
Climb:	16,405ft in 6min 43sec
Service ceiling:	32,810ft
Range:	620nm (963nm max)

NOTES: This aircraft was conceived by the navy in 1940 as a single-seat fighter seaplane to provide air cover in the early stages of amphibious landings in the Japanese offensives in Southeast Asia and the southwestern Pacific, or on small islands, such as Tulagi in the Solomons, where construction of airfields was not practical. Under navy instructions it was produced by Nakajima as a floatplane version of the Mitsubishi A6M2. In this offensive role it served effectively at the outset of the Pacific War, but functioning defensively as an interceptor when the tide of war turned against Japan, it was hardly a match for land-based Allied fighters.

FLYING BOATS

Kawanishi H6K4

Official designation:	Type 97 flying boat
Subsequent Allied code name:	"Mavis"
Description:	4-engined long-range reconnaissance flying boat; also produced in transport version (H6K2-L and H6K3)
Crew:	8
Power plant:	4 Mitsubishi Kinsei 46 14-cylinder air-cooled radials, 930hp at takeoff, driving 3-bladed propellers
Armament:	1 flexible 7.7mm Type 92 machine gun in an open bow position, 1 flexible 7.7mm Type 92 machine gun in an open dorsal position, 1 × 7.7mm Type 92 machine gun in each beam blister, and 1 flexible 20mm Type 99 Model 1 cannon in a tail turret
Bomb load:	2 × 800kg (1,764lb) torpedoes or up to 1,000kg (2,205lb) of bombs

Dimensions

Span:	131ft 2in
Length:	84ft 0in
Height:	20ft 6in

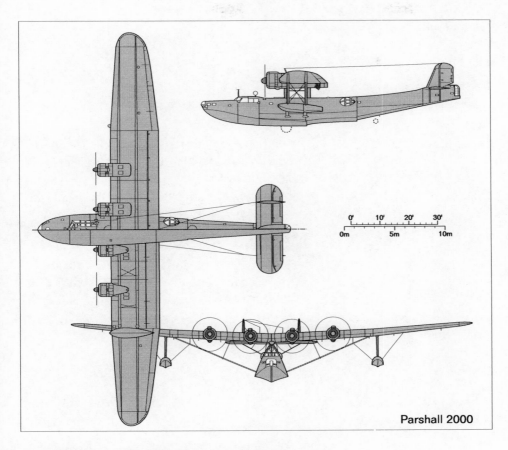

Fig. A6-21. Kawanishi H6K4 Type 97 flying boat

	Weight
Empty:	25,810lb
Loaded:	37,479lb

	Performance
Maximum speed:	211mph at 13,125ft
Cruising speed:	138mph at 12,125ft
Climb:	16,405ft in 13min 31sec
Service ceiling:	31,530ft
Range:	2,590nm (3,283nm max)

NOTES: The H6K4 (Type 97 Model 2-2) was the major production version of this aircraft at the beginning of the Pacific War. Earlier variants included H6K2 and H6K3.

Kawanishi H8K1

Official designation:	Type 2 flying boat
Subsequent Allied code name:	"Emily"
Description:	4-engined long-range reconnaissance flying boat
Crew:	9
Power plant:	4 Mitsubishi MK4A Kasei 12 14-cylinder air-cooled radials, 1,530hp at takeoff, driving 4-bladed propellers
Armament:	20mm Type 99 Model 1 cannon in dorsal and tail turrets, and 7.7mm Type 92 machine guns in 2 beam blisters, ventral and cockpit hatches, and bow turret
Bomb load:	2 × 800kg (1,764lb) torpedoes, or 8 × 250kg (551lb) bombs, or 16 × 60kg (132lb) bombs, or depth charges

Dimensions

Span:	124ft 8in
Length:	92ft 3in
Height:	30ft 0in

Weight

Empty:	34,176lb
Loaded:	54,013lb

Performance

Maximum speed:	269mph at 16,405ft
Cruising speed:	184mph at 13,145ft
Climb:	16,405ft in 14min 33sec
Service ceiling:	25,035ft
Range:	3,888nm

NOTES: The first production versions of this aircraft were just being delivered as war broke out.

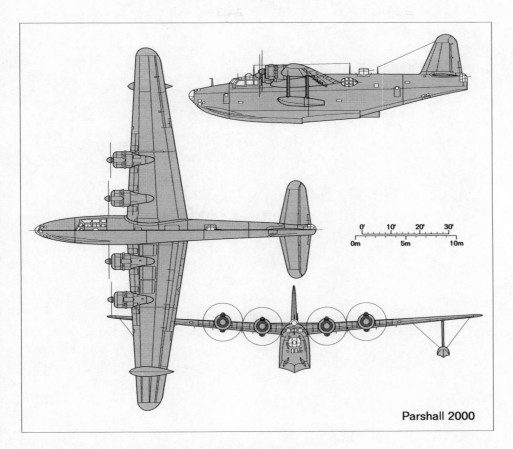

Parshall 2000

Fig. A6-22. Kawanishi H8K1 Type 2 flying boat

LAND-BASED ATTACK BOMBERS

Mitsubishi G3M2 Model 22

Official designation:	Type 96 attack bomber
Subsequent Allied code name:	"Nell"
Description:	Twin-engined land-based bomber; transport variant (L3Y) also produced
Crew:	7
Power plant:	2 Mitsubishi Kinsei 42 14-cylinder air-cooled radials, 1,075hp at takeoff, driving either 4-bladed fixed-pitch propellers or 3-bladed variable-pitch propellers; or 2 Mitsubishi Kinsei 45 14-cylinder air-cooled radials, 1,075hp at takeoff, driving 3-bladed variable-pitch propellers
Armament:	1 flexible 20mm Type 99 Model 1 cannon in a dorsal turret, and 1 flexible 7.7mm Type 92 machine gun in each of the beam blisters and a retractable dorsal turret; a flexible 7.7mm Type 92 machine gun could also be fired from the cockpit windows
Bomb load:	1 × 800kg (1,764lb) torpedo or 800kg (1,764lb) of bombs carried externally

Dimensions

Span:	82ft 0in
Length:	53ft 11in
Height:	12ft 1in

Weight

Empty:	10,936lb
Loaded:	17,637lb

Performance

Maximum speed:	232mph at 13,715ft
Cruising speed:	173mph at 13,125ft
Climb:	9,845ft in 8min 19sec
Service ceiling:	29,950ft
Range:	2,365nm

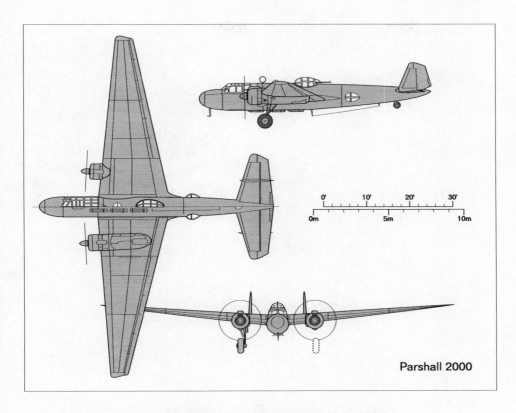

Parshall 2000

Fig. A6-23. Mitsubishi G3M2 Model 22 Type 96 attack bomber

Mitsubishi G4M1 Model 11

Official designation:	Type 1 attack bomber
Subsequent Allied code name:	"Betty"
Description:	Twin-engined land-based bomber
Crew:	7
Power plant:	2 Mitsubishi MK4A Kasei 11 14-cylinder air-cooled radials, 1,530hp at takeoff, driving 3-bladed propellers; or 2 Mitsubishi MK4E Kasei 15 14-cylinder air-cooled radials, 1,530hp at takeoff, driving 3-bladed propellers
Armament:	7.7mm Type 92 machine guns in nose, dorsal blister, and beam blister positions, and 20mm Type 99 Model 1 cannon in tail turret
Bomb load:	1 × 800kg (1,764lb) torpedo or 800kg (1,764lb) of bombs carried internally

Dimensions

Span:	82ft 0in
Length:	65ft 7in
Height:	19ft 8in

Weight

Empty:	14,991lb
Loaded:	20,944lb

Performance

Maximum speed:	276mph at 13,780ft
Cruising speed:	196mph at 9,845ft
Climb:	22,965ft in 18min
Service ceiling:	30,000ft (approx)
Range:	3,256nm

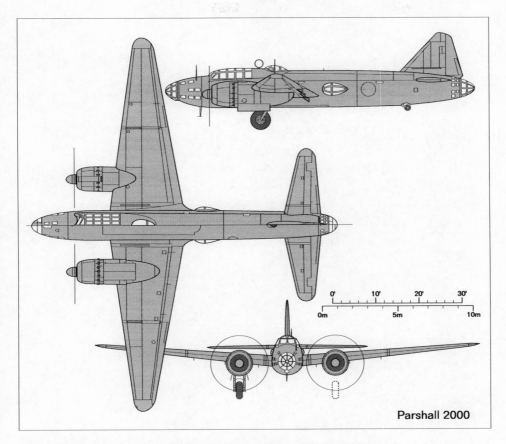

Parshall 2000

Fig. A6-24. Mitsubishi G4M1 Model 11 Type 1 attack bomber

Appendix 7

Naval Aircraft Designation Systems

Information for this appendix was drawn from the following sources: Mikesh and Abe, *Japanese Aircraft*, 1-3; Francillon, *Japanese Aircraft*, 46-59; and consultation with Osamu Tagaya.

The systems used by the Japanese army and navy to identify their aircraft can be extremely confusing. For the purposes of explaining how the navy identified the aircraft discussed in this study, however, only three designation systems need to be understood: the type-number system, the short-designation system, and the *shi-* (experimental-) number system.

TYPE-NUMBER SYSTEM

Beginning in 1921, a number was assigned to all aircraft that had been accepted for production for the Japanese navy. From 1921 through 1928, these numbers were based on the year of the current emperor's reign. (There were only two emperors in the period covered by this study, the Taishō emperor, whose reign began in 1912, and the Shōwa emperor [the emperor Hirohito], whose reign began in 1926. In each case, the first year of reign counted as year 1.) Thus, an aircraft adopted by the navy for production in 1924 would be known as a Type 13 (thirteenth year of the reign of the Taishō emperor).

Then in 1929 the Japanese government, while not displacing the reign dates, adopted a calendar based on the supposed (but wholly mythological) founding of the Japanese state in 660 B.C. The navy implemented this system by assigning to its aircraft the last two digits of the calendar year in which the aircraft was adopted for production. Thus, according to this method of calculation, the Western calendar year 1930 was reckoned to be the Japanese year 2590, and any aircraft adopted for production in that year was identified as a Type 90. An exception to this system was made for aircraft adopted in 1940—in the Japanese calculation, 2600—which were given only a single-digit designation. Thus, the famed Mitsubishi fighter of the Pacific War was identified by the navy as the Type 0 fighter, from which is derived its Western designation, the Zero. The type-number system was the aircraft designation system most widely used at the operational level by the Japanese naval air service.

SHORT-DESIGNATION SYSTEM

Beginning in the late 1920s, the navy introduced a designation system that identified each aircraft, once its design was fairly far advanced, by a block of symbols setting forth its category, pedigree, and status. The aircraft's function was indicated by a letter, its "generation" by a number, its manufacturer by a letter, its model by a number, and its modification by a letter. The following explanation breaks this system down into its component parts:

1. *Functional identification.* This letter identified the aircraft as to its principal operational use:

A	carrier fighter
B	carrier attack bomber (used for either horizontal or torpedo bombing)
C	reconnaissance aircraft
D	carrier bomber (usually functioning as a dive bomber)
E	reconnaissance seaplane
G	(land-based) attack bomber (in U.S. parlance, a medium land-based bomber)
H	flying boat
J	land-based fighter
K	trainer
L	transport
M	special floatplane
MX	special-purpose aircraft
N	seaplane fighter
P	(land-based) bomber
Q	patrol plane
R	land-based reconnaissance aircraft
S	night fighter

2. *Generation identification.* This number simply indicated the place of the aircraft in the chronology of production of naval aircraft of a similar function.

3. *Manufacturer's identification.* This letter identified the aircraft firm that designed the aircraft and was usually its principal producer. The following letters represent the principal manufacturers of aircraft described in this study: A = Aichi; H = Hirō; K = Kawanishi; M = Mitsubishi; N = Nakajima; Y = Yokosuka.

4. *Model identification.* This number indicated the particular design configuration of an aircraft. As significant changes or improvements were made in the aircraft, the model number would be changed upward.

5. *Modification identification.* Minor changes in the design or construction of an aircraft not justifying a change in the model number would be indicated by a letter in Japanese phonetic spelling (equating to the English *a, b, c,* etc.) following the model number.

In rare cases when an aircraft used for a particular operational function was adapted for use in an entirely different function, a letter drawn from the functional list would be appended after the model number or the modification letter.

Putting all these symbols together, the following short designation identifies a particular model of the famed Mitsubishi fighter aircraft of the Pacific War:

Shi- (EXPERIMENTAL-) NUMBER SYSTEM

As explained in the text, every specific aircraft design in the Japanese navy began its life as a set of required specifications set forth by the Navy General Staff and released to aircraft manufacturers interested in bidding for the contract to design and produce it. Beginning in 1931, the navy initiated a system that identified as "experimental" each projected aircraft whose design was still being let for bid or that was still in the prototype stage. It was, in effect, a temporary identification similar to the "X" and "Y" designations used in the United States for aircraft in preliminary stages of development.

This *shi* (experimental) number was based upon the reign date of the Shōwa emperor. Thus, an aircraft projected by the navy in 1937 was given a 12-*shi* number (twelfth year of Shōwa), and an aircraft let out for bid in 1940 would be designated a 15-*shi* (fifteenth year of Shōwa). To tell apart various naval aircraft that had been planned in the same year, each aircraft was also identified under this system by a functional designation. Thus, the famed Mitsubishi fighter plane of the Pacific War was initially identified as a 12-*shi* carrier fighter.

In addition to these three systems, beginning in 1943 the Japanese navy began officially assigning more popular names to its aircraft in lieu of type numbers. These were poetic in nature and represented various meteorological or natural phenomena. For example, as briefly mentioned in the text, the fighter aircraft that was supposed to succeed the Zero was called the Shiden—"Violet Lightning."

Finally, mention should be made of the designation system with which Americans are most familiar, the Pacific code-name system. Initiated in 1942 by the Allied Air Forces Directorate of Intelligence, Southwest Pacific Area, this system used personal names, either male or female, to identify Japanese aircraft. Fighters and reconnaissance seaplanes were given male names and bombers, attack bombers, dive bombers, all reconnaissance aircraft, and flying boats were given female names. In the postwar decades, however, American writers on the Pacific War have tended to use the Pacific code-name system overwhelmingly without acknowledgment that it was entirely alien to any Japanese terminological concepts during the war. Western studies that have eschewed the use of these artificial names have tended, like this study, to use the short-designation system, which combines the merits of simplicity and accuracy. But it should be recognized that during the war the Japanese navy, which most commonly used the type-number system in its records of operations, gave the short-designation system only a narrow and highly technical application.

Appendix 8

Principal Naval Aircraft Engines

This appendix describes the principal Japanese naval aircraft engines in use at the opening of the Pacific War. The information was drawn from the following sources: *KSS,* 409; Mikesh, *Zero,* 21; USSBS, Economic Studies, *Japanese Aircraft Industry,* 98–99; Milford, "Note on Japanese Naval Aircraft Engines"; Bergerud, *Fire in the Sky,* 168, 170; *NKKS,* 3:586–602; and H. Smith, *History of Aircraft Piston Engines,* 131–34.

The design heritage of Japanese aircraft engines, even more than that of Japanese airframes, was largely foreign. Until the early 1930s, Japanese aircraft used either imported engines or engines of foreign design produced under Japanese license. During the decade, Japanese manufacturers began to produce Japanese-designed engines, though these were in part based on foreign models, particularly those of Pratt and Whitney and Curtiss-Wright. As in the United States Navy, nearly all the power plants used in Japanese naval aircraft were radial air-cooled engines. The higher power-to-weight ratio of these engines as compared with liquid-cooled engines provided added design flexibility. For example, they were able to carry more fuel and more ordnance or to deliver improved flight performance. The usual approach in both navies was to use the added flexibility to improve the most needed aspect of any particular design. For carrier operations, shorter takeoff runs and lower landing speeds were important. In addition, naval aircraft designers believed and later demonstrated that radial air-cooled engines were superior to liquid-cooled engines in terms of reliability and maintainability. Most of the navy's engines were produced by Mitsubishi and Nakajima, Japan's two largest airframe and engine manufacturers.

Basically, the original foreign models were excellent power plants, and some of the Japanese engines developed from them, like the wartime 1,800-hp Homare, were quite good. But within a few years the performance of Japanese aircraft engines was being greatly overshadowed by far more powerful American power plants, and the development of engines rated over 2,000 hp proved difficult for Japanese manufacturers.

As discussed at the end of chapter 4, this situation stemmed largely from Japan's technological isolation and lack of access to strategic metals. American progress in metallurgy in the immediate prewar and war years was phenomenal, and of this Japanese engineers had scant knowledge. Furthermore, by the late 1930s Japan was restricted in its access to the strategic alloying metals, such as nickel, chromium, and vanadium, essential to the production of the high-tensile steel used in larger engines. The limitations under which Japanese aero-engineers had to labor were also a factor. There were too few of these skilled specialists, and they had little freedom or flexibility, forced to work as they were within the dictates of a rigid bureaucracy. Moreover, the onrush of war, beginning in 1937, absorbed their energies and attention, leaving them no time for the development of new designs. For all these reasons, no Japanese engine designed and produced for the two services ever matched the American Pratt and Whitney R-2800 or the Curtiss-Wright R-3350 engines. During the Pacific War the smaller, lighter engines of Japanese aircraft, unable to operate efficiently at high altitudes, were often a fatal handicap to Japanese navy pilots.

Like much Japanese military equipment, Japanese aircraft engines were assigned several different designations, seemingly used interchangeably in much of the literature on the subject. During the Pacific War the two armed services developed a mutual designation system to aid in the rationalization of aircraft engine production, though the system itself was extremely complicated. Identification of aircraft engines used by the Japanese navy at the beginning of the war is simpler, however, since the navy relied on three main engine types described below, each of which went through various models. The figures for horsepower are rated for takeoff.

THE NAKAJIMA SAKAE ENGINE. An air-cooled radial engine of fourteen cylinders and a volume of 1,710 cubic inches. The Sakae ("Prosperity") powered the Mitsubishi A6M (Type 0) carrier fighter, the Nakajima A6M2-N (Type 2) seaplane fighter, and the Nakajima B5N (Type 97) carrier attack bomber. Its design derived from earlier Gnome-Rhone engines that Japan produced under license in the mid-1930s. It was reasonably reliable and was able to run for long periods on a very lean fuel mixture, a feature that provided the Zero with what was, at the time of its appearance, an unprecedented range. The first version was rated at 940 hp, a later version at 1,000 hp.

The Mitsubishi Kinsei engine. An air-cooled radial engine of fourteen cylinders and a volume of 1,980 cubic inches. Based originally on a Pratt and Whitney design, the Kinsei ("Venus") powered the Aichi D3A (Type 99) carrier bomber, the Mitsubishi G3M (Type 96) land-based medium bomber, the Aichi E13A (Type 0) reconnaissance seaplane, and the Kawanishi H6K (Type 97) flying boat. It was produced throughout the war and was increased in horsepower from an initial 730 hp to as much as 1,560 hp.

The Mitsubishi Kasei engine. An air-cooled radial engine of fourteen cylinders and a volume of 2,576 cubic inches. Derived originally from an earlier Pratt and Whitney power plant, the Kasei ("Mars") was the largest Mitsubishi fourteen-cylinder engine at the beginning of the Pacific War. It was used aboard such aircraft as the Mitsubishi G4M (Type 1) land-based medium bomber and the Kawanishi H8K (Type 2) flying boat. It was originally rated at 1,530 hp; wartime versions increased this figure to as high as 1,850 hp.

In addition to these three main engine types, there were a number of smaller power plants produced by both Mitsubishi and Nakajima, as well as by lesser manufacturers. The fourteen-cylinder Mitsubishi Zuisei and the nine-cylinder Nakajima Kotobuki and Hikari engines, for example, powered aircraft that either were no longer first line by the time of the Pacific War or were placed in aircraft, principally floatplanes and trainers, that were not the mainstay of the navy's offensive power at the time of the war. The largest engines, such as the eighteen-cylinder Nakajima Homare, were not in production at the time the Pacific War broke out.

Appendix 9

The Hineri-komi ("Turning-in") Maneuver

The information for this appendix was drawn from the following sources: Osamu Tagaya, communication with author, 1 February 1999; Genda, *Kaigun kōkūtai,* 1:119–20; Mikesh, *Zero,* 75; and Hattori and Sugiuchi, "Kūkyoku no hissatsugi," 68–74.

The *hineri-komi* tactic was designed to give an advantage to Japanese fighter pilots engaged in dogfighting, particularly when pitted against an enemy flying an aircraft of superior turning performance. It appears to have been developed in the mid-1930s by pilots of the Yokosuka Naval Air Group. According to the renowned navy airman Genda Minoru, the tactic was developed by Petty Officer (later Lieutenant) Mochizuki Isamu.

In repeated aerial training duels with Mochizuki, Genda, who early in the decade had already become famed in the navy as the head of one of the "flying circus" acrobatic teams, found himself repeatedly beaten by Mochizuki, despite his frenzied efforts to outmaneuver him. One day Genda suggested that they start out a dogfight with Genda already on Mochizuki's tail. Genda then followed Mochizuki on several loop-the-loops and in each case noticed that just before he reached the apex of the loop, Mochizuki's wings would begin to sideslip—to describe a sort of twist *(hineri)*—which cut down the turning radius considerably and changed the

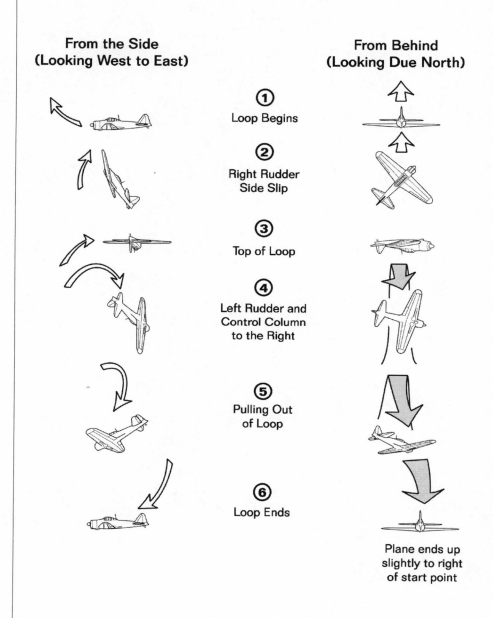

**From the Side
(Looking West to East)**

**From Behind
(Looking Due North)**

① Loop Begins

② Right Rudder
Side Slip

③ Top of Loop

④ Left Rudder and
Control Column
to the Right

⑤ Pulling Out
of Loop

⑥ Loop Ends

Plane ends up
slightly to right
of start point

Fig. A9-1. The *hineri-komi* acrobatic maneuver
Sources: Hattori and Sugiuchi, "Kūkyoku no hissatsugi," 68–73; Tagaya Osamu,
letter to author, 1998.

Usage in Combat

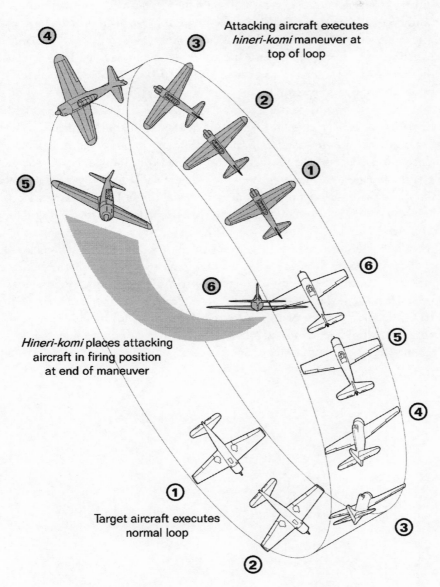

Attacking aircraft executes *hineri-komi* maneuver at top of loop

Hineri-komi places attacking aircraft in firing position at end of maneuver

Target aircraft executes normal loop

Parshall 2000
Adapted from drawings by Hattori Shugo, Sugiuichi Yukiko, and Tagaya Osamu

direction of the nose of his plane by about 90 degrees, followed by a diving curve, inscribing a sort of screw pattern. Genda now realized that, using this technique, a pilot followed by an enemy close on his tail could quickly turn the tables on his tormentor and become the hunter instead of the hunted. Now clearly understood by Genda, the tactic was taught to the other pilots of the Yokosuka Naval Air Group. As Yokosuka was the mecca of fighter tacticians in the Japanese navy, by the opening of the China War the *hineri-komi* maneuver had been adopted by all navy fighter pilots and had even spread to the pilots of the navy's sister service.

For the first few months of the Pacific War, in combination with the superb maneuverability of the Zero fighter and the inexperience of Allied airmen in dealing with it, the *hineri-komi* was among the deadliest assets possessed by Japanese navy fighter pilots. But as Osamu Tagaya has pointed out, the maneuver was an example of the Japanese military penchant for accepting a basic element of warfare as a given and—without ongoing consideration as to its utility in changing circumstances—perfecting it through the application of tremendous effort and skill far beyond the effort accorded it in other countries, but always within the same conceptual box. When confronted by such an example of perfected but self-enclosed thinking about warfare, the American response was to step out of the box to develop new approaches to warfare that played to American rather than enemy advantages. Thus, with the entry of American aircraft whose performance were both different from and superior to that of the Zero, and with the appearance of American pilots who understood this, those pilots simply refused to play the dogfighting game, and the *hineri-komi* became a tactical footnote.

Notes

ATIG	U.S. Department of the Navy, Office of Naval Intelligence, Air Technical Intelligence Group
CincPac/CincPOA	U.S. Department of the Navy, Commander-in-Chief, Pacific and Pacific Ocean Areas, Joint Intelligence Center, Pacific Ocean Area
KG	*Kaigun gunsembi,* in *SS* series
KHI	Kaigun Henshū Iinkai
KKG	*Kaigun kōkū gaishi,* in *SS* series
KS	*Kaigun suiraishi,* Kaigun Suiraishi Kankōkai, ed.
KSS	*Kaigun sentōkitaishi,* Reisen Tōjō Iinkai, ed.
NKK	*[Shashin zusetsu] Nihon kaigun kōkūtai,* Sonokawa Kamerō, ed.
NKKS	*Nihon kaigun kōkūshi,* Nihon Kaigun Kōkūshi Hensan Iinkai, ed.
NKS	*Nihon kōkū sōshū,* Nozawa Tadashi, ed.
SS	*Senshi sōsho,* Japan, Bōeichō Bōeikenshūjō Senshibu, ed.
SZ	*Shōwa zōsenshi,* Nihon Zōsen Gakkai, ed.
TS	Tsūshō Sangyōshō
USNTMJ	U.S. Naval Technical Mission to Japan
USSBS	U.S. Strategic Bombing Survey

CHAPTER 1. THE NAVY TESTS ITS WINGS

1. The original terms for this type of aircraft were "hydroplane" or "hydroaero-plane" and then "floatplane." The word "seaplane" was supposedly coined by Winston Churchill during his tour at the British Admiralty. Layman, *Before the Aircraft Carrier*, 34.

2. Wragg, *Wings over the Sea*, 9–25; Melhorn, *Two-Block Fox*, 6–10.

3. Wragg, *Wings over the Sea*, 18, 24, 29–34; Popham, *Into Wind*, 52–55.

4. Kuwabara, *Kaigun kōkū kaisōroku, sōsō-hen*, 42–44.

5. Yamamoto Eisuke, *Nana korobi*, 219–20; *NKKS*, 1:53; KHI, *Kaigun*, 13:24–25.

6. Yamamoto Eisuke, *Nana korobi*, 229; Sekigawa, *Pictorial History*, 10.

7. *NKKS*, 1:58–59.

8. KHI, *Kaigun*, 13:25–26; *NKKS*, 1:61–63, 2:772. Curtiss, a pioneer industrialist in American aviation, had opened a flight school at Hammondsport, N.Y., in 1910. At the end of that year he also set up operations at North Island in San Diego, where flight training could continue during the winter months. Though Curtiss began with the training of U.S. Army and Navy pilots, he soon opened his doors to foreign students, and by the time the Japanese officers arrived in the spring of 1912 the school had developed a truly international student body. Kirk House (curator, Curtiss Museum, Hammondsport), letter to author, August 1996.

9. Mōro, *Ijin Nakajima Chikuhei hiroku*, 162–63.

10. Studer, *Sky Storming Yankee*, 300–302; Kirk House, letter to author, July 1996. The two instructors at the school were Francis Wildman and Lansing J. Callan, who had learned to fly at the Curtiss schools two years before. Callan eventually entered the United States Navy and went on to attain flag rank. His large collection of photos of the early aviation history at Hammondsport is housed at the Curtiss Museum there, along with a newspaper clipping dating from the early months of the Pacific War in which Callan, reflecting on the early flight training he gave to Nakajima Chikuhei, was quoted as saying, "I should have dunked him!"

11. *NKKS*, 1:59, 63; KHI, *Kaigun*, 13:27; Mikesh and Abe, *Japanese Aircraft*, 8.

12. These included Vice Adm. Shimamura Hayao, the father of modern Japanese naval tactics, who, as commander of Japanese naval units participating in the international naval review held in Britain in honor of the coronation of King George V, crossed over to Le Havre to inspect the flying school being run by Maurice Farman. While there he was invited by Farman to go up in one of his aircraft. His flight was the first such venture by a flag officer of any navy. *NKKS*, 1:61.

13. Ibid., 63–65.

14. Ibid.

15. Ikeda, *Nihon no kaigun*, 2:37; Jentschura et al., *Warships of the Imperial Japanese Navy*, 63. The *Wakamiya Maru* had been launched in Glasgow in 1900 as the 7,720-ton freighter *Lethington* and leased to Russia. Early in the Russo-Japanese War she was captured by the Japanese and was taken into service as a

navy transport and renamed the *Wakamiya Maru*. She was leased to the NYK line in 1908 but reentered Japanese naval service in 1913 as an auxiliary and in that capacity operated one or two seaplanes. Inactive for a time after that, she was recommissioned as a seaplane carrier in August 1914 and dispatched to Tsingtao the next month to take part in the reduction of that German base. Damaged by a mine off Tsingtao shortly afterward, she returned to Japan and in 1915 was rerated as an aircraft depot ship, the mercantile suffix *Maru* being dropped from her name. Retrofitted with a platform over her forecastle in 1920, she was reclassified as an aircraft carrier, and it was from her decks that the first Japanese shipboard takeoff was accomplished. Put on inactive reserve in 1925, the *Wakamiya* was broken up in 1931. Layman, *Before the Aircraft Carrier*, 87.

16. *NKKS*, 1:66; KHI, *Kaigun*, 13:28.
17. Wada, *Kaigun kōkū shiwa*, 70.
18. *NKKS*, 4:25.
19. *KKG*, 3–4; Wada, *Kaigun kōkū shiwa*, 93–94.
20. *NKKS*, 4:33–34; Burdick, *Japanese Siege of Tsingtau*, 77, 81.
21. Mikesh and Abe, *Japanese Aircraft*, 10.
22. *NKKS*, 4:49–65; Mikesh and Abe, *Japanese Aircraft*, 9–10.
23. Burdick, *Japanese Siege of Tsingtau*, 197.
24. For an analysis of the influence of naval aviation by 1918, see Layman, *Naval Aviation in the First World War*, 200–205.
25. *NKKS*, 1:71–72.
26. Ibid., 68–70.
27. Ibid., 75–77.
28. Ibid., 77–78.
29. Ibid., 61–63.
30. Ibid., 56–57.
31. The memorandum itself, *Kōkō kaizō ni kansuru shiken* [A personal opinion concerning aircraft construction], is reproduced in full in ibid., 106–7.
32. Ibid., 73–74.
33. Ibid., 2:73, 4:653–54; Ikeda, *Nihon no kaigun*, 2:161.
34. *NKKS*, 3:147–49.
35. *NKK*, 288; Ikeda, *Nihon no kaigun*, 2:161–62; *NKKS*, 2:653.
36. *NKKS*, 3:23–32; Ikeda, *Nihon no kaigun*, 2:160.
37. *NKKS*, 1:302–12.
38. Ibid., 334–36. Considering the valuable service of the "blimps" of the United States Navy during World War II, the Japanese navy obviously erred in deciding to discontinue the use of airships. But because the Japanese either envisioned the airship in the rather unimaginative role of naval gunfire spotting or exaggerated its potential as an offensive weapon, they never did think through its uses as an element in antisubmarine patrolling, uses that were to be demonstrated so effectively by the Americans in the Atlantic during the war.
39. Ibid., 87–89.
40. Ibid., 78, 80, 86.
41. Wada, *Kaigun kōkū shiwa*, 264–67; Layman, *Before the Aircraft Carrier*, 86.
42. Daitō Bunka Daigaku Tōyō Kenkyūjō, *Shōwa shakai-keizai-shi shiryō shūsei*,

1:96–97; Kuramatsu Tadashi (specialist in Japanese naval policy between the world wars), communication to author, 29 July 1998.

43. *SS: Rikugun kōkū no gumbi to unyō*, 89–96.

44. Unless otherwise noted, the discussion in this and the next two paragraphs draws heavily on Ferris, "British Unofficial Aviation Mission," 416–39.

45. The Sempill Mission was not without its difficulties. Particularly frustrating to the British was the lack of enthusiasm conveyed by the base commander, who was not a pilot and had little air experience. Because he could not lead by example, morale sagged. The atmosphere improved greatly upon the appointment as base commander of Lt. Kuwabara Torao, an enthusiastic observer of British naval aviation during World War I and one of the pioneers of Japanese naval air power. Brackley, *Brackles*, 194; Osamu Tagaya, letter to author, 31 March 1998.

46. *NKK*, 54; *NKKS*, 2:715.

47. Ikeda, *Nihon no kaigun*, 2:190, 192; Brackley, *Brackles*, 173–77.

CHAPTER 2. AIRBORNE

1. Wildenberg, "In Support of the Battle Line," 1–11.

2. In this and the succeeding paragraph I have been greatly informed by the insights of both Thomas Wildenberg, author of several studies on U.S. naval aviation used in this work, and Comdr. Alan D. Zimm, USN Ret., a longtime student of naval tactics.

3. Extensive discussion of Japanese plans between the world wars for the decisive surface battle is to be found in chaps. 7 and 8 of Evans and Peattie, *Kaigun*.

4. For a summary of Lanchester's theories, see ibid., 143–44. For a fuller explication of the "pulsed power" model of firepower, see Hughes, "Naval Tactics," 11–13. Thomas Wildenberg tends to see the N^2 Law as carrying over into the carrier age, the carrier deck load becoming the equivalent of the big-gun salvo. Wildenberg, letter to author, 31 August 1999.

5. An excellent summary of the development of the Japanese aircraft industry before and during World War II is provided by Samuels, *Rich Nation, Strong Army*, 108–29.

6. Ikeda, *Nihon no kaigun*, 2:168.

7. Mikesh and Abe, *Japanese Aircraft*, 93, 101; Ferris, "British Unofficial Aviation Mission," 424.

8. Mikesh and Abe, *Japanese Aircraft*, 161; Sekigawa, *Pictorial History*, 23–24. For an explanation of the navy's aircraft designation systems, see app. 7.

9. Mikesh and Abe, *Japanese Aircraft*, 61, n. 37.

10. Ibid., 226.

11. Ibid., 198–99, 224–26.

12. Ibid., 124–25, 135–36.

13. *KG*, 1:54.

14. The name of this organization, Kaigun Kōkū Hombu, is sometimes translated as Naval Air Headquarters, but as it had an administrative rather than a command function, I believe that the translation used here is more appropriate.

15. *NKK,* 66.
16. Ikari, *Kaigun kūgishō,* 1:17–18.
17. These matters are discussed in Evans and Peattie, *Kaigun,* 233–37.
18. *KG,* 1:451.
19. *KKG,* 67; Ikari, *Kaigun kūgishō,* 1:17–24. In 1939 the name of the Air Arsenal was changed to Naval Air Technical Arsenal (Kaigun Kōkū Gijutsushō) and in early 1945 to First Technical Arsenal (Dai-ichi Gijutsushō); the common appellation for the arsenal during the war was the abbreviation Kūgishō. See Mikesh, "Rise of Japanese Naval Air Power," 110–11, and Genda, *Kaigun kōkūtai,* 1:103–4.
20. Samuels, *Rich Nation, Strong Army,* provides an illuminating insight into the continuities of Japanese military industrial policy. His discussion of the prototypes policy is on 116–18.
21. Ibid., 121–26.
22. Hone and Mandeles, "Interwar Innovation," 77–80; Samuels, *Rich Nation, Strong Army,* 127–28.
23. For an explanation of the Circle plans, see Evans and Peattie, *Kaigun,* chaps. 8 and 10.
24. *NKKS,* 2:51; air group total is derived from *KG,* 1:435.
25. Ōmae, "Nihon kaigun no heijutsu shisō," 2:37; Ōmae and Pineau, "Japanese Naval Aviation," 75.
26. *KKG,* 8–9.
27. Kuwabara, *Kaigun kōkū kaisoroku,* 117.
28. *NKK,* 67; *KKG,* 65–66; Lundstrom, *First Team: Pacific Naval Air Combat,* 455; Hata and Izawa, *Japanese Naval Aces,* 417.
29. *NKKS,* 2:906–10; Hata and Izawa, *Japanese Naval Aces,* 422; Ōhama and Ozawa, *Teikoku rikukaigun jiten,* 98.
30. *NKKS,* 2:163; Agawa, *Reluctant Admiral,* 86–87.
31. *NKKS,* 1:93–95.
32. This was only the first of a series of aerial bombardment experiments conducted by the navy on overage Japanese warships, the last being carried out in 1936 on the hull of the *Mishima. NKKS,* 1:721, 726–29.
33. *NKK,* 222; *NKKS,* 1:716–17.
34. *NKK,* 220; *NKKS,* 1:749–51.
35. *NKK,* 220.
36. *KS,* 23; USSBS, Military Analysis Division, *Japanese Air Weapons and Tactics,* 55–56.
37. *KG,* 1:175; *NKKS,* 1:757; Genda, *Kaigun kōkūtai,* 1:153.
38. J. Campbell, *Naval Weapons,* 209.
39. Ibid.; *NKKS,* 1:757–61; *KS,* 607–8; USNTMJ, Report 0-01-2, "Japanese Torpedoes and Tubes," Article 2, "Aircraft Torpedoes."
40. The term "attack" *(kōgekki)* used after a type number for one of the navy's bombers meant that the aircraft could be employed either for torpedo attacks or horizontal bombardment, depending upon the kind of ordnance it carried.
41. *KG,* 1:175.
42. *NKKS,* 1:756–57.

43. Genda, *Kaigun kōkūtai*, 1:157; Alan D. Zimm, letter to author, 8 August 1992.
44. *NKKS*, 1:116–17, 204–5, 756; *NKK*, 221; *KKG*, 193; Genda, *Kaigun kōkūtai*, 1:153.
45. Van Deurs, "Aviators Are a Crazy Bunch of People," 96–97.
46. Wildenberg, *Destined for Glory*, 10–11.
47. Ibid., 30–35, 52–54, 68–70, 73.
48. It should be understood, however, that by the 1930s floatplanes launched from battleships and cruisers had come to be seen not only as having a role in tactical scouting and spotting for friendly surface batteries, but also as carrying out these tasks while driving off enemy fighters. While their pontoons were known to put them at a disadvantage compared with wheeled aircraft in a dogfight, they adjusted their tactics accordingly and devoted rigorous training to perfecting them, an effort that was to pay off well in the early days of the China air war. *KKG*, 196.
49. Wildenberg, *Destined for Glory*, 158; *NKK*, 68; *KG*, 1:175.
50. *NKK*, 68; *NKKS*, 1:683–85.
51. Okumiya, *Tsubasa-naki sōjūshi*, 114–16.
52. Genda, *Kaigun kōkūtai*, 1:151–52.
53. *NKKS*, 1:690.
54. P. Smith, *Into the Assault*, 1–34.
55. Okumiya, *Saraba kaigun kōkūtai*, 66–67.
56. My use of the term "dive bomber" does not conform to the Japanese terminology of the time. The aircraft used for this purpose were initially called "special bombing aircraft" *(tokushu bakugekki)* and later were known as "carrier bomber aircraft" *(kanjō bakugekki)*. Mikesh and Abe, *Japanese Aircraft*, 280, assert that these vaguer designations were applied because the Japanese navy wished to keep secret its progress in the revolutionary tactic of dive bombing. On the other hand, in the United States Navy the terminology for dive bombing was similarly vague at first, and the tactic was referred to as "light bombing," "strafing with light bombs," and "diving bombing" before someone coined the term "dive bombing." See also Tillman, *Dauntless Dive Bomber*, 4. For an understanding of aircraft terminology in the Japanese navy, see app. 2.
57. Francillon, *Japanese Aircraft*, 268–69.
58. Okumiya, *Saraba kaigun kōkūtai*, 68.
59. *NKKS*, 1:773–74.
60. *NKK*, 68, 221.
61. *NKKS*, 1:79; Ikari, *Kaigun kūgishō*, 1:103.
62. *NKKS*, 1:654–55, 660.
63. Hata and Izawa, *Japanese Naval Aces*, 233.
64. *NKKS*, 1:661–62; Hata and Izawa, *Japanese Naval Aces*, 233; Reynolds, "Remembering Genda," 52–56.
65. Osamu Tagaya, letter to author, 17 December 1997; Genda, *Kaigun kōkūtai*, 1:119–20; Hata and Izawa, *Japanese Naval Aces*, 342; Mikesh, *Zero*, 75.
66. Genda, *Kaigun kōkūtai*, 1:112–19.
67. Shibata, *Genda Minoru ron*, 56.
68. The superiority of the land-based bomber in the 1930s was a widespread phe-

nomenon among the world's air forces. It was abundantly obvious in the United States Army Air Corps, for example. Once the USAAC developed the Martin XB-10 monoplane bomber, the aircraft's performance immediately outclassed any pursuit plane then in army service. Wagner, *American Combat Aircraft,* 101–14. The United States Navy did somewhat better than the Army Air Corps in developing fighter aircraft because of an early decision for radial engines and mechanical superchargers. Frederick J. Milford, letter to author, June 1992.

69. Extremely agile and popular with pilots and ground crews, the A2N was used by acrobatic teams like the "Genda Circus." The later model, the A4N, had greater speed, increased wingspan, and a more powerful engine, but it was generally rated inferior to the earlier version. By 1937 the A4N, the last biplane fighter to serve with the navy, had proved unable to deal with Soviet-built Chinese planes in the China War and was quickly replaced by the Mitsubishi A5M all-metal monoplane fighter. Mikesh and Abe, *Japanese Aircraft,* 225–26; Polmar, *Aircraft Carriers,* 80; Munson, *Fighters between the Wars,* 116–17.

70. *NKKS,* 1:287–88, 294; *KKG,* 59.

71. *NKKS,* 1:666–67. The navy once again adopted the expedient of using fighters as dive bombers when Zeros were used for this purpose in 1943–44, but they were ineffective in this role.

72. Shibata, *Genda Minoru ron,* 50–62.

73. *NKKS,* 1:293.

74. Genda, *Kaigun kōkūtai,* 1:104–8; *KSS,* 386–89.

75. Genda, *Kaigun kōkūtai,* 1:109–10.

76. *NKKS,* 1:288–90, 294; Caidin, *Zero Fighter,* 28–30.

77. An attempt to translate the relevant Japanese terminology within this field of aerial activity can be frustrating, given the confusing tendency in the Japanese accounts to use the terms "reconnaissance" *(teisatsu),* "patrolling" *(shōkai),* and "searching" *(sōsaku)* interchangeably. Considerable study of the problem leads me to conclude that "reconnaissance" in the Japanese navy context implies long-distance search, "patrolling" implies defensive scouting activity, and "searching" is a general term that can be applied to either activity.

78. *NKKS,* 1:780–81.

79. Unless otherwise noted, the information in this and the following two paragraphs is based on Osamu Tagaya, letter to author, 31 March 1998.

80. Mikesh and Abe, *Japanese Aircraft,* 162–63, 236–37.

81. This paragraph draws heavily on opinions expressed by Thomas Wildenberg in a letter to the author, 31 August 1999.

82. Francillon, *Japanese Aircraft,* 408–10.

83. For a discussion of the development of American flying boats to fill this long-range requirement during this same period, see Miller, *War Plan Orange,* 175–79.

84. *NKK,* 68; *NKKS,* 4:96–97; Thorne, *Limits of Foreign Policy,* 209.

85. Sekigawa, *Pictorial History,* 39; *NKKS,* 4:99–104, 114–15; Hata and Izawa, *Japanese Naval Aces,* 17–18, 24.

86. While the A1N2 seemed to do well against most of the Chinese planes encountered, Japanese pursuit pilots were shocked at its marked inferiority to the

Boeing 218, a fact that hastened the development of the Type 90. Genda, *Kaigun kōkūtai*, 1:91–92.

87. *NKK*, 68.

CHAPTER 3. FLIGHT DECKS

1. A profile, data, and history for each of the Japanese aviation vessels (carriers, seaplane carriers, and seaplane tenders) discussed in this study are provided in app. 4.
2. These matters, as they affected all carrier design in the interwar period, are analyzed by Friedman in *Carrier Air Power*, 9–23; Chesneau in *Aircraft Carriers of the World*; and D. Brown in *Aircraft Carriers*, 2–7.
3. Fukui, *Nihon no gunkan*, 38; *NKKS*, 2:190; Jentschura et al., *Warships of the Imperial Japanese Navy*, 41; Watts and Gordon, *Imperial Japanese Navy*, 169–71; Chesneau, *Aircraft Carriers*, 157–58.
4. *SZ*, 1:472–73; Nagamura, *Zōkan kaisō*, 136.
5. *SZ*, 1:472–73; Snow, "Japanese Carrier Operations."
6. Originally it had been planned to embark Mitsubishi 1MT1N (Navy Type 10) carrier attack aircraft, but the height—more than 4 meters (14 feet)—of this, the navy's only triplane, proved too great for the *Hosho*'s hangar, and the scheme was dropped. *SZ*, 1:472.
7. Chesneau, *Aircraft Carriers*, 157–58.
8. Discussion of these two warships in this and the next six paragraphs is derived principally from the following sources: *SZ*, 1:473–79; Hasegawa, *Nihon no kōkūbōkan*, 22–24; and Lengerer, "Akagi and Kaga," pt. 1, 127–39.
9. Chesneau, *Aircraft Carriers*, 159.
10. Lengerer, "Akagi and Kaga," pt. 1, 130.
11. Ibid., 131.
12. In the 1933 and 1934 USN fleet problems, for instance, carriers were caught and "shelled" by "enemy" surface units because they had strayed too close to the opposing force while conducting recovery operations. This starkly illustrated the predicament in which carriers could find themselves because of the continuing need to put the wind over their flight decks. Hone et al., *American and British Aircraft Carrier Development*, 135.
13. Lengerer, "Akagi and Kaga," pt. 1, 131.
14. Ibid., 134.
15. Ibid., 136–37.
16. Ibid., 134.
17. Ibid., 138–39; *SZ*, 1:481.
18. Lengerer, "Akagi and Kaga, pt. 1, 138–39; *SZ*, 1:481.
19. Lengerer, "Akagi and Kaga," pt. 1, 136–37; Okada, "Kaga/Akagi," 86–89.
20. Chesneau, *Aircraft Carriers*, 163–64.
21. *SZ*, 1:479–80; Chesneau, *Aircraft Carriers*, 163; Watts and Gordon, *Imperial Japanese Navy*, 177–78.
22. For a discussion of the impact of this incident upon construction in the Japanese navy generally, see Evans and Peattie, *Kaigun*, 24–45.

23. Evans and Peattie, "Ill Winds Blow," 70–73.
24. *SZ*, 1:479–80.
25. Jentschura et al., *Warships of the Imperial Japanese Navy*, 46, provides diagrams of the several designs for this class. One recent study has asserted that this design was intended as a response to the flight-deck cruisers the United States was then rumored to be building. See Lengerer and Rehm-Takahara, "Japanese Aircraft Carriers *Junyō* and *Hiyō*," pt. 1, 11.
26. The Navy General Staff requirements for the new class included the following: a displacement of 10,500 standard tons; capacity for sixty-eight aircraft; machinery equal to that of the cruiser *Kumano;* a maximum speed of 35 knots; a range of nearly 8,000 nautical miles at 18 knots; six 12.7-centimeter (5-inch) antiaircraft guns; armor around the magazine to withstand a 20-centimeter (8-inch) shell fired at a range of 12,000–20,000 meters (13,000–22,000 yards); and armor around the boiler sufficient to withstand shellfire from an average-sized destroyer. *SZ*, 1:480; Fukui, *Nihon no gunkan,* appendix chart showing aircraft carriers.
27. Fukui, *Nihon no gunkan,* appendix chart showing aircraft carriers; Chesneau, *Aircraft Carriers*, 165–66; *SZ*, 1:480.
28. Chesneau, *Aircraft Carriers,* 166.
29. See Friedman, *Carrier Air Power,* 9–10; Lengerer and Rehm-Takahara, "Japanese Aircraft Carriers *Junyo* and *Hiyo*," pt. 1, 9, 11.
30. In this connection, it is worth noting that horsepower per ton required to achieve a given speed is generally smaller for large ships than for small ones. Thus, large ships require a smaller fraction of their total displacement for propulsive machinery and have more available for other functions. In the case of aircraft carriers, the larger carrier can devote greater displacement to air group storage, ordnance, and aircraft support elements. These matters are discussed in Pugh, *Cost of Seapower,* 183–212.
31. *SZ*, 1:536; Watts and Gordon, *Imperial Japanese Navy,* 182; Dickson, "Fighting Flat-tops," 16–18.
32. *SZ*, 1:536.
33. Fukaya with Holbrook, "Shokakus," 639.
34. At the Battle of the Coral Sea, the *Shōkaku* and *Zuikaku* helped to sink the American *Lexington.* But the *Shōkaku* was seriously damaged in the process and was under repair at the time of the Midway battle. The *Zuikaku* was not at the Battle of Midway largely because she lacked a viable air group, since her air group could not prepare the inexperienced pilots assigned to it in time for the Midway operation.
35. Polmar, *Aircraft Carriers,* 69–70; Dickson, "Fighting Flat-tops," 15.
36. The navy's shadow building program using Japanese merchant shipping is discussed in some detail in Lengerer and Rehm-Takahara, "Japanese Aircraft Carriers *Hiyō* and *Junyō*," pt. 1, 12–19.
37. *SZ*, 1:490–92, 540–41; Hasegawa, *Nihon no kōkūbōkan,* 34, 36, 42; Watts and Gordon, *Imperial Japanese Navy,* 184–87, 193–94, 199–200, 491–92.
38. *SZ*, 1:537–39; Hasegawa, *Nihon no kōkūbōkan,* 44; Watts and Gordon, *Imperial Japanese Navy,* 191–92.
39. *SZ*, 1:548–49; Hasegawa, *Nihon no kōkūbōkan,* 40; *KKG*, 89–90; Watts and

Gordon, *Imperial Japanese Navy*, 187–91; Lengerer and Rehm-Takahara, "Japanese Aircraft Carriers *Junyo* and *Hiyo*," pt. 2, 107, 111.

40. Osamu Tagaya, letter to author, 31 March 1998.
41. The upper hangar deck was the strength deck of most Japanese fleet carriers, beginning with the *Sōryū* and continuing through the *Hiryū*, the *Shōkaku*-class carriers, and into the *Unryū* class. The *Taiho* was a notable exception, with her armored flight deck being the strength deck. D. Brown, *Aircraft Carriers*, 5, 18, 30.
42. Friedman, *Carrier Air Power*, 20; Willmott, *Barrier*, 415; Marder, *Old Friends*, 1:300; USNTMJ, Report S-06-2, "Report of Damage to Japanese Warships," 25; author's conversation, 18 October 1989, with Yoshida Akihiko, an informed authority on the prewar Japanese navy.
43. USNTMJ, Report A-11, "Aircraft Arrangements," 12.
44. This practice was pioneered aboard the USS *Yorktown* before the Battle of the Coral Sea. John B. Lundstrom, e-mail to Jon Parshall, 27 March 2000.
45. USNTMJ, Report A-11, "Aircraft Arrangements," 20–23.
46. Friedman, *Carrier Air Power*, 20; Willmott, *Barrier*, 415; Marder, *Old Friends*, 1:300; USNTMJ, Report S-06-2, "Report of Damage to Japanese Warships," 25; author's conversation with Yoshida Akihiko, 18 October 1989.
47. Lengerer, "Akagi and Kaga," pt. 1, 130.
48. Hasegawa, *Nihon no kōkūbōkan*, 165; Snow, "Japanese Carrier Operations." This information corrects a serious error in Evans and Peattie, *Kaigun*, 324, which implies that Japanese carriers had no crash barriers.
49. Hasegawa, *Nihon no kōkūbōkan*, 135–40; Friedman, *U.S. Aircraft Carriers*, 139. As Friedman notes, this capability seems bizarre to the modern reader, yet it represented a means of ensuring that a carrier could at least land its air complement in the event of a bomb hit aft. The ability to conduct landing operations over the bow had been a feature of early American carriers, and it was an important formal design consideration for the *Essex*-class carriers, which (unlike their earlier counterparts) could steam long distances going astern without causing damage to their machinery. Fore-mounted arresting gear was not removed from U.S. carriers until 1944. The Japanese mounted such gear on many of their fleet carriers, including the late-war *Taiho*-, *Unryū*-, and *Shinano*-class vessels.
50. Popham, *Into Wind*, 143.
51. Japanese carriers were supposed to maneuver independently when launching and recovering aircraft, except in those cases where enemy naval or air bases were within 300 miles; ATIG Report no. 1, 2. However, it is unclear whether this practice was strictly followed under combat conditions, such as the Battle of Midway. I am grateful to John B. Lundstrom for drawing my attention to the ATIG material. The reports cited were largely based on interviews with naval officers who had responsible positions aboard Japanese carriers at Midway, including captains Aoki Taijirō, who commanded the *Akagi*; Amagai Takahisa, air officer of the *Kaga*; and Kawaguchi Susumu, air officer of the *Hiryū*.
52. Okumiya, *Saraba kaigun kōkūtai*, 72; Hasegawa, *Nihon no kōkūbōkan*, 172; Fuchida and Okumiya, *Midway*, 135. On occasion, there were apparently take-off cycles of as little as ten seconds. ATIG Report no. 2, 2.

53. ATIG Report no. 1, 3.
54. An underdeck air-propelled catapult design was apparently developed in 1935 but was not adopted owing to its complexity and to the belief at the time that such gear was unnecessary. In the latter half of the Pacific War, this lack of foresight would hamper Japanese carrier operations using heavier aircraft. ATIG Report no. 2; ATIG Report no. 7, 1.
55. ATIG Report no. 1, 5; ATIG Report no. 2, 2; ATIG Report no. 5, 3.
56. ATIG Report no. 1, 5; ATIG Report no. 2, 2; ATIG Report no. 5, 2.
57. ATIG Report no. 5, 3.
58. Snow, "Japanese Carrier Operations"; Hasegawa, *Nihon no kōkūbōkan,* 167; USNTMJ, Report A-11, "Aircraft Arrangements," 15–18.
59. ATIG Report no. 2, 2.
60. ATIG Report no. 5, 3.
61. In the early stages of the Pacific War, aircraft arresting hooks were controlled by the pilot (in single-seat aircraft) or the observer crewman (in multiseat aircraft). However, later in the war the hook apparatus was modified so that the deck crew was made responsible for releasing the hook. This was done because the decline in the quality of aircrew training had led to an increase in deck accidents due to premature hook release. ATIG Report no. 3, 1.
62. Each arresting wire was controlled by enlisted crewmen, whose stations were staggered port and starboard down the length of the flight deck. All crash barriers were controlled by a single enlisted man stationed on the port side of the flight deck, who received signals from the air operations officer to raise and lower the barrier. ATIG Report no. 2, 2.
63. Okumiya, *Saraba kaigun kōkūtai,* 78.
64. Typical elevator cycles to the lower hangar deck and back were around forty seconds for the *Shōkaku,* including unloading time. Dickson, "Fighting Flat-tops," 18. However, older carriers, such as the *Akagi* and *Kaga,* had slower elevators.
65. Friedman, *Carrier Air Power,* 13–15; Prange, with Goldstein and Dillon, *Miracle at Midway,* 214–15, 264. I am also grateful for the insights of Thomas C. Hone and Mark A. Campbell on these matters.
66. Okumiya, *Saraba kaigun kōkūtai,* 74. In order of frequency, the most common landing accidents on Japanese carrier flight decks were (1) missing the deck astern (too low); (2) damaged landing gear from hard landings; (3) barrier crashes; (4) hitting the wing against the carrier island; and (5) going over the side. At night, mishaps 2 and 4 were apparently the most prevalent. ATIG Report no. 1, 5.
67. The First Carrier Division (Rear Adm. Takahashi Sankichi commanding) initially consisted of the *Hōshō* and *Akagi,* with the *Kaga* joining the division in November 1929.
68. Sekigawa, *Pictorial History,* 29; NKKS, 1:203–4.
69. Ōmae, "Nihon kaigun heijutsu shisō," 1:47; NKKS, 1:114, 203–4; Genda, "Evolution," 23. Thomas Wildenberg points out that in the United States Navy such carrier-vs.-carrier scenarios had been part of the Fleet Problems since 1929. Wildenberg, letter to author, 31 August 1999.
70. The Battle Instructions were a set of principles for fleet maneuvers and tactics

that represented the heart of tactical doctrine in the Japanese navy and were thus among its most closely guarded secrets. The instructions were revised five times: in 1910, 1912, 1920, 1928, and 1931. See Evans and Peattie, *Kaigun*, 550, n. 44.

71. Ōmae, "Nihon kaigun heijutsu shisō," 1:51; *KKG*, 48–49; *KG*, 1:135–36.

72. I refer to the concept of a preemptive strike at several points in this chapter. Because of the inadequacy of the Japanese documentary record, it is impossible to say with any precision just when the Japanese navy first incorporated this concept into its doctrine, though it certainly appears in the Naval Staff College study of November 1936 mentioned later in this chapter. My discussion of the navy's thinking on carrier strikes in the mid-1930s is drawn almost entirely from *KKG*, 202–4, which in turn is drawn from the recollections of former IJN commander Tsunoda Hitoshi,[†] whose career was almost entirely in naval aviation. After the war Tsunoda was on the research and editorial staff of the War History Institute of the Japanese Self-Defense Agency, a position that would have given him access to whatever relevant documents exist concerning Japanese naval doctrine; this fact, added to his long naval air service, gives his views considerable authority.

73. Genda, *Shinjuwan sakusen*, 42–43; *KG*, 1:176–78; *KS*, 502.

74. *KKG*, 50. While this source is not specific on the matter, Thomas Wildenberg has pointed out that a doctrine that called for nearly simultaneous attacks on enemy carriers and battleships indicates that the Japanese navy assumed that American carriers would be operating closely with the battleship main body. He further suggests that this assumption in turn may have led the Japanese navy to believe that it did not need to develop any sophisticated reconnaissance arrangements, since such a large concentration of fleet units could be easily discovered. Wildenberg, letter to author, 31 August 1999.

75. Dickson, *Battle of the Philippine Sea*, 221; Bergerud, *Fire in the Sky*, 9.

76. When operating with a protecting cruiser force, the actual position of carriers in relation to the cruiser force and the main body of the fleet was, of course, determined in part by the direction of the wind for the launching and recovery of aircraft. For a discussion, illustrated by diagrams, of the actual positioning of Japanese carriers in various cruising formations, see Fioravanzo, "Japanese Military Mission," 26–29.

77. *NKKS*, 1:205; Friedman, *Carrier Air Power*, 54; Genda, *Shinjuwan sakusen*, 42–43.

78. *KKG*, 202–3.

79. *NKKS*, 1:205–6; Genda, *Shinjuwan sakusen*, 43–46.

80. *KG*, 1:169.

81. *KKG*, supplement chart no. 2; Larkins, *U.S. Navy Aircraft*, 243–44.

82. John B. Lundstrom, letter to author, 15 March 1997.

CHAPTER 4. SOARING

1. *NKKS*, 1:101.
2. Ibid., 113.

3. *NKK,* 69.

4. Agawa, *Reluctant Admiral,* 104–5; Mikesh and Abe, *Japanese Aircraft,* 100–101.

5. Mikesh and Abe, *Japanese Aircraft,* 175; Bueschel, *Mitsubishi/Nakajima G3M1/2/3,* 4–5.

6. The noted British naval historian Stephen Roskill, for example, has written of the Japanese navy's "freedom from the controversies which so long plagued naval aviation in Britain." Roskill, *Naval Policy between the Wars,* 1:531.

7. Genda, "Tactical Planning," 46–47.

8. Ko Ōnishi Takijirō Kaigun Chūjō Den Kankōkai, *Ōnishi Takijirō,* 38–40, 50; *NKKS,* 1:116.

9. *NKKS,* 1:119–20; Genda, *Kaigun kōkūtai,* 1:137–47.

10. Quoted in *KKG,* 48.

11. Ibid.

12. *NKKS,* 1:123–24.

13. Agawa, *Reluctant Admiral,* 93.

14. *NKKS,* 1:124–25.

15. *KKG,* 74–79.

16. I realize that my use of the term "medium bomber," in the context of the G3M and its successor the G4M, will upset some purists in correct Japanese aircraft terminology. The term does not translate exactly from the common Japanese *rikkō* appellation, and admittedly the Japanese developed no operational *heavy* bomber with which to compare its size. Nevertheless, for a Western audience, the term "medium bomber" for the G3M seems more appropriate, since it brings to mind the Mitchell B-25 and the Marauder B-26, which were also twin-engined and which were roughly comparable in size. It is true, of course, as Osamu Tagaya points out (letter to author, July 2000), that the navy's original purpose in the design of the G3M was to develop a land-based long-range aircraft that could deliver torpedo—not bombing—attacks against a distant enemy fleet. Yet despite a few dramatic exceptions early in the Pacific War, over the entire operational span of both the G3M and the G4M, these aircraft were used primarily for bombing missions.

17. Iwaya, *Chūkō,* 1:38–47; *NKS,* 1:142; Francillon, *Imperial Japanese Navy Bombers,* 41–45.

18. Iwaya, *Chūkō,* 1:51–52, 115–16.

19. Bueschel, *Mitsubishi/Nakajima G3M1/2/3,* 4–5. In the development of the G3M1 a serious controversy had arisen over its armament. Specifically, the question was whether to put a machine gun in the nose of the aircraft, along with a position for an observer who would fire it, or whether to omit the gun from the nose assembly and place the observer behind the pilot. For easier communication between the pilot and observer, the second arrangement was eventually adopted (perhaps because the observer was often the commander of the aircraft), but this left a dead space for defensive fire forward. Undetected in peacetime exercises, this was to prove a dangerous defensive weakness in combat. Iwaya, *Chūkō,* 1:45–47.

20. *NKKS,* 4:26.

21. *NKS*, 1:132, 134; Horikoshi and Okumiya, *Reisen*, 54–55; Francillon, *Japanese Aircraft*, 342–43.
22. *NKKS*, 1:297–98.
23. *NKKS*, 3:412, 414; *NKS*, 1:128–34; Francillon, *Japanese Aircraft*, 342–43.
24. Horikoshi, *Eagles of Mitsubishi*, 19–23; Mikesh and Abe, *Japanese Aircraft*, 173–74; *NKKS*, 1:293; Francillon, *Japanese Aircraft*, 342–43; *NKKS*, 3:414; Genda, *Kaigun kōkūtai*, 1:122–26.
25. *NKKS*, 1:293; Francillon, *Japanese Aircraft*, 342, 345.
26. Leary, "Assessing the Japanese Threat," 274.
27. *NKS*, 1:156; Horikoshi, *Eagles of Mitsubishi*, 3–7; Caidin, *Zero Fighter*, 36–37.
28. Horikoshi, *Eagles of Mitsubishi*, 48–51; Caidin, *Zero Fighter*, 37–41; USSBS, Military Analysis Division, *Japanese Air Weapons and Tactics*, 10–12.
29. Horikoshi, *Eagles of Mitsubishi*, 34–46; Thompson, "Zero," 33–34.
30. *NKS*, 1:156–66; Caidin, *Zero Fighter*, 41, 48–49; Bueschel, *Mitsubishi A6M1/2*, 4. The most comprehensive and detailed study of the Zero in English is without doubt Robert Mikesh's *Zero*, but perhaps the most insightful analysis is to be found in Bergerud, *Fire in the Sky*, which discusses the aircraft's strengths and weaknesses at great length. There is, of course, a wealth of information on the genesis of this aircraft in *Eagles of Mitsubishi* by Horikoshi, as well as in Okumiya and Horikoshi, with Caidin, *Zero!*, which is a translation and adaptation of the original work, *Reisen*, by Horikoshi and Okumiya. The Squadron/Signal publication of Shigeru Nohara's *A6M Zero in Action* contains numerous and interesting schematics and line drawings of the many models of the aircraft as well of its various components.
31. In this connection, Gary Boyd, a historian for the United States Air Force, has written a highly interesting monograph in which he argues that the design of the Zero was largely based on the Chance-Vought V-143 fighter plane. The V-143 had been turned down by the United States Army Air Corps but was purchased from that company by Mitsubishi in 1937, about the time Horikoshi and his team began design work on the Zero. Boyd asserts that the Horikoshi design adhered closely to the V-143 across an array of configurations and equipment. But Boyd's evidence is largely circumstantial, and he admits that Japanese documentation concerning the V-143 is completely lacking. Boyd, "Vought V-143," 28–37.
32. Thompson, "Zero," 32.
33. Unless otherwise indicated, this and the following three paragraphs are based largely on Bergerud, *Fire in the Sky*, 199–212.
34. Horikoshi, *Eagles of Mitsubishi*, 139.
35. See app. 8 for a discussion of the nature and significance of the development of the principal aircraft engines developed by the Japanese navy.
36. *KKG*, 195; Thompson, "Zero," 32; Spick, *Fighter Pilot Tactics*, 86. The Zero carrier fighter went through eight major model changes from its adoption to the end of the Pacific War. A floatplane version was built by Nakajima during the war. For details, see Mikesh, *Zero*, 88–97, and Francillon, *Japanese Aircraft*, 362–77.
37. *NKS*, 1:176–82; Francillon, *Japanese Aircraft*, 317–19, 320–27, 388–95, 417–22; *NKS*, 3:121–24, 126–34; Osamu Tagaya, letter to author, July 2000.

38. Bergerud, *Fire in the Sky*, 211.

39. Francillon, *Imperial Japanese Navy Bombers*, 21–29; Francillon, *Japanese Aircraft*, 271–75; Bergerud, *Fire in the Sky*, 218–19.

40. Bergerud, *Fire in the Sky*, 218–19.

41. *NKS*, 5:161–65; Francillon, *Imperial Japanese Navy Bombers*, 11–16.

42. *NKS*, 5:166; Francillon, *Japanese Aircraft*, 412–14.

43. This and the next two paragraphs are based largely on Bergerud, *Fire in the Sky*, 212–15, 218; *NKS*, 1:166–68, 172–75; Francillon, *Japanese Aircraft*, 378–79; and Francillon, *Imperial Japanese Navy Bombers*, 45–49.

44. *NKS*, 1:168–75.

45. Osamu Tagaya believes that the G6M1 was originally developed as an escort for the projected G4M, not for the G3M as asserted in Francillon, *Japanese Aircraft*, 380. Tagaya points out that the superiority in cruising speed of the G4M over the G3M was such that no aviation professionals would have considered the two aircraft an effective match. Indeed, in the early days of the Pacific War when the two types of aircraft were used together for bombing attacks on the Philippines and Singapore from bases near Saigon, the G3Ms were obliged to take off one hour ahead of the G4Ms. The latter, with their faster cruising speed, would then automatically catch up with the G3Ms just as they approached the target, allowing the two types to deliver combined attacks. Tagaya, letter to author, August 2000.

46. Lundstrom, *First South Pacific Campaign*, 66–67.

47. Francillon, *Japanese Aircraft*, 307–12. Some examples of the aircraft's range and ruggedness: flying from Wotje Atoll in the Marshalls, an H8K carried out a night bombing of Hawai'i; flying across the Bay of Bengal, another reconnoitered the port of Columbo, Ceylon, engaged a B-17 Flying Fortress, and shot it down; and, in a tangle with a Curtiss P-40 fighter plane, an H8K drove off the attacker and returned safely to base with seventy bullet holes in the fuselage. *NKS*, 3:106–16.

48. Francillon, *Japanese Aircraft*, 358–61; *NKKS*, 3:498–500.

49. Francillon, *Japanese Aircraft*, 277–79.

50. *NKS*, 5:184–88; Francillon, *Japanese Aircraft*, 429–32, 454–55; Francillon, *Imperial Japanese Navy Bombers*, 28–40.

51. USSBS, Economic Studies, *Japanese Aircraft Industry*, 1.

52. Ibid.

53. TS, *Shōkō seisaku shi*, 18:427; Mikesh and Abe, *Japanese Aircraft*, 262–63.

54. USSBS, Economic Studies, *Japanese Aircraft Industry*, 7; TS, *Shōkō seisaku shi*, 18:427.

55. USSBS, Economic Studies, *Japanese Aircraft Industry*, 7.

56. TS, *Shōkō seisaku shi*, 18:431; USSBS, Economic Studies, *Japanese Aircraft Industry*, 27.

57. TS, *Shōkō seisaku shi*, 18:436–37.

58. As measured by an efficiency index worked out by the Aircraft Resources Control Office of the U.S. War Production Board during World War II. USSBS, Economic Studies, *Japanese Aircraft Industry*, 27–28.

59. TS, *Shōkō seisaku shi*, 18:438; USSBS, Economic Studies, *Japanese Aircraft Industry*, 22–23; Bergerud, *Fire in the Sky*, 204.

60. USSBS, Economic Studies, *Japanese Aircraft Industry,* 7; TS, *Shōkō seisaku shi,* 18:436.
61. Krebs, "Japanese Air Forces," 233, n. 11.
62. *KKG,* 208-9.

CHAPTER 5. ATTACKING A CONTINENT

1. Tsutsui, "Shina jihen," 19, 25.
2. There is as yet no comprehensive and authoritative English-language study of the navy's air war in China. Until such a work appears, the reader will have to make do with a slender and popular account, *Prelude to Pearl Harbor: Air War in China, 1937–1941,* by Ray Wagner.
3. The best English-language overview of the outbreak of Japanese hostilities with China is provided in Hata, "Marco Polo Bridge Incident."
4. Kusaka, *Ichi kaigun shikan no hanseiki,* 266.
5. *NKKS,* 4:261–62.
6. *KKG,* 113–14; Nagaishi, *Kaigun kōkūtai nenshi,* 18–19.
7. *NKKS,* 1:283.
8. *NKKS,* 4:191–95; U.S. Department of the Army, Japan Monographs no. 166, 21–23; Caidin, *Ragged Rugged Warriors,* 58–65.
9. Izawa, *Rikkō to Ginga,* 43–46.
10. Ibid., 78–79.
11. I base this opinion on an incident in Takahashi et al., *Kaigun rikujō kōgekki-tai,* 212–13, which, though dealing with Japanese medium-bomber operations in the Pacific War, would seem to hold true for similar operations in the China War. I am indebted to Osamu Tagaya for this reference.
12. Hata and Izawa, *Japanese Naval Aces,* 17–19, 30–31.
13. *NKKS,* 4:266–67.
14. Okumiya and Horikoshi, with Caidin, *Zero!,* 12; Bergerud, *Fire in the Sky,* 562.
15. *NKKS,* 4:264–70.
16. Ibid., 269–72.
17. Ibid., 271–72.
18. *KKG,* 115.
19. U.S. Department of the Army, Japan Monographs no. 166, 27–30, 38–39.
20. *NKKS,* 4:265–66; *NKS,* 1:156.
21. *NKKS,* 4:262.
22. Ibid., 443–44.
23. Nakayama, *Chūgoku-teki tenkū,* 241. I am indebted to Osamu Tagaya for bringing this source and reference to my attention.
24. My narrative here is based on a balancing of conflicting assertions made in *NKKS,* 1:235–38, and Hsu and Chang, *History of the Sino-Japanese War,* 268–69.
25. *NKK,* 94; Okumiya and Horikoshi, with Caidin, *Zero!,* 27.
26. Hata and Izawa, *Japanese Naval Aces,* 426.
27. Although internationally the term "ace" has been applied to pilots who have

shot down five or more aircraft, the Japanese services had no tradition of recording kills by individual pilots. On their part, Hata and Izawa provide biographies only of those pilots who had eleven or more victories to their credit. Hata and Izawa, *Japanese Naval Aces*, ix, 344.

28. *KSS*, 392. As Osamu Tagaya has noted, it was during these years that Japanese pilots first began to encounter tactics that would neutralize and overcome their cherished dogfighting style. In the skies over western Manchuria during the heavy aerial combat of the Nomonhan "Incident" of 1939, Soviet I-16 fighter planes learned to avoid swirling dogfights with the more maneuverable Japanese Army Type 97 fighter (similar to the Navy A5M) and began to use "hit-and-run" tactics with great success. In a harbinger of what was to come for the Japanese navy in the Pacific War, army pilots found it difficult to counter this tactic, and their losses began to mount. Tagaya, communication to author, 1 February 2000.

29. Most fighter units in the Japanese navy used the three-plane *shōtai* until late 1943, a source of wide criticism by students of air combat history. The charge has been that, like the RAF "vic," which it supposedly resembled, it was vulnerable to attack and led to collisions between its aircraft. But John B. Lundstrom points out that the Japanese *shōtai* was nothing like the constricted "vic" that, beginning in the Spanish civil war, was tried and rejected by every major European air force. The Japanese flew a much looser formation, often line astern or staggered, which reduced the danger of collision and allowed for much greater lookout on the part of the wingmen. In 1941–42, very rarely was a formation of Japanese navy fighters surprised, which was certainly not true of the RAF. John B. Lundstrom, letter to author, 10 January 1994.

30. Izawa, *Rikkō to Ginga*, 57–61; *SS: Chūgoku hōmen*, 1:522–23.

31. Caidin, *Ragged Rugged Warriors*, 72.

32. *NKK*, 94; *NKKS*, 4:387–88; *KKG*, 115–16; Caidin, *Ragged Rugged Warriors*, 106–7; Cornelius and Short, *Ding hao*, 87–88.

33. On the problem of exaggerated Japanese kills, see USSBS, Military and Naval Intelligence Division, *Japanese Military and Naval Intelligence*, 24, and Hsu and Chang, *History of the Sino-Japanese War*, 269.

34. In March 1938 the Kisarazu and Kanoya naval air groups were returned to their home bases in Japan and were placed under the command of the Combined Fleet for training and operational purposes, while the Thirteenth Air Group was reconstituted as a purely medium-bomber unit and sent to China for operations there. Iwaya, *Chūkō*, 1:112.

35. *KKG*, 116; Hata and Izawa, *Japanese Naval Aces*, 101; Caidin, *Ragged Rugged Warriors*, 99.

36. *NKK*, 95.

37. Bueschel, *Mitsubishi/Nakajima G3M1/2/3*, 8.

38. *NKKS*, 1:478; Bueschel, *Mitsubishi/Nakajima G3M1/2/3*, 8.

39. Iwaya, *Chūkō*, 1:160–61; *KKG*, 117.

40. Caidin, *Ragged Rugged Warriors*, 99–100.

41. *NKKS*, 4:552–63; *NKK*, 95; Caidin, *Ragged Rugged Warriors*, 99–100, 151–53; Sekigawa, *Pictorial History*, 70.

42. *NKKS,* 4:368–69, 510–11.
43. Iwaya, *Chūkō,* 1:154–62.
44. *NKKS,* 4:563; Iwaya, *Chūkō,* 1:164, 166.
45. Iwaya, *Chūkō,* 1:166–67.
46. These were the Mitsubishi C5M2 (Type 98) reconnaissance planes, a navy version of a single-engined army aircraft that as a civilian plane had set a speed record for a Japan-to-Britain flight in 1937. Equipped with special radio and camera equipment, the plane was used for deep penetrations into Chinese territory. *NKS,* 1:152, 154; Francillon, *Japanese Aircraft,* 152–53.
47. Iwaya, *Chūkō,* 1:161–71.
48. Yokoyama, *Aa reisen ichidai,* 74.
49. Ibid., 80; Horikoshi and Okumiya, *Reisen,* 155.
50. Yokoyama, *Aa reisen ichidai,* 82–88; Horikoshi and Okumiya, *Reisen,* 155–58. Once again, my tabulation of losses on each side is a composite of Japanese and Chinese accounts: *NKKS,* 4:560, 571; Mikesh, *Zero,* 39; Hsu and Chang, *History of the Sino-Japanese War,* 512; and a communication from D. Y. Louie, an amateur specialist in the air war over China, citing a memoir of a Chinese pilot who participated in the engagement.
51. There remains a good deal of uncertainty as to when reliable information concerning the Zero first reached the United States. William Leary has asserted that in the autumn of 1940 the Chinese captured a Japanese light-bomber pilot stationed at Hankow who related to his Chinese captors considerable information about the Zero that he had gleaned from Zero pilots also based at Hankow. This information was supposedly passed on to the Office of Naval Intelligence in Washington in November 1940. Leary goes on to state that additional data on the Zero arrived in Washington in late June 1941, again from the Chinese, who, it is claimed, shot down a Zero, recovered its wreckage fairly intact, and from it compiled a detailed technical report that confirmed the intelligence passed to Washington the previous November. Leary concludes that the United States had early and accurate information on the Zero before the Pacific War yet through complacency, chauvinism, and ignorance simply disbelieved it. Leary, "Assessing the Japanese Threat," 272–77.

    One does not know what to make of the recollection of Stephen Jurika, former assistant naval attaché in Tokyo in the years immediately prior to the Pacific War, who in later years claimed that in 1940 he actually sat in the cockpit of a Zero that was on display at the Haneda International Airport. Jurika asserted that the serial plate inside the cockpit was printed in English and provided important information about the aircraft, such as the weight of the aircraft and the horsepower of its engine. Jurika papers, Hoover Archives, Stanford University, file 10, 348. This account is relayed without comment by John Prados in his *Combined Fleet Decoded.* Given the Japanese obsession with military secrecy and the fact that this was one of the Japanese navy's newest and most valuable technologies, Jurika's claim is incredible.
52. *KKG,* 119–20; Caidin, *Zero Fighter,* 54–58.
53. *NKK,* 95; Iwaya, *Chūkō,* 1:173; *KKG,* 120.
54. *NKK,* 95.

55. Ibid.
56. *SS: Chūgoku hōmen kaigun sakusen,* 2:276–78.
57. *KKG,* 121–22. In this summary of losses I have set aside those caused by air accidents in Japan due to accelerated and intensified training. While I have no figures on the number of fatalities caused by these accidents, the number of accidents themselves jumped from 22 in 1937 to 206 in 1941. It is impossible to say whether the accident rate was increasing, or whether the higher number just reflects the larger number of trainees. *KKG,* 145.
58. Overy, "Air Power," 9.
59. *NKK,* 95.
60. KHI, *Kaigun,* 13:70; *KKG,* 88.
61. KHI, *Kaigun,* 13:70; *KKG,* 89; Genda, *Shinjuwan sakusen,* 46–47.
62. KHI, *Kaigun,* 13:71; *KKG,* 89.
63. Iwaya, *Chūkō,* 1:41.
64. Of the 150 fighter aces in the Japanese navy listed in Hata and Izawa, *Japanese Naval Aces,* fully one-third achieved their first victories in air combat over China, 1937–41.
65. *KKG,* 194.
66. Ōmae, "Nihon kaigun no heijutsu shisō," 1:51–52; *KKG,* 189, 192. Although the navy's air groups proved in the China War that they could cooperate effectively with the army in land operations, army air groups were almost completely ineffective in operations at sea, for which they had very little training. When the Pacific War began, this weakness was glaringly revealed and stands in sharp contrast to the reasonably effective long-range, overwater operations of the United States Army Air Force in the Pacific. Iwaya, *Chūkō,* 1:113–14.
67. Iwaya, *Chūkō,* 1:161.
68. *KKG,* 88, 142–43; *NKK,* 221.
69. Bergerud, *Fire in the Sky,* 17, 194–99, 327, 412–13.
70. *KSS,* 394, 397–98.
71. Bergerud, *Fire in the Sky,* 17.

CHAPTER 6. FORGING THE THUNDERBOLT

1. Because of their somewhat more advanced educational qualifications, these recruits, now designated *Kō-* (A-) category students within the Yokaren system, would have to undergo only twelve to fourteen months of general training, instead of the two and a half years required of the primary-school graduates under the old system. Some of the latter type of students were still recruited by the navy under the same conditions as formerly, but they were now designated to be *Otsu-* (B-) course students. In 1940, recruits brought into the naval air service from noncommissioned ranks under the old *Sōren* (Pilot Trainee) system were placed in what was now called the *Hei-* (C-) course category. *KKG,* 105, 152; Hata and Izawa, *Japanese Naval Aces,* 410.
2. Wildenberg, *Destined for Glory,* 87–88.
3. Lundstrom, *First Team: Pacific Naval Air Combat,* 454–55; Prange, with

Goldstein and Dillon, *At Dawn We Slept,* 265; Osamu Tagaya, letter to author, 31 March 1998.

4. Hata and Izawa, *Japanese Naval Aces,* 417.

5. Lundstrom, *First Team: Pacific Naval Air Combat,* 456; USSBS, Military Analysis Division, *Japanese Air Power,* 34.

6. *KKG,* 152; USSBS, Military Analysis Division, *Japanese Air Power,* 35.

7. *KKG,* 13; *KSS,* 361–68.

8. *KSS,* 364.

9. Kusaka, *Rengō kantai,* 318.

10. Sakai, with Caidin and Saito, *Samurai,* 10, 13–15, 17.

11. Ōmae, "Nihon kaigun no heijutsu shisō," 2:40; Marder, *Old Friends,* 1:315–16.

12. Van Fleet, *United States Naval Aviation,* 382.

13. Accurate figures for both sides are elusive. For the Japanese side, *KG,* 2:202, states that there were about seven thousand total aircrew in December 1941. The most authoritative postwar source on Japanese naval aviation, *KKG,* asserts that no reliable records providing such statistics for that period survived the Pacific War. Fragmentary evidence from an official record kept by the Naval Aviation Department indicates that in 1940 the navy had 3,371 pilots, of whom 2,516 were assigned to operational air groups and 855 were in the pipeline, attached to training air groups. The same report notes that in March 1941 there was a "shortfall" in navy pilots of 20 percent, but it gives no target figure (*KKG,* 106). I estimate that even if the navy had added another one thousand pilots by December 1941, it is unlikely that there would have been more than thirty-five hundred operational pilots in the Japanese navy by that time. Of these, of course, a sizable number, having just completed flight training, would not have been combat-ready. Thus the figure of nine hundred for carrier aviators suggested by James Sawruk, who has spent considerable time estimating aircrew figures for both navies. Sawruk, communication to author, 7 April 1998.

For the American side, Furer, *Administration,* 385, drawing on an unpublished history of U.S. naval administration in World War II, states that as of 1 December 1941, there were 6,206 naval aviators in the United States Navy, Marine Corps, and Coast Guard (not including trainees). But more authoritatively, Van Fleet, *United States Naval Aviation,* 461, asserts that there were somewhat fewer than eight thousand active-duty pilots in the United States Navy and Marine Corps in December 1941.

14. Another source of tactical inspiration for the navy's fighter squadrons was the information brought back by a small number of naval air officers who were detached to observe the fierce air combat between air units of the Japanese army and the Soviet air force along the border between Mongolia and western Manchuria in the spring and summer of 1939. *NKKS,* 4:677.

15. Unless otherwise noted, this and the next paragraph are based on the authoritative discussion of Japanese fighter tactics in Lundstrom, *First Team: Pacific Naval Air Combat,* 486–89.

16. Spick, *Fighter Pilot Tactics,* 86; *NKKS,* 1:678.

17. *KKG,* 195.

18. John B. Lundstrom, letter to author, 6 January 1994; Cook and Cook, *Japan at War,* 139; Osamu Tagaya, letter to author, 31 March 1998.

19. These points were made to the author by Frederick J. Milford, 6 April 1993.
20. *NKKS,* 1:79.
21. *KKG,* 186; U.S. War Department, *Handbook on Japanese Military Forces,* 315.
22. Prange, with Goldstein and Dillon, *At Dawn We Slept,* 163.
23. *KKG,* 198.
24. Prange, with Goldstein and Dillon, *Miracle at Midway,* 373. It is possible to chart the Japanese navy's fluctuating emphasis on fighter aircraft by noting the composition of carrier air groups at different points in time. Off Shanghai in 1932, the *Kaga*'s air group consisted of twenty-four fighters and thirty-six attack aircraft. In the mid-1930s it consisted of twelve fighters and sixty dive and torpedo bombers, and for the Pearl Harbor strike it comprised eighteen fighters and fifty-four dive and torpedo bombers.
25. *KKG,* 189–90.
26. Okumiya, *Tsubasa-naki sōjūshi,* 190.
27. Prange, with Goldstein and Dillon, *At Dawn We Slept,* 160–61. In this connection, some fragmentary but instructive data remains from the Combined Fleet bombing exercises of 1939. During daylight, on a target moving at 14 knots, level bombing runs by land-based G3Ms from heights of 400–4,100 meters (1,300–13,000 feet) resulted in 18 hits out of 139 bombs dropped, or 12 percent; level bombing runs by carrier-based attack planes from heights of 1,000–3,000 meters (3,000–10,000 feet) resulted in 17 hits out of 152 bombs, or 11.2 percent; dive-bombing runs by carrier dive bombers from heights of 350–700 meters (1,000–2,000 feet) resulted in 66 hits out of 123 bombs, or 53.7 percent; and torpedo attacks by thirty carrier attack planes (accompanied by both dive bombers and land-based twin-engined bombers) resulted in 49 hits out of 74 torpedoes launched, or 76 percent (but because some of the torpedoes were oxygen-driven, their wakes could not be traced). *KKG,* 144. Of course, it must be noted that exercise conditions are rarely good indices of combat results, and that in the Pacific War, Japanese bombing attacks rarely achieved the percentages given above.
28. Prange, with Goldstein and Dillon, *At Dawn We Slept,* 259–60.
29. Okumiya, *Saraba kaigun kōkūtai,* 147–50.
30. Prange, with Goldstein and Dillon, *At Dawn We Slept,* 161–63, 268–69, 323.
31. *KKG,* 190; J. Campbell, *Naval Weapons,* 215. According to John De Virgilio, a specialist in the ordnance used by the Japanese in the Pearl Harbor attack, the Type 99 No. 80 Mk-5 bomb was a reshaped 41 centimeter (16-inch) AP naval shell normally used for the main batteries of the battleships *Nagato* and *Mutsu.* It was produced by machining the shoulders back to make the nose of the shell more pointed for better penetration. It was then machine-tapered from just above the midbody to the base of the shell for better aerodynamics. The internal cavity of the shell, which contained the bursting charge, was widened slightly by machine-shaving. This process was hard on the heavy machinery doing the work, and for that reason only 150 of these bombs were produced before the machinery broke down. De Virgilio, e-mail to Jon Parshall, 20 May 1998.
32. Prange, with Goldstein and Dillon, *At Dawn We Slept,* 513; *KKG,* 191.
33. *NKKS,* 1:693–94.
34. In directing training of dive bomber units at Kasanohara, near Kanoya in

southern Kyūshū, Comdr. Egusa Takashige gained approval for bomb release as low as 450 meters (about 1,500 feet) in order to increase the chances of a direct hit. Prange, with Goldstein and Dillon, *At Dawn We Slept*, 271.

35. *NKKS*, 1:694; *KKG*, 192; CincPac/CincPOA, "Know Your Enemy," 21.

36. CincPac/CincPOA, "Know Your Enemy," 19, 21–22.

37. *KKG*, 193; *NKKS*, 1:707–8. Prior to the outbreak of the Pacific War, the navy considered using an entirely new bombing technique—skip bombing *(hanchō bakugeki)*—by which the bombing aircraft actually bounced their bombs off the water and onto the sides or decks of enemy ships. Apparently it was not practiced by the navy, which used it only once, in February 1942, when G3M bombers of the Genzan Air Group based at Kuching, Borneo, employed it with some success against Allied merchant ships trying to flee Singapore Harbor. However, it was used by American army bombers with devastating effect against Japanese shipping in the Battle of the Bismarck Sea in March 1943. *NKKS*, 1:714–15.

38. *KG*, 1:175.

39. *NKK*, 222–23.

40. *KKG*, 194; *NKKS*, 1:764; Evans and Peattie, *Kaigun*, 49.

41. *KKG*, 194; *KS*, 611; USSBS, Military Analysis Division, *Japanese Air Weapons and Tactics*, 56–57; CincPac/CincPOA, "Know Your Enemy," 22–23.

42. Recent studies have tended to downplay the influence of the Taranto attack on the Japanese plans for Pearl Harbor. See, for example, Marder, *Old Friends*, 1:315, and Chapman, "Tricycle Recycled," 276–77, 291–92.

43. *KS*, 621–26; *NKKS*, 1:765–66.

44. *NKKS*, 1:757–61; *KS*, 607–8; USNTMJ, Report 0-01-2, "Japanese Torpedoes and Tubes," Article 2, "Aircraft Torpedoes."

45. Yamamoto Teiichirō, *Kaigun damashii*, 165–69; Prange, with Goldstein and Dillon, *At Dawn We Slept*, 104–6, 159–60, 270–71, 320–22; De Virgilio, "Japanese Thunderfish," 61–68; Genda Minoru's analyses of the Pearl Harbor operation in Goldstein and Dillon, *Pearl Harbor Papers*, 17–44.

46. Marder, *Old Friends*, 1:443–44.

47. Initially the navy attempted to settle on the single best aerial offensive tactic, and to this end the Yokosuka Naval Air Group devoted intensive study to the relative merits of torpedo and dive bombing. Not surprisingly, its staff reached the conclusion, around 1940, that each tactic had its advantages, and thus the staff eventually confirmed the value of each. *NKKS*, 1:773–74.

48. Ibid., 707; *KKG*, 193, 203; Genda, *Shinjuwan sakusen*, 47–48.

49. *KG*, 1:136–37, 142.

50. *NKKS*, 4:262.

51. Genda, "Evolution," 24.

52. *NKKS*, 1:42, 153–54, 189–90; Genda, *Kaigun kōkūtai*, 1:144.

53. Polmar, *Aircraft Carriers*, 131–32; Friedman, *Carrier Air Power*, 56.

54. Genda, *Shinjuwan sakusen*, 24.

55. The position of the carrier fleet, vis-à-vis its cruiser escorts and the main body of capital ships, was to depend largely on the strength and direction of the wind. Fioravanzo, "Japanese Military Mission," 26–29.

56. Genda, *Shinjūwan sakusen,* 62; Polmar, *Aircraft Carriers,* 132; Friedman, *Carrier Air Power,* 56.

57. While Genda's claim to the authorship of this important tactical innovation may indeed be valid, it is worth noting that it rests entirely on his own account. One finds no corroboration of his assertion in two of the most authoritative works on Japanese naval aviation, *KKG* and *NKKS.* For his part, Yoshida Akihiko is skeptical of Genda's claim and believes that the innovation of the Japanese box formation, like all developments in the navy's operational doctrine, was probably the result of discussions, over time, among a number of leading naval officers—in this case, men like Genda, Yamamoto, Ōnishi, Kusaka Ryūnosuke, Yamaguchi Tamon, Ozawa Jisaburō, and Miwa Yoshitake. Yoshida, letter to author, 6 November 1990.

58. Prange, with Goldstein and Dillon, *At Dawn We Slept,* 102.

59. Ibid., 101–2; Ozawa Teitoku Den Kankōkai, *Kaisō no Teitoku Ozawa,* 20–22.

60. Within a few months the reorganization led to a renumbering of the navy's air units whereby all aircraft carrier divisions were numbered from one to ten, seaplane carrier divisions from eleven to nineteen, and air flotillas from twenty to twenty-nine. *KKG,* 149–50.

61. Ibid., 149–50.

62. *KKG,* 207; Prange, with Goldstein and Dillon, *At Dawn We Slept,* 101–2, 106.

63. Polmar, *Aircraft Carriers,* 132; Friedman, *Carrier Air Power,* 56. At the Battle of the Coral Sea, the first fleet action that pitted carrier against carrier, the Japanese had only two fleet carriers at hand, not the assembled assets of the First Air Fleet.

64. *KKG,* 204.

65. Ibid., 203–4; *NKKS,* 1:704–5.

66. Genda, "Evolution," 27.

67. Dickson, *Battle of the Philippine Sea,* 25.

68. This and the next two paragraphs are based on *KKG,* 185–89, and *NKKS,* 1:27–28.

69. *KKG,* 186.

70. Dallas Isom, using *SS (Senshi sōsho)* documentation, takes sharp exception to the accepted wisdom that Japanese aerial reconnaissance was sloppy at Midway. He argues that cloud cover had much to do with the Japanese failure to discover the American carrier force, and that the causes of the disaster to the Japanese fleet lie elsewhere. Isom, "Battle of Midway," 87–94.

71. Bergerud, *Fire in the Sky,* 555.

72. Morison, *New Guinea and the Marianas,* 316–17.

73. *KKG,* 205.

74. Unless otherwise noted, my understanding and analysis of fleet air defense as it existed in December 1941 derive directly from ibid., 205–6.

75. Even after the advent of radar, of course, its effective coordination with fleet air defense took time. Moreover, the damage wrought by Japanese kamikaze aircraft late in the Pacific War demonstrated that it was impossible to defeat a determined air attack completely. John B. Lundstrom, letter to author, 16 August 1994.

76. Spick, *Fighter Pilot Tactics*, 90; Lundstrom, *First Team: Pacific Naval Air Combat*, 228.

77. USSBS, Military Analysis Division, *Interrogations*, 1:3. Yoshida Akihiko, however, insists that the control of the CAP over a carrier formation was usually the responsibility of the flag carrier's air officer. Yoshida, letter to author, 5 May 1993.

78. Except where otherwise noted, I am indebted for information in this paragraph and the three that follow it to Jonathan Parshall.

79. The two best technical overviews of Japanese antiaircraft defenses are to be found in J. Campbell, *Naval Weapons*, and Itani et al., "Anti-aircraft Gunnery," 81–101.

80. David Dickson, unpublished monograph.

81. A case in point was the critically poor air defense provided for the *Shōhō* at the Battle of the Coral Sea, which cost the Japanese the loss of the carrier. In that portion of the battle when the *Shōhō* was under air attack, the overall tactical commander, Rear Adm. Gotō Aritomo, deployed his four heavy cruisers 8,000 yards (7,300 meters) from the carrier, which had only a single destroyer as plane guard nearby. H. P. Willmott has written, "It was almost as if the cruisers were trying to disassociate themselves from the carrier in the hope that they might escape attack themselves. They were certainly not in positions to provide the *Shōhō* with flak support." Willmott, *Barrier*, 244.

82. I am indebted to Alan Zimm, USN Ret., for making this point. Zimm, letter to author, 26 May 1993.

83. Dickson, *Battle of the Philippine Sea*, 129.

84. *KKG*, 206; Garzke and Dulin, *Axis and Neutral Battleships*, 113.

85. Interview by David Evans with Yoshida Akihito, 18 October 1989.

86. Evans and Peattie, *Kaigun*, 482–86.

87. Shimada, "Opening Air Offensive," 72–82.

88. It is true that certain of the navy's prewar planning documents contain references to an extended war of attrition to be fought behind an impregnable barrier that the navy would supposedly create against an anticipated American counteroffensive in the Pacific. Yet the navy's technological innovations, its force structure, the decades-long evolution of its tactics, and its specific plans for the Pearl Harbor assault were all obviously developed with the underlying assumption that Japan must achieve immediate and decisive superiority over the enemy. These matters are discussed in greater detail in Evans and Peattie, *Kaigun*, 447–86.

89. Marder, *Old Friends*, 1:315.

90. *KKG*, 105, 288, 211.

91. At the opening of hostilities, it appears there were no more than twenty land-based and flying-boat transport aircraft within the Eleventh Air Fleet, the force that spearheaded the Japanese invasion of Southeast Asia. Favorite with Kawamoto, *Japanese Air Power*.

92. *SS: Nantō hōmen kaigun sakusen*, 2:642.

93. At the opening of the war, not counting the fuels already distributed to its individual air groups, the navy believed that it had on hand 477,500 tons of aviation

gas, 6,470 tons of aviation lubricants, 26,926 tons of iso-octane, and over 61 tons of ethyl fluid. *KKG,* 109–10.

Chapter 7. Descending in Flame

1. Among the mountains of literature in English on the Japanese navy's attack on Oahu, Prange, with Goldstein and Dillon, *At Dawn We Slept,* continues to be the nearest thing to a definitive history of the operation.
2. The most extensive English-language account of the sinking of the *Repulse* and *Prince of Wales* is Middlebrook and Mahoney, *Battleship: The Loss of the Prince of Wales and the Repulse.* The most authoritative English-language account is Marder, *Old Friends,* 1:465–90. Unless otherwise noted, the discussion in the following four paragraphs is based on Marder.
3. *SS: Hitō-Marē hōmen kaigun shinkō sakusen,* 464.
4. The Japanese claimed twenty-one torpedo hits on the two ships, but British records assert that there were only eleven, five on the *Repulse* and six on the *Prince of Wales.* Marder, *Old Friends,* 470.
5. Ibid., 493.
6. Ibid., 482–93.
7. *SS: Hitō-Marē hōmen kaigun shinkō sakusen,* 491.
8. To date, the best English-language treatment of the Japanese aerial sweep of Southeast Asia from December 1941 through February 1942 is Shores and Cull, with Izawa, *Bloody Shambles,* vol. 1. A critical look at the nature of the Japanese aerial offensive is provided in Harvey, "Japanese Aviation and the Opening Phase of the War in the Far East," 174–204.
9. Osamu Tagaya notes that fighter combat practice in the prewar United States Army Air Corps was also essentially dogfighting, and even the United States Navy, though it emphasized a greater degree of deflection shooting than its sister service, largely practiced turning combat. Faced with an enemy flying superior aircraft and using superior tactics for this type of combat, American pilots could not hope to be effective. Tagaya, communication to author, 1 February 2000.
10. U.S. Department of the Navy, Office of Naval Intelligence, "Quality of Japanese Naval Pilots," 3342.
11. Lundstrom, *First Team: Pacific Naval Air Combat,* 188.
12. Ibid., 300–305; Lundstrom, *First Team and the Guadalcanal Campaign,* 92; James Sawruk, letter to author, 7 April 1998.
13. Lundstrom's *First Team: Pacific Naval Air Combat* is the most detailed and authoritative English-language source for the tactical aspects of air combat at Midway.
14. Rearden, *Cracking the Zero Mystery,* details the recovery of a reasonably intact Zero that had crash-landed in the Aleutians in the summer of 1942 and that was subsequently refurbished and flight-tested in the United States. Supposedly this recovery was a tremendous Allied windfall, revealing as it did the critical secrets of the Zero and thus leading to its extermination at the hands of Allied fighter

pilots. But John Lundstrom deflates this myth by explaining how American fighter pilots had already analyzed the Zero's strengths and weaknesses in actual combat against it. Lundstrom argues that it was the loss of good Japanese pilots through attrition, not the loss of technical secrets, that ultimately led to the downfall of the navy's Zero fighter units. Lundstrom, *First Team and the Guadalcanal Campaign*, 533–36. Other models of the aircraft were captured during the later course of the war and evaluated against Allied aircraft at the naval air stations at Anacostia, Va., and Patuxent River, Md. Mikesh, *Zero*, 70.

15. Lundstrom, *First Team and the Guadalcanal Campaign*, 92.
16. *SS: Midowei kaisen*, 598.
17. Prados, *Combined Fleet Decoded*, 337; James Sawruk, communications to author, 31 March, 1 April, and 7 April 1998. Sawruk has devoted intensive study over the years to the great carrier battles of 1942. In compiling this figure he used, among other sources, Sawachi Hisae's *Midowei kaisen*, which provides a wealth of statistical data concerning aircraft and personnel losses on both sides at Midway drawn from published accounts, unpublished Japanese navy reports, shrine records at Yasukuni Jinja, newspapers, records of veterans associations, and personal interviews with survivors and survivors' families. Sawruk tabulates the Japanese aircrew losses as follows: *Akagi*, seven (three in the air and four aboard ship); *Kaga*, twenty-one (eight in the air and thirteen aboard ship); *Sōryū*, ten (six in the air and four aboard ship); and *Hiryū*, seventy-two (sixty-four in the air and eight aboard ship). Sawruk, communication to author, 31 March 1998.
18. Prados, *Combined Fleet Decoded*, 337. The recollections of Genda Minoru and Lt. Comdr. Yoshioka Chūichi, both on the staff of the First Air Fleet during the Midway operation, support these contentions. *SS: Midowei kaisen*, 598–99.
19. *KG*, 1:270–72.
20. Genda, "Tactical Planning," 48; Friedman, *Carrier Air Power*, 56.
21. With the establishment of the Third Fleet in July 1942, the standard loading by aircraft type for its three carriers was as follows (prior aircraft complements in parentheses):

CARRIER NAME	FIGHTERS	DIVE BOMBERS	TORPEDO BOMBERS
Shōkaku and *Zuikaku* each	27 (21)	27 (21)	18 (21)
Zuihō	21 (12)	—	6 (12)

Source: *SS: Midowei kaisen*, 639.

22. Moore, "Shinano," 147.
23. John Lundstrom's *First Team and the Guadalcanal Campaign* provides the most authoritative and lavishly detailed English-language source for the study of the air war in the Solomons, though it gives greater attention to the American side of the conflict than to the Japanese. Eric Bergerud's recently published *Fire in the Sky* complements, but does not supersede, Lundstrom's study.
24. Lundstrom, *First Team and the Guadalcanal Campaign*, 41–44.

25. For a discussion of the paucity and backwardness of the navy's base construction forces, see Evans and Peattie, *Kaigun*, 400–401.

26. *KKG*, 265–66; *KSS*, 407; McKearney, "Solomons Naval Campaign," 60–61; U.S. Department of the Army, Japan Monographs no. 122, 4.

27. Lundstrom, *First Team and the Guadalcanal Campaign*, 173.

28. *KKG*, 267; Lundstrom, *First Team and the Guadalcanal Campaign*, 190. It is impossible to determine with precision the losses suffered by Japanese naval air units in the Solomons. Perhaps the most thorough analysis of the casualty figures, compiled both from Japanese accounts and records, including the Japanese Defense Agency *SS (Senshi sōsho)* volumes, and from American records and reports, is to be found in Frank's *Guadalcanal*, 761–63. Frank estimates that the navy lost something over nine hundred aircrew in combat from 1 August 1942 to 15 November but admits this figure may be conservative.

29. *SS: Nantō hōmen kaigun sakusen*, 2:309–12; Lundstrom, *First Team and the Guadalcanal Campaign*, 454. Those few experienced aircrews who survived through the autumn of 1942 were apparently sent home to rest and in most cases became instructors in naval air training units. Their return to combat by the summer of 1943 marked a brief resurgence in the quality of aircrews encountered by Allied pilots. U.S. Department of the Navy, Office of Naval Intelligence, "Quality of Japanese Naval Pilots," 3343–44.

30. Ninety aircraft were lost at the Battle of the Coral Sea (47 from the *Shōkaku*, 33 from the *Zuikaku*, 10 from the *Shōhō*); 110 were lost at Midway (7 from the *Akagi*, 21 from the *Kaga*, 10 from the *Sōryū*, 72 from the *Hiryū*); 61 were lost at the Battle of the Eastern Solomons (27 from the *Shōkaku*, 21 from the *Zuikaku*, 13 from the *Ryūjō*); and 148 off the Santa Cruz Islands (55 from the *Shōkaku*, 57 from the *Zuikaku*, 9 from the *Zuihō*, 27 from the *Jun'yō*). At the end of the Pacific War only 20 percent of the original Pearl Harbor participants had survived. James Sawruk, communications to author, 1 and 7 April 1998, 27 January 2000.

31. *SS: Nantō hōmen kaigun sakusen*, 1:642; Mikesh, *Zero*, 89; Lundstrom, *First Team and the Guadalcanal Campaign*, 45, 190; *KSS*, 405–6; McKearney, "Solomons Naval Campaign," 59–60; Okumiya and Horikoshi, with Caidin, *Zero!*, 164.

32. Lundstrom, *First Team and the Guadalcanal Campaign*, 45, 57.

33. *KSS*, 408; Bergerud, *Fire in the Sky*, 522–23.

34. Lundstrom, *First Team and the Guadalcanal Campaign*, 529; Hata and Izawa, *Japanese Naval Aces*, 132–38.

35. Okumiya and Horikoshi, with Caidin, *Zero!*, 246–49.

36. *KSS*, 406; *KKG*, 266.

37. *KSS*, 394–98.

38. Ibid., 407–8.

39. Bergerud, *Fire in the Sky*, 459–60.

40. Ibid., 478–79.

41. All these elements are analyzed in Lundstrom's *First Team and the Guadalcanal Campaign*, 477–85.

42. From 1942 through 1944 the United States carried out a series of flight

evaluations of captured Zeros to compare their performance with that of U.S. fighter aircraft of the time. The results of these tests demonstrated that even though the Zero was inferior in some respects to later Allied fighters, it could never be discounted as a lethal fighting machine. By inference, then, it is probable that the severe losses to which Japanese naval air groups had been subjected by the end of 1942 were more the result of changing balances in the skills of Japanese and American pilots and their use of tactics than to any deficiencies in the Zero. Mikesh, *Zero*, 83.

43. *KKG*, 266.
44. Bergerud, *Fire in the Sky*, 505–7.
45. U.S. Department of the Navy, Office of Naval Intelligence, "Quality of Japanese Naval Pilots," 3342.
46. Osamu Tagaya, letter to author, 31 March 1998.
47. Bergerud, *Fire in the Sky*, 329.
48. Morison, *Breaking the Bismarcks Barrier*, 117–18, 125–27; *KKG*, 310; Okumiya and Horikoshi, with Caidin, *Zero!*, 191–95; Ugaki, *Fading Victory*, 328–29.
49. Sakaida, *Siege of Rabaul*, 6.
50. Morison, *Breaking the Bismarcks Barrier*, 347.
51. Sakaida, *Siege of Rabaul*, 6–8, 22, 27–31; Morison, *Breaking the Bismarcks Barrier*, 284–93; Dull, *Battle History*, 293; Bergerud, *Fire in the Sky*, 647–48, 653–54.
52. Dickson, *Battle of the Philippine Sea*, 28–29.
53. *SS: Mariana-oki kaisen*, 636.
54. Dickson, *Battle of the Philippine Sea*, 29.
55. Dull, *Battle History*, 303–4.
56. Ibid., 303–10; Dickson, *Battle of the Philippine Sea*, 115, 168; quotation from Tillman, *Carrier Battle in the Philippine Sea*.
57. Morison, *New Guinea and the Marianas*, 317–18.
58. See Fukui, *Japanese Naval Vessels at the End of the War*.
59. Mikesh, *Broken Wings of the Samurai*, 28.
60. Agawa, *Reluctant Admiral*, 105.
61. By March 1944 the number of navy aviators had nearly doubled to fourteen thousand (as compared with combat deaths of almost four thousand). Most of these were enlisted personnel. *KG*, 2:202.
62. Fuchida and Okumiya, *Midway*, 208.
63. These considerations were suggested by Osamu Tagaya in a letter to the author, 31 March 1998.
64. Bergerud, *Fire in the Sky*, 189, 429–32.
65. John B. Lundstrom, letter to author, 6 December 1993. In the Pacific War, picket submarines, occasionally stationed in projected combat areas, as in the Pearl Harbor, Midway, and Guadalcanal operations, were also given sea rescue as part of their mission. However, these arrangements hardly constituted a consistent air-sea rescue system, particularly since there were no direct communications between submarines and aircraft. USNTMJ, Report S-17, "Japanese Submarine Operations," 12.

66. Okumiya and Horikoshi, with Caidin, *Zero!*, 172.
67. *KKG*, 210, 266; Bergerud, *Fire in the Sky*, 141–42.
68. *KKG*, 209.
69. Ibid., 336, 343.
70. *KG*, 1:818.
71. *KKG*, 209–10.
72. Ibid., 341–42; *NKKS*, 2:634–36. For a more detailed discussion of the navy's general prewar and wartime fuel problems, see Evans and Peattie, *Kaigun*, 406–11.
73. *KKG*, 270.
74. These thoughts are provoked by comments in ibid., 267–70.
75. See, for example, Bergerud, *Fire in the Sky*, 554–55.
76. Bergerud makes this point in ibid.
77. Prange, with Goldstein and Dillon, *At Dawn We Slept*, 542–44.
78. See, for example, the comments in Okumiya and Horikoshi, with Caidin, *Zero!*, 248–49.
79. Horikoshi and Okumiya, *Reisen*, 245–46. Beginning in 1943, Nakajima worked sporadically with the navy to develop a four-engined strategic bomber, the G8N Renzan, and a prototype was developed in October 1944. But a shortage of light alloy metals and constant interruption of the project by American air attacks meant that only two or three of these aircraft were ever produced. *NKS*, 5:198–202.
80. Horikoshi and Okumiya, *Reisen*, 244.
81. *KKG*, 212–13.
82. Evans and Peattie, *Kaigun*, 487–517.
83. Guerlac, *Radar in World War II*, 925–33.
84. Evans and Peattie, *Kaigun*, 411–15. During the war the Navy Technical Department authorized the Naval Air Arsenal to research and mass-produce airborne radar sets, but the effort never materialized because the Technical Department failed to provide the arsenal with sufficient personnel or support to undertake the task. Matsui, "Nihon kaigun no dempa tanshingi," 454.
85. For a discussion of the operation of the VT fuze, see Friedman, *U.S. Naval Weapons*, 88–89.
86. Bergerud, *Fire in the Sky*, 562–68; Baldwin, *Deadly Fuze*, 233–49.
87. See app. 8 for a discussion of the principal engines used by the Japanese navy at the opening of the Pacific War.
88. General Motors Corporation, *Engine Design*, 67–68.
89. Horikoshi, *Eagles of Mitsubishi*, 141.

Bibliography

Note: Unless otherwise noted, all Japanese-language titles were printed in Tokyo.

Agawa Hiroyuki. *The Reluctant Admiral: Yamamoto and the Imperial Navy.* Translated by John Bester. Kōdansha International, 1979.

Akimoto Minoru. *Nihon gunyōki kōkūsen zenshi* [A complete history of the air combat of Japan's military aircraft]. Guriin Arō Shuppansha, 1994–95.

Baldwin, Ralph B. *The Deadly Fuze: The Secret Weapon of World War II.* Princeton, N.J.: Princeton University Press, 1947.

Bekker, Cajus. *The Luftwaffe Diaries.* Translated and edited by Frank Ziegler. New York: Doubleday, 1967.

Bergerud, Eric M. *Fire in the Sky: The Air War in the South Pacific.* Boulder, Colo.: Westview Press, 1999.

Boyd, Gary. "The Vought V-143: 1930s Technology Transfer." *Air Power History* 43 (Winter 1996): 28–37.

Brackley, Frida H. *Brackles: Memoirs of a Pioneer in Civil Aviation.* London: W. and J. Mackay, 1952.

Brown, David. *Aircraft Carriers.* New York: Arco, 1977.

Brown, Eric. *Duels in the Sky: World War II Naval Aircraft in Combat.* Annapolis, Md.: Naval Institute Press, 1988.

Bueschel, Richard M. *Mitsubishi A6M1/2 Zero-sen in Imperial Japanese Naval Air Service.* Arco-Aircam Aviation Series no. 18. New York: Arco, 1970.

————. *Mitsubishi/Nakajima G3M1/2/3 and Kusho L3Y1 in Imperial Japanese Naval Air Service*. Arco-Aircam Aviation Series no. 35. Berkshire, England: Osprey, 1972.

Burdick, Charles B. *The Japanese Siege of Tsingtau: World War I in Asia*. Hamden, Conn.: Archon Books, 1976.

Caidin, Martin. *The Ragged Rugged Warriors*. New York: Ballantine Books, 1966.

————. *Zero Fighter*. New York: Ballantine Books, 1969.

Campbell, John. *Naval Weapons of World War Two*. London: Conway Maritime Press, 1985.

Campbell, Mark. "The Influence of Air Power upon the Evolution of Battle Doctrine in the U.S. Navy." Master's thesis, University of Massachusetts at Boston, 1992.

Chapman, John. "Tricycle Recycled: Collaboration among the Secret Intelligence Services of the Axis States." *Intelligence and National Security* 7 (July 1992): 268–99.

Chesneau, Roger. *Aircraft Carriers of the World, 1914 to the Present: An Illustrated Encyclopedia*. Annapolis, Md.: Naval Institute Press, 1992.

Cook, Theodore, and Haruko Cook, eds. *Japan at War: An Oral History*. New York: Free Press, 1992.

Cornelius, Wanda, and Thayne Short. *Ding hao: America's Air War in China, 1937–1945*. Gretna, La.: Pelican, 1980.

Daitō Bunka Daigaku Tōyō Kenkyūjō, ed., *Shōwa shakai-keizai-shi shiryō shūsei* [Compilation of materials relating to the social and economic history of the Shōwa era]. Vol. 1, *Kaigunshō shiryō* [Navy ministry materials]. Ochanomizu Shobō, 1978.

Dean, Francis H., ed. *America's One Hundred Thousand: Report of the Joint Fighter Conference, NAS Patuxent River, Maryland, October 16–23, 1944*. Atglen, Pa.: Schiffer, 1998.

De Virgilio, John F. "Japanese Thunderfish." *Naval History* 5 (Winter 1991): 61–68.

Dickson, W. David. *Battle of the Philippine Sea, June 1944*. Surrey, U.K.: Ian Allen, 1974.

————. "Fighting Flat-tops: The Shōkakus." *Warship International*, no. 1 (1977): 15–44.

Dull, Paul S. *A Battle History of the Imperial Japanese Navy, 1941–1945*. Annapolis, Md.: Naval Institute Press, 1978.

Ellis, John. *Brute Force: Allied Strategy and Tactics in the Second World War*. New York: Viking Press, 1990.

Evans, David C. *The Japanese Navy in World War II in the Words of Former Japanese Naval Officers*, 2d ed. Annapolis, Md.: Naval Institute Press, 1982.

Evans, David C., and Mark R. Peattie. "Ill Winds Blow." United States Naval Institute *Proceedings* 123 (October 1997): 70–73.

————. *Kaigun: Strategy, Tactics, and Technology in the Imperial Japanese Navy, 1887–1941*. Annapolis, Md.: Naval Institute Press, 1997.

Favorite, Martin, with Kawamoto Minoru. *Japanese Air Power at the Outbreak of the Pacific War* (website; URL: http://www.star-games.com/).

Ferris, John. "A British Unofficial Aviation Mission and Japanese Naval Developments, 1919–1929." *Journal of Strategic Studies* (September 1982), 5:416–39.

Fioravanzo, Vice Adm. Giuseppe. "The Japanese Military Mission to Italy in 1941." United States Naval Institute *Proceedings* 8 (January 1956): 24–31.

Francillon, René J. *Imperial Japanese Navy Bombers of World War II*. Windsor, Berkshire, England: Hilton Lacy, 1969.

———. *Japanese Aircraft of the Pacific War*. Annapolis, Md.: Naval Institute Press, 1987.

Frank, Richard. *Guadalcanal*. New York: Penguin Books, 1990.

Friedman, Norman. *Carrier Air Power*. Greenwich, England: Conway Maritime Press, 1981.

———. *U.S. Aircraft Carriers: An Illustrated Design History*. Annapolis, Md.: Naval Institute Press, 1983.

———. *U.S. Naval Weapons: Every Gun, Missile, Mine, and Torpedo Used by the U.S. Navy from 1883 to the Present Day*. Annapolis, Md.: Naval Institute Press, 1982.

Fuchida, Mitsuo, and Masatake Okumiya. *Midway: The Battle That Doomed Japan*. Annapolis, Md.: Naval Institute Press, 1955.

Fukaya, Hajime, with M. E. Holbrook. "The Shokakus—Pearl Harbor to Leyte Gulf." United States Naval Institute *Proceedings* 78 (June 1952): 638–44.

Fukui, Shizuo. *Japanese Naval Vessels at the End of the War*. Old Greenwich, Conn.: We, 1970.

———. *Nihon no gunkan: waga zōkan gijutsu no hattatsu to kantei no hensen* [Japanese warships: our development of ship construction technology and changes in warships over time]. Shuppan Kyōdōsha, 1959.

———. *Shashin Nihon kaigun zen kantei shi* [A photographic history of all the ships in the Japanese navy]. 3 vols. Best Sellers, 1994.

Furer, Julius. *Administration of the Navy Department in World War II*. Washington, D.C.: GPO, 1959.

Gardiner, Robert. *Warship, 1991*. London: Conway Maritime Ltd., 1991.

Garzke, William H., Jr., and Robert O. Dulin Jr. *Axis and Neutral Battleships in World War II*. Annapolis, Md.: Naval Institute Press, 1985.

Genda Minoru. "Evolution of Aircraft Carrier Tactics of the Imperial Japanese Navy." In *Air Raid: Pearl Harbor!* Edited by Paul Stillwell. Annapolis, Md.: Naval Institute Press, 1981, 23–27.

———. *Kaigun kōkūtai shimatsuki* [A record of the particulars of the Japanese naval air service]. 2 vols. Bungei Shunjū, 1961–62.

———. *Shinjuwan sakusen kaikoroku* [Recollections of the Pearl Harbor operation]. Yomiuri Shimbunsha, 1972.

———. "Tactical Planning in the Imperial Japanese Navy." *Naval War College Review* 22 (October 1969): 45–50.

General Motors Corporation. *Engine Design as Related to Airplane Power*. Detroit, Mich.: General Motors, 1943.

Goldstein, Donald, and Katherine V. Dillon, eds. *The Pearl Harbor Papers: Inside Japanese Plans*. New York: Brassey's, U.S., 1993.

Guerlac, Henry. *Radar in World War II*. Los Angeles, Calif.: Tomash, 1987.

Harvey, A. D. "Army Air Force and Navy Air Force: Japanese Aviation and the Opening Phase of the War in the Far East." *War in History* 6, no. 2 (1999): 174–204.

Hasegawa Tōichi. *Nihon no kōkūbōkan* [Japanese aircraft carriers]. Grand Prix Shuppan, 1997.

Hata, Ikuhiko. "The Marco Polo Bridge Incident, 1937." In *The China Quagmire*:

Japan's Expansion on the Asian Continent, 1933–1941. Edited by James William Morley. Translations from *Taiheiyō sensō e no michi* [Road to the Pacific war] Series (1962–63). New York: Columbia University Press, 1983, 243–86.

————, ed. *Nihon riku-kaigun sōgō jiten* [Comprehensive encyclopedia of the Japanese army and navy]. Tokyo Daigaku Shuppankai, 1991.

Hata, Ikuhiko, and Yasuho Izawa. *Japanese Naval Aces and Fighter Units in World War II*. Translated by Don Gorham. Annapolis, Md.: Naval Institute Press, 1989.

Hattori Shōgō and Sugiuchi Yukihiko. "Kūkyoku no hissatsugi: 'hineri-komi' sempō to wa?" [The ultimate killing tactic: what was the 'turning-in' maneuver?]. *Rekishi Gunzō*, no. 23 (February 1996): 68–74.

Hayashi Katsunari. *Nihon gunji gijutsu shi* [A history of Japanese military technology]. Haruki Shobō, 1972.

Hone, Thomas C. "Destruction of the Battle Line at Pearl Harbor." U.S. Naval Institute *Proceedings* 103 (December 1977): 49–59.

Hone, Thomas C., Norman Friedman, and Mark D. Mandeles. *American and British Aircraft Carrier Development, 1919–1941*. Annapolis, Md.: Naval Institute Press, 1999.

Hone, Thomas C., and Mark D. Mandeles. "Interwar Innovation in Three Navies: U.S. Navy, Royal Navy, Imperial Japanese Navy." *Naval War College Review* 40 (Spring 1987): 63–83.

Horikoshi, Jirō. *Eagles of Mitsubishi: The Story of the Zero Fighter*. Translated by Shojiro Shindo and Harold N. Wantiez. Seattle: University of Washington Press, 1981.

Horikoshi Jirō and Okumiya Masatake. *Reisen* [Zero fighter]. Marason Asahi, 1975.

Hsu Long-hsuen and Chang Ming-kai. *History of the Sino-Japanese War (1937–1945)*. Translated by Wen Ha-hsiung and revised by Kao Ching-chen et al. Taipei: Chung Wu, 1971.

Hughes, Wayne P., Jr. "Naval Tactics and Their Influence on Strategy." *Naval War College Review* 39 (January–February 1986).

Ikari Yoshirō. *Ikite iru reisen* [The Zero lives]. Yomiuri Shimbunsha, 1970.

————. *Kaigun kūgishō: zunō shudan no eikō to shuppatsu* [The Naval Air Technical Arsenal: the origins and the glory of a praiseworthy group of experts]. 2 vols. Kōjinsha, 1985.

Ikeda Kiyoshi. *Nihon no kaigun* [The Japanese navy]. 2 vols. Isseido, 1967.

Isom, Dallas W. "The Battle of Midway: Why the Japanese Lost." *Naval War College Review* (Summer 2000), 60–100.

Itani Jirō, Hans Lengerer, and Tomoko Rehm-Takara. "Anti-aircraft Gunnery in the Imperial Japanese Navy." In *Warship, 1991*. Edited by Robert Gardiner. London: Conway Maritime Press, 1991, 81–101.

Iwaya Fumio. *Chūkō: kaigun rikujō kōgekiki taishi* [The medium bomber: a unit history of the navy's land-based attack aircraft]. 2 vols. Shuppan Kyōdōsha, 1956–58.

Izawa Yasuho. *Rikkō to Ginga* [The rikkō and Ginga navy bombers]. Asahi Sonorama, 1995.

Japan, Bōeichō Bōeikenshūjō Senshibu [originally, Bōeichō Boeikenshūjō Senshishitsu]. *Senshi sōsho* [War history] series. *Chūgoku hōmen kaigun sakusen* [Naval operations in the China theater]. 2 vols. Asagumo Shimbunsha, 1974–75.

————. *Hirippin-Marai hōmen: kaigun shinko sakusen* [The Philippine-Malaya theater: the naval offensive]. Asagumo Shimbunsha, 1969.

————. *Hitō-Marē hōmen kaigun shinkō sakusen* [The navy's offensive operations in the Philippines-Malaya theater]. Asagumo Shimbunsha, 1969.

————. *Kaigun gunsembi* [Naval armaments and war preparations]. 2 vols. Asagumo Shimbunsha, 1969–75.

————. *Kaigun kōkū gaishi* [A historical overview of Japanese naval aviation]. Asagumo Shimbunsha, 1976.

————. *Mariana-oki kaisen* [Naval battle off the Marianas]. Asagumo Shimbunsha, 1968.

————. *Midowei kaisen* [Battle of Midway]. Asagumo Shimbunsha, 1971.

————. *Nantō hōmen kaigun sakusen* [Naval operations in the southeast theater]. 2 vols. Asagumo Shimbunsha, 1971–75.

————. *Rikugun kōkū no gumbi to unyō: Shōwa jūsannen shōki made* [Army air weapons and their use: up to early 1938]. Asagumo Shimbunsha, 1971.

Jentschura, Hansgeorg, Dieter Jung, and Peter Mickel. *Warships of the Imperial Japanese Navy, 1869–1945.* Annapolis, Md.: Naval Institute Press, 1977.

Kaigun Henshū Iinkai, ed. *Kaigun* [The navy]. Vol. 13, *Kaigun kōkū, kōkūtai, kōkūki.* Seibun Yosho, 1981.

Kaigun Rekishi Hōzonkai, ed. *Nihon kaigun shi* [A history of the Japanese navy]. 11 vols. Daiichi Hōki Shuppan, 1995.

Kaigun 705 Kūkai, ed. *Dai 705 Kaigun Kōkūtai shi: Rabauru kōkūtai chūkō shitō no kiroku* [History of the 705th air group: a record of the desperate struggle of the medium bombers of the Rabaul air group]. Kaigun 705 Kūkai, 1975.

Kaigun Suiraishi Kankōkai. *Kaigun suiraishi* [History of mines and torpedoes of the navy]. Shinkōsha, 1979.

Katō Sadatoshi, ed. *Nihon kaigun kantei zumen. Shū 3: kōkū bōkan, suijōki bōkan, sensuikan* [Drawings of Japanese naval vessels. No. 3: aircraft carriers, seaplane carriers, and submarines]. Model Art, 1999.

Ko Ōnishi Takijirō Kaigun Chūjō Den Kankōkai, ed. *Ōnishi Takijirō* [Ōnishi Takijirō]. Ko Ōnishi Takijirō Chūjō Den Kankōkai, 1963.

Kōkūshō Kankōkai, ed. *Kaigun no tsubasa* [Wings of the navy]. 3 vols. Kōkūshō Kankōkai, 1989.

Krebs, Gerhard. "The Japanese Air Forces." In *The Conduct of the Air War in the Second World War: An International Comparison.* Edited by Horst Boog. New York: Berg, 1992, 228–34.

Kusaka Ryūnosuke. *Ichi kaigun shikan no hanseiki* [A naval officer's record of half a lifetime of service]. Kōwadō, 1973.

————. *Rengō kantai: moto sambō-chō no kaiso* [The Combined Fleet: recollections of a former staff officer]. Mainichi Shimbun Sha, 1952.

Kuwabara Torao. *Kaigun kōkū kaisoroku, sōsō hen* [Recollections of naval aviation, early years]. Kōkū Shimbun Sha, 1964.

Larkins, William T. *U.S. Navy Aircraft, 1911–1941.* New York: Orion, 1961.

Layman, R. D. *Before the Aircraft Carrier: The Development of Aviation Vessels, 1849–1922.* London: Conway Maritime Press, 1989.

————. *Naval Aviation in the First World War: Its Impact and Influence.* Annapolis, Md.: Naval Institute Press, 1996.

Leary, William M. "Assessing the Japanese Threat: Air Intelligence Prior to Pearl Harbor." *Aerospace Historian* (December 1987), 34:272–77.

Lengerer, Hans. "Akagi and Kaga." Parts 1–3. *Warship: A Quarterly Journal of Warship History,* no. 22 (April 1982): 127–39; no. 23 (July 1982): 170–77; no. 24 (October 1982): 305–10.

Lengerer, Hans, and Tomoko Rehm-Takahara. "The Japanese Aircraft Carriers *Junyo* and *Hiyo.*" Parts 1–3. *Warship International,* no. 33 (January 1985): 9–19; no. 34 (April 1985): 105–14; no. 35 (July 1985): 188–93.

Lundstrom, John. *The First South Pacific Campaign.* Annapolis, Md.: Naval Institute Press, 1976.

———. *The First Team and the Guadalcanal Campaign: Naval Fighter Combat from August to November 1942.* Annapolis, Md.: Naval Institute Press, 1994.

———. *The First Team: Pacific Naval Air Combat from Pearl Harbor to Midway.* Annapolis, Md.: Naval Institute Press, 1984.

Mainichi Shimbun, ed. *Nihon no senshi* [Japanese military history]. Vols. 3–5, comprising a three-volume set, *Nitchū sensō* [The Sino-Japanese war of 1937–1945], numbered parts 1–3. Mainichi Shimbun Sha, 1979.

Marder, Arthur. *Old Friends, New Enemies: The Royal Navy and the Imperial Japanese Navy.* 2 vols. New York: Oxford University Press, 1981–90.

Maru Magazine, ed. *Nihon kaigun kantei shashinshū* [Photographic collection of Japanese warships]. Kōjinsha, 1996. No. 5, *Akagi, Kaga, Hōshō, and Ryūjō.* No. 6, *Shōkaku, Zuikaku, Sōryū, Unryū, and Taihō.*

Matsui Muneaki. "Nihon kaigun no dempa tanshingi" [Japanese navy radar]. In *Kaisō no Nihon kaigun* [The Japanese navy recollected]. Edited by the Suikōkai. Hara Shobō, 1985.

McKearney, T. J. "The Solomons Naval Campaign: A Paradigm for Surface Warships in Maritime Strategy." Thesis, Naval Postgraduate School, Monterey, Calif., 1985.

Melhorn, Charles. *Two-Block Fox: The Rise of the Aircraft Carrier, 1911–1929.* Annapolis, Md.: Naval Institute Press, 1974.

Middlebrook, Martin. *Battleship: The Loss of the Prince of Wales and the Repulse.* London: Allen Lane, 1977.

Mikesh, Robert. *Broken Wings of the Samurai: The Destruction of the Japanese Air Force.* Annapolis, Md.: Naval Institute Press, 1993.

———. *Zero: Combat and Development History of Japan's Legendary Mitsubishi A6M Zero Fighter.* Osceola, Wisc.: Motorbooks International, 1994.

Mikesh, Robert C., and Shorzoe [sic] Abe. *Japanese Aircraft, 1910–1941.* Annapolis, Md.: Naval Institute Press, 1990.

———. "The Rise of Japanese Naval Air Power." In *Warship 1991.* Edited by Robert Gardiner. Greenwich, England: Conway Maritime Press, 1994.

Milford, Frederick J. "A Note on Japanese Naval Aircraft Engines." Unpublished monograph, 1994.

Miller, Edward S. *War Plan Orange: The U.S. Strategy to Defeat Japan, 1897–1945.* Annapolis, Md.: Naval Institute Press, 1991.

Moore, Lynne Lucius. "Shinano: The Jinx Carrier." U.S. Naval Institute *Proceedings* 79 (February 1953): 142–49.

Morison, Samuel Eliot. *Breaking the Bismarcks Barrier, 23 July 1942–1 May 1944.* Vol.

6 of *History of United States Naval Operations in World War II*. Boston: Little, Brown and Company, 1951.

———. *New Guinea and the Marianas, March 1944–August 1944*. Vol. 8 of *History of United States Naval Operations in World War II*. Boston: Little, Brown and Company, 1953.

Mōro Masanori. *Ijin Nakajima Chikuhei hiroku* [Confidential record concerning the illustrious Nakajima Chikuhei]. Jōmō Ijin Denki Kankōkai, 1960.

Munson, Kenneth. *Fighters between the Wars, 1919–1939*. New York: Macmillan, 1970.

Nagaishi Masataka. *Kaigun kōkūtai nenshi* [Chronological record of Japanese naval air groups]. Shuppan Kyōdōsha, 1961.

Nagamura Kiyoshi. *Zōkan kaisō* [Recollections of naval construction]. Shuppan Kyōdōsha, 1957.

Nakamura Masao, ed. *Taiheiyō sensō shi shirizu* [Pacific war history series]. Cakushū Kenkyūkai, 1999. No. 13, *Shōkaku gata kūbō* [Shōkaku-class carriers]. No. 14, *Kūbō kidō butai* [Carrier strike force].

Nakayama Masahiro. *Chūgoku-teki tenkū: chimmoku no kōkū senshi* [China skies: an untold account of aerial combat]. Sankei Shuppan, 1981.

Nihon Kaigun Kōkūshi Hensan Iinkai, ed. *Nihon kaigun kōkūshi* [The history of Japanese naval aviation]. 4 vols. Jiji Tsushinsha, 1969.

Nihon Zōsen Gakkai, ed. *Shōwa zōsenshi* [A history of ship construction in the Shōwa era]. 2 vols. Hara Shobō, 1977.

Nohara, Shigeru. *A6M Zero in Action*. Carrolton, Tex.: Squadron/Signal Publications, 1983.

Nozawa Tadashi, ed. *Nihon kōkū sōshū* [Encyclopedia of Japanese aircraft, 1900–1945]. 8 vols. Shuppan Kyōdōsha, 1958–83. [Vol. 1, *Mitsubishi*. Vol. 2, *Aichi and Kugishō*. Vol. 3, *Kawanishi and Hirō*. Vol. 5, *Nakajima*.]

O'Connell, Robert. *Sacred Vessels: The Cult of the Battleship and the Rise of the U.S. Navy*. Boulder, Colo.: Westview Press, 1991.

Ōhama Tetsuya and Ozawa Ikurō, eds. *Teikoku rikukaigun jiten* [Dictionary of the Imperial Japanese Army and Navy]. Dōseisha, 1995.

Okada Heiichirō. "Kaga/Akagi no hikō kampan dai kaizō no keii" [Particulars concerning the general reconstruction of the flight decks of the *Kaga* and *Akagi*]. In *Kaisō no Nihon kaigun* [The navy recollected]. Edited by the Suikōkai. Hara Shobō, 1985.

Okamura Jun and Iwaya Eichi. *Kōkū gijutsu no zembo* [Complete outline of aviation technology]. Shuppan Kyōdō Sha, 1954.

———. *Nihon no kōkūki* [Japanese aircraft]. *Kaigun hen* [Navy volume]. Shuppan Kyōdō Sha, 1960.

Okumiya Masatake. *Saraba kaigun kōkūtai* [Farewell, the naval air groups]. Asahi Sonorama, 1979.

———. *Tsubasa-naki sōjūshi* [Pilot without wings]. Shuppan Kyōdō Sha, 1956.

Okumiya, Masatake, and Jiro Horikoshi, with Martin Caidin. *Zero! The Air War in the Pacific from the Japanese Viewpoint*. Washington, D.C.: Zenger, 1956.

Ōmae Toshikazu. "Nihon kaigun no heijutsu shisō no hensen to gumbi oyobi sakusen" [Changes in tactical thought in the Japanese navy in relation to armaments and operations]. Parts 1–4. *Kaigun Bunko geppō,* no. 6 (April 1981); no. 7 (July 1981); no. 8 (September 1981); and no. 9 (December 1981).

Ōmae Toshikazu and Roger Pineau. "Japanese Naval Aviation." U.S. Naval Institute *Proceedings* 98 (December 1972): 70–77.

Overy, Richard. "Air Power in the Second World War: Historical Themes and Theories." In *The Conduct of the Air War in the Second World War: An International Comparison.* Edited by Horst Boog. New York: Berg, 1992, 7–28.

Ozawa Teitoku Den Kankōkai, ed. *Kaisō no Teitoku Ozawa Jisaburō* [Recollections concerning Adm. Ozawa Jisaburō]. Hara Shobō, 1971.

Polmar, Norman. *Aircraft Carriers: A Graphic History of Carrier Aviation and Its Influence on World Events.* London: MacDonald, 1969.

Popham, Hugh. *Into Wind: A History of British Naval Flying.* London: Hamish Hamilton, 1969.

Prados, John. *Combined Fleet Decoded: The Secret History of American Intelligence and the Japanese Navy in World War II.* New York: Random House, 1995.

Prange, Gordon W., with Donald Goldstein and Katherine Dillon. *At Dawn We Slept: The Untold Story of Pearl Harbor.* New York: McGraw Hill, 1981.

———. *God's Samurai: Lead Pilot at Pearl Harbor.* New York: Brassey's, U.S., 1990.

———. *Miracle at Midway.* New York: McGraw Hill, 1982.

Pugh, Philip. *The Cost of Seapower: The Influence of Money on Naval Affairs from 1815 to the Present Day.* London: Conway Maritime Press, 1986.

Rearden, Jim. *Cracking the Zero Mystery: How the U.S. Learned to Beat Japan's Vaunted World War II Fighter Plane.* Harrisburg, Pa.: Stackpole Books, 1990.

Reisen Tōjō Iinkai, ed. *Kaigun sentōkitaishi* [History of the navy's fighter units]. Hara Shobō, 1987.

Reynolds, Clark. *The Fast Carriers: The Forging of an Air Navy.* Huntingdon, N.Y.: R. E. Krieger, 1968.

———. "Remembering Genda." United States Naval Institute *Proceedings* 116 (April 1990): 52–56.

Roskill, Stephen. *Naval Policy between the Wars.* 2 vols. Annapolis, Md.: Naval Institute Press, 1968–76.

Sakai, Saburo, with Martin Caidin and Fred Saito. *Samurai!* New York: Sutton, 1957. Reprint, Bantam Books, 1975.

Sakaida, Henry. *Imperial Japanese Navy Aces, 1937–1945.* London: Osprey, 1998.

———. *The Siege of Rabaul.* St. Paul, Minn.: Phalanx, 1996.

Samuels, Richard. *Rich Nation, Strong Army: National Security and the Technological Transformation of Japan.* Ithaca, N.Y.: Cornell University Press, 1994.

Sawachi Hisae. *Middowei kaisen: kiroku* [The naval battle of Midway: a record]. Bungei shunjū, 1986.

Sekigawa, Eiichirō. *A Pictorial History of Japanese Military Aviation.* Translated by C. Uchida and edited by David Mondey. London: Ian Allen, 1974.

Shibata Takeo. *Genda Minoru ron* [On Genda Minoru]. Omoikane Shobō, 1971.

Shimada, Kōichi. "The Opening Air Offensive against the Philippines." In *The Japanese Navy in World War II.* Edited by David Evans. Annapolis, Md.: Naval Institute Press, 1986, 71–104.

Shores, Christopher, and Brian Cull, with Yasuho Izawa. *Bloody Shambles.* Vol. 1, *The Drift to War to the Fall of Singapore.* London: Grub Street Press, 1992.

Smith, Herschel. *A History of Aircraft Piston Engines.* Manhattan, Kans.: Sunflower University Press, 1986.

Smith, Peter C. *Into the Assault: Famous Dive Bomber Aces of the Second World War.* Seattle, Wash.: University of Seattle Press, 1985.

Snow, Carl. "Japanese Carrier Operations: How Did *They* Do It?" *The Hook* (Spring 1995), 17.

Sonokawa Kamerō, ed. *Shashin zusetsu Nihon kaigun kōkūtai* [An illustrated compendium of the Japanese naval air service]. Kodansha, 1970.

Spick, Mike. *Fighter Pilot Tactics: The Technique of Daylight Air Combat.* Cambridge, England: Patrick Stephens, 1983.

Stilwell, Paul. *Battleship Arizona: An Illustrated History.* Annapolis, Md.: Naval Institute Press, 1991.

Studer, Clara. *Sky Storming Yankee: The Life of Glenn Curtiss.* New York: Stackpole and Sons, 1937.

Suikōkai, ed. *Kaisō Nihon kaigun* [Recollections about the Japanese navy]. Hara Shobō, 1985.

Sumida, Jon Tetsuro. "The Best Laid Plans: The Development of British Battle-Fleet Tactics, 1919–1942." *International History Review* 14 (November 1992): 681–700.

Takahashi Shōsaku et al. *Kaigun rikujō kōgekki-tai* [The navy's medium bomber units]. Konnichi-no-wadai Sha, 1976.

Tanaka Etsutarō. *Reisen ichidai* [The Zero era]. Sankei Shimbun Shuppankyoku, 1966.

Thompson, Steven L. "The Zero: One Step Beyond." *Air and Space Smithsonian* 4 (February–March 1990): 28–38.

Thorne, Christopher. *The Limits of Foreign Policy.* London: Hamilton, 1972.

Till, Geoffrey. *Air Power and the Royal Navy, 1914–1945: A Historical Survey.* London: Jane's, 1979.

Tillman, Barrett. *Carrier Battle in the Philippine Sea: The Marianas Turkey Shoot, June 19–20, 1944.* St. Paul, Minn.: Phalanx, 1994.

———. *The Dauntless Dive Bomber of World War II.* Annapolis, Md.: Naval Institute Press, 1976.

Toyama Misao, ed. *Riku-kaigun shōkan jinji sōran* [Brief resumés of army and navy officers]. 2 vols. Eiyō Shobō, 1981.

Tsūshō Sangyōshō, ed. *Shōkō seisaku shi* [A history of commercial and industrial policy]. Vol. 18, *Kikai kōgyō, senzen hen* [The machine industry, prewar]. Shōkō Seisaku-shi Kenkyūkai, 1976.

Tsutsui Mitsuru. "Shina jihen boppatsuji ni okeru rikukaigun kōkō heiryoku" [Japanese military and naval air strength at the outbreak of the China war]. *Gunji Shigaku,* no. 42 (September 1975).

Uehara Mitsuhara. *Kambaku taichō Egusa Takashige* [Carrier bomber leader Egusa Takashige]. Kōjinsha, 1989.

Ugaki, Matome. *Fading Victory: The Diary of Matome Ugaki, 1941–1945.* Translated by Masataka Chihaya and edited by Donald M. Goldstein and Katherine V. Dillon. Pittsburgh, Pa.: University of Pittsburgh Press, 1991.

U.S. Department of the Army, Office of the Chief of Military History. Japan Monographs no. 120, *Outline of Southeast Theater Naval Air Operations.* Part 1, *December 1941–August 1942.* Washington, D.C.: Library of Congress, 1964.

————. Japan Monographs no. 121, *Outline of Southeast Theater Naval Air Operations*. Part 2, *August–October 1942*. Washington, D.C.: Library of Congress, 1964.

————. Japan Monographs no. 122, *Outline of Southeast Theater Naval Air Operations*. Part 3, *November 1942–June 1943*. Washington, D.C.: Library of Congress, 1964.

————. Japan Monographs no. 166, *China Incident Naval Operations (July–November 1937)*. Washington, D.C.: Library of Congress, 1964.

U.S. Department of the Navy, Commander-in-Chief, Pacific and Pacific Ocean Areas, Joint Intelligence Center, Pacific Ocean Area. "Aerial Tactics." *Weekly Intelligence Bulletin,* no. 87–45.

————. "Know Your Enemy: Japanese Aerial Tactics against Ship Targets." *Weekly Intelligence Bulletin* 1 (20 October 1944).

U.S. Department of the Navy, Office of Naval Intelligence, Air Technical Intelligence Group. Reports 1, 2, 5, and 7.

U.S. Department of the Navy, Office of Naval Intelligence, Publications Branch. "Quality of Japanese Naval Pilots." *The O.N.I. Weekly* 2 (10 November 1943): 3342–45.

U.S. Naval Technical Mission to Japan. Report 0-01-2, "Japanese Torpedoes and Tubes." Article 2, "Aircraft Torpedoes." Washington, D.C.: Operational Archives, Naval History Division, January 1946.

————. Report A-11, "Aircraft Arrangements and Handling Facilities in Japanese Naval Vessels." Washington, D.C.: Operational Archives, Naval History Division, January 1946.

————. Report S-06-2, "Report of Damage to Japanese Warships." Washington, D.C.: Operational Archives, Naval History Division, January 1946.

————. Report S-17, "Japanese Submarine Operations." Washington, D.C.: Operational Archives, Naval History Division, January 1946.

U.S. Strategic Bombing Survey, Aircraft Division. *Army Air Arsenal and Navy Air Depots*. Washington, D.C.: GPO, 1947.

————. *Kawanishi Aircraft Company*. Washington, D.C.: GPO, 1947.

————. *Mitsubishi Heavy Industries Ltd*. Washington, D.C.: GPO, 1947.

U.S. Strategic Bombing Survey, Economic Studies. *Japanese Aircraft Industry*. Washington, D.C.: GPO, 1947.

U.S. Strategic Bombing Survey, Military Analysis Division. *Interrogations of Japanese Officials*. 2 vols. Washington, D.C.: GPO, 1946.

————. *Japanese Air Power*. Washington, D.C.: GPO, 1946.

————. *Japanese Air Weapons and Tactics*. Washington, D.C.: GPO, 1947.

U.S. Strategic Bombing Survey, Military and Naval Intelligence Division. *Japanese Military and Naval Intelligence*. Washington, D.C.: GPO, 1946.

U.S. Strategic Bombing Survey, Naval Analysis Division. *The Allied Campaign against Rabaul*. Washington, D.C.: GPO, 1946.

————. *Reduction of Truk*. Washington, D.C.: GPO, 1947.

U.S. War Department. *Handbook on Japanese Military Forces, Technical Manual E 30-480*. Washington, D.C.: GPO, 1944.

Van Deurs, George. "Aviators Are a Crazy Bunch of People." In *The Golden Age*

Remembered: U.S. Naval Aviation, 1919–1941. Edited by E. T. Woolridge. Annapolis, Md.: Naval Institute Press, 1998, 78–91.

Van Fleet, Clarke. *United States Naval Aviation, 1910–1980.* 3d ed. Washington, D.C.: GPO, 1981.

Wada Hideho. *Kaigun kōkū shiwa* [An account of naval aviation]. Meiji Shōin, 1944.

Wagner, Ray. *American Combat Aircraft.* Garden City, N.Y.: Doubleday, 1968.

———. *Prelude to Pearl Harbor: The Air War in China, 1937–1941.* San Diego, Calif.: San Diego Aerospace Museum, 1991.

Watts, Anthony J., and Brian G. Gordon. *The Imperial Japanese Navy.* Garden City, N.Y.: Doubleday, 1971.

Wildenberg, Thomas. *Destined for Glory: Dive Bombing, Midway, and the Evolution of Carrier Air Power.* Annapolis, Md.: Naval Institute Press, 1998.

———. "In Support of the Battle Line: Gunnery's Influence on the Development of Carrier Aviation in the USN." Unpublished paper presented at the Fourteenth Naval History Symposium, Annapolis, Md., 25 September 1999.

Willmott, H. P. *The Barrier and the Javelin: Japanese and Allied Pacific Strategies, February to June 1942.* Annapolis, Md.: Naval Institute Press, 1982.

Wilson, Eugene. "The Navy's First Carrier Task Force." U.S. Naval Institute *Proceedings* 76 (February 1950): 159–69.

Woolridge, E. T. *Carrier Warfare in the Pacific: An Oral History Collection.* Washington, D.C.: Smithsonian Institution Press, 1993.

Wragg, David. *The Offensive Weapon: The Strategy of Bombing.* London: Robert Hale, 1986.

———. *Wings over the Sea: A History of Naval Aviation.* Newton Abbot, England: David and Charles, 1979.

Yamamoto Eisuke. *Nana korobi yaoki no chijin yū* [The vicissitudes of life: wisdom, goodness, and bravery]. Sankei Shuppan, 1979.

Yamamoto Teiichirō. *Kaigun damashii: wakaki raigeki-ō Murata Shigeharu* [The spirit of the navy: the young king of torpedo attack, Murata Shigeharu]. Kōjinsha, 1985.

Yokomori Chikanobu. *Kaigun rikujō kōgekki* [Navy land bombers]. Sankei Shuppan, 1979.

Yokoyama Tamotsu. *Aa reisen ichidai: reisentai kūsen shimatsuki* [Ah, the Zero era: a record of the air combat of Zero fighter units]. Kojin Sha, 1969.

Index

About the Author

Mark Peattie served for nine years with the U.S. Information Agency in Japan, receiving intensive Japanese-language training in Tokyo. After earning his Ph.D. in modern Japanese history from Princeton University, he taught Japanese history at Pennsylvania State University, the University of California at Los Angeles, and the University of Massachusetts at Boston. For many years Peattie was a research fellow at the Edwin O. Reischauer Institute of Japanese Studies at Harvard University. He currently serves on the research staff of the Hoover Institution on War, Revolution, and Peace at Stanford University.

Peattie is the author, coauthor, and co-editor of eight books on Japanese imperialism and colonialism and modern Japanese military and naval history, including the award-winning *Kaigun: Tactics, and Technology in the Imperial Japanese Navy, 1887–1941*, coauthored with the late David Evans. He is currently researching Japan's involvement with Southeast Asia from the late nineteenth century to the present.